Linguistic Typology:

Morphology and Syntax

Jae Jung Song

Longman

An imprint of **Pearson Education**

Harlow, England · London · New York · Reading, Massachusetts · San Francisco · Toronto · Don Mills, Ontario · Sydney
Tokyo · Singapore · Hong Kong · Seoul · Taipei · Cape Town · Madrid · Mexico City · Amsterdam · Munich · Paris · Milan

Pearson Education Limited
Edinburgh Gate
Harlow
Essex CM20 2JE
England

and Associated Companies throughout the world

Visit us on the World Wide Web at:
www.pearsoneduc.com

First published 2001

© Pearson Education Limited 2001

The right of Jae Jung Song to be identified as author of
this work has been asserted by him in accordance with
the Copyright, Designs and Patents Act 1988.

ISBN 0-582-31220-5 CSD
ISBN 0-582-31221-3 PPR

British Library Cataloguing-in-Publication Data
A catalogue record for this book is available from the British Library.

Library of Congress Cataloging-in-Publication Data
A catalog record for this book is available from the Library of
Congress.

Set by 35 in 10/12pt Janson Text
Produced by Pearson Education Asia Pte Ltd.
Printed in Singapore

LONGMAN LINGUISTICS LIBRARY

In memoriam
Jin Sun Yu

Aber welcher Gewinn wäre es auch, wenn wir einer Sprache auf den Kopf zusagen dürften: Du hast das und das Einzelmerkmal, folglich hast du die und die weiteren Eigenschaften und den und den Gesammtcharakter! – wenn wir, wie es kühne Botaniker wohl versucht haben, aus dem Lindenblatte den Lindenbaum construiren könnten.

Georg von der Gabelentz (1901: 481)

Linguistic typology is an inference from the science of languages for the science of language.

Roman Jakobson (1958: 24)

The hypothesis that typology is of theoretical interest is essentially the hypothesis that the ways in which languages differ from each other are not entirely random, but show various types of dependencies among those properties of languages which are not invariant differences stateable in terms of the 'type'.

Joseph H. Greenberg (1974: 54–5)

Contents

Preface

No doubt authors will give readers plenty of reasons as to why they have written their books. I am no exception, but I am content to offer one here. The currently available introductory literature on linguistic typology is in need of updating, addition and revision in the light of recent developments in the field. The classic introductory volumes, Mallinson and Blake (1981), Comrie (1989) and Croft (1990), were published nine or more years ago, although each of them continues to be a great source of inspiration and information for students and professional linguists alike and, I must add, did indeed set an excellent example for me. These texts must thus be supplemented by a substantial amount of additional reading, which not everyone has access to, or has time for. Whaley (1997), a more recent and equally outstanding book, may be suitable only for beginners because by design it does not treat each topic in sufficient detail – its coverage of an admirably wide range of topics notwithstanding. I have thus written this book with a view to providing readers with detailed up-to-date critical discussion of a few carefully selected topic areas, and of related theoretical issues. In contrast to Whaley (1997), therefore, I have opted for depth of discussion in preference to breadth of coverage. By the time they have reached the last page of this book, readers will have a good understanding of important theoretical issues in current linguistic typology, and a good deal of exposure to 'exotic' languages. My expectation is that they will also have a greater appreciation of the unity, and diversity of human language.

Brief words are in order to explain why certain topic areas, and not others, have been chosen for the present book. Originally, I had intended to address topic areas other than the ones discussed in the introductory texts referred to above, but I very quickly abandoned that idea. I realized that in order to present a good overview of linguistic typology within the usual limitations of space I would have to focus primarily on the areas in which most important theoretical developments have taken place. Furthermore, in the true spirit of modern linguistic typology, I needed to select topic areas so that at least some of them would 'hang together', as it were, with the effect that discussion of one topic area could at least partially mesh conceptually with discussion of another. For instance, it has been demonstrated that there are such significant correlations between word order on the one hand, and case marking and relative clauses on the other. Hence a chapter each on basic word order, case marking and relative clauses. I have also included discussion of causative constructions because they are one of the most recurrent research topics in the history of modern linguistics and, admittedly, also because I personally have much research interest in them. Moreover, I felt the need to address the utility of linguistic typology in other areas of linguistics because it is very important for linguistic typologists to inform fellow linguists that their research is of much relevance to other areas of interest in linguistics. Thus one of the chapters has been devoted to the role of linguistic typology in historical reconstruction, linguistic prehistory and language acquisition. There is also a chapter-length discussion of non-Greenbergian or European approaches to linguistic typology, because I am of the view that those interested in linguistic typology must also be given an opportunity to become aware of the existence of at least some of the 'minor' approaches to linguistic typology.

Books like this one cannot be completed without the assistance and generosity of many people. I am indebted to those who kindly sent me copies of their work, procured obscure references, or answered questions about languages or areas of their specialization: Keith Allan, Peter Austin, Barry Blake, Hilary Chappell, Kaoru Horie, Mary Laughren, Mingchen Liu, Ng Bee-Chin, Patrizia Pacioni, Masayoshi Shibatani, Kenneth Shields, Anna Siewierska, Jane Simpson, John Taylor, Viktor Xrakovsky and Jaehoon Yeon. I am most grateful to the readers of my manuscript for their insightful comments and suggestions: Barry Blake, Anna Siewierska and an anonymous reviewer from the *Longman Linguistics Library Series* editorial board. They read and commented on the whole draft of the book, and to them should be attributed the better ideas rather than the remaining errors, inconsistencies and misinterpretations, for which I bear the full responsibility. I also wish to take this opportunity to thank my students for asking numerous awkward questions, forcing me to think hard about what I took for granted and also 'teaching' me how to teach what I know. There are too many to thank each one here, but the following students deserve a special mention: William Samuel Appadurai, Katie Brannan, Tanya Fernandez, Pamela Gordon, Jessica Green, Mell Hodge, Elizabeth Hogbin, Lorraine Johnston, Jacqui Jones, Kapka Kasabova, Michelle Lazar, Arlette Mason, Rachel Milburn, Rajan Nair, Megan Nicholl, Vickie Saunders, Vera Scurr and Helen Sommerville. This is a better book because of their input. I cannot forget to thank Vickie Saunders for her assistance in checking the Bibliography. A word of gratitude must go to Maureen Bruce, Treena Daly, Jane Hinkley, Muriel King and Fiona McDonald for their logistical assistance, and smiles. The writing of the present book commenced when I spent the second half of 1997 as Honorary Visiting Fellow in the Department of Linguistics at La Trobe University, Melbourne. I would like to record here my gratitude to the then Head of Department, Hilary Chappell and my host, Barry Blake for their support, without which I would have found it very difficult to initiate the writing process. Special thanks must go to Ng Bee-Chin, who not only introduced me to Ping's at La Trobe University, but also quite often made time to talk with me over Ping's first-class Chinese food. On a more personal level I wish to thank Barry and Maree, Bee and Francesco, Keith and Wendy, Mr and Mrs Kyu Hong Lee, Mr and Mrs Sung Su Lee, and Dr and Mrs Mingchen Liu for their hospitality during my study leave in Melbourne. Special mention must be made of Assistant Vice Chancellor Alistair Fox, who has over the last ten years supported the discipline of linguistics in the Division of Humanities at the University of Otago with such foresight and distinction; to him I am greatly indebted for being able to pursue my research interests. My brother, Jae Tak, must be thanked for his encouragement of interests very remote indeed from his own. Last but not least my sincere thanks go to my family for having the courage to agree once again to put up with my writing a book. What you are about to read is as much the product of their support and tolerance as that of my work.

Jae Jung Song
Dunedin, NZ
May 2000

Abbreviations

ABS	absolutive	FUT	future
ACC	accusative	GEN	genitive
A(GT)	agent	IMP	imperative
APASS	antipassive	INC	inclusive
APPL	applicative	INCMP	incompletive
ASP	aspect	IND	indicative
AUX	auxiliary	INST	instrumental
BEN	benefactive	INTR	intransitive
C	causative affix	INV	inverse
CL	classifier	IO	indirect object
CLT	clitic	IPFV	imperfective
CMP	completive	LOC	locative
COM	comitative	M	masculine
COMP	complementizer	MVT	movement affix
CONJ	conjunction	NFUT	nonfuture
CP	causative prefix	NOM	nominative
CREL	correlative	NP	noun phrase
CS	causative suffix	NR	nominalizer
D	deictic	OBJ	object
DAT	dative	OBL	oblique
DECL	declarative	OBV	obviative
DEF	definite	OPT	optative
DEM	demonstrative	P	patient
DEP	dependency	PART	participle
DET	determiner	PASS	passive
DO	direct object	PFV	perfective
DR	direct	PL	plural
ERG	ergative	POSS	possessive
F	feminine	PROG	progressive
FIN	finite	PROX	proximate

PRS	present	SR	subordinator
PRT	particle	SUBJ	subjunctive
PRTV	partitive	TA	tense/aspect
PST	past	TNS	tense
PURP	purposive	TOP	topic
Q	question	TR	transitive
REL	relativizer	V	verb
RLS	realis	1	1st person
RPRO	relative pronoun	2	2nd person
SBJ	subject	3	3rd person
SG	singular		

Acknowledgements

We are grateful to the following for permission to reproduce copyright material:

Table 1.1 from Rijkhoff, J. et al. in *Studies in Language* 17(1): 169–203 (1993), Tables 2.23, 2.24 and 2.25 from Bybee et al. *Studies in Typology and Diachrony* (1990) and Table 2.27 from Siewerska, A. et al. in *Studies in Language* 20: 115–161 (1990), all reproduced by permission of John Benjamins Publishing Co.; Tables 2.1, 2.2, 2.4 and 4.3 from Greenberg, J. *Universals of Language* (1963), reproduced by permission of the MIT Press; Tables 2.5, 2.6 and 4.4 from Dryer, M. in *Journal of Linguistics* 27: 443–482, reproduced by permission of the author and Cambridge University Press; Tables 2.8, 2.17 from Tomlin, R. *Basic Word Order* (1986), reproduced by permission of Croom Helm; Tables 2.13, 2.14 and 2.16 from Dryer, M. in *Language* 68: 81–138 (1992) and Tables 4.1 and 4.2 from Fox, B. in *Language* 63: 856–870 (1987), all reproduced by permission of Linguistic Society of America; Tables 2.15, 2.18 and 2.21 from Hawkins, J. *A Performance Theory of Order and Consistency* (1994), reproduced by permission of the author and Cambridge University Press; Table 2.22 from Hawkins, J. et al. in *Lingua* 74: 219–257 (1988), reproduced by permission of Elsevier Science; Tables 3.1 and 3.5 from Nichols, J. *Linguistic Diversity in Space and Time* (1992), reproduced by permission of The University of Chicago Press; Tables 3.2 and 3.6 from Siewierska, A. *Sprachtypologie und Universalienforschung* 49: 149–176 (1996), reproduced by permission of Akademie Verlag; Table 6.2 from Gass, S. *On TESOL '81* (1982), reproduced by permission of TESOL.

While every effort has been made to trace the owners of copyright material, in a few cases this has proved impossible and we take this opportunity to offer our apologies to any copyright holders whose rights we have unwittingly infringed.

1

Introducing linguistic typology

1.1 What do linguistic typologists study?

There are generally estimated to be about 4,000 to 6,000 languages in the world. Depending on where the distinction between languages and dialects is drawn, the total number of the languages of the world may easily shoot up to 7,000.[1] This sheer number alone gives one at least a rough idea of the immense diversity of the languages of the world. A moderate example of this diversity comes from basic word order – which will be discussed in detail in Chapter 2. Consider the following six sentences, each exhibiting one of the six basic word orders.

(1) Korean (SOV)
     kiho-ka   saca-lĭl   cha-ass-ta
     Keeho-NOM lion-ACC kick-PST-IND
     'Keeho kicked the/a lion.'

(2) Thai (SVO)
     khon níi kàt mǎa tua nán
     man this bite dog CL that
     'This man bit that dog.'

(3) Welsh (VSO)
     Lladdodd draig   ddyn
     killed   dragon man
     'A dragon killed a man.'

(4) Malagasy (VOS)
     manasa ny lamba ny vehivavy
     wash   the clothes the woman
     'The woman is washing the clothes.'

(5) Panare (OVS)
     pi?   kokampö unkï?
     child washes   woman
     'The woman washes the child.'

(6) Nadëb (OSV)
     samǔ̈ǔy   yi   qa-wùh
     howler-monkey people eat
     'People eat howler-monkeys.'

What is most intriguing about these examples is the way the three main
expressions – denoting the entity which initiates an action (S), the entity at
which that action is directed (O) and the action itself (V) – occur in all six
logically possible permutations, i.e. SOV, SVO, VSO, VOS, OVS and OSV.
The diversity evident in basic word order will further increase with the order
of constituents at other levels also taken into consideration, e.g. the word
order within noun phrases, prepositional or postpositional phrases, and the
like. With the six logically possible basic word orders all realized in the
languages of the world, however, it may not immediately be clear whether
or not there is anything significant about basic word order which can shed
light on the nature of human language. (See 2.1 for discussion of the concept of basic word order, and also of flexible or free word order languages, as
opposed to languages with basic word order.)

   Despite the differences among them there must be certain properties
whereby the languages of the world are all recognized as falling into the
category of human languages – perhaps an obvious point to make. There must,
therefore, be an underlying unity to human languages. There are linguists
who are concerned directly with discovering this unity by studying the rich
structural variation found in the languages of the world. These linguists are
known as *linguistic typologists*, or *typologists* for short. Their investigation of
cross-linguistic variation is referred to as *linguistic typology*, or *typology* for short.
For instance, having observed the existence of the six logically possible basic
word orders in the languages of the world, linguistic typologists will ask
questions such as: what is the actual distribution of the six basic word orders
in the languages of the world?, is each of the basic word orders more or less
equally distributed in the languages of the world?, if not, what is the frequency of each basic word order?, and which basic word order(s) is (are) the
most or least common in the languages of the world? As cross-linguistic
research has so far shown, there is, in fact, a preponderance of the two basic
word orders exemplified in (1) and (2), that is SOV, and SVO. This suggests
strongly that the distribution of the basic word orders cannot possibly be
random or arbitrary because otherwise the six basic word orders should
be more or less evenly distributed among the languages of the world, that
is about 16.6 per cent for each basic word order. More importantly, the

distinct preference for SOV and SVO points the way towards the existence
of (a) certain motivating factor(s) for the skewed distribution of basic word
order. Linguistic typologists will thus also raise the question as to why the
distribution of the basic word orders is the way it is.

Furthermore, linguistic typologists compare two or more structural properties with a view to ascertaining whether there exists a (statistically significant) correlation between them and, if so, how strong that correlation is.
For instance, basic word order has been compared with the presence (or
absence) of prepositions, or postpositions. Verb-initial languages (or languages with the verb appearing first in the sentence, i.e. VSO and VOS) are
always found to be equipped with prepositions, not with postpositions.[2] This
means that verb-initial word order does not co-occur with postpositions.
Welsh is a typical language exhibiting this correlation, as in (7) and (8):

(7)   Welsh
       Gwelodd y   bachgen ddyn ddoe
       saw   the boy   man yesterday
       'The boy saw a man yesterday.'

(8)   Welsh
       a.   trwy   Gaerdydd
             through Cardiff
             'through Cardiff'
       b.   yn y   cōr
             in the choir
             'in the choir'

This finding constitutes one important property of human language in that
it does represent a constraint on possible variation within human language:
no verb-initial languages are predicted to have postpositions instead of prepositions. There is no reason why the two independent properties, basic word
order, and the presence of prepositions or postpositions, should correlate
with each other to the effect that the presence of verb-initial word order
implies that of prepositions. Logically speaking, there should also be verb-
initial languages with postpositions, which is not the case. The question that
directly confronts linguistic typologists is, why should such a correlation
exist at all? In more general terms, the primary task for linguistic typologists
is to identify and explain the properties that make human language what
it is. The question can thus be rephrased: what is a possible, as opposed to
impossible, human language? But, as has already been demonstrated with
respect to the distribution of the basic word orders (that is, with all the
six logical possibilities of word order attested to different degrees in the
languages of the world), linguistic typologists may also address an attenuated
form of the question: what is a more probable, as opposed to less probable,
human language?

1.2   Typological analysis

In order to reach the stage of asking and, hopefully, answering the question posed at the end of the previous section, linguistic typologists will need to go through the following four stages in typological analysis: (i) identification of a phenomenon to be studied; (ii) typological classification of the phenomenon being investigated; (iii) the formulation of (a) generalization(s) over the classification; and finally (iv) the explanation of the generalization(s).

First, linguistic typologists must determine what they would like to investigate. There are, of course, no theoretical restrictions on what structural properties or grammatical phenomena should or should not be studied. Nor are there any restrictions on how many properties should simultaneously be studied at a given time. Some linguistic typologists may choose one feature of language as an object of inquiry, whereas others may at once probe into more than one. But what one must exercise circumspection about is which of the properties selected for typological analysis is actually worthwhile investigating, with some properties proving to be more interesting or revealing than others. Said differently, some are more likely than others to lead to linguistically significant typological generalizations. For instance, compare the typological property of basic word order with the presence of question particles. As has already been hinted at, the selection of basic word order as a typological property has led to a number of empirically or theoretically interesting questions and issues. But what about use of question particles? The languages of the world will be typologized into two groups: those with question particles and those without. But what is there to be understood from this bland typological classification? There does not seem to be much more to be done or learned about it. It is difficult to imagine that this typological classification can be put to much use at all in understanding the nature of human language – unless perhaps it is studied in conjunction with some other structural properties. In a way, therefore, the first stage of typological analysis may depend crucially on the investigator's insight or intuition to a great extent just as in any kind of scientific endeavour. Furthermore, the first and second stages of typological analysis may have to be carried out concurrently to a certain degree. This is because, unfortunately, one does not know in advance whether or not the chosen property is going to be a typologically significant one.

Once a property (or properties) has (or have) been chosen for typological analysis, structural types pertaining to that property (or those properties) will be identified or defined so that the languages of the world can eventually be classified into those types. In the case of basic word order, for instance, six (logically possible) types are identified, whereby languages are typologized according to the basic word order type that they exhibit. Some languages will be grouped as SOV, others as VSO, and so forth. The identification of the six basic word order types, and the classification into those types of the languages of the world will then constitute the linguistic typology of basic word order. The skewed distribution of the six basic word orders emerging from this typological classification is such that there is concluded to be a distinct tendency towards SOV, and SVO in the languages of the world. This can then be taken to be a significant generalization over the data classified – representing stage (iii) above. It will also ultimately lead to the question as to why there is this strong tendency, i.e. stage (iv). At this final stage, linguistic typologists will make every attempt to explain the structural tendency in question.

Similar comments can be made of the correlation between verb-initial word order, and prepositions, which was alluded to in 1.1. First, the languages of the world are surveyed in terms of basic word order on the one hand, and the presence (or absence) of prepositions or postpositions on the other. There are four different logical combinations of these two properties (2 × 2): (i) verb-initial languages with prepositions; (ii) verb-initial languages with postpositions (i.e. non-prepositions); (iii) non-verb-initial (i.e. verb-medial or verb-final) languages with prepositions; and finally (iv) non-verb-initial languages with postpositions. The languages of the world will then be classified into these four types. As it turns out, all the types except for that in (ii) are well represented in the languages of the world as illustrated by the following examples:

(9)   Tzotzil (VOS & prepositions)
    a.   ʔi-s-pet   lok'el ʔantz ti t'ul-e
        CMP-3-carry away woman the rabbit-CLT
        'The rabbit carried away the woman.'
    b.   xchiʔuk s-malal
        with   3-husband
        'with her husband'

(10) Yoruba (SVO & prepositions)
    a.   bàbá ra   bàtà
        father bought shoes
        'Father bought shoes.'
    b.   ní ọjà
        at market
        'at the market'

(11) Canela-Krahô (SOV & postpositions)
    a.   hũmre te   rop cakwĩn
        man   PST dog beat
        'The man beat the dog.'
    b.   pur kam
        field in
        'in the field'

This classification will eventually give rise to the generalization: the presence of verb-initial word order implies that of prepositions. This will in turn call for an explanation as to why this implicational relationship exists between verb-initial word order and prepositions.

1.3   Typology of language universals

Properties such as the preponderance of SOV and SVO, and the correlation between verb-initial word order and prepositions are often referred to as language universals in linguistic typology. Strictly speaking, however, language universals must be true of all languages. Under this strict definition of the term, neither the preference for SOV and SVO, nor the correlation between verb-initial word order and prepositions may qualify as a language universal since the former is merely a structural tendency in human language, albeit a strong one, and since the latter makes explicit reference only to verb-initial languages with prepositions. In other words, only properties which all human languages have in common may be taken to be language universals. In linguistic typology, however, whatever statistically significant patterns or tendencies that are found in the languages of the world are also referred to as language universals.[3] The correlation between verb-initial word order, and prepositions *is* a language universal in the sense that it embodies one significant statement about the nature of human language. (So is the preponderance of SOV, and SVO.) Thus, while not making explicit reference to non-verb-initial languages, the correlation between verb-initial word order and prepositions does capture a fundamental structural property of human language by excluding the logically possible co-occurrence of verb-initial word order and postpositions from the domain of human language as will presently be explained in more detail. In the present book, then, it is this broad interpretation of language universals that will be adopted (but cf. Ramat 1987).

Interestingly enough, language universals can themselves be typologized into four different types, by using two parameters: (i) absolute vs. non-absolute; and (ii) implicational vs. non-implicational. Absolute universals are exceptionless by definition. An example of this type of universal is: all languages have ways to turn affirmative sentences into negative ones (e.g. *James kicked the dog* → *James did not kick the dog*). Non-absolute universals – also known as universal tendencies, or statistical universals – are not without exceptions but the empirical validity of this type of universal does far outweigh the number of exceptions that may exist. The preponderance of SOV and SVO in the languages of the world is a non-absolute universal. More often than not, various statistical methods are employed in order to determine whether or not a given tendency is statistically significant (cf. 1.5.3).

Implicational universals take the form of 'if p, then q'. Thus the presence of one property (i.e. the *implicans*) implies that of another (i.e. the *implicatum*). A good example of this type of universal has already been provided: verb-initial languages are always found to be equipped with prepositions. This can be rewritten as follows: if a language is verb-initial, then it is also prepositional. By design implicational universals will be based on interaction of more than one property. Thus there may also be implicational universals, involving more than two properties. One such example is Greenberg's (1963b) Universal 5: if a language has dominant SOV order and the genitive follows the governing noun, then the adjective likewise follows the noun. In this implicational universal two properties are needed to predict a third. It is also possible that the implicatum can be more than one property. Again, Greenberg (1963b) offers an example of this kind: if some or all adverbs follow the adjective they modify, then the language is one in which the qualifying adjective follows the noun and the verb precedes its nominal object as the dominant order (Universal 21). It is not difficult to see that, other things being equal, implicational universals that predict the presence of multiple properties on the basis of a single property are more highly valued than those that predict the presence of a single property on the basis of multiple properties. To put it differently, it is preferable to predict as much as possible on the basis of as little as possible (Moravcsik 1997: 107). By this criterion of economy alone Greenberg's Universal 21 is of more value than his Universal 5.

The predicting power of implicational universals is not confined solely to the properties to which they make explicit reference. Thus given the implicational universal 'if a language is verb-initial, then it is also prepositional', there are two other situations that fall out from that universal (in addition to the impossibility of verb-initial languages with postpositions). By making no claims about them, it, in effect, has the advantage of saying something about non-verb-initial languages with prepositions or with postpositions, thereby recognizing these languages also as possible human languages. In other words, the implicational universal in question rules out only verb-initial languages with postpositions as impossible human languages – that is, p & $-q$ (or not q), contradicting the original statement of 'if p, then q'. What is referred to as a *tetrachoric* table is often used to indicate clearly which of the logically possible combinations of two (or more) properties is allowed or disallowed.

(12)   *prepositions   postpositions*
    verb-initial   Yes   No
    non-verb-initial   –   –

The tetrachoric table in (12) shows that the combination of verb-initial word order, and postpositions is an impossibility in human language. Thus the implicational universal effectively serves as a constraint on possible variation within human language.

Non-implicational universals, on the other hand, do not involve the predicting of property X on the basis of property Y. They involve only a single typological property. They do not appear in the form of 'if p, then q'. The preponderance of SOV, and SVO is such a universal. Note that this particular universal is not only non-implicational but also non-absolute, thereby illustrating that universals may cut across the distinction between the absolute/non-absolute, and implicational/non-implicational parameters. Thus, in addition to non-absolute non-implicational universals, there may also be (i) absolute implicational universals, (ii) absolute non-implicational universals, and (iii) non-absolute implicational universals. An example of (i) has already been provided: if a language is verb-initial, it is also prepositional; an example of (ii) comes from the fact that all languages have ways to convert affirmative sentences into negative ones, and finally (iii) is exemplified by Greenberg's Universal 21 (see above).

1.4   Language universals and linguistic typology

Language universals are properties which must at least be true of the majority of the human languages. They also impose constraints or limits on possible variation within human language. Linguistic typology, on the other hand, is concerned with classification of languages into different structural types (i.e. individual structural properties, or correlations between them).[4] Therefore, 'it may seem to the uninitiated something of a contradiction in terms to handle these apparently quite distinct areas of investigation together' (Mallinson and Blake 1981: 7). But, as may be gleaned from previous sections, the contradiction is more apparent than real. Language universals research, in fact, thrives on linguistic typology. This is because in order to discover language universals linguistic typologists first need typological classification on which to work. Thus linguistic typology 'provides material for establishing language universals' (Mallinson and Blake 1981: 7). With languages classified into different types, linguistic typologists may be able to discern patterns or regularities in the distribution of the types, for example, with some types being significantly more common than others, or with one (or more) of the logically possible types completely unattested or only marginally attested in the languages of the world.

This close relationship between language universals and linguistic typology can be most clearly demonstrated by one of the language universals that have been discussed in brief in previous sections: the strong tendency towards SOV and SVO. If the languages of the world had not been surveyed in terms of all possible six basic word orders, this structural tendency would never have been brought to light in the first place. To put it differently, the typological classification in terms of basic word order of the languages of the world is a prerequisite for the significant statement to be made about human language. Imagine the prospect of discovering the tendency in question by examining only one language, or even a handful of languages! This may be too extreme an example but the point could not be made more strongly. Language universals underlying structural tendencies are statistical in nature. Thus it comes as no surprise that they demand statistical data.

Further demonstration of the symbiotic interaction between language universals research and linguistic typology comes from implicational universals. Recall that the presence of verb-initial word order implies that of prepositions (or p & q). This universal also makes indirect reference to the two other logical possibilities ($-p$ & q, and $-p$ & $-q$; cf. (12)). While making no negative claims about non-verb-initial languages, it does not only sanction verb-initial languages with prepositions as possible human languages but it also rules out verb-initial languages with postpositions as impossible human languages. In order to arrive at the actual formulation of this implicational universal, however, it first needs to be ascertained which of the four logical possibilities is attested or unattested in the languages of the world. That can be achieved only on the basis of initial typological classification of the languages of the world in terms of basic word order, and also in terms of the distribution of prepositions and postpositions.

The interaction between language universals and linguistic typology also highlights one of the virtues of formulating language universals on the basis of typological classification. Typological classification naturally calls for data from a wide range of languages (see 1.5.3 on how languages are selected or sampled for this purpose). Only by working with such a wide range of data is one able to minimize the risk of misinterpreting some of the least common structural properties as being (part of) language universals. This risk is more real than some linguists may be willing to admit because, when deciding to work with a small number of familiar or well-known languages (for whatever reasons), one is likely to deal with structural properties which may not in any real sense be representative of the languages of the world. For instance, use of relative pronouns in relative clauses is very common in European languages but it has been pointed out that it is a cross-linguistically infrequent type (Comrie 1989: 149). Therefore, universal claims about, or universal theories of, relative clauses which are put forth on the basis of these European languages alone should immediately be suspect.

1.5 Assumptions and problems in typological analysis

There are at least two theoretical assumptions which must be made in typological analysis: *cross-linguistic comparability* and *uniformitarianism*. In addition there are at least two practical problems that linguistic typologists must address and, if possible, make explicit statements as to how they are going to deal or have dealt with in their typological investigation. These are problems of *language sampling* and *data collection*. It seems at least that, while the two assumptions are deemed reasonably uncontroversial, the problems of language sampling and data collection are far from resolved although, as will be seen in 1.5.3 and 1.5.4, the problem of language sampling has over the years attracted a good deal of attention from linguistic typologists. These issues and problems will in turn be discussed with a view to laying the groundwork for the chapters that follow.

1.5.1   Cross-linguistic comparability

Linguistic typologists study cross-linguistic variation in order to understand the nature of human language. The best way to gain access to the cross-linguistic variation of a grammatical phenomenon is to study as wide a range of languages as possible. Because they study a large number of languages all at once, linguistic typologists must therefore ensure that what they are comparing across languages be the same grammatical phenomenon, not different grammatical phenomena. It goes without saying that languages should be studied against one another in terms of the same property. Otherwise one will never be able to achieve what one sets out to: the description of cross-linguistic variation of the same grammatical phenomenon. If one wants to construct a typology of, for example, comparative constructions, how does one then actually make sure that one is comparing the comparative construction in language X with the same construction, and not something else, in language Y? To ask it differently, how does one identify the same grammatical phenomenon across languages? This is what Stassen (1985: 14) refers to aptly as *the problem of cross-linguistic identification*.

There are basically two ways of dealing with the problem of cross-linguistic identification (cf. Stassen 1985: 14–15; Croft 1995: 88–9). First, one may choose to carry out cross-linguistic identification on the basis of purely formal or structural criteria. A set of formal properties, e.g. verbal marking, adpositions (i.e. prepositions and postpositions), etc., may first be put together in order to identify a given grammatical phenomenon. Alternatively, one can opt for functional – i.e. semantic, pragmatic and/or cognitive – definitions of the grammatical phenomenon to be studied.

Which of the two types of definition – formal or functional – will meet the needs of typological analysis better? Croft (1995: 88) gives two reasons as to why formal definitions do not work for cross-linguistic comparison. First, structural variation across languages is so great that it cannot serve as the basis of cross-linguistic identification. As an example, Croft takes note of the fact that the subject relation in English may be expressed by means of two different grammatical relations in languages such as Quiché, Lakhota and Spanish. Second, formal definitions are internal to the structural system of a single language, thereby again failing to constitute the basis of a language-independent definition. In a similar vein Stassen (1985: 14) also points out that language-dependent formal definitions do not tie in with linguistic typology, one of the primary aims of which is to characterize structural variation across languages. In addition, there are two fundamental reasons why formal definitions are not deemed appropriate for the resolving of the problem of cross-linguistic identification. Structural variation itself is what in the first place linguistic typologists want to identify for cross-linguistic comparison. In other words, one cannot make use of the structural variation which has not yet been established in order to identify that structural variation. It will be tantamount to using a (non-existent) description of X in order to describe X. Moreover, there can hardly be any *purely* formal definitions. Formal definitions of grammatical phenomenon X can only be identified and thus understood in the context of the function that X carries out. One cannot simply examine a given grammatical property and predict what function that grammatical property is used to carry out. This would be possible only if functions were inherent in, and thus deducible from, grammatical phenomena themselves. Rather, functions do arise out of what linguistic expressions are utilized for. For example, if one wants to study comparative constructions across languages, one cannot infer the function of comparison only from the linguistic expression in which that function is encoded (e.g. the use of adpositions, grammatical marking, etc.). One will not know what grammatical properties to look for in the first place, thereby being unable to recognize a comparative construction when one sees it.

In view of the foregoing objections to formal definitions, linguistic typologists opt for functional definitions for purposes of cross-linguistic identification. However, functional definitions may not be without problems, either. Far more frequently than not, functional definitions themselves tend to be based on pre-theoretic concepts, or ill-defined notions. This is not to say, of course, that the problem is unique to this type of definition. The definition of a given concept is always dependent on the understanding of other concepts which make up that definition – unless these other concepts are undefined theoretical primitives. For example, consider the semantic definition of comparison utilized by Stassen (1985: 15):

> a construction counts as a comparative construction (and will therefore be taken into account in the typology), if that construction has the semantic function of assigning a graded (i.e. non-identical) position on a predicative scale to two (possibly complex) objects.

In order to understand this definition fully one needs to have an understanding of what a predicative scale, a graded position, etc. are. Also note that the definition has nothing to say about what form or shape the construction in question will take. Thus functional definitions are more of heuristics for cross-linguistic identification than of definitions in the strict sense of the word. For this reason it may not always be entirely clear how wide a range of grammatical phenomena may be 'permitted' to fall under a given functional definition. As an example, take the semantically based definition of relative clauses adopted in Keenan and Comrie (1977: 63), which runs as follows:

> Our solution to [the problem of cross-linguistic identification] is to use an essentially semantically based definition of RC [relative clause]. We consider any syntactic object to be an RC if it specifies a set of objects (perhaps a one-member set) in two steps: a larger set is specified, called the *domain* of relativization, and then restricted to some subset of which a certain sentence, the *restricting* sentence, is true. The domain of relativization is expressed in surface structure by the *head NP*, and the restricting sentence by the *restricting clause*, which may look more or less like a surface sentence depending on the language.

As Mallinson and Blake (1981: 266) correctly point out, it is not the case that Keenan and Comrie's definition of the RC 'sets a lower limit on the degree to which the RC can resemble a simple sentence or full clause and still be an RC.' Whatever structure is seen to perform the relative clause function as described above will be taken to be an RC, no matter how little resemblance it may bear to the relative clause in well-known languages, e.g. English. Note that the definition contains no distinct structural properties by which to identify RCs, other than the mention of the restricting clause and the head NP. Thus one may not always be certain whether or not a given grammatical structure in language X is a relative clause. It may well be nothing more or less than a 'general' structure which happens to be taken pragmatically or contextually as having a relative clause interpretation. Consider the following example of a so-called adjoined clause from Warlpiri (Hale 1976), which is susceptible to both relative clause and temporal interpretations as the English translation of (13) indicates (also Mallinson and Blake (1981: 266–8)). (The same structure can also have a conditional interpretation.)

(13) Warlpiri
     ŋatjulu-ḷu ø-ṇa   yankiri pantu-ṇu,
     I-ERG   AUX-I emu   spear-PST
     kutja-lpa   ŋapa ŋa-ṇu
     COMP-AUX water drink-PST
     'I speared the emu which was/while it was drinking water.'

There is evidence that calls into question the grammatical status as a genuine relative clause of (13). First, the adjoined clause as a whole can be positioned before the main clause as in (14).

(14) Warlpiri
      yankiri-ḷi kutja-lpa ŋapa   ŋa-ṇu,
      ŋatjulu-ḷu ø-ṇa   pantu-ṇu
      'The emu which was drinking water, I speared it.' *or*
      'While the emu was drinking the water, I speared it.'

Moreover, the adjoined clause need not have an NP co-referential with an NP in the main clause (in which case a relative clause interpretation is not possible) as in (15).

(15) Warlpiri
      ŋatjulu-ḷu lpa-ṇa kaḷi   tjaṇtu-ṇu,
      I-ERG   AUX-I boomerang trim-PST
      kutja-ø-npa ya-nu-ṇu   njuntu
      COMP-AUX walk-PST-hither you
      'I was trimming a boomerang when you came up.'

Also note that the syntactic linkage of the adjoined clause with respect to the main clause is, as Hale (1976: 78) puts it, 'marginal [or very loose] rather than embedded'. In fact, how the adjoined clause is interpreted 'is not determined by the grammar, but rather by a subset of the system of maxims, which are presumably observed in the construction of felicitous discourse, involving such notions as "relevance", "informativeness", and the like' (Hale 1976: 88). Given these pieces of evidence, the question does immediately arise as to whether or not the adjoined clause in (13) should really be regarded as a relative clause although under Keenan and Comrie's semantically based definition of RCs it may still qualify as an RC.

This is exactly the same question that Comrie and Horie (1995) raise as to the status as the relative clause of grammatical structures like the one in Warlpiri. They (1995) observe that in Japanese relative clauses do not behave as they do in languages such as English. In English relative clauses behave distinctly from other types of complement clause, whether with verbal or nominal heads.[5] In Japanese, on the other hand, relative clauses are akin to complement clauses with nominal heads, distinct from complement clauses with verbal heads. In other words, there do not seem to be clear grammatical differences between relative clauses and complement clauses with nominal heads, with sentences potentially interpreted either as relative clauses or as complement clauses, 'depending on such factors as the semantics of the head noun (e.g. only certain head nouns allow the complement clause interpretation), and the plausibility of interpreting the head noun semantically as a constituent of the subordinate clause' (Comrie and Horie 1995: 69). They (1995: 73) also point out that in Khmer the grammatical marker used in relative clauses is 'not specifically a relative clause marker, but rather a general marker for associating subordinate clauses with head nouns'. They (1995: 74) thus draw the conclusion from these observations that, there being no clear distinction between relative clauses and complement clauses of head nouns, the basic notion of relative clauses may not be of universal validity if it is meant by that notion that relative clauses are a distinct syntactic construction correlating highly with relative clause interpretations. In other words, they suggest that languages which lack relative clauses, such as Japanese and Khmer, make use of a general syntactic construction for relating subordinate clauses to head nouns, which is in turn subject to a wide range of pragmatic, not semantic, interpretations including that of relative clauses.

When confronted with such a problem as this, individual investigators may ultimately have to make up their own mind as to whether or not the structures in Warlpiri, Japanese and Khmer should be taken to be relative clauses. However, such a decision should not be taken in an arbitrary or random manner. One must, in fact, take into account at least two criteria, one language-internal and the other cross-linguistic, when making that kind of decision: (i) *functional-structural consistency*, and (ii) *measure of recurrence* or, more accurately, *measure of cross-linguistic recurrence*. Without supporting evidence from these two, it may hardly be justifiable to interpret the functional definition of relative clauses too broadly, that is to accept the adjoined clause in Warlpiri, or the 'relative clause' in Japanese or Khmer as a genuine relative clause.

First, one must determine whether or not relative interpretations are mapped consistently onto the adjoined clause in languages like Warlpiri. Thus, if the adjoined clause is the option or strategy used consistently for the expressing of relative clause function, it must be regarded as a genuine example of relative clauses. If, on the other hand, the adjoined clause is associated only on an *ad hoc* basis with relative clause interpretations, its status as a relative clause will be very doubtful. Being one of the two structures employed consistently for the expressing of relative clause function in Warlpiri (Mary Laughren, personal communication), the adjoined clause must be taken to be none other than the relative clause construction *par excellence* in that language.[6]

Even if the criterion of functional-structural consistency has been met, one cannot be too cautious about the status as the relative clause of the adjoined clause in Warlpiri, for instance. One should also be circumspect enough to take the structure to be an exemplar of the relative clause if and only if it recurs with relative clause function in language after language. This is the criterion of measure of recurrence. Of course, it cannot categorically be said in how many languages the structure in question should appear in order to be classified as a relative clause construction. But what can be said is this: the more languages make use of the structure for the expressing of relative clause function, the stronger one's confidence grows in accepting that structure as constituting one of the types of relative clause construction.

The measure of recurrence may sound to some ears too 'commonsense' to be legitimate in serious scientific investigation. This kind of measure of recurrence, however, is also adopted in other types of scientific investigation, albeit in much more rigorous form. For example, water is predicted to boil at 100 degrees Celsius at one atmosphere pressure (i.e. 760 torr, or about 14.7 lb/sq in) and, in fact, we know that it does so precisely because of its *recurrent* physical behaviour of reaching the boiling point at that temperature. Similarly, if a given structure is used recurrently, and recurrently enough across languages to express relative clause function, it must be regarded as exemplifying one of the types of relative clause construction available in human language.

1.5.2   The Principle of Uniformitarianism

Linguistic typologists often study not only currently spoken languages but also extinct ones, provided that they have been documented. This may perhaps strike one as odd, if not surprising, because one may expect typological classification to be concerned only with the currently spoken languages of the world. One may be inclined to think that language universals represent constraints or limits on structural variation within human language as it *is*, not as it *was* (or for that matter as it *will be*). But then why do linguistic typologists also include extinct languages in their typological investigation? The assumption underlying this inclusion is what is generally known as *the Principle of Uniformitarianism* in linguistics (see Lass (1980: 53–7, 1997: 24–32) for discussion thereof in the context of historical linguistics).[7] Basically, what it means is that human languages of the past – or of the future for that matter – are not essentially different in qualitative terms from those of the present. It claims, therefore, that the fundamental properties of human language have remained invariable over time. There are believed to be no differences in evolutionary terms between languages of the past – as far back as one can go and claim the existence of human languages – and those spoken today. In other words, human language of today is at the same level of evolution as that of, say, 60,000 years ago.

This assumption is, of course, something that has never been subjected to empirical verification, and cannot be put to the test for obvious reasons; one simply cannot go back in time and examine languages spoken 60,000 years ago to see whether or not they were qualitatively different from those of today. Nor is there any logical reason why the principle should be correct. Nonetheless it plays an important role in typology (and equally in historical linguistics). The primary aim of typology is to discover universal properties of human language. Language universals should by definition be true of all human languages. If human languages were spoken 60,000 years ago, then these languages must also be included in any typological study, which is utterly impossible. In the absence of the Principle of Uniformitarianism, then, no typological analysis will be possible or, more accurately, complete simply because it is impossible to 'recover' all unrecorded extinct languages from oblivion. With the Principle of Uniformitarianism in place, however, linguistic typologists can examine languages spoken today and, if and where possible, attested extinct languages as well – since they are available for inclusion in typological study, anyway – and can still make claims about the nature of human language. Similar comments can also be made of languages of the future. Since it is expected that they will also be human languages, any typological study must in principle include them as well, which is out of the question. But the Principle of Uniformitarianism also works in the opposite direction of time from the present, thereby allowing linguistic typologists to extend to languages of the future such universal properties as they may have discovered on the basis of currently available data. After all, under the Principle of Uniformitarianism the nature of human language is assumed not to change over time.

There are also rather practical reasons why the Principle of Uniformitarianism is adhered to in linguistic typology. Without this principle, languages must be seen to evolve constantly as time passes by. But if languages were evolving through time, and were conceived of as being at different stages of linguistic evolution, grammatical descriptions that linguistic typologists employ for their research would be completely useless for typological research because they invariably – and inevitably – record languages at different points in time, or at different stages of evolution, with some grammars being descriptions of languages of more than a few hundred years ago, and others being far more recent ones.

The absence of the principle will also lead to the view – which incidentally is generally not accepted in linguistics – that some languages should be at a more advanced stage of evolution than others because one would not be able to claim that all human languages have evolved to the same level. If languages were at different stages of linguistic evolution, it would be impossible to engage in any typological research since one would (arbitrarily) have to target at one particular stage of evolution which all human languages have reached at one time or another, and to study all grammatical descriptions of the languages of the world at *that* stage of evolution (assuming, of course, that it is possible to select such a stage, and also to have access to all grammatical descriptions at once).[8]

The Principle of Uniformitarianism, then, provides a kind of frame of reference within which fruitful typological research can be carried out productively without being hindered unduly by the intractable methodological issue, which does not necessarily have to be resolved at the current stage of development of linguistic typology as an empirical approach to the study of language (see Croft (1995: 86–7) for typology as a linguistic theory).[9]

1.5.3   Approaches to language sampling

Intuitively speaking, the best way to discover language universals is perhaps to examine all languages of the world.[10] For obvious reasons, however, it is very easy to see why it is out of the question to do so. As was pointed out at the beginning of this chapter, there are about 4,000–7,000 languages currently spoken in the world. Individual linguistic typologists (or even a team of linguistic typologists for that matter) are unable to compare such a large number of languages or even a small fraction thereof in a reasonable span of time. In fact, economic considerations alone will rule the large-scale survey out as wholly unfeasible. What makes it even more unrealistic is the fact that not all languages of the world have been studied and described and are thus available for inclusion in typological research. It is correct to say that, as things stand, there are far more languages which await linguistic documentation than those which have been described. It is also true that many languages are so inadequately or poorly documented that linguistic typologists may not be able to find anything about the grammatical phenomena in which they are interested. In fact, it is plainly impossible to study all languages of the world because many languages have already died out, with some of them leaving little or no record, although their existence may be known to us (e.g. Arin, Assan, Kassitic, Illyrian, etc.). There may also be many other languages which are not even known to have existed. Furthermore, with dialects developing in separate languages over time, there will also be 'new' languages coming into being. If one's aim is to study all languages of the world, there must certainly also be room for these new languages in one's investigation. But, needless to say, there is no taking these 'future' languages into account before their birth, or emergence (cf. 1.5.2).

In view of these practical limitations of time, money, existence and descriptions (Perkins 1989: 297), linguistic typologists often work with a practically manageable set of languages or what is referred to commonly as a language sample. Naturally, questions arise as to how many languages should be included in a given sample, and how languages should be selected for that sample. A few researchers have over the years addressed these and other related questions but it seems that some of them 'unfortunately remain unresolved' (Croft 1995: 89).

Bell (1978) is the first to raise the issue of language sampling for typological research. In his programmatic yet most influential paper he explains the role of stratification in language sampling (i.e. the process of placing languages into different strata, e.g. genetic affiliation, geographic location, word order types, etc.) and discusses genetic, areal and bibliographic biases to be avoided in language sampling.

First, his discussion points the way towards the major methodological advantage of using stratified language samples. As Perkins (1989: 300) correctly points out, language sampling has two contradicting requirements to meet. A language sample must have as many languages as possible so that any inferences or generalizations drawn from that sample can be extended in an empirically sound manner to language in general. At the same time it must have as few languages as possible because that is the whole idea of using the sample in the first place. Pertinent to this second requirement is the risk of including more languages from each stratum than required, thereby introducing 'variables that are not independent of [genetic] affiliation and location'. In stratified samples the number of cases to be studied can be more substantially reduced than the number of cases required in other types of sample. This suggests strongly that one can at least in principle learn as much about the nature of human language from a sample with a few languages as from a sample with many languages (Perkins 1989: 298). Equally important is the fact that stratification in language sampling ensures at least in principle that languages to be chosen be independent, and 'not [be] identical cases that should more properly be considered different instances of the same case' (Perkins 1980: 60–61; 1992: 124). This is known as the issue of the independence of cases, which, as will presently be seen, has perhaps been the most intractable problem that linguistic typologists have to deal with in language sampling. Bell (1978: 127–9, 137–40) also highlights the importance of probability or random sampling. Use of probability or random samples does not only enable researchers to run various tests in order to ascertain whether or not their findings are statistically significant (or whether or not they are due to chance). But it also makes it possible 'to estimate the extent of the error from a single sample' (Bell 1978: 157). 'Evaluating risks [of sampling error] involved in inferences from a sample to the population of all languages is extremely desirable in ascertaining the precision of the results obtained in a particular test of a theory' (Perkins 1980: 59–60; 1992: 127). Indeed Tomlin (1986: 25–6), for instance, is able to choose the 'best' sample from a number of potential ones precisely because he employs this kind of stratified probability sampling technique.

Second, Bell (1978: 145–9) calls for language samples to be accurately representative of the actual distribution of the languages of the world. In order to achieve such a representative sample one must make every effort to overcome certain sampling biases. He refers specifically to genetic and areal biases that should be eliminated from language samples. Languages of a single language family have structural properties or features in common by virtue of having derived from the same source. They are bound to have inherited structural properties from their parent or ancestor language. Moreover, languages of different genetic lineages are also known to share structural properties or feature when they have long been in contact with one another. In other words, structural features may come to diffuse across genetic boundaries to the effect that they may be shared by various languages which are unrelated to one another or at least are from different subgroups within a family. Such an area of linguistic convergence is technically called a linguistic area or *Sprachbund*. For example, Meso-America is reported to be a fine example of Sprachbund (Campbell, Kaufman and Smith-Stark 1986). There are a number of features which the languages of Meso-America have in common but which are absent from languages outside the area: e.g. nominal possession; use of relational nouns; vigesimal numeral systems; non-verb-final basic word order; several widespread semantic calques; etc. Properties that languages share due to their common genetic heritage or contact are what may be called 'chance' or accidental structural properties of language families or linguistic areas, respectively (Comrie 1989: 10). They must be carefully distinguished from those properties which truly represent language universals, and should not be taken to be characteristic of human language. Special care must, therefore, be taken to ensure that particular language families or groups not be over-represented (or under-represented) in language samples but that languages be selected equitably from all known language families, or groups. Suppose one wants to study relative clause constructions on a cross-linguistic basis. If a given sample contains too many European languages at the expense of other groups or families, the use of relative pronouns will be given more weight or importance in one's investigation than it should be because, as was pointed out earlier, the use of relative pronouns is most frequently found in European languages and is, in fact, infrequent in other languages of the world. Any generalizations to be drawn from that sample will consequently suffer from over-representation of European languages, and the over-estimation of the relative pronoun type in universal theory of relative clause constructions. Conversely, if a language family is under-represented in a given sample, then it means that structural properties associated with that language family will in turn be afforded less significance than they should be, and also that other language families will end up being over-represented – even if it were only for the sake of making up for the predetermined size of the sample. Too many languages from a single Sprachbund may also be included in a sample, in which case there is a grave danger of misinterpreting as language universals structural properties which are characteristic of that Sprachbund. This danger looms larger when one is dealing with a linguistic area much greater than is conventionally known to exist. For instance, it was widely believed that there was a linguistic tendency for O(bject-)V(erb) languages to place modifying adjectives (or A) before nouns (or N). However, Dryer (1989: 274–5) finds that the putative correlation between OV and AN is due largely to the fact that it is the dominant pattern in Eurasia – which is not normally thought to constitute a Sprachbund. He points out that the tendency in the languages of the world is, in fact, the opposite pattern, i.e. OV and NA. Thus over-representation of languages of Eurasia must carefully be guarded against in the setting up of language samples.

Linguistic typologists often find themselves in an unenviable situation where they are forced to select languages for a sample, depending mainly on whether or not grammatical descriptions or grammars are available. This is indeed a very unfortunate situation but sometimes cannot be avoided. For instance, Indo-European languages are very well documented in both breadth and depth, whereas the coverage of the languages of New Guinea and South America is very meagre. Even if linguistic typologists are willing to incorporate a representative number of languages from New Guinea or South America in their samples, they may thus be unable to have a reasonable amount of access to them simply because there are not enough (detailed) grammars of languages of these regions available in the first place. This is something that cannot easily be remedied, and will continue to create a certain amount of distortion or tension in linguistic typologists' samples 'even where the existence of the skewing and of its disadvantages are [sic] recognized' (Comrie 1989: 11).

Linguistic typologists may also work in a place where already published grammars are unfortunately not readily accessible to them; the libraries that they rely on for their research may hold mainly Indo-European or Oceanic languages and not much else, for instance. This is what Bell (1978: 145) refers to aptly as bibliographic bias. If this kind of bias is unavoidable and present in a sample, the least that the investigator can do is to state openly the existence of the problem for the benefit of other linguists.

For the foregoing pragmatic reasons linguistic typologists often opt for so-called *convenience* or *opportunity samples* (Bell 1978: 128). They may only select languages which they are familiar with or have ready access to through grammatical descriptions or language consultants. In fact, a good number of ground-breaking typological works are based on such convenience samples (e.g. Greenberg (1963b); Comrie (1976); Keenan and Comrie (1977); Nichols (1986) *inter alia*). The obvious shortcomings in their samples notwithstanding they did not only provide much insight into the nature of human language, which continues to play an important role in typological research. But, more often than not, they also gave impetus to subsequent large-scale research. Needless to say, any generalizations or inferences based on such convenience samples should only be taken as what they are – suggestions or preliminary findings concerning cross-linguistic patterns, or language universals – and they should naturally undergo further empirical verification, or revision on the basis of more languages, or more adequately constructed language samples.

How can languages then be selected equitably from all language families of the world? Bell (1978: 145–9) puts forth a specific proposal as to how this can be achieved. He sets an arbitrarily controlled time depth of genetic relatedness at 3,500 years so that all languages of the world can fall into a number of delimitable genetic groups, in fact a total of 478 groups. For example, the Indo-European family is regarded as consisting of twelve groups, whereas the Australian stock produces about twenty-seven groups. The use of the controlled time depth of 3,500 years, albeit hopelessly arbitrary, is intended in no small measure to reflect genetic diversity within language families, or stocks (Bell 1978: 146). The more genetic groups there are within a family, or stock, the more genetic diversity that family, or stock exhibits. For instance, in Bell's calculation the Niger-Kordofanian, and Amerind stocks contain 900 languages each. But the genetic diversities of these two stocks are not comparable, with the former being less genetically complicated than the latter. The Niger-Kordofanian stock is allocated forty-four groups, while the Amerind stock is estimated to contain 150 groups. Bell's approach is based crucially on what may be termed *proportional representation*. Each language family contributes to a given sample in proportion to the number of the genetic groups in that family, or stock. Thus given the total number of 478 genetic groups in the languages of the world, each language family, or stock will take up a certain fraction of that total according to the number of genetic groups which that family, or stock encompasses. The Niger-Kordofanian stock will then be represented in a given sample at the ratio of 44/478 (or 9.2 per cent), whereas the Amerind stock will be given a much larger representation in the sample at the ratio of 150/478 (or 31.4 per cent). These same ratios of representation will apply regardless of the size of the sample. In a sample of 100 languages, for example, the Niger-Kordofanian stock will contribute about nine languages ($100 \times 44/478$), whereas the Amerind stock will be represented by about thirty-one languages ($100 \times 150/478$). Basically, this is a top-down approach in that the size of a sample is normally predetermined, and each language family or stock is proportionally represented in the final sample according to its share of the total number of genetic groups (Nichols 1992: 38).

Bell (1978) does not actually specify how areal bias is to be avoided in language sampling but it follows from his general discussion of sampling that it is possible to control for areal bias in much the same way as genetic bias has been dealt with. Thus no inordinate number of languages should be selected from the same geographical area for a given sample. To this end the whole world can be carved up into a number of geographical areas, for each of which only a representative number of languages can be selected. In this way the investigator can at least make a deliberate attempt to refrain from choosing too many languages from the same area since languages spoken in the same area are known to borrow from, or influence, one another, undergoing similar innovations.

Tomlin (1986: 24) follows Bell's (1978) sampling approach in that his primary aim in language sampling is also to produce a language sample which is representative of the languages of the world in both genetic and areal terms. But he makes a further attempt to hone the sampling technique by performing a statistical measurement known as *the Kolmogrov goodness-of-fit test* on his language sample. What this particular statistical test does is to evaluate the degree of disparity between the known theoretical genetic or areal distribution of the languages of the world (e.g. the overall genetic classification of the languages of the world as presented in Voegelin and Voegelin (1977) or Ruhlen (1987)) and proposed language samples. Only when its deviance from the theoretical distribution is found to be statistically non-significant, will a given sample be adopted and implemented for typological research. By making use of the information on genetic affiliation of the languages of the world as provided in Voegelin and Voegelin (1977), Tomlin (1986: 27) creates a genetic frame which consists of a large number of 'cells', or genetic groups of approximately the level of Italic/Romance of the Indo-European family. In principle, these cells are supposed to be comparable to one another in terms of time depth, or level of genetic classification. This is, then, Tomlin's equivalent to Bell's controlled time depth of genetic relatedness, i.e. 3,500 years.

In addition Tomlin sets up an areal frame which consists of twenty-six 'cells', or linguistic areas. Basically, most of these areas are uncontroversially recognized linguistic or cultural areas, e.g. South Asia, Meso-America, New Guinea, etc. Where no such linguistic or cultural areas are evident, negative definition is employed. For example, after Southeast Asia, East Asia, Europe and Mid Central Asia having each been taken up as cells, one is left with a vast area, which is then identified as North and Northeastern Asia. Tomlin then derives a sample of 402 languages from his database of 1063 languages, and runs the Kolmogrov test of goodness-of-fit on the sample to measure the extent of its deviance from the 'characteristics' of the theoretical genetic and areal frames. Note that Tomlin does not start with a predetermined sample size but rather arrives at a sample of 402 languages in the process of 'approximat[ing] the genetic and areal distribution of the world's languages using his sampling technique' (Nichols 1992: 39), i.e. a bottom-up approach. Tomlin (1986) is an improvement on Bell's (1978) approach to controlling for genetic and areal biases in that his sampling technique demands of language samples a statistically acceptable level of genetic and areal representativeness.

There is at least one fundamental issue that must be addressed with respect to the proportionally representative language sample as outlined by Bell (1978) and further refined by Tomlin (1986): the independence of cases. The issue is related directly to the question – in fact, a fundamental question in all statistical procedures – as to whether or not languages selected for a given sample are indeed independent of one another or, in other words, are independent cases or units of analysis (Bell 1978: 146; Dryer 1989: 261–3; Perkins 1989: 299–301; Perkins 1992: 123–5). This is essentially what is known as *Galton's problem* or *Galton's objection* in cultural anthropology: anthropological traits which are related to cultures must be independent of one another since such traits often diffuse through migration and/or borrowing.

Perhaps the independence of cases is well illustrated by the often discussed weakness of proportionally representative language samples: the effect on representation of the actual sample size. That is, whether or not small language families, or stocks can be taken into consideration hinges crucially on how many languages are going to be sampled. For instance, in Bell (1978) the Khoisan stock is thought to have five genetic groups. In order for this particular stock to contribute a single language to a sample the investigator must have no fewer than ninety-six languages in that sample. To put it differently, in samples of fewer than ninety-six languages there is no possibility of stocks like Khoisan being considered for typological research. This means that not all independent cases may have a chance of being included in a small sample. But the independence of cases certainly cannot be upheld when some independent cases are included in, but others are excluded from, the final sample because it will not be clear from that sample what the languages chosen are independent of. Even worse is the situation where small stocks that have been excluded from the sampling happen to possess exceptional or rare linguistic types because 'exceptional types test the rule' (Perkins 1988: 367). The weakness in question can actually be demonstrated by means of one of the samples discussed in Bell's (1978: 149) own paper. In his hypothetical sample of thirty languages, five out of the sixteen stocks (or 31.2 per cent) have nil representation!

Large language samples are generally not without problems, either. In a sample of, for example, 500 languages, there is no absolute guarantee that some of the languages chosen are not somehow remotely related to one another. There may be deeper genetic relatedness among the languages of the world than is generally believed (but cf. Nichols (1992: 40), who is not too much perturbed by this because she is of the view that there is much less deep relatedness among the languages of the world than is widely assumed). One can perhaps point out that there is not much one can do about deep genetic relatedness since there is at present no obvious way of detecting it. The independence of cases in language sampling is not just confined to genetic relatedness. Indeed it must also apply to linguistic areas since it proves very difficult not to include in large samples languages which may in one way or another have been in contact or may come from the same linguistic areas especially when these areas are not generally recognized in the literature. It is impossible, therefore, to extricate completely from large samples variables or factors that are not independent of genetic affiliation or geographical location. In fact, Dryer (1989: 263) goes so far as to suggest that it may not be possible to construct a sample of many more than ten languages if one decides to be really strict about the independence of cases in language sampling (but see Perkins (1989: 308)). Needless to say, a sample of ten languages is plainly unlikely to produce any significant generalizations about the nature of human language.

To sum up, in small samples where some language stocks are left out of consideration the independence of cases demanded of statistical sampling is not maintained because languages may not be independent of one another, with some being included in, and others being excluded from, the final sample. In the case of large samples as well, languages chosen may not be independent, with some being remotely related to one another or coming from the same linguistic area(s). Therefore, both the validity, and reliability of conclusions or inferences drawn from samples will necessarily be compromised unless the independence of cases is upheld strictly in the constructing of those samples.

Related to the independence of cases in language sampling is the distinction between linguistic preferences and actual frequencies of different linguistic types in the languages of the world. It is the former, not the latter, that language universals should be equated with. Some linguistic types may be the most frequently found in the languages of the world simply because they are utilized in *large* language families. Such linguistic types are not necessarily related to language universals, or linguistic principles which make up human language. The distinction in question is most clearly demonstrated by Dryer (1989: 259–60). He puts forward a scenario in which there are 1,000 languages in the world. In this world there is one large language family of 900 languages, with the remaining 100 languages evenly distributed among ten small language families (i.e. ten languages in each of these small families). All the 900 languages in the large family are SVO, and all the languages of the other ten small families are SOV. As Dryer asks, do we conclude from this distribution that there is a linguistic preference for SVO over SOV? Of course not. We will instead come to the conclusion that SOV represents a linguistic preference in basic word order. The basis of the conclusion is very clear. The fact that 900 out of the 1,000 languages are SVO is merely a non-linguistic historical accident. These 900 languages are SVO because, for example, they must have inherited the same basic word order from their parent language. There are ten SOV families as opposed to only one SVO family. The distinction between linguistic preferences and actual frequencies of linguistic types is an important one, which is often not recognized and made in the typological literature. Since it will be discussed in detail in Chapter 2, suffice it to mention that Tomlin's (1986) large-scale study of basic word order reveals that there is no statistical difference between the frequency of SOV and that of SVO, both being the most frequent basic word order types. It is tempting to draw the conclusion from this that there is no linguistic preference for SOV to the exclusion of SVO. But Dryer (1989: 269–70) demonstrates that there is indeed a linguistic preference for SOV over SVO, and that the lack of a statistical difference between SOV and SVO in Tomlin's investigation is due to the distinction between linguistic preferences and actual frequencies of different linguistic types not being maintained. For example, in Tomlin's sample about 40 per cent of the SVO languages come from Niger-Congo, and there is also a large contingent of SVO languages from Austronesian (Dryer 1989: 260, 270).

Perkins (1980) deals with the independence of cases by adding a 'qualitative' dimension to language sampling. He derives a probability or random sample of fifty languages/cultures from the population or universe of all cultures using as a frame the list of cultures proposed in Murdock's (1967) *Ethnographic Atlas*. He takes into consideration the languages which are spoken in the cultures listed by Murdock.[11] He further informs his selection of the fifty languages/cultures by ensuring on the basis of Voegelin and Voegelin (1966) and Kenny (1974) that they not be (substantially) close to each other in terms of genetic and cultural relatedness. He is acutely aware of the fact that in a large sample it is unavoidable to include closely related languages/cultures (see above). But this should not be permitted in all statistical procedures because, as has already been pointed out, these procedures 'presuppose the independence of cases' (Perkins 1992: 367). He thus establishes his sample of fifty languages in such a way that no two languages/cultures are from the same language family, or the same cultural area. Clearly, this is a significant improvement over the previous sampling attempts in that it is specifically designed to maximize the genetic (or cultural) distance between the languages of the sample. Therefore, Perkins's sampling strategy contrasts with Tomlin's, for instance, in that one and only one language will be selected for each language family regardless of the actual size of language families. For example, insofar as sampling is concerned, there is no 'qualitative' difference between a language family of ten languages, and a language family of 100 languages because both will contribute only one language each to the sample.

Perkins's deliberate attempt to maximize genetic distance within his sample is indeed a welcome step in the right direction of the discovering of linguistic preferences, rather than of the actual frequencies of different linguistic types, a point which was adequately illustrated by Dryer's example above. Furthermore, his sampling technique – at least in principle – makes a serious attempt to meet the requirement of the independence of cases in language sampling for purposes of statistical inferences. As Whaley (1997: 39) points out, a sample of fifty languages is also practically manageable in size for a single investigator; it may not be too difficult to collect fifty languages for typological research.

Dryer (1989: 261–3), however, casts doubt on whether or not the languages in Perkins's sample are truly independent of one another. In particular, he takes issue with the inclusion in the fifty language sample of three Nilo-Saharan languages (i.e. Ingassana, Maasai and Songhai) and six languages which are considered to be Mon-Khmer (Car, Semai, Khasi, Khmer, Palaung and Vietnamese).[12] Independence being a relative notion (Dryer 1989: 262), one may with little reservation accept the presence of the Nilo-Saharan languages in the same sample because Nilo-Saharan is a very remote grouping. But Dryer (1989: 262) is absolutely correct to raise the question as to how remotely related languages have to be in order to be admitted as independent for sampling purposes. Moreover, Dryer alludes to the fact that the notion of independence actually depends on what linguistic property is being investigated. Word order, for example, changes quite easily, whereas morphological properties may be less susceptible to change. Thus 'a pair of languages that one might consider independent for the purposes of word order might not be properly treated as independent for the purposes of morphology' (Dryer 1989: 262).

A potential problem specific to Perkins's sample is its lack of control for areal bias. In a way his decision not to include two languages from the same cultural area can perhaps be regarded as an attempt to guard against areal bias (Dryer 1989: 263) because cultural relatedness may possibly be indicative of geographical proximity. This, in fact, seems to be Perkins's rationale for deciding not to control for areal bias when he (1992: 126) says that

> [t]he sampling plan used insures that cultures included in the final sample are not closely related culturally. This is some insurance that languages that are similar *due to contact* and cultural borrowing are not included in the sample [emphasis added].

This assurance notwithstanding, Dryer (1989: 262) identifies in Perkins's sample a number of languages that come from well-defined linguistic areas, e.g. Southeast Asia, Pacific Northwest of North America, Meso-America, etc (cf. Tomlin (1986)), and he comes to the conclusion that the cultural frame that Perkins uses in lieu of an areal frame is far too fine for the purposes of controlling for areal bias. It is not clear at the moment whether or not Perkins's assumption is a sound or reasonably acceptable one to make in language sampling. But in this context it is worthwhile commenting, along with Dryer (1989: 283–4), that in general linguistic properties are not borrowed as easily as cultural ones (e.g. Driver and Chaney (1970) for discussion of the Yurok, Karok and Hupa tribes in California with their languages belonging to different stocks, yet their cultures being almost identical). Perhaps it may be judicious not to equate linguistic borrowing with cultural borrowing.

Perkins's sampling technique has taken a few innovative steps towards the basic requirements of statistical procedures. But the issue of the independence of cases does not seem to have been resolved completely in his fifty language sample. There is still room for suspecting that some of the fifty languages may at least be remotely related to one another in either genetic or areal terms. As has already been pointed out, Dryer (1989: 263) is of the opinion that no language sample with more than ten languages may be able to meet the requirement of the independence of cases. But for obvious reasons samples of ten or so languages are very unlikely to produce anything interesting or insightful about the nature of human language. This harks back to Perkins's observation that in language sampling a balance has to be struck between the two contradicting requirements: a language sample must have as many languages as possible so that any inferences or generalizations drawn from that sample can be extended in an empirically sound manner to language in general, while for practical, conceptual and statistical reasons it must also have as few languages as possible (see Perkins 1992: 123–4). In the final analysis, then, Perkins's sampling technique is also beset with the fundamental problem of the independence of cases, although it is designed to resolve that problem.

Dryer (1989) puts forward a novel yet ingenious method in language sampling. One of his aims is to achieve the independence of cases at the level of large *linguistic areas*, which are continental or almost continental in size though he (1989: 267) claims that his sampling method is able to control for 'the most severe genetic bias' as well. Note that Dryer's concept of *linguistic areas* should be distinguished from the conventional concept of linguistic areas or Sprachbund. (For the sake of distinction Dryer's *linguistic areas* will appear in italics in the present book.) In Dryer's work a *linguistic area* refers to 'an area in which at least one linguistic property is shared more often than elsewhere in the world to an extent which is unlikely to be due to chance, but which is probably due either to contact or remote genetic relationships' (Dryer 1989: 266). He also invokes the concept of a *genus*, which is analogous to Bell's (1978) genetic group. Genera are supposed to be comparable to the sub-families of Indo-European, e.g. Germanic or Romance – or a time depth of 3,500 to 4,000 years. The languages of a given sample are then placed into 322 genera in total, largely in line with the genetic classification of Ruhlen (1987) (cf. Bell's (1978) 478 genetic groups; in his actual sample of 542 languages, however, Dryer (1989: 267–9) only operates with 218 genera). Thus only genera, not individual languages, are counted and taken into consideration for purposes of typological investigation. Note that the independence of cases, which is vital for all statistical procedures, is not at all demanded at the level of genera, which are only identified and utilized in order to control for the most severe genetic bias, the assumption underlying this decision being that 'languages within genera are generally fairly similar typologically' (Dryer 1989: 267; but see below). The independence of cases is required strictly at the next stage of Dryer's sampling method, where the world is divided into five large continental (or almost continental) areas: Africa, Eurasia, Australia-New Guinea, North America and South America.[13] These five *linguistic areas* are then assumed to be independent of one another. It is thus at this level of the *linguistic areas* that the independence of cases is claimed to be achieved or maintained in Dryer's language sampling. The purpose of using these five *linguistic areas* is, therefore, to control not only for areal bias of the proportion that has not hitherto been understood to have a bearing on language sampling but also for remote genetic relatedness, which may not be amenable to conventional historical methods. Unless this type of areal bias – the underlying cause of which may possibly be partly or largely genetic (Dryer 1989: 266) – is controlled for in language sampling, there is indeed a distinct possibility of failing to realize when 'apparently statistically significant results . . . may simply reflect areal [or remotely genetic] phenomena rather than linguistic preferences' (Dryer 1989: 283).

The ingenuity of Dryer's approach lies precisely in the fact that the independence of cases is sought – to the extent that this is possible – at the level of the five *linguistic areas*, not at the level of genera, the number of which may be rather unwieldy for purposes of such statistical manipulation. His technique thus makes it possible 'to take into consideration all of the data at hand' (Croft 1995: 91), while dealing with only the five *linguistic areas* for purposes of controlling for areal *and* genetic biases. Moreover, the most severe genetic bias is claimed to be controlled for at the level of genera particularly because '[i]n some areas of the world, these genera are the maximal level of grouping whose genetic relationship is uncontroversial' (Dryer 1989: 267). It also seems that Dryer's decision to achieve the independence of cases at the level of *linguistic areas* makes much sense because the divisions between the five *linguistic areas* 'are rather well defined physically' (Dryer 1989: 268), and, should thus be far less controversial than the divisions between the 322 genera.

For further illustration of how Dryer's method actually works, the preference of SOV over SVO can be referred back to. Recall that Tomlin (1986) does not recognize any statistical difference, or significance between the actual frequency of SOV, and that of SVO in the languages of the world. Dryer (1989: 269–70), on the other hand, provides evidence in support of SOV being a linguistic preference over SVO as exemplified below (N.B.: Afr = Africa, Eura = Eurasia, A-NG = Australia-New Guinea, NAm = North America, SAm = South America).

(16)

	Afr	Eura	A-NG	NAm	SAm	Total
SOV	[22]	[26]	[19]	[26]	[18]	111
SVO	21	19	6	6	5	57

The numbers in both rows represent the number of generas exhibiting SOV, or SVO for each of the five *linguistic areas*. The larger of the two figures for each of the columns appears in square brackets (or in a box in Dryer (1989)). Though the difference between SOV and SVO in Africa is far from significant, there does clearly emerge a generalization to the effect that SOV outnumbers SVO by five *linguistic areas* to none, thereby confirming that there indeed is a linguistic preference of SOV over SVO. The logic here is that, since the five areas are assumed to be independent of one another both genetically and areally, there would only be one chance in thirty-two – one chance in sixty-four in Dryer (1992), wherein six areas are recognized, with Southeast Asia & Oceania teased out from Eurasia – for all five areas to display the given property if there were no linguistic preference for the more frequently occurring language type (Dryer 1992: 85).

Another universal claim that can easily be checked using Dryer's sampling method concerns the correlation between the position of the verb, and the distribution of adpositions, partly discussed earlier in the present chapter. (Dryer (1992) opts for OV and VO instead of verb-finality and verb-initiality.) Dryer (1989: 271) provides the following results, which, in fact, strongly support the correlation in question (N.B.: Po = postposition, Pr = preposition).

(17)

	Afr	Eura	A-NG	NAm	SAm	Total
OV&Po	[13]	[27]	[15]	[20]	[12]	87
OV&Pr	2	2	1	0	0	5

(18)

	Afr	Eura	A-NG	NAm	SAm	Total
VO&Pr	[14]	[23]	[5]	[15]	[5]	62
VO&Po	4	1	0	2	2	9

Note that Dryer (1989: 269, 271) takes a very conservative attitude towards interpreting his results, e.g. (16), (17) and (18). Only if and when all the five *linguistic areas* conform to the hypothesis being tested, that hypothesis is considered to be a language universal. For instance, if only four of the five conform to the hypothesis, then he prefers to speak of 'trends', short of statistical significance. By his standards, then, some of the language universals that other linguistic typologists would happily accept will have to be relegated to trends (Whaley 1997: 41).

Attractive as Dryer's sampling method may seem, there may be a number of problems associated with it, some being of a general nature, and others being unique to his approach. The use of genera in his sampling approach is to control for the most severe genetic bias especially when caused by large language families which only constitute a single genus, e.g. Bantu and Malayo-Polynesian. But, as Croft (1995: 91) points out, Dryer's technique cannot help eliminate completely genetic bias which would have existed in the linguistic situation prior to the time depth of a genus to which that technique can bring one back. As Croft (1995: 91) himself admits, however, this is 'essentially an inescapable problem'. It is almost impossible to imagine if any sampling technique or method can actually overcome this problem. Perhaps it is not really necessary to be overly concerned about the linguistic situation beyond the time depth of, say, Dryer's genus, if one adopts Nichols's (1992: 40) assumption that 'throughout human prehistory most languages have left few descendants, stock have usually had at most one sister, and at any time about half of the world's lineages have been isolates'. It follows from this that '[t]here is much less deep relatedness among the world's languages than is widely assumed'.

Whaley (1997: 41) thinks that there are two 'problems' with Dryer's approach: (i) difficulty with determining to which genus a given language belongs; and (ii) the large sample size required for the method to be effective.

The first is caused by the simple fact that there are many languages whose genetic classification is 'unknown, unclear, or under dispute' (Bybee, Perkins and Pagliuca 1994: 28). This, however, cannot be said to be a problem unique to Dryer's approach. All designers of language samples will have to live with this problem, which is only emblematic of the state of the art in genetic classification (see below). The second problem is not really a problem as such. In Dryer (1989), a sample of 542 languages is used. This is, of course, a much larger sample compared with, for example, Perkins's sample of fifty languages. Tomlin's (1986) database, on the other hand, consists of 1,063 languages, and his database could potentially have been used as a sample, if not for genetic and areal biases contained in it (Tomlin 1986: 29). The point is, different researchers have access to varying amounts of resources. It makes little sense to say that one's sample is too small or too large (by whose standards, anyway?). More importantly, it should not be forgotten that Dryer only deals with a far smaller number of genera (i.e. 218 of them), not 542 individual languages in his database, in order to control for genetic bias.

In addition to the foregoing there are four specific problems with Dryer's sampling method that need to be discussed in some detail. The first problem concerns selection of sample languages. It is not entirely clear how (and which) languages are chosen for each genus. For instance, when setting up her sample Nichols (1992: 27) carefully avoids languages considered by specialists as linguistically divergent or atypical of the family so that the language(s) chosen can be representative of the whole family. There is nothing in Dryer's discussion concerning the actual selecting of sample languages. Is there a set of uniform criteria for selecting sample languages for genera? Related to this is also the issue of the minimum or maximum number of languages to be selected for each of the genera. Unfortunately, Dryer is not explicit on this point, either. It may thus depend on the actual number of languages to be chosen whether a given genus may turn out to be of type X, type Y or whatever (cf. Dryer 1989: 270). It seems that too much is left to chance. More detrimental to his method is, however, that the languages used to make up genera 'are not randomly chosen so that independence is not assured by his method but is undercut by the prior problem of lack of randomness used to choose his languages' (Perkins 1989: 299). This certainly is a serious problem from a statistical point of view alone.

It also needs to be confirmed or verified to reasonable satisfaction whether or not the five continental *linguistic areas* are comparable to one another in terms of diversity, typological and/or genetic. For instance, Nichols (1992: 39) expresses her doubt that the standard continents such as Africa, North America and Australia are the same kind of unit. She is of the opinion that they are not of the same order. For example, the entire Old World – comprising Africa, Ancient Near East, Northern Eurasia and South and Southeast Asia (Nichols 1992: 27) – behaves like the same kind of unit as the single island of New Guinea in terms of diversity (cf. 6.2.3). This leads her

(1992: 39) to suggest that in order to ensure that the units or areas to be compared really be comparable, one needs to devise a 'bottom-up' areal survey in which units or areas are first objectively defined or identified by using the same set of criteria (it is not clear what these may be), and these units or areas are then put together to 'complete' the whole world, as it were. Dryer's approach, on the other hand, is top-down in that the five *linguistic areas* are first assumed to be comparable, and each of the languages in the sample is then pigeonholed into one and only one of these areas through the medium of genera. As a result, his intention to treat these areas as independent cases can be called into question because independent cases must also be comparable.

In Dryer (1989) the existence of large *linguistic areas* is identified by one continental area patterning differently from the rest of the world (Dryer 1989: 284). For example, the putative correlation between OV and AN, which was once widely thought to be a language universal, is demonstrated to be owing largely to the dominance of that correlation in Eurasia. The data in support of this finding are presented below (Dryer 1989: 274).

(19)	Afr	Eura	A-NG	NAm	SAm	Total
OV&AN	6	[22]	5	9	6	48
OV&NA	[17]	9	[15]	[17]	[10]	68

Note that except for Eurasia there is, in fact, a clear tendency towards OV and NA in all *linguistic areas*. According to Dryer, the standing out from the rest of the world of Eurasia points to the possibility that the co-occurrence of OV and AN is an areal phenomenon which is associated only with Eurasia. He (1989: 284–5) then poses himself a hypothetical yet interesting question as to whether or not the entire world may constitute one huge *linguistic area*. This naturally leads to a further question as to whether the linguistic preferences as reported in (16), (17) and (18) may not be genuine linguistic preferences but rather due to remote genetic or areal factors (i.e. all languages deriving from a single parent language, or Proto-World). Of course, there is no way of knowing that this is not the case as Dryer (1989: 284) admits. However, one can actually go even further and extend this line of thinking to a situation such as in (19). If one really cannot determine whether the linguistic universals in (16), (17) and (18) represent linguistic preferences, or common histories, how can one be completely sure whether the correlation between OV and NA in four of the five *linguistic areas* is a linguistic preference, or is due to remote genetic or areal factors. There being – strictly speaking – nothing in Dryer's method that can in principle tell linguistic preferences and areal phenomena apart, one cannot be certain about this question. In that case only the pattern in Eurasia could well reflect the linguistic preference of OV and AN, with the other four *linguistic areas* simply exhibiting what they have inherited from their common source, or what they have assumed through diffusion, or even both.

Finally, Dryer (1989: 267) claims that in his sampling method counting genera rather than individual languages makes it possible to control for the most severe genetic bias 'since languages within genera are generally fairly similar typologically'. However, this assumption is somewhat questionable in view of a great deal of variation that does exist between different linguistic properties in terms of innovation or conservatism. For example, as Dryer (1989: 262) himself acknowledges, basic word order properties change fairly easily, whereas morphological ones may be far more resilient to change. In other words, the assumption that languages within genera are generally fairly similar typologically may not apply equally to all different types of linguistic property. Prior to the adopting of that assumption one may then be well advised to ascertain first whether or not the linguistic property being studied is a relatively stable one over time and/or in the context of contact. Furthermore, one needs to find out how stable a given linguistic property has to be in order to uphold the assumption in question. Of course, these are totally different areas of study yet to be undertaken elsewhere on a large scale (cf. Nichols 1992).

1.5.4   Determining language sample sizes

There are two additional pieces of research in language sampling that need to be reviewed here: Perkins (1989), and Rijkhoff, Bakker, Hengeveld and Kahrel (1993). These works do not concern directly language sampling *per se* but rather the determining of optimum language sample sizes.

Perkins (1989: 294) addresses the question as to what is the appropriate basis for selecting sample sizes. He puts forward a statistical method whereby (i) appropriate sample sizes can be determined with the requirements of representativeness and independence met; and (ii) the extent to which linguistic properties being studied are dependent on the variables of stratification or classification used for sampling purposes can be statistically measured. He chooses to take advantage of a statistic known as tau_{RIC} (Light and Margolin 1971; Bishop *et al.* 1975), for which a test of significance – called U^2 which has a chi-square distribution – can be employed. This statistic also generates an analysis of variance measure for categorical variables where one variable is taken to be independent, and the other dependent (Perkins 1989: 301). It thus enables one to determine, for example, whether or not in a given sample the dependence on the genetic affiliation of basic word order is statistically significant. For the sake of demonstration, he runs the statistic on Tomlin's database of 1,063 languages, and finds that the statistical significance of the association between the independent and dependent variables is substantial, suggesting that, if Tomlin's database itself were used as a sample, it would include 'cases . . . that show obvious effects due to [genetic] inheritance or borrowing' (Perkins 1989: 298). Inclusion of such cases in a sample will indeed be very detrimental to the criterion of independence of case. The tau$_{RIC}$ can also produce two limiting numbers of the size of the sample in which the dependent variable (e.g. basic word order) is not significantly associated with the independent variable (e.g. genetic affiliation). The mean of these two limiting numbers is then taken to be the size of an optimum language sample. Another advantage of using this statistic is that it also makes it possible to choose the level of stratification, or categorization that requires the smallest number of languages without compromising the requirements of representativeness and independence. By using the statistic, for example, Perkins (1989: 305–9) evaluates three different levels of geographical stratification – (i) Tomlin's (1986) twenty-six cells in his areal frame; (ii) Dryer's five *linguistic areas*; and (iii) the division of the world into the two hemispheres (i.e. eastern and western). The statistic of tau$_{RIC}$ indicates that the levels of geographical stratification in (i), (ii) and (iii) require about 90, 40 and slightly over 100 languages, respectively. The smallest number of languages is required of the level of stratification in (ii): the five continental *linguistic areas* identified in Dryer (1989). Thus the highest level of strata for a language sampling frame for basic word order should be the five continents, not the twenty-six areas or cells in Tomlin (1986) or the two hemispheres.

Perkins's sampling design method can prove to be 'a heuristic suggesting plausible language sample sizes that meet the criterion of independence of cases' (Perkins 1989: 301). He (1989: 294) thus comes to the conclusion that '50 to 100 languages are most appropriate for a variety of linguistic variables [including basic word order].' But, as Perkins (1989: 302) himself notes, it can also serve as a kind of post-mortem on language samples that have been used in typological research especially when the dependence on the type of stratification of linguistic properties investigated has not been statistically tested.

There are, however, two points that can be made about Perkins's sampling design method, one practical and the other theoretical. First, Perkins's method requires a rather large database (Perkins 1989: 301). In order to arrive at optimum sample sizes, all languages of the database must be genetically classified, and analysed in terms of structural properties. That may also depend to an extent on the nature of linguistic properties to be studied. Perhaps this may be unavoidable since, as Bell (1978: 141) perceptively notes, '[t]he investigator is always faced with the paradox that the optimum sample requires the very knowledge that he seeks'. What really is required of Perkins's sampling design method seems to be some kind of ready-made databank, wherein a large number of languages have been recorded with various linguistic properties or variables having already been identified for each of these languages without any specific research topics in mind (e.g. GRAMCATS at the University of New Mexico or Matthew Dryer's database at the SUNY at Buffalo). Most investigators do not have access to such a large databank, however.

More problematic for Perkins's method is that the results of the tau_{RIC} analysis seem to hinge on the actual distribution of a given linguistic variable in the database from which an optimum language sample is to be derived as Perkins (1989: 303–5) himself demonstrates. This suggests that the optimum language sample size to be calculated may actually vary from a database which contains too many VSO languages to another one which includes too few VSO languages, for instance. To put it differently, the tau_{RIC} analysis seems to be sensitive at least to the actual constitution of the database in terms of the linguistic variable being investigated. If this is the case, the validity of 'optimum' sample sizes arrived at by means of Perkins's sampling design method cannot but be in dispute.

Rijkhoff, Bakker, Hengeveld and Kahrel (1993) describe two different types of language sample (or two different approaches to language sampling): (i) samples used to identify tendencies or correlations (i.e. *probability samples*); and (ii) samples set up to discover 'all possible realizations of a certain meaning or structure across languages' (i.e. *variety samples*). Following both Bell (1978), and Perkins (1980), they develop a sampling design procedure which falls under the second type. They (1993: 172) believe that genetic relatedness is the most important criterion in language sampling because languages that are closely related in time also tend to be closely related in space, culture and typology (but see above). In other words, they are concerned with controlling for genetic bias alone.

Rijkhoff *et al.* (1993: 172) point out that the best way to avoid genetic bias is to ensure that all languages in the sample come from different phyla. They thus agree with Perkins (1980) that a sample must include at least one representative from each phylum so that there is minimal representation of all phyla in that sample. But at the same time they note that this way to control for genetic bias will only give rise to a sample of fewer than thirty languages – assuming that there are twenty-seven phyla (cf. Ruhlen 1987). They point out that such a small sample does not make a good variety sample, the primary goal of which is 'to maximize the amount of variation in the data' (Rijkhoff *et al.* 1993: 171). A good variety sample must then reflect the greatest possible structural diversity so that even cases of the rarest structural type can have a chance of representation (Rijkhoff *et al.* 1993: 171). Clearly, a sample consisting of fewer than thirty languages will hardly be likely to achieve this. Rijkhoff *et al.*'s (1993: 179–80, 196) sampling method thus makes an attempt to incorporate Bell's (1978) call for appropriate representation of genetic diversity in a sample (i.e. variation *within* phyla), and the insight of Perkins's (1980) sampling technique (i.e. variation *across* phyla).

Rijkhoff *et al.* (1993: 171) also attempt to replace Bell's notion of genetic groups, or his 'age-criterion' (or the time depth of 3,500 years) with an 'objectively' computable measure of genetic diversity by taking advantage of the internal structure of genetic language trees. This is intended to reflect Bell's (1978) observation that '[i]f the strata [e.g. genetic groups] are not

Figure 1.1: *A hypothetical language family tree*

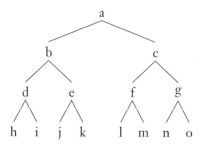

equally homogeneous, some increase in sampling efficiency may be achieved by weighting [. . .] samples according to strata variability'. Thus the number of languages to be selected for a phylum in a sample must be proportional to the internal genetic diversity of that phylum. In Rijkhoff *et al.*'s weighted sampling procedure the internal structure of the family tree is translated mathematically into a diversity value, which will in turn be utilized in order to calculate the exact number of languages to be selected for each of the twenty-seven phyla (including language isolates, and pidgins and creoles), based largely on Ruhlen (1987).

The diversity value (or DV) is computed on the basis of the number of nodes at the intermediate levels between the top node, and the terminal nodes at the bottom end in a language tree. Top nodes, e.g. *a* in the hypothetical family tree in Figure 1.1, are excluded from computation because they do not contribute to internal diversity. So are terminal nodes, e.g. *h*, *i*, *j*, *k*, *l*, *m*, *n* and *o* in Figure 1.1. Only the internal structure of a language family tree, or the intermediate nodes, e.g. *b*, *c*, *d*, *e*, *f*, *g*, in Figure 1.1, must be taken into consideration for purposes of computation because it is possible, for example, that a language family of 300 languages is far less complicated internally than a language family of fifty languages.

Rijkhoff *et al.* (1993: 181–2) also recognize that high-level splits, or branchings are more significant in terms of contribution to diversity value than low-level splits because the former preceded the latter in time or because the former had more time to develop into distinct languages than the latter. Therefore, they build into the DV formula in (20) a factor of significance which decreases as the depth of intermediate levels increases, that is by steps of *1/n* where *n* is the maximum number of intermediate levels found in any phylum, e.g. sixteen in the Niger-Kordofanian phylum in the case of Ruhlen's (1987) genetic classification.[14]

(20) $Cy = Cx + ((n - x)/n * (Ny - Nx))$, where $x = y - 1$

Cy represents the contributing DV at any given level, which is computed by combining the contribution of the immediately preceding level (or *Cx*), and the difference between the number of nodes at Cy and that at Cx (or $Ny - Nx$), which is in turn multiplied by the factor of decreasing significance referred to above (or $(n - x)/n$). The contributions of all intermediate levels of a given phylum are then computed according to the formula in (20), and then averaged out to derive the mean DV for that phylum.

Once the mean DVs of the twenty-seven phyla have been worked out, they will *invariably* be used to decide how many languages must be selected from each phylum in order to construct samples of predetermined sizes as is presented in Table 1.1. Thus Rijkhoff *et al.*'s sampling procedure is top-down. Recall that in common with Perkins (1980), Rijkhoff *et al.* recognize the need to have at least one representative from each of the phyla in a sample irrespective of actual sample sizes. In a sample of 100 languages, for example, each phyla will first be allocated at least one language (i.e. twenty-seven languages in total) regardless of its DV score, with the remaining seventy-three languages being divided up among the twenty-seven phyla according to their DVs.

Rijkhoff *et al.*'s (1993: 192, 196) quantification of internal diversity is claimed to be an improvement over Bell's age-criterion, or genetic groups in that their DV computation 'can be seen as an objectivization of Bell's language groups', the basis of which is the time depth of 3,500 years. They argue that this arbitrary time depth is difficult to apply equally to all phyla especially when the histories of many phyla are not well understood due mainly to lack of documentation. This is a fair point to make but then Rijkhoff *et al.*'s objectivization of Bell's age-criterion hardly escapes the same criticism and does rather highlight one of the intractable problems associated with all approaches to language sampling. The way language family trees are constructed is due as much to lack of understanding of, or uncertainty about, internal genetic relations as to actual internal diversity. In fact, this point has not at all been missed completely by Rijkhoff *et al.* when they (1993: 177–8) point out: '[w]hat strikes us is that the number of languages (t) per non-terminal (nt) and preterminal (pt) node is low for relatively well-explored phyla like Indo-Hittite (ratios 1.67 and 2.65), and rather high for phyla for which our knowledge still leaves much to be desired, such as Indo-Pacific (ratios 2.93 and 4.65)'. The reason for this difference is that phyla whose internal genetic relatedness is well understood tend to have more intermediate groups recognized, with their trees being more hierarchical or less flat, whereas phyla whose histories cannot easily be accessed tend to contain fewer intermediate groups, thereby resulting in flatter or less hierarchical trees. The problem is exacerbated by the undeniable fact that the genetic classifications on the basis of which many samples have been set up are in turn based on different sets of criteria being applied to different genetic groupings. Rijkhoff *et al.* (1993) rely heavily on the genetic classification list provided in Ruhlen (1987), with DVs computed on the basis of the internal structure of genetic language trees. But how can one lay claim to comparability of the

Table 1.1: *Number of languages in samples of different sizes*

Phylum/Sample size	30	40	50	60	70	80	90	100	125	150	175	200	225	250
Afro-Asiatic	1	2	2	3	4	5	5	6	8	9	11	12	14	16
Altaic	1	1	1	1	1	1	2	2	2	3	3	3	4	4
Amerind	2	5	7	9	12	14	16	18	24	29	35	40	45	51
Australian	1	2	3	4	4	5	6	7	9	11	13	15	17	19
Austric	2	4	5	7	9	11	12	14	19	23	27	31	35	39
Caucasian	1	1	1	1	1	1	1	1	1	2	2	2	2	3
Chukchi-Kamchatkan	1	1	1	1	1	1	1	1	1	1	1	1	1	1
Elamo-Dravidian	1	1	1	1	1	1	1	1	1	1	1	2	2	2
Eskimo-Aleut	1	1	1	1	1	1	1	1	1	1	1	1	1	1
Indo-Hittite	1	1	2	2	3	3	4	4	5	7	8	9	10	11
Indo-Pacific	2	3	5	7	8	10	11	13	17	20	24	28	32	35
Khoisan	1	1	1	1	1	1	1	1	1	1	1	2	2	2
Sumerian	1	1	1	1	1	1	1	1	1	1	1	1	1	1
Ket	1	1	1	1	1	1	1	1	1	1	1	1	1	1
Nahali	1	1	1	1	1	1	1	1	1	1	1	1	1	1
Hurrian	1	1	1	1	1	1	1	1	1	1	1	1	1	1
Burushaski	1	1	1	1	1	1	1	1	1	1	1	1	1	1
Meroitic	1	1	1	1	1	1	1	1	1	1	1	1	1	1
Basque	1	1	1	1	1	1	1	1	1	1	1	1	1	1
Etruscan	1	1	1	1	1	1	1	1	1	1	1	1	1	1
Gilyak	1	1	1	1	1	1	1	1	1	1	1	1	1	1
Na-Dene	1	1	1	1	1	1	1	1	1	2	2	2	2	3
Niger-Kordofanian	1	3	4	5	6	7	8	9	12	15	18	20	23	26
Nilo-Saharan	1	1	2	3	3	4	4	5	6	7	8	10	11	12
Pidgins and Creoles	1	1	1	1	1	1	2	2	2	2	3	3	4	4
Sino-Tibetan	1	1	2	2	3	3	4	4	5	6	7	9	10	11
Uralic-Yukaghir	1	1	1	1	1	1	1	1	1	1	1	1	1	1
TOTALS	30	40	50	60	70	80	90	100	125	150	175	200	225	250

(Rijkhoff *et al.* 1993: 186)

internal structure of genetic language trees across the twenty-seven phyla when the conceptual basis of that internal structure differs from one genetic grouping to another? These, of course, are not criticisms levelled at Rijkhoff *et al.*'s sampling approach *per se* but rather they are intended to emphasize the problem which Bybee, Perkins and Pagliuca (1994: 28) succinctly summarize in the following way:

> [f]irst, there are many languages for which genetic classification is unknown, unclear, or under dispute. Second, more is being learned each day about genetic relations, so that some of the information published in 1978 may be incorrect. Third, different criteria were used in establishing the groupings in different parts of the world. In some cases, genetic grouping is based on extensive historical documentation and historical-comparative work (as in the case of Indo-European languages); in other cases, the groupings are based on lexicostatistical surveys; and in still others, it is admittedly only a geographical region that is being identified as a group.

Thus Rijkhoff *et al.*'s objectivization of Bell's age-criterion can only be as sound as the genetic classification on which it is based. It must also be borne in mind that what is at issue is not objectivization of the internal diversity of phyla *per se* but objectivization of the internal structure of genetic language trees with their weaknesses, flaws, gaps, and all because, as Rijkhoff *et al.* (1993: 178, 198, *passim*) themselves reiterate, only the internal structure as *represented or reflected in the form of a tree diagram* is 'exploited to measure linguistic diversity among genetically related languages'.

This uncertainty about genetic classification brings back to the fore perhaps the most important of the issues in language sampling. How can one ensure the independence of cases in one's sample when one cannot be completely certain whether or not some of the languages being studied are genetically independent? For example, languages that are classified into different genetic families in a given genetic classification list may turn out to be genetically related to one another; languages whose genetic relations are still in dispute may simply be assumed to belong to the same language family. Languages like these will have a greater chance of inclusion in a large language sample than in a small one because it is more difficult to maximize genetic distance in the former than in the latter. In view of this it may not always be possible to determine to which genus a language belongs. Recall that this is precisely the difficulty that Whaley (1997: 41) associates with Dryer's (1989) notion of genera.

There is also a related – equally, if not more serious – issue of whether or not languages really are 'clearly definable objects' (Perkins 1989: 295) – which is a necessary condition for all statistical procedures. Croft (1990: 22), in fact, views this as a fundamental problem that has not properly been addressed in the sampling literature (but cf. Tomlin 1986: 35). For example, how many languages are there in Austronesian, Indo-European, or Niger-Kordofanian? We do certainly have rough figures. But is there a uniform or universally agreed on set of criteria for identifying individual languages as opposed to dialects of a single language? These questions cannot be answered because the solution to the problem of definability of languages is unlikely to be found. This is why linguists put the total number of the languages of the world at 4,000 to 7,000. As is well known, the defining of a language in contrast to a dialect is beset with a number of practical difficulties (e.g. how do we measure mutual intelligibility?), and is also susceptible to non-linguistic, e.g. political, cultural, etc., considerations.

In view of all this it may seem to be an impossible task to achieve the independence of cases required of language sampling. But it must also be emphasized that despite all these difficulties linguistic typologists have over the years made a number of significant generalizations about the nature of human language as will be demonstrated in the following chapters. Perhaps it may offer a modicum of assurance about language sampling to note, along with Bybee *et al.* (1994: 28), that a genetic classification list such as Ruhlen (1987), or Voegelin and Voegelin (1977), 'provides an objective basis for sampling that was established independently of any hypotheses that [one sets out] to test'.

1.5.5 Problems with data

As can be seen from the foregoing, linguistic typologists work with a large amount of data from a large number of languages. It is, therefore, unrealistic to expect them to have a sound firsthand understanding of all sample languages that they deal with. They normally rely on primary sources: grammatical descriptions, or grammars in monograph (e.g. (*Lingua*) *Descriptive Series* by Routledge (previously by North-Holland and by Croom Helm) or journal article form (e.g. notably *International Journal of American Linguistics*, and *Oceanic Linguistics*). The most frequent problem with this kind of data source is that grammars are not always sufficient enough in detail, and/or broad enough in scope. Far more frequently than not, grammars may just gloss over or fail to examine the grammatical phenomena that linguistic typologists wish to study, although this often depends on what grammatical phenomena are being investigated. For instance, information on basic word order can probably easily be retrieved from most grammars, whereas that on the comparative construction 'is often not found in even the most minute grammars' (Stassen 1985: 13). There may exist only texts, not grammars, for some languages. These texts may not be glossed sufficiently enough – if glossed at all – to be easily amenable to linguistic or typological analysis. In a situation like this, linguistic typologists may have to work through texts by carrying out basic linguistic analysis themselves. If they are lucky, they may manage to find good examples but, as Stassen (1985: 13) laments, 'one often despairs of the fact that two days of deciphering a grammatical text has not resulted in finding one good and clear example of the comparative construction'. Stassen's plight is not uncommon in typological research. Finding that a grammar does not deal with the phenomenon being studied often proves to be more difficult and time-consuming than finding that a grammar does indeed deal with the phenomenon. This is because one has to study a grammar from cover to cover in order to make sure that it does not deal with the phenomenon in question, whereas discovery of the phenomenon may not require perusal of a whole grammar. Moreover, one cannot just rely on the table of contents, and the subject index – if they are provided – to ascertain whether or not a grammatical description provides information on the phenomenon because, although the table of contents, or subject index does not make mention of it, one or more good examples of the phenomenon may be hidden in a most unlikely place in the grammar. To make matters worse, some grammars may be biased towards certain grammatical aspects, e.g. morphology, thereby providing no information whatsoever on linguistic typologists' areas of interest, e.g. syntax.

Linguistic typologists may also have to rely on secondary sources. But, as Croft (1990: 25) sounds a cautionary note, these materials may already be biased by the hypothesis or theoretical orientation of original analysts. Thus a great deal of discretion must be exercised in using secondary sources. For instance, they must, whenever possible, if not always, be checked by referring to the primary sources on which they are based. The reliability of secondary sources has also not proven to be particularly commendable because errors of citation are not unheard of, and can actually be repeated in subsequent works (Mallinson and Blake (1981: 14–15) for one such perpetuating error of citation).

Linguistic typologists may also need to work with language consultants. But this also poses an enormous amount of practical difficulty. Even if one can manage to find consultants for each of one's sample languages, it will be completely unfeasible economically, given the normal size of a language sample in typological research. What is worse, it will be unwise to work with only one consultant for each language. One may need to work with more than one consultant for each language for the sake of verification, or confirmation. Working with consultants in typological research also involves the same host of problems that are encountered in any research based on interaction with (live) human subjects. Perhaps one may wish to have this option as a last resort especially when certain subtle grammatical points in primary or secondary sources need clarification.

Whaley (1997: 42) also discusses use of questionnaires (e.g. Dahl 1985; also discussion of the role of questionnaires within the Leningrad Typology Group in 7.2). A set of written questions about the grammatical phenomenon to be studied can be sent out to language specialists, or language consultants. Despite its apparent advantages (e.g. the possibility of obtaining more detailed information about the phenomenon than is available in grammars), this kind of data collection has its own share of difficulties, too. For one thing, it may be very time-consuming and costly to implement such a questionnaire especially when one is operating with a large language sample, *and* a small budget. But with the advent of electronic technology (e.g. e-mail, or electronic discussion lists such as the *LINGUIST-LIST* and the *ASSOCIATION FOR LINGUISTIC TYPOLOGY-LIST*, to which a good number of linguists around the world subscribe), execution of a questionnaire may no longer be so time-consuming and expensive as it used to be.[15] Through an electronic network, one can instantly get in touch with a number of language specialists – provided that they are willing enough to respond to one's request (within a reasonable span of time). But there may still be problems with carrying out electronic questionnaires. Often the reliability, or credibility of respondents may be in doubt or in need of confirmation. Of course, this problem can be assuaged if a selection of qualified respondents can first be made by means of careful planning, screening, etc., and if only those who pass muster can then be approached in much the same way that a written questionnaire is administered. Mention must also be made of potential difficulties with electronic transmission of data from different languages, e.g. special fonts.

For practical reasons, however, most linguistic typologists prefer to work with primary sources. When in doubt, they may seek assistance from consultants, access secondary sources or draw upon questionnaires. But, as has already been noted, the use of primary materials is not without problems. Thus Croft (1990: 25) is led to declare that 'the typologist has to rely on faith in the qualities of the materials at hand', and that 'most of those materials do not inspire faith'. Inspire faith as they may not, the situation may not be so hopeless as this. One of the virtues of working with a large number of languages in typological research is that it does to a certain extent offset the problem of faith about which Croft is pessimistic. Recall that in section 1.5.1 mention was made of the measure of recurrence in cross-linguistic comparison. If a certain pattern or structural type occurs in language after language, one can be reasonably assured that this is a real phenomenon to be identified as such. Primary materials may fail to inspire faith individually but they may inspire faith collectively. This is due to the power of the measure of recurrence in cross-linguistic research.

1.6   Partial typology vs. holistic typology

References have been made in the preceding sections to cross-linguistic comparison of a wide range of languages in typological research. In those references languages are treated as if they were units of comparison. But, as has been pointed out in passing, this does not mean that languages in their entirety are being compared but rather that structural properties, or constructions found in languages constitute objects of comparison. Consequently, when languages are typologized or classified, it must be understood that properties, or constructions, not whole languages, are put into different types. Said differently, 'languages' are simply being used here for indexing purposes, or as 'addresses' at which the different types of construction are located. Thus specific grammatical domains, e.g. basic word order, relative clause constructions, comparative constructions, etc., are chosen for typological research, and individual languages are then studied or analysed in terms of these selected domains, and classified into different types. This is an important point to bear in mind in the context of modern linguistic typology, at least in the mainstream thereof. This kind of typology – the analytical units of which are grammatical domains, not entire languages – is referred to as partial typology. What is more frequently done in partial typology is, however, to examine concurrently a cluster of properties in one and the same grammatical domain with a view to ascertaining whether or not these properties exhibit significant connections. For example, basic clausal word order is studied in conjunction with, for example, the distribution of adpositions: the presence of verb-initiality implies that of prepositions. Investigation of a cluster of properties such as basic clausal word order, adpositions, etc. is also an example of partial typology (cf. multi-feature, polythetic typology (Ramat 1986: 6)) despite the fact that multiple properties are under scrutiny. Partial because the investigation still deals with only part of grammar or language. Most of the modern typological works including the ones to be surveyed in the bulk of the present book are, in fact, subsumed under partial typology.

As opposed to partial typology is holistic typology. This kind of typology is no longer widely practised but commanded a great deal of popularity in the nineteenth century (see Horne (1966), Robins (1997), Greenberg (1974), Skalička and Sgall (1994), Sgall (1995) and Ramat (1995) for historical perspectives on this) when the dominant mode of intellectual thinking came from natural science (especially botanical science) (Ramat (1986: 3); also see Plank (1991) for possible input from anatomy; but see below, and also discussion of the Prague School Typology in 7.4).[16] Scholars of this period – e.g. August Wilhelm Schlegel (1767–1845), Friedrich von Schlegel (1772–1829), Wilhelm von Humboldt (1767–1835) and August Schleicher (1821–68) – believed that language was a (natural) organism which possessed an 'inner form' (Robins (1997: chapter 7) for an overview of linguistics in the nineteenth century). This inner form was thought to be a manifestation of the spirit (*Geist*) of the people who spoke it (cf. Greenberg (1974: chapter 3); Robins (1997: 192–5)). In the words of Wilhelm von Humbolt (Finck 1899; Lehmann's (1978c: 423) translation), '[t]he characteristic intellectual features and the linguistic structure of a people stand in such intimacy of fusion with each other that if the one were presented the other would have to be completely derivable from it'. The inner form was in turn assumed to be reflected in 'variation in grammatical mechanisms employed in relating lexical concepts to each other [or relational meaning]' (Shibatani and Bynon 1995: 4). Thus 'each language [was] a distinct revelation of the spirit (*Geist*)' (Greenberg 1974: 38). Coupled with growing interest in etymology (i.e. comparative-historical linguistics), this point of view led directly to the emergence of the morphological (or classical) typology, wherein three different basic strategies in the encoding of relational meaning were recognized: inflectional, agglutinative and isolating – Wilhelm von Humboldt later added a fourth, incorporating, to Schlegel's tripartite classification (for an example of the classical typology, see 5.2).[17] The unit of analysis in this typology was undoubtedly the word, the structure of which 'was seized upon as in some sense central to the attempt to characterize the language as a whole' (Greenberg 1974: 36) so that 'the description of the entire grammatical system [could] be annexed to an exact description of the structure of the word in every language' (Lewy 1942: 15, cited in Greenberg 1974: 36). They believed that it was possible to characterize the *entire* language on the basis of a single grammatical parameter, or even a small number of grammatical features in much the same way that, for example, one could reconstruct the entire skeleton of an animal on the basis of a fossil jaw (Ramat 1986: 3). (This intellectual wish is what Shibatani and Bynon (1995: 16) term *the Gabelentzian ideal* since the formulation of this ambitious typological approach is generally attributed to Georg von der Gabelentz (1901).) In other words, the single property of morphology was assumed to constitute the ultimate basis of typological classification of all languages of the world. The classical typology is, therefore, a true exemplar of holistic typology.

But the adequacy of holistic typology as a classificatory scheme was subsequently called into question (Sapir (1921); cf. Greenberg (1954) for a quantitative approach to this type of classification). It was soon realized that languages in their entirety are not amenable to neat pigeonholing because most languages are in fact mixed types or hybrids in that they employ more than one type of morphological mechanism, e.g. Polynesian languages better characterized as 'agglutinative-isolating', and Cambodian as 'inflectional-isolating' (Shibatani and Bynon 1995: 5–9). As a consequence, holistic typology began to give way to far more modest partial typology in the twentieth century.

As Ramat (1986: 4) points out, however, holistic typology is 'perfectly understandable and reasonable' from a theoretical point of view. There are no theoretical or logical reasons why the Gabelentzian ideal cannot be retained as the ultimate – albeit probably unattainable – goal in typological research. The possibility – however remote that may be – of reducing a host of grammatical phenomena at all linguistic levels to a single underlying principle or even a handful of them is extremely attractive and tempting especially to the theoretically minded because, admittedly, '[t]he best possible typology . . . would be one that refers all manifestations of language to one single underlying principle'. With such a holistic typology in hand, for example, one should be in a position to predict on the basis of basic word order what type of relative clause construction is used, whether or not morphological causativization of transitive, as opposed to intransitive, verbs is permitted, what type of case marking system is employed, whether or not verbs have aspect rather than tense, and so forth (Shibatani and Bynon 1995: 12). But, as Comrie (1989: 40) puts it succinctly, 'experience to date is rather against this possibility: while we can state often wide-ranging correlations among logically independent parameters, these correlations are not sufficiently strong or sufficiently wide-ranging to give holistic types rather than cross-classification of languages on different parameters'. This probably explains the paucity of holistic typology in the current typological literature.

That is not to say that there have recently been no attempts at holistic typology. Since the bulk of the present book only deals with partial typology, it perhaps is worthwhile very briefly surveying two holistic works in the present chapter. (Members of the Prague School of linguistics or the Prague School Typology do also practise holistic typology by continuing with the nineteenth-century classical typology; but their work deserves separate discussion (cf. 7.4 and 7.5) in the context of Chapter 7).

W.P. Lehmann (1973, 1978b, 1978c), for instance, entertains the possibility of drawing certain phonological and morphological implications from basic word order typology: many OV order languages are claimed to have certain phonological characteristics such as (C)CV (or open) syllable structure, vowel harmony and pitch accent. To the best of the present writer's knowledge, however, Lehmann's claim has never seriously been put to the test. Interesting as it may be, it still remains nothing more than a hypothesis, if not a total conjecture (refer to Ramat's (1986: 5) sceptical view on this holistic typology).

Perhaps better known in the context of modern holistic typology is the work of the Russian linguist G.A. Klimov (1977, 1983). The basis (or the underlying principle) of his holistic typology is 'a language's predications and its categorization of basic nominal and verbal notions'. (Nichols 1992: 7–11). There are four basic types: (i) the accusative type, (ii) the ergative type, (iii) the active type and (iv) the class type. The types in (i)–(iv) are based on subject-object relations, agent-patient relations, an active/inactive distinction and referential properties of nominals, respectively. For example, the active type is claimed to be associated with a cluster of grammatical properties of different linguistic levels: lexical properties such as binary division of verbs into active and inactive, inclusive/exclusive distinction in first person pronouns, etc., morphological properties such as alienable/inalienable possession distinction, more verbal inflection than nominal inflection, etc., and syntactic properties such as SOV basic word order, direct object incorporation into verb, etc. (also see Klimov 1974). Interestingly enough, Nichols

(1992: 11) reports that her own results partly confirm some of the predictions drawn from, or the claims made in, Klimov's holistic typology although she argues that the morphological distinction between head and dependent marking (see 3.13) is a better predictor of other features than Klimov's notion of type.

The theoretical attractiveness of the Gabelentzian ideal notwithstanding, holistic typology is beset with at least one fundamental problem as Ramat (1986: 8–9) correctly identifies it: diachronic dynamics of language. Languages do shift from type X to type Y while retaining some features of type X. This fundamental fact of language alone casts much doubt on the feasibility of holistic typology, with there necessarily being languages of mixed types. A single underlying principle, which in holistic typology is used to classify the whole of a language into a given type, will not easily take adequate account of such mixed languages. This problem indeed harks back to the difficulty inherent in the classical typology as discussed above (Sapir 1921).

1.7   Organization of the rest of the book

In Chapter 2, beginning with Greenberg's (1963b) ground-breaking article, a number of cross-linguistic word order studies will be discussed and critically examined. In so doing, word order patterns and relevant correlations between different word order parameters will be investigated not only at the clausal and phrasal levels but also at the morphological level (e.g. suffixing vs. prefixing). Reference will also be made to a number of factors ranging from structural ones to processing efficiency as plausible avenues of explanation of observed word order patterns and correlations.

In Chapter 3 attention is directed to the ways in which the languages of the world deal with the fundamental 'problem' of expressing 'who is doing X to whom'. A comprehensive survey of case marking systems will first be provided with a view to understanding each of these systems and also to gaining insight into possible functional factors underlying not only these case marking systems but also their distribution. Moreover, correlations between case marking and word order types will be explored.

In Chapter 4 various relativization strategies will be exemplified with special reference to the expression of the head NP. In addition a brief cross-linguistic survey of accessibility to relativization will be carried out based on the hierarchy of grammatical relations. Furthermore, discourse and processing motivations will be appealed to in attempting to explain a number of observed cross-linguistic patterns or propensities in relativization. Possible correlations between relative clause and basic word order types will also be discussed as a prelude to functional explanation of cross-linguistic patterns in relativization.

In Chapter 5, following discussion of the morphologically based typology of causative constructions, the hierarchy of grammatical relations (cf. Chapter 4) will be revisited in slightly modified form with particular reference to the syntax of the causee NP, especially in the context of morphological causativization. Also included in this chapter is discussion of causative types, and causation types, the interaction between which is most clearly reflected in the actual case marking of the causee NP, for instance.

In Chapter 6 possibilities of applying linguistic typology to other areas of linguistics will be explored, where and if possible, referring back to relevant discussions in the preceding chapters. The areas of linguistics to be discussed in this chapter are historical linguistics (especially linguistic reconstruction), first language acquisition and second language acquisition, the latter two in the context of accessibility to relativization – perhaps the most researched topic of language acquisition, with direct reference to linguistic typology. Discussion is also provided of potential contributions of linguistic typology – i.e. what Nichols (1992) refers to as population typology – to a better understanding of linguistic prehistory, the time depth of which may be inaccessible by means of the classic comparative-historical method.

Finally, in Chapter 7 a survey of non-Greenbergian approaches to modern linguistic typology is offered with a view to helping the reader to become aware of the basic aims, assumptions and achievements of three prominent European schools of linguistic typology: the Leningrad Typology Group, the Cologne UNITYP Group and the Prague School Typology. A comparison of the European schools, and the Greenbergian/American tradition of linguistic typology will also be provided with a view to highlighting both strengths, and weaknesses of these different approaches to modern linguistic typology, all having their roots in the nineteenth-century European tradition of linguistic typology.

Notes

1. The distinction between languages and dialects is a notoriously difficult one to draw. For instance, one of the most widely used criteria is *mutual intelligibility*. But that notion itself is a difficult one to define, adding to the difficulty of defining the distinction in question.
2. This example is often cited as an exceptionless language universal. But it is correct to say that there are a few verb-initial languages with postpositions, e.g. Yagua (Comrie 1988: 146). Dryer (1991: 448) adds three more counter-examples: N. Tepehuan, Cora and Guajajara. But it will be kept here as an exceptionless language universal for the sake of illustration.

3. Nichols (1992: 42) describes universal tendencies as properties or correlations favoured in languages independent of geography and genetic affiliation, and thus as universal preferences of the languages of the world.

4. It must be borne in mind that languages are not being compared and classified in their entirety, but only in terms of structural properties in question (see 1.6 for discussion of partial and holistic typology).

5. Examples of a complement clause with a verbal head, and that with a nominal head are exemplified within square brackets in (i) and (ii), respectively (Comrie and Horie 1995: 65–6).

   (i)   The teacher knows [that the student bought the book].
   (ii) the declaration/knowledge/fact [that the student bought the book].

6. In fact, Warlpiri has one additional construction that is employed consistently for the expression of relative clause function, i.e. the nominalized non-finite clause (Mary Laughren, personal communication). Being subject to aspectual or temporal restrictions, however, this construction seems to be marked as opposed to the adjoined clause (Hale 1976: 83).

7. This principle was first introduced into the study of language by Neogrammarians from the natural science thesis of Hutton and Lyell. Karl Brugmann is quoted as saying (Collinge 1994: 1561): '[t]he psychological and physiological nature of man as speaker must have been essentially identical at all epochs'.

8. A related question will be: which stage of evolution in human language should be chosen as the 'target' stage?

9. One may choose to use the descriptive label 'an escape hatch', rather than 'a frame of reference'.

10. Perkins (1980: 56, 1992: 123–4), however, points out that this is not the best way of studying language universals because the assumption of the independence of cases (see below) is clearly not met in the universe of languages.

11. Perkins (1980) uses a universe of cultures in order to derive a sample of languages because 'it is more reasonable to expect that linguistic materials exist for cultures that have been studied by ethnographers than those that have not[;] the appearance of a culture on Murdock's list makes it considerably more likely that the corresponding linguistic materials exist than for languages chosen from a language list [e.g. Voegelin and Voegelin (1966)]' (Perkins 1992: 125).

12. Perkins (1992: 179–81) argues that Dryer's criticism is far from damaging to his sampling procedure because, although possibly related, the Mon-Khmer languages, for example, diverge in terms of the relationship between deictic grammaticalization and cultural complexity in the way that is predicted by his hypothesis. In other words, this divergence despite genetic relatedness is claimed instead to strengthen the proposed association between the linguistic, and cultural properties. Be that as it may, Perkins's argument is beside the point because Dryer's criticism is directed at Perkins's sampling procedure in general, not to a particular application

of that procedure (i.e. Perkins's own investigation). Therefore, Dryer's criticism remains valid.

13. In his subsequent work (1992), Dryer removes Southeast Asia & Oceania from Eurasia, and treats them as an independent *linguistic area*. Thus in Dryer (1992) there are six, not five, large areas.

14. The reason why the highest number of intermediate levels is taken as the basis of the factor of decreasing significance in (20) is for corresponding levels in each phylum to be treated alike (Rijkhoff *et al.* 1993: 200).

15. The *LINGUIST-LIST*, and its related resources are now accessible on the internet (http://www.linguistlist.org/), and the *ALT-LIST* and its resources are also accessible on the internet (http://148.88.14.7:80/alt/).

16. Shibatani and Bynon (1995b: 16), however, see the difference between partial and holistic typology to be largely a matter of degree.

17. Comrie (1989: 45), on the other hand, adopts 'fusional' in lieu of 'inflectional' because 'both [agglutinative] and fusional languages, as opposed to isolating languages, have inflection, and it is [. . .] misleading to use a term based on *(in)flection* to refer to one only of these two types'.

2

Basic word order

2.1 What is basic word order?

References to basic word order were made in Chapter 1 in relation to the types of language universals and sampling procedures. Basic word order at the clausal level consists of the three major constituents, S, O and V. There are six logical permutations of S, O and V, each of which has indeed been attested in the languages of the world (see 1.1 for actual examples).[1] Basic word order is also observed at other grammatical levels (e.g. phrasal) as will be discussed below. The importance of basic word order study in the development of modern linguistic typology cannot be overstated with the appearance in 1963 of Greenberg's seminal paper on word order typology, which not only generated insightful statements about the nature of human language which have stood the test of time but also laid the solid groundwork for linguistic typology as is practised today.

But what is basic word order? That is, what is understood by 'basicness' of basic word order? Perhaps the best way to answer this question is to explain how basic word order actually is identified in linguistic typology. It is generally thought that basic word order at the clausal level is found 'in stylistically neutral, independent, indicative clauses with full noun phrase (NP) participants, where the subject is definite, agentive and human, the object is a definite semantic patient, and the verb represents an action, not a state or an event' (Siewierska 1988: 8). Thus pragmatic neutrality – in conjunction with transitivity (Hopper and Thompson 1980) – may make it possible to identify basic word order. Other criteria may also include textual frequency and formal markedness (Mallinson and Blake 1981: 125–9; Hawkins 1983: 12–16; Comrie 1989: 88–9; Whaley 1997: 100–4). Given two competing word orders, the more frequent one is taken to represent basic word order. Moreover, one word order may be grammatically unmarked, whereas the other is marked. For instance, the marked order may be subject to grammatical or distributional restrictions, or may display a higher degree of formal complexity than the unmarked one.

Unfortunately, it is not always a straightforward matter to determine basic word order based on these criteria. Siewierska (1988: 8–14) offers a good discussion of some of the problems associated with frequency and markedness (also see Payne 1985b, Mithun 1992, and Dryer 1995, 1997). For instance, in many languages heavy use of bound pronouns, pronominal clitics, or noun incorporation results in transitive clauses with full noun phrases being extremely infrequent or even rare. She (1988: 12) also points to the observation often made by text linguists (e.g. Dressler 1969, 1981; Garciá-Berrio 1980; Longacre 1980; Quakenbush 1992) that the most frequent word order may actually vary from one type of text to another – e.g. VSO and SVO in Biblical Hebrew narratives and expository texts, respectively; and verb-initial order and subject-verb order in Agutaynon narratives and expository texts, respectively. Thus frequency may perhaps not be a reliable parameter in the determining of basic word order in these languages (also see Hawkins (1994: 430)). Markedness may not always serve as a useful diagnostic for basic word order, either. Whaley (1997: 103–4), for instance, makes reference to Yagua, wherein the morphologically marked word order VSO turns out to be basic in terms of frequency and pragmatic neutrality as opposed to SVO, which is the morphologically unmarked order (Payne 1985a). This leads him to decide that in general markedness is the most unreliable of the three criteria.

These problems notwithstanding, linguistic typologists make judicious use of these criteria in determining basic word order. More frequently than not these criteria do tend to converge toward a particular word order, which will then be taken to be basic. They also rely on language specialists' expertise, or experience in the matter, if and where available. This is the case with, for instance, Mallinson and Blake's (1981: 133) survey of basic word order at the clausal level. This is not to say that these problems, and others – e.g. the notion of subject and object in a language with ergative morphology or syntax (Payne 1985b: 464; Comrie 1989: 88) – can safely be swept under the rug. Rather one needs to bear this inadequacy in mind when evaluating existing works on basic word order, or when carrying out similar research. In a nutshell, the criteria in question are not deterministic by any means but rather largely heuristic.

It must also be made clear at the outset that the foregoing criteria used in determining basic word order are not applicable to so-called flexible or free word order languages. The word order in these languages, at least at the clausal level, is qualitatively different from the syntactically defined word order in that the former reflects pragmatic factors or functions, not semantic roles and/or grammatical relations. For instance, Mithun (1992) identifies languages such as Cayuga, Ngandi and Coos as exhibiting flexible word order. She suggests that in these 'pragmatically based' languages whatever constituent is 'newsworthy' – introducing pertinent new information, presenting a new topic or indicating a contrast – is placed initially in sentences, thereby giving rise to a range of orderings of the major constituents. As she (1992: 50) is at pains to demonstrate, the criteria of frequency, markedness and pragmatic neutrality 'provide little evidence for any underlying [basic] order in these languages'. To put it differently, the concept of basic word order (at the clausal level) is simply irrelevant to flexible word order languages just as the concept of tone is inapplicable to non-tonal languages (Comrie 1989: 36). Needless to say, the consequences of applying the criteria (inadvertently) to pragmatically based languages and then pigeonholing them into basic word order types as if they were syntactically based are to the detriment of the study of language universals since (syntactically defined) basic word order has no place in these languages (Mithun 1992: 59). Said differently, data from pragmatically based languages cannot be taken to provide evidence for or against language universals concerning basic word order.

There are also basic word order patterns at the non-clausal level. Among the most frequently discussed patterns are: PrN/NPo (preposition (Pr) + noun (N) and noun (N) + postposition (Po)), NA/AN (the order of noun (N) and adjective (A)), NG/GN (the order of noun (N) and genitive (G)), and NRel/RelN (the order of noun (N) and relative clause (Rel)). Examples of these patterns are as follows:

(1) Niuean (PrN)
     To   fano a   au apogipogi ki Queen Street
     FUT go   ABS I   tomorrow to Queen Street
     'I am going to Queen Street tomorrow.'

(2) Urubu-Kaapor (NPo)
     kaninde rehe
     Canindé to
     'to Canindé (a place name)'

(3) Malay (NA)
     rumah besar itu
     house big   that
     'that big house'

(4) Sinhalese (AN)
     hoňdə eloolu
     good vegetable
     'good vegetables'

(5) Spanish (NG)
     el   coche de la   mujer
     the car   of the woman
     'the woman's car'

(6) Ket (GN)
ob   da-quś
father his-tent
'father's tent'

(7) Luganda (NRel)
ekitabo kye   n-a-gula   kirungi
book   REL I-PST-buy good
'The book that I bought is good.'

(8) Basque (RelN)
gizon-a-k   liburu-a eman dio-n   emakume-a
man-the-SBJ book-the give   has-REL woman-the
'the woman that the man has given the book to.'

2.2   Early research on basic word order

The different word order pairs in (1) to (8), including the six permutations of S, O and V, are all independent of, or distinct from, one another. Logically speaking, there is no reason why they should be otherwise. For instance, what does basic word order at the clausal level have to do with the distribution of prepositions and postpositions? Not much, it seems. But, as research has over the years shown, there are certain significant correlations among these word order patterns. In this section Greenberg's (1963b) pioneering paper on word order typology, and later works based directly on it, i.e. W.P. Lehmann (1973), Vennemann (1974a) and Hawkins (1983), will be surveyed with a view to exploring these word order correlations and to evaluating critically the proposed theories, or explanations of them. The discussion will also serve as a prelude to the review in 2.3, 2.4 and 2.5 of more recent research on basic word order, i.e. Tomlin (1986), Dryer (1992) and Hawkins (1994).

2.2.1   The inception of word order typology

It was Greenberg (1963b) who first recognized word order as a potentially rich area of typological investigation. In fact, it is not an exaggeration to say that he initiated probably the most prominent and productive typology known in modern linguistics. He not only identified word order patterns systematically on the basis of a modest 30 language convenience sample but also discovered that certain correlations hold between the seemingly logically distinct word order properties.[2] In so doing he also 'established the validity and importance of a new type of universal statement, the implicational universal, thereby setting a precedent for the discovery of other universals of this logical form [$p \supset q$ (where '$\supset$' is to be understood to mean 'implies')]' (Hawkins 1983: 19). Greenberg's (1963b) pioneering paper also laid the solid groundwork for later research on basic word order. It actually served as the empirical basis for a number of subsequent works including notably W.P. Lehmann (1973), Vennemann (1974a) and Hawkins (1983). But, more importantly, his work on basic word order 'opened up a whole field of [typological] research' (Hawkins 1983: 23) by revamping and revitalizing linguistic typology, which had until then been ignored more or less completely in linguistics (see Horne 1966; and Greenberg 1974 for further discussion).[3] His emphasis on word order did not just spearhead a distinct move from the traditional morphology-based typology to a syntax-based one in line with the contemporary development in linguistics (i.e. Chomskyan linguistics; for further discussion see Newmeyer (1986 [1986])) but also reflected a clear preference for partial typology over (idealistic) holistic typology (cf. 1.6).

Greenberg (1963b) puts forth forty-five separate putative 'universal' statements – enumerated in Appendix III of his paper – based on his thirty language sample, and also on his observations of a considerably larger number of languages – identified in Appendix II of his paper.[4] By one count (Hawkins 1983: 22) there are twenty-five implicational statements that have to do with basic word order, involving as many as thirty-four logically distinct claims. Some of his universal statements have in fact stood the test of time and data, which in itself is very remarkable, given that he had only thirty languages to work on in his sample. For example:

(9)   *UNIVERSAL 1*
       In declarative sentences with nominal subject and object, the
       dominant order is almost always one in which the subject precedes
       the object.

(10)   *UNIVERSAL 3*
       Languages with dominant VSO order are always prepositional.

The validity of (9) and (10) has been confirmed many times over (e.g. Mallinson and Blake (1981); Hawkins (1983); Tomlin (1986); Dryer (1989, 1992) *inter alia*; but cf. the caveat against (10) in Chapter 1, note 2). Greenberg's Universal 3 also indicates that, where possible, his universal statements are formulated as exceptionless (i.e. 'always'). Hawkins (1983: 22) points out that forty-two out of a total of fifty-six logically distinct claims (75 per cent) made in Greenberg's (1963b) paper are meant to be exceptionless. Producing such exceptionless universals is a very important desideratum of theory building – even if they may eventually prove to have exceptions – because they represent strict constraints or limitations within which the languages of the world can be seen to vary. If the primary goal of linguistic typology is to define possible human language, every attempt must be made to pursue exceptionless universals or to render universal statements exceptionless (also see Hawkins 1983: 60–3 for a clear exposition of this view).

Greenberg's (1963b) implicational universal statements, which take the logical form of $p \supset q$, are all unilateral, that is non-reversible implicational statements. Thus $p \supset q$ can never be read alternatively as $q \supset p$. Take Universal 25 as an example:

(11) *UNIVERSAL 25*
      If the pronominal object follows the verb, so does the nominal object.

The universal in (11) should not be interpreted bilaterally as in (12).

(12) If the nominal object follows the verb, so does the pronominal object.

The reason why Greenberg formulates his implicational universals only unilaterally is very simple: bilateral interpretations of the universal statements in question are empirically unwarranted. For instance, there are many languages in which the pronominal object precedes the verb when the nominal object follows the verb, e.g. Romance languages such as French, Spanish and Italian but none in which the nominal object precedes the verb when the pronominal object follows the verb. This explains why the reverse interpretation of $p \supset q$, that is $q \supset p$, is not permitted in Greenberg (1963b).

Another laudable aspect of Greenberg's pioneering work on word order is his insistence on employing different word order parameters in order to predict other word order properties (Comrie 1989: 93). As will presently be seen, however, later researchers, W.P. Lehmann and Vennemann, diverge radically from this position in an effort to reduce various word order co-occurrences to a simple elegant generalization or principle. Consider the following universal statements put forth by Greenberg (1963b).

(10) *UNIVERSAL 3*
      Languages with dominant VSO order are always prepositional.

(13) *UNIVERSAL 4*
      With overwhelmingly greater than chance frequency, languages with normal SOV order are postpositional.

(14) *UNIVERSAL 2*
      In languages with prepositions, the genitive almost always follows the governing noun, while in languages with postpositions it almost always precedes.

Word order at the clause level is taken into account to predict the distribution of adpositions, whereas it is the distribution of adpositions that is used as the predictor of the relative position of the genitive (G) and the governing noun (N).

Greenberg (1963b: 93) also sheds light on the relationship between word order and morpheme order, thereby broadening the scope of word order typology. This is reflected most clearly in his Universal 27.

(15)   *UNIVERSAL 27*
        If a language is exclusively suffixing, it is postpositional; if it is exclusively prefixing, it is prepositional.

This particular insight has subsequently also led to work by others, who venture to relate morpheme order to the OV-VO parameter – OV favouring suffixes and VO prefixes (e.g. Cutler, Hawkins and Gilligan (1985), and Hawkins and Cutler (1988); but cf. Hawkins and Gilligan (1988)) – or to the position of equivalent non-bound morphemes (Bybee, Pagliuca and Perkins 1990). For further discussion refer to section 2.6.

In the concluding section of his paper Greenberg (1963b: 96–104) discusses the notions of dominance and harmony in an attempt to provide an explanation of the observed word order correlations. For example, Universals 3 and 4 (see (10) and (13)) indicate that prepositions occur regardless of whether word order at the clausal level is VSO or SOV, whereas there is a strict restriction as to where postpositions occur. That is, postpositions are found in SOV, not VSO, languages. This means that because of their unrestricted distribution prepositions are 'dominant' over postpositions, which are in turn regarded as 'recessive'. It turns out that in general, dominant orders are also the cross-linguistically more common permutations, appearing in the implicatum of implicational universal statements (or q in $p \supset q$) (Dryer 1988; Croft 1995: 99–100). The reason why postpositions can co-occur with SOV, not with VSO, is that they are harmonic with the order of both SV and OV. This also explains why postpositions are avoided in VSO languages: postpositions are disharmonic with VS or VO. Thus Greenberg (1963b: 97) claims that '[a] dominant order may always occur, but its opposite, the recessive, occurs only when a harmonic construction is likewise present'. If V and adpositions are taken to be modified elements, and O and N to be modifiers, then OV and NPo can both be seen to be based on the modifier-before-modified template, as it were. Harmonic relations may thus be based on the 'polarizing' of modifiers and non-modifiers (i.e. modified), with all of the modifiers placed on one side of the modified (for a comprehensive list of dominant orders and harmony patterns, refer to Croft 1990: 56). Thus Greenberg (1963b: 100) cautiously puts forth the notion of harmony as a possible explanation of some of the observed word order correlations (cf. Vennemann 1974a; see below).

Finally, Greenberg's (1963b: 76) Universal 1 (in (9)) predicts the dearth of object-before-subject languages in the world, i.e. VOS, OVS and OSV. In his investigation these three word orders 'do not occur at all or at least are excessively rare' (but see Keenan 1978; and Derbyshire and Pullum (1981, 1986) for the existence of object-before-subject languages). He thus only deals with the remaining three basic word order types, namely VSO, SVO and SOV. He (1963b: 77) also interprets this tripartite word order typology in terms of the position of the verb by symbolizing VSO, SVO and SOV as I, II and III, respectively (where the Roman numerals indicate the positions of the verb relative to S and O). It must be mentioned, however, that he never actually makes reference to I, II or III in formulating his universal statements though he does so in some of the tables used in his paper. This verb-based typology led later researchers, notably W.P. Lehmann (1973, 1978a, 1978b) and Vennemann (1974a), to make an attempt to reduce the tripartite typology to the bipartite OV–VO typology – the latter in conjunction with Greenberg's appeal to the 'polarization' of modified and modifier.

2.2.2   The OV–VO typology

Building on Greenberg's (1963b) work on basic word order, W.P. Lehmann (1973, 1978a, 1978b) puts forth what he calls *the Fundamental Principle of Placement*, or FPP. This principle assumes that the primary syntactic construction is made up of the verb and object (noun phrase), which are in turn 'primary concomitants' of each other in the sentence. In W.P. Lehmann's work subject is left out of consideration because in many languages 'subjects are by no means primary elements in sentences', e.g. subjectless sentences in so-called 'expletive' expressions such as Sanskrit *varṣati*, Greek *húei*, Latin *pluit* all meaning 'It is raining' (W.P. Lehmann 1973: 51; also W.P. Lehmann 1978b: 7–8). He thus reduces Greenberg's tripartite typology to two basic word order types, namely OV (i.e. **S**OV) and VO (i.e. **V**SO and **S**VO). When taken into account, the three less common word orders, VOS, OVS and OSV will also be collapsed similarly to the ordering of O and V. The FPP stipulates that modifiers be placed on the opposite side of a basic constituent, V or O, from its primary concomitant. Thus if one knows that a given language is OV or VO, one can predict the following: in OV languages verbal elements – e.g. negation, causation, reflexive or reciprocal action, etc. – all appear to the right of the verb, whereas in VO languages they appear to the left of the verb; similarly, in OV languages nominal elements – adjective, genitive and relative expressions – are placed to the left of the noun, and in VO languages to the right of the noun. For example, Greenberg (1963: 84, 90) provides the following distributions of auxiliary verbs (Table 2.1), and relative clauses (Table 2.2) in his sample.

In Table 2.1, VSO (or VO in W.P. Lehmann's scheme) has three exponents of the AuxV order, and nil representation of the VAux order, whereas

Table 2.1: *Distribution of AuxV/VAux in the three most common basic word orders*

	VSO	SVO	SOV
AuxV	3	7	0
VAux	0	1	8

(Adapted from Greenberg 1963b: 84)

SOV (or OV in W.P. Lehmann's scheme) has eight VAux languages, and none of the AuxV order. Furthermore, SVO – which is expected to pattern like VSO according to the FPP – is, in fact, represented by seven AuxV languages as opposed to one with the VAux order. Insofar as Greenberg's data in Table 2.1 are concerned, they all fall out very neatly from the FPP. The same can also be said of the data in Table 2.2. The relative clause is also placed on the opposite side of O from the latter's primary concomitant, V. The ordering of the two primary concomitants of the sentence thus forms the parameter on the basis of which predictions can be made about all other word order properties down to morpheme order, e.g. the position of causative, reflexive or reciprocal affixes.

Table 2.2: *Distribution of RelN/NRel in the three most common basic word orders*

	VSO	SVO	SOV
RelN	0	0	7
NRel	6	12	2
Both	0	1	1

(Adapted from Greenberg 1963b: 90)

W.P. Lehmann's (1973, 1978b, 1978c) FPP should not be thought to operate on the basis of the categorial distinction of head and dependent, or, in other words, the analogical linearization of constituents as assumed in Siewierska (1988: 17), for instance. As indicated above, the verbal modifier – be it a causative affix or a negative marker – in OV languages comes after V, whereas that in VO languages comes before V. The adjective (a nominal modifier), on the other hand, is placed before the noun in OV languages, and after the noun in VO languages. This can be represented schematically as in Table 2.3 (vm = verbal modifier).

As can be seen in Table 2.3, the ordering of O and its nominal modifier A is at odds with that of V and its verbal modifier. But this is exactly what

Table 2.3: *Position of nominal and verbal modifiers in W.P. Lehmann's scheme*

OV	VO
AN	NA
V-vm	vm-V

the FPP predicts with respect to the verbal and nominal modifiers. The FPP is never meant to represent the analogical linearization of constituents or, to borrow Greenberg's (1963b: 100) term, the polarization of modifier and modified, as in the case of, for example, Vennemann (1974a). The FPP makes quite different predictions about word order properties, depending on whether modifiers are verbal or nominal. As W.P. Lehmann (1978b: 19) himself points out, the real net effect of the FPP is the uninterrupted contiguity between the noun and verb, regardless of whether OV or VO, because it predicts that modifiers, whether verbal or nominal, will be placed on either side of the complex of V and O, but never inside it (cf. Tomlin 1986; also Mallinson and Blake 1981: 393; Siewierska 1988: 17).

W.P. Lehmann (1973: 55; 1978b: 34) is well aware of a large number of languages that do not behave as the FPP predicts. This is apparent when the FPP is tested in the light of Greenberg's expanded list of languages in Appendix II. For instance, languages may display properties of both OV and VO. He accounts for the existence of such 'inconsistent' or 'ambivalent' languages by claiming that they are undergoing a typological change from OV to VO, or *vice versa* due to contact, or internal development (W.P. Lehmann 1978b: 32–7). But even if inconsistent languages were discounted, why do verbal and nominal modifiers position themselves in the first place in the way that the FPP predicts? W.P. Lehmann (1973: 65), however, does not offer any answer to this question. In fact, he chooses to refrain from giving an explanation for the FPP because he thinks that it is premature to do so. At best, therefore, the FPP is no more than a generalization that is designed to take account of Greenberg's (1963b) word and morpheme order correlations (Comrie 1989: 96–7). The task of providing an explanation of Greenberg's findings is taken up by Vennemann (1974a).

Like W.P. Lehmann, Vennemann (1974a) is firmly of the opinion that subject is of no importance or relevance to word order typology, thereby pursuing the OV–VO typology. But, unlike W.P. Lehmann, Vennemann makes an explicit attempt to explain Greenberg's universal statements on basic word order in terms of categorial analogy. The thrust of his explanation is embodied in what he (1974a: 80) calls *the Principle of Natural Serialization*, or PNS (cf. Bartsch and Vennemann (1972)): the order of operators (i.e. dependents or modifiers in traditional parlance) and operands (i.e. heads or modified in traditional parlance) tends to be serialized in one direction, namely either operators before operands, or operands before operators, as schematized in (16).

(16)   {operator {operand}} $\Rightarrow \begin{cases} [\text{operator [operand]}] \text{ in OV languages} \\ [[\text{operand] operator}] \text{ in VO languages} \end{cases}$

Various categories are assigned to either of these two meta-categories, operators and operands, as in the following.

(17)   OPERATOR   OPERAND
       object   verb
       adverbial   verb
       main verb   auxiliary
       adjective   noun
       relative clause   noun
       genitive   noun
       numeral   noun
       determiner   noun
       adjective   comparison marker
       standard of comparison   comparative adjective
       noun phrase   adposition

The status of some of the operators and operands has, however, been called into question by others (Mallinson and Blake 1981: 384–5; Hawkins 1983: 37–40; Comrie 1989: 98; Dryer 1992: 88–9). For instance, W.P. Lehmann (1973, 1978b, 1978c) takes the auxiliary category to be a verbal modifier (as in Table 2.1) or an operator. But in Vennemann's operand–operator theory, it is regarded as a head/modified or an operand. Whether a given category is an operator or an operand may, of course, depend to a considerable extent on one's theoretical orientation. The status of some of the categories in (17) may thus be more or less controversial than others. But at least insofar as Greenberg's observations are concerned – and if (17) is accepted as valid – Vennemann's PNS takes account of them in a principled manner. For instance, NRel is far more likely to be found in VO languages than in OV languages because the relative positions of the N and the Rel are to be determined in the exactly same way as those of V and O are (cf. Table 2.2). Similarly, being an operand the Aux is expected to occupy the same position as V (in relation to O); AuxV is found in VO, and VAux in OV (cf. Table 2.1) (cf. Dryer 1988, 1992; also see 2.4).

As has already been noted, there are as many as thirty-four logically distinct claims about basic word order in Greenberg's (1963b) paper. The rather unwieldy number of these claims alone is a good enough reason for making an attempt to discover (an) 'organizing principle(s)' that ultimately explain(s) all these universal statements (Hawkins 1983: 23; but cf. Croft 1995: 103–4). The possibility of reducing the multiple claims about word order to a single elegant principle as in (16) does indeed seem a highly attractive option. Regardless of its validity the major advantage of Vennemann's PNS is, therefore, that it is far 'less atomistic and potentially more explanatory than Greenberg's universal statements' (Hawkins 1983: 36).

The position of V relative to O is the core of Vennemann's theory as he (1974a: 79) emphasizes that 'all word order rules are dependent on the relative position of the verb, V, and its object, O, in such a way that in a syntactically consistent language all grammatically functional word order relationships can be predicted from the relative order of V and O'. Accordingly, he (1974a) speaks of OV and VO languages. This in turn gives rise to the OV–VO typology. But, as Hawkins (1983: 36) correctly points out, the verb ends up losing its special role within Vennemann's theory because categories are reduced across the board to either operators or operands. Thus in terms of operand status the verb relative to O is not different from any other categories on the right-hand side of the list in (17).

Vennemann's reductionist theory has more serious implications for the interpretation within the PNS of Greenberg's implicational universal statements (Hawkins 1983: 35–6; Comrie 1989: 99). As can be recalled from 2.2.1, Greenberg's implicational universal statements are all unilateral, not bilateral, that is $p \supset q \neq q \supset p$. However, now that all word order patterns are converted into either the operator-operand or operand-operator sequence, Greenberg's implicational universal statements, e.g. Universal 3, will have to be interpreted bilaterally. Thus the correlation between VSO – or, more accurately, VO since S is irrelevant – and PrN in Universal 3, renumbered here as (18), is reduced likewise to an instance of the operand-operator sequence as in (19).

(18)   *UNIVERSAL 3*
        Languages with dominant VSO order are always prepositional.

(19)   a.   VO ⊃ PrN *read as*
        b.   operand-operator ⊃ operand-operator

Part (b) of (19) is an implication between the two instances (or tokens) of the same sequence (or type), thereby effectively rendering the original unilateral statement into a bilateral one. In other words, the direction of implication can be reversed without complications to the effect of $p \supset q = q \supset p$. But, as has been noted in 2.2.1, this is neither Greenberg's intention nor is it empirically justified because there are prepositional languages that are not VO, e.g. Iraqw, Amharic and Khmati among others.

Furthermore, the transformation of Greenberg's unilateral statements into bilateral ones gives rise to complete obliteration of the distinction between strong (or high-grade) universal statements and weak (or low-grade) ones (cf. Hawkins 1983: chapter 4; Comrie 1989: 99–100) because all implicational universal statements are simply understood in terms of the ordering of operators and operands, that is either operand-operator ⊃ operand-operator, or operator-operand ⊃ operator-operand. For example, compare Universal 3 in (18) with Universal 17, which depicts the correlation between VSO and NA.

(20)   *UNIVERSAL 17*
       With overwhelmingly more than chance frequency, languages with dominant order VSO have the adjective after the noun.

The validity of the latter universal statement (and others which are also concerned with the verb position, and NA/AN for that matter) has been called into serious question. Dryer (1988: 189–91) finds, contrary to the once widely held view, that the order of noun and adjective does not correlate with that of verb and object (also see Dryer 1991: 461–2). For instance, he discovers that in his large sample only four of thirteen families with V-initial languages behave in compliance with Greenberg's Universal 17, and that there is no evidence for V-initial languages (including VSO) being more likely to be NA than SVO or SOV languages.[5] Thus Universal 17 is, if valid at all, an extremely weak universal statement. But in Vennemann's theory this statement will equally be reinterpreted as operand-operator ⊃ operand-operator, thereby failing to distinguish itself from truly high-grade universal statements such as Universal 3. Recall that Greenberg (1963b) appeals to different word order properties to predict other word order properties, e.g. VSO and adpositions as the predictors of prepositions, and the order of genitive and noun, respectively.

Even within Greenberg's expanded list of Appendix II, Vennemann's PNS runs into a similar difficulty. Hawkins (1983: 42) notes that the PNS predicts the ideal co-occurrence of OV & GN & AN, but there are two types of exception in Appendix II: one with NG & NA, and another with GN & NA. In other words, there are no OV languages in which the position of the genitive *alone* is an exception to the PNS. That is to say, OV & NG & AN – Greenberg's Types 18 and 22 – is unattested in Appendix II. A similar comment can also be made of VSO languages: the unattested co-occurrence of VO & GN & NA, or Greenberg's Types 4 and 8. Again, what is out of sync with the other word order properties in the *unattested* co-occurrence is the G. To put it differently, it is the A, not the G, that runs counter to the PNS if there is only a single noun ordering exception. This suggests strongly that '[t]he adjective is evidently a more unstable operator relative to its operand [i.e. the N] than is the genitive, a pattern that generalizes across the two ideal operator-operand types' (Hawkins 1983: 42). But within the PNS the one operator (i.e. G) is no different qualitatively from the other (i.e. A).

To wit, the elegance and simplicity of the PNS could only be achieved 'at the expense of [the] descriptive power [of Greenberg's atomistic formulations]' (Hawkins 1983: 36, 63).

In Appendix II of his paper Greenberg (1963b: 108–10) lists twenty-four logically possible combinations of the four word order parameters, (i) VSO/SVO/SOV, (ii) PrN/NPo, (iii) NG/GN and (iv) NA/AN (i.e. $3 \times 2 \times 2 \times 2 = 24$). But Vennemann's PNS positively sanctions only two combinations: the operator-operand and operand-operator sequences, or OV/NPo/GN/AN and VO/PrN/NG/NA. These two PNS-sanctioned sequences can be mapped onto only three of the twenty-four logical possibilities in Appendix II:

(21)   Type 1:   VSO/PrN/NG/NA
       Type 9:   SVO/PrN/NG/NA
       Type 23:   SOV/NPo/GN/AN

By one estimation (Hawkins 1983: 40), however, these three types account for only 68 of the 142 languages (48 per cent) in the expanded list of Appendix II – which is revised slightly in Hawkins (1983: 52–3) in the light of new data. In Appendix II there are no fewer than sixteen attested combination types, which means that 52 per cent of the sample languages belong to the remaining thirteen types. In other words, more than half of the sample languages do deviate from the predictions of the PNS, or, as Hawkins (1983: 40) puts it, 68 languages have no inconsistency, 50 languages 25 per cent inconsistency and 24 languages 50 per cent inconsistency. Therefore, granted that the sample is a reasonably representative one, 'over half of the world's languages turn out to be exceptions although, admittedly, some of them [i.e. five out of the sixteen types] deviate only marginally [i.e. one inconsistency] from the norms of operator-operand or operand-operator languages, so that some kind of norm does still exist' (Comrie 1989: 100; also see Mallinson and Blake 1981: 379; but cf. Hawkins 1983: 56–8).[6]

The completely ignored status of subject, and the collapsing of VSO and SVO into the single type VO in Vennemann's work have also drawn severe criticism from a number of linguists (Mallinson and Blake 1981: 379; Comrie 1989: 97; Siewierska 1988: 18; Payne 1990: 19). Comrie (1989: 97), for instance, points out correctly that what is true of object noun phrases is also true of other types of noun phrase, be they subject noun phrases or noun phrases in adverbials. This is an important linguistic fact that should be captured in any theory of basic word order, for which there is no room within Vennemann's theory – the same comment applies to W.P. Lehmann (1973, 1978b, 1978c). But, of course, it is the elimination of subject from word order typology that has enabled Vennemann to lump VSO and SVO together without much difficulty because, with subject taken into consideration, SVO would simultaneously fall under both XV (for SV) and VX (for VO) – X standing for either S or O – which would indeed make it impossible for the PNS to make consistent predictions about other word order properties of SVO in particular.

Greenberg's (1963b: 76) Universal 1 (in (9)) predicts the paucity of object-before-subject languages in the world, namely VOS, OVS and OSV. Indeed in his thirty-language sample and expanded list in Appendix II these three permutations of the major constituents 'do not occur at all or at least are excessively rare'. He thus only deals with the remaining three basic word order types, namely VSO, SVO and SOV. But, as Hawkins (1983: 29, 42–3, 114–16) points out, all fifteen implicational universal statements which refer to the verb position as either the antecedent (or p) or consequent (or q) property involve VSO or SOV, but not SVO. Therefore, although Greenberg's tripartite typology of VSO, SVO and SOV can be interpreted to be verb-based – VSO → V-initial, SVO → V-medial and SOV → V-final – it is clear from his discussion that SVO plays no significant role in the predicting of other word order properties (but see Hawkins (1983: 135–6) for SVO languages with prepositions patterning like VSO languages with prepositions in terms of the numerical distribution of languages across the attested types; also see 2.2.3). In fact, when all word order co-occurrences in Greenberg's (1963b) sample are examined with respect to the verb position (Hawkins 1983: 30), SVO can only be seen as a kind of mixed type between VSO and SOV, albeit inclining slightly towards VSO (Hawkins 1983: 30). For example, consider the distribution of adpositions, which is perhaps most indicative of the alleged mixed status of SVO in Greenberg's (1963b) work:

Table 2.4: *Distribution of PrN/NPo in the three most common word orders*

	VSO	SVO	SOV
PrN	6	10	0
NPo	0	3	11

(Adapted from Greenberg 1963b: 77)

SVO has both PrN and NPo exponents, whereas it is either PrN or NPo for VSO and SOV. This typologically ambivalent position of SVO thus leads to Comrie (1989: 96) to claim that:

> [k]nowing that a language is VSO or VOS, we can predict its value for other word order parameters; knowing a language is SOV, we can with considerable reliability predict its other word order parameter values; knowing that a language is SVO, we can predict *virtually nothing else* [emphasis added].

Hawkins (1983: 16, 29–30) echoes this view by stating that 'nothing cor-relates with SVO in a unique and principled way'. He (1983: 114–16) thus abandons the verb-based (and hence OV–VO) typology in favour of the distribution of adpositions being elevated to preferential status as will be discussed in 2.2.3.

Dryer (1991), however, has demonstrated on the basis of a sample of 603 languages that the ambivalence as a basic word order type of SVO is over-stated, with the validity of the OV–VO typology underestimated. He argues that both W.P. Lehmann, and Vennemann were essentially correct in advan-cing the OV–VO typology. His evidence does show, contrary to the widely held view, that in general the word order properties of SVO languages differ little from those of the other two VO languages, i.e. VSO and VOS. He (1991: 443) thus comes to the conclusion in full favour of the OV–VO typology: with respect to a large number of word order properties there is 'a basic split between VO and OV languages'.

Dryer's evidence in support of that split comes basically from two sources: (i) it is as difficult to come up with exceptionless universals about V-initial languages as about SVO languages; and (ii) where there is a tendency for V-initial languages to possess a property, SVO languages also possess that property.[7] Since there are a large number of word order properties that are characteristic of both V-initial and SVO languages, the basic distinction between OV and VO languages is fully justifiable, thereby providing a sur-feit of support for the OV–VO typology itself as initiated by W.P. Lehmann (1973, 1978b, 1978c) and Vennemann (1974a).

First, Dryer (1991: 445–51) tests the nine word order properties that are claimed on the basis of Greenberg's sample to correlate with V-initial languages in an exceptionless way: (i) PrN; (ii) AN; (iii) GN; (iv) AuxV; (v) intensifier-A order; (vi) yes/no question particle in initial position; (vii) wh-word in initial position; (viii) NRel; and (ix) adjective-standard of comparison order. Dryer finds that in his large sample there are counter-examples to the first seven properties although the last two have no exceptions. In fact, there are many V-initial languages that are at odds with the pro-perties listed in (i)–(vii). He (1991: 451) concludes, therefore, that SVO lan-guages are similar to V-initial (and perhaps V-final) languages because few exceptionless universal statements can be made about them. He (1991: 446) also draws attention to the fact that the properties that are unknown in V-initial languages, e.g. RelN and standard of comparison-adjective order, are also extremely rare in SVO languages and, in fact, only found in the Chinese languages in his sample.

Second, Dryer (1991: 451–68) sets out to determine whether or not SVO languages are an in-between or mixed type by examining the properties that SVO and V-initial languages have in common. The reasoning is that, if the distribution of SVO languages is between those of V-initial and V-final languages with respect to a number of word order properties, then SVO is indeed intermediate between V-initial and V-final. If not, the question arises as to which of the two SVO languages align themselves with. For instance, he scrutinizes the correlation between the distribution of adpositions and V-initial/-final order. This is, in fact, more or less captured in Greenberg's Universals 3 and 4 (see above), that is V-initial ⊃ PrN and V-final ⊃ NPo. Dryer (1991: 452) confirms the validity of these co-occurrence patterns as in Table 2.5 (also Dryer (1992: 83)). As the reader can recall from 1.5.3, Dryer's sampling technique involves the counting of genera in the six large continental areas (cf. five areas in Dryer 1989). For a linguistic pattern to be statistically significant (or strong enough to be accepted as a language universal), it must be dominant in each of the six large areas; said differently, the rule is that for *each* area the number of genera containing languages with the pattern in question must *exceed* that of genera containing languages without it. The figures in both rows represent the number of genera exhibiting the correlations in question, with the larger of the two figures for each area or column appearing in square brackets (Afr = Africa, Eura = Eurasia, SEAsia & Oc = Southeast Asia and Oceania, A-NG = Australia-New Guinea, NAm = North America and SAm = South America).

Table 2.5: *Distribution of NPo/PrN in V-final, SVO and V-initial languages*

	Afr	Eura	SEAsia&Oc	A-NG	NAm	SAm	Total
V-final&NPo	[15]	[22]	[5]	[16]	[23]	[16]	97
V-final&PrN	3	2	0	0	0	0	5
Proportion NPo	0.83	0.92	1.00	1.00	1.00	1.00	Avg. = 0.96
SVO&NPo	3	1	0	0	0	2	6
SVO&PrN	[15]	[5]	[12]	[4]	[4]	2	42
Proportion NPo	0.17	0.17	0.00	0.00	0.00	0.50	Avg. = 0.14
V-initial&NPo	0	0	0	0	2	2	4
V-initial&PrN	[5]	[1]	[6]	[1]	[15]	[3]	31
Proportion NPo	0.00	0.00	0.00	0.00	0.12	0.40	Avg. = 0.09

(Dryer 1991: 452)

It is abundantly clear from Table 2.5 that in all the six areas the co-occurrence of the V-final order and postpositions is the dominant pattern, with the very few exceptions confined to the two areas, Africa and Eurasia. On the other hand, V-initial languages are far more likely to co-occur with prepositions than with postpositions in each of the six areas. Again, there are very few exceptions, restricted to the two Americas. These two correlations are even more clearly indicated by the average figures (in the far right-hand column) of the 'proportion of genera' for V-final/-initial & NPo: 0.96, and 0.09 for V-final and V-initial, respectively. In the present case these proportion figures represent the numerical values of the total number of genera containing languages with postpositions over the total number of genera containing V-final or V-initial languages as the case may be. These figures mean that 96 out of randomly chosen 100 V-final languages (Avg. = 0.96) are estimated to be postpositional, whereas only 9 out of randomly chosen 100 V-initial languages (Avg. = 0.09) are postpositional. To put it differently, choose one V-final language and one V-initial language randomly, and there is a 96 per cent chance of the V-final language being postpositional but only a 9 per cent chance of the V-initial language being postpositional. This discrepancy (0.96 vs. 0.09) simply is too huge to be attributed to accident, chance or sampling error (Dryer 1991: 454).

Far more relevant to the issue at hand is the behaviour of SVO languages with respect to the distribution of adpositions: it is almost as likely for SVO languages as V-initial languages to be prepositional, with the difference of 0.05 between the proportion of SVO & NPo (0.14) and that of V-initial & NPo (0.09) being due to chance or random variation. The average figure of the proportion of genera for SVO & NPo (0.14) is literally intermediate between those for V-final & NPo (0.96) and V-initial & NPo (0.09). But it is closer by a decisive margin to that for V-initial languages, thereby providing evidence for SVO patterning like V-initial languages. Dryer (1991: 455–60) carries out a similar investigation of SVO languages in terms of ten additional word order properties: NRel/RelN, adjective-standard of comparison order, copula-predicate order, position of adverbial subordinators, position of plural words, adpositional phrase-verb order, manner adverb-verb order, AuxV/VAux, negative-verb order and position of complementizers. He finds that in all these word order properties SVO languages do behave like V-initial languages in opposition to V-final languages.

However, Dryer (1991: 464–7) also points to at least three word order properties for which SVO is like a mixed type between V-initial and V-final: NG/GN, position of question particles and position of wh-words. For instance, consider the data in Table 2.6 for the distribution of NG/GN in V-final, SVO and V-initial languages.

The first section of Table 2.6 indicates clearly that V-final languages have a strong preference for GN, the average proportion of genera being 0.89. The preference of V-initial languages, albeit not as strong as that of V-final ones for GN, is NG, the average proportion figure for GN standing at 0.28; there is only one large area which exhibits a preponderance of GN, namely Australia-New Guinea. But the preference of SVO is divided more or less equally between GN and NG, with two areas favouring GN, another two NG and the remaining two equally split between GN and NG. The raw figures of genera with SVO & NG are much higher than those of genera with SVO & GN (34 vs. 22), but this is due mainly to the presence of a high number of SVO & NG genera in Africa. What is more interesting here is, however, that the average proportion figures for V-final, SVO and V-final

Table 2.6: *Distribution of GN/NG in V-final, SVO and V-initial languages*

	Afr	Eura	SEAsia&Oc	A-NG	NAm	SAm	Total
V-final&GN	[17]	[18]	[5]	[15]	[28]	[19]	102
V-final&NG	5	3	1	2	0	0	11
Proportion GN	0.77	0.86	0.83	0.88	1.00	1.00	Avg. = 0.89
SVO&GN	5	3	4	[5]	2	[3]	??
SVO&NG	[20]	3	[9]	0	2	0	34
Proportion GN	0.20	0.50	0.31	1.00	0.50	1.00	Avg. = 0.59
V-initial&GN	0	0	1	[2]	2	2	7
V-initial&NG	[6]	[1]	[6]	0	[17]	[3]	33
Proportion GN	0.00	0.00	0.14	1.00	0.11	0.40	Avg. = 0.28

(Dryer 1991: 464)

are almost equidistant from one another by 0.30. Dryer (1991: 465) thus takes the order of noun and genitive to be one of the three word order properties for which SVO languages are genuinely intermediate between V-initial and V-final languages.

The unavoidable conclusion that can be drawn from the foregoing analysis is that in terms of word order properties SVO languages are more aligned with V-initial languages than they can ever be regarded as intermediate between V-initial and V-final languages (Dryer 1991: 467–8). When SVO does behave like an in-between type, it is 'localized in certain characteristics' (Dryer 1991: 467) (cf. 3.13, and 3.14 for the behaviour of different word order types relative to case marking). Nonetheless there are far more other characteristics for which SVO and V-initial languages behave likewise as opposed to V-final languages. The distinction between OV and VO languages is undeniably justifiable. So is the OV–VO typology itself.

It bears brief mention that Dryer (1997) has recently called for the SV–VS typology in addition to the OV–VO typology. He argues that there are a number of advantages of using this new typology as well. First, intransitive subjects, which have so far been ignored completely in word order typology, can now be taken into consideration. Second, the additional typology makes it possible to collapse VSO and VOS into a single VS&VO type because these two word order types have many characteristics in common. This in turn has the effect of strengthening the validity of the OV–VO typology itself by reducing VSO and VOS into the two parameters of VO and VS. Third, it incorporates into word order typology those languages which are unclassifiable by means of the traditional typology based on S, O and V. Lastly, the SV–VS typology does not depend on the transitive clause type, which proves to be very infrequent in actual language use in certain languages (e.g. Du Bois (1987: 818) for Sacapultec, Weber (1989: 15–16) for Huallaga Quechua and Payne (1990: 222) for Yagua). It will certainly take some time to understand fully implications, or ramifications of the SV–VS typology. There are also some issues in the SV–VS and OV–VO typology that need to be clarified. For instance, Fijian, with two normal word orders, VSO and VOS, cannot be assigned to one of the six traditional clausal word order types. It must otherwise be identified as possessing the hybrid type of VSO/VOS. Dryer (1997: 75) thus points out that the SV–VS, and OV–VO typology treat Fijian as a VS&VO language. It is not entirely clear, however, what is exactly the conceptual difference between the VSO/VOS type, and VS&VO type because the latter also seems to be a kind of hybrid type. At any rate, it remains to be seen whether or not this new typology will lead to the discovery of word order or structural correlations not hitherto envisaged, especially in the context of the conventional word order typology.

2.2.3   Making language universals exceptionless

In 2.2.1 Greenberg's (1963b) paper is not critically examined in the light of the detailed discussion of different sampling techniques in 1.5.3. As he himself acknowledges (1963b: 74–5), both his sample and expanded list of languages (i.e. Appendix II) are genetically and areally unrepresentative of the languages of the world. But perhaps its exploratory, pioneering nature makes it unreasonable to evaluate his work by current rigorous standards of language sampling. Both W.P. Lehmann's (1973, 1978b, 1978c) and Vennemann's (1974a) research derive directly from Greenberg's (1963b) paper and his sample. Thus what can be said of Greenberg (1963b) with respect to sampling may also apply unreservedly to them, their unwarranted overgeneralizations notwithstanding.

Hawkins (1983: 319), on the other hand, works with an expanded 336 language sample of his own although he frequently makes use of not only Greenberg's thirty-language sample but also *his* expanded list in Appendix II for purposes of testing, for example. The importance of having access to a representative sample cannot be overemphasized for work such as Hawkins (1983: 62), one of the main objectives of which is to define attested co-occurrences of word order properties and to distinguish them from unattested co-occurrences in *quantitative* terms. Needless to say, without a reasonably unbiased sample that objective is almost impossible to achieve. However, Hawkins's expanded sample cannot but be faulted on two counts. First, his sample is largely a convenience sample although he (1983: 281) notes that his contributors to his sample were encouraged not to provide data from the same language family or group in order to maximize genetic distance. Nonetheless it 'reflect[s] the interests and expertise of the contributors, the availability of sources of information, and the original Greenberg['s] sample[, and] [n]o attempt was made to collect fixed numbers of languages from the various language families, from the various geographical regions, or from the various language types'. Thus, as Payne (1985b: 464–5) rightly observes, Hawkins's sample suffers from the lack of representation from, for example, the Eskimo-Aleut family and also the Ge-Pano-Carib phylum, which obviously consists of 'a large number of genetically and typologically diverse languages'; some phyla or families are grossly under-represented, with others over-represented. Equally problematic is the fact that Hawkins's sample is far from random. As has been pointed out in 1.5.3, the use of random samples does not only enable researchers to run various tests in order to ascertain whether or not their findings are statistically significant – or whether or not they are due to chance. But it also allows one to estimate or minimize the extent of sampling error (Bell 1978: 157). In a nutshell, the use of a non-representative, non-random sample utterly defeats Hawkins's own aim to define attested co-occurrences of word order properties in the languages of the world. Second, Hawkins's basic procedure of arriving at exceptionless universals – in order to discover absolute properties of human language – is to count individual languages (e.g. 100 languages for p & q, but none for p & $-q$). But, as Perkins (1980, 1992) and Dryer (1989) have demonstrated, there are serious problems associated with 'counting languages in a sample containing more than one language per family . . . since actual language numbers are also the effect of various non-linguistic factors' (Dryer 1988: 206; see 1.5.3). Unless non-linguistic factors are sifted from linguistic ones, Hawkins's (exceptionless) universals are only suspect. Despite these problems, however, Hawkins's work will be reviewed here on its own merit if only as a *theoretical* contribution to the study of basic word order correlations. More-over, it is the first major work on word order typology after Greenberg, in which an attempt is made to strike a balance between Greenberg's data-driven multiple generalizations (or lack of (an) organizing principle(s)), and W.P. Lehmann's and Vennemann's empirical inadequacy (or zeal for abstract generalizing).

First, Hawkins (1983: 60–3) highlights the importance and role of excep-tionless or non-statistical universals in constructing a theory of basic word order. Indeed if one's goal is to characterize possible human language with respect to basic word order, it goes without saying that one needs to be able to define all and only the attested word order co-occurrence types. Although it proposes a large number of exceptionless universal statements, Greenberg's original work contains a fair number of statistical universal statements (i.e. with exceptions). Of a total of fifty-six logically distinct claims made by Greenberg forty-two are exceptionless and fourteen are statistical (Hawkins 1983: 22). Hawkins (1983: chapter 3; also Hawkins (1980: 200–4)) sets out to demonstrate that statistical universals can actually be strengthened or con-verted into exceptionless ones. For instance, Hawkins (1983: 66–72) comes up with the following three basic observations, or universals (one of which is statistical, i.e. (22a)):[8]

(22) a. Pr ⊃ (NA ⊃ NG)
      b. Pr ⊃ (NDem ⊃ NA)
      c. Pr ⊃ (NNum ⊃ NA)

Encoded in (22) are the (statistical) implicational universal statements: (a) if a language has preposition word order, then if the adjective follows the noun, the genitive follows the noun; (b) if a language has preposition word order, then if the demonstrative determiner (or Dem) follows the noun, the adjective follows the noun; and (c) if a language has preposition word order, then if the numeral (or Num) follows the noun, the adjective follows the noun. By transitivity, two additional implicational universals can be drawn as in (23).

(23) a. Pr ⊃ (NDem ⊃ NG)
      b. Pr ⊃ (NNum ⊃ NG)

The implicational statements in (23) predict that Pr & NDem & GN and Pr & NNum & GN are non-attested co-occurrence patterns. But there are two counterexamples to each of (23a) and (23b) in Hawkins's expanded sample, namely Kaliai-Kove and Karen, which are not only Pr & NDem & GN, but also Pr & NNum & GN. The small number of these counterexamples can perhaps be brushed aside as insignificant but Hawkins (1983: 128–9) observes that these two languages happen to be SVO. By requiring prepositional languages to be non-SVO, or –SVO in (23), Hawkins is able to 'eliminate' the two counterexamples safely, and to reformulate the statistical universals in (23) into complex yet exceptionless ones as in (24).

(24) a. Pr & –SVO ⊃ (NDem ⊃ NG)
      b. Pr & –SVO ⊃ (NNum ⊃ NG)

The exceptionless statements in (24) thus read: (a) if a language has prepositions and any clausal word order other than SVO, then if the demonstrative determiner follows the noun, the genitive follows the noun; and (b) if a language has prepositions and any clausal word order other than SVO, then if the numeral follows the noun, the genitive follows the noun.

Note that Hawkins manages to develop exceptionless universals from the originally statistical ones by 'increasing the [antecedent or] conditioning property [i.e. the implicans p in $p \supset q$] from one word order specification [e.g. Pr] to at least two [e.g. Pr & –SVO]' (Hawkins 1980: 204). This is one of the hallmarks of Hawkins's (exceptionless) universals: multi-valued or multi-termed implicational universals, involving at least three word order properties. Greenberg (1963b) also relies on similar multi-valued implicational statements (e.g. Universal 5), albeit very sparingly, but it is the norm in the case of Hawkins (1983), with most of his twenty odd universals formulated as multi-valued. Also note that all of Hawkins's universal statements are unilateral, not bilateral, as in Greenberg's (1963b) original work (cf. the earlier discussion of Vennemann (1974a)).

As has already been noted, Vennemann's PNS may only be able to account for less than half of the languages of the world (or at least insofar as the evidence available to Hawkins (1983) is concerned); conversely, more than half of the languages of the world are counterexamples to the PNS. One of Hawkins's major contributions to word order typology is to bring these 'counterexamples' back into word order typology as something to be explained in a principled way. In Hawkins's theory of basic word order there are two ways in which this reinstatement of the counterexamples can be carried out. First, he puts forth two (competing) principles that have a bearing on word order correlation patterns: *the Heaviness Serialization Principle* (HSP), and *the Mobility Principle* (MP). Second, he makes a conceptual distinction between two different types of universals, implicational and distributional, the latter adding a quantitative dimension to language universals research.

Hawkins (1983: 75) finds that only seven of the thirty-two mathematically possible co-occurrences of the five nominal modifiers in prepositional languages ($2^5 = 32$) are attested in Greenberg's data, and in his own as enumerated below.

(25) a. Pr & NDem & NNum & NA & NG & NRel
      b. Pr & DemN & NNum & NA & NG & NRel
      c. Pr & NDem & NumN & NA & NG & NRel
      d. Pr & DemN & NumN & NA & NG & NRel
      e. Pr & DemN & NumN & AN & NG & NRel
      f. Pr & DemN & NumN & AN & GN & NRel
      g. Pr & DemN & NumN & AN & GN & RelN

What (25) clearly illustrates is that the nominal modifiers are preposed or placed before the head N 'in a fixed and predictable pattern: first the demonstrative determiner or the numeral; then both; then the adjective; then the genitive; and finally the relative clause' (Hawkins 1983: 75). Said differently, if the Rel is preposed, all the other modifiers, the G, A, Num and Dem, must also be preposed; if the G is preposed, so are the A, Num and Dem; and so forth. Hawkins claims that the nominal modifiers behave in this manner precisely because some modifiers are heavier or lighter than others, and because heavier modifiers tend to occur to the right of lighter ones. For instance, the Rel is heavier than the Dem or the Num because the former contains more words (or more morphemes or syllables) than the latter, and the Rel, which is a clause in its own right, may dominate other constituents including the Dem/Num, the A and so forth. This rightward preference of heavy modifiers (or constituents for that matter) can, in fact, easily be seen in the different orderings of adjectives and adjectives coupled with prepositional phrases in English, e.g. *a rich country* (AN) vs. *a country rich in natural resources* (NA), or in so-called Heavy NP shift in English, e.g. *Teresa gave the car to a pauper* vs. *Teresa gave to a pauper the car that her husband had won in a raffle organized by the primary school that her daughter goes to.* Hawkins (1983: 90–1) thus proposes the HSP with respect to nominal modifiers in the following form (cf. Mallinson and Blake 1981: 151):

(26)   *Heaviness Serialization Principle (HSP)*
        Rel $\geq_R$ G $\geq_R$ A $\geq_R$ {Dem, Num}
        where '$\geq_R$' means 'exhibits more or equal rightward positioning relative to the head noun across languages'.

In terms of Vennemann's PNS, only (25a) will be consistent or fully serialized, with the rest being inconsistent in one or more respects in terms of the ideally serialized operand–operator sequence (cf. (16) and (17)). Thus languages belonging to the patterns in (25b)–(25g) will all be counterexamples to the predictions of the PNS. But under Hawkins's HSP not only the completely consistent co-occurrence in (25a) but the inconsistent ones in (25b)–(25g) can also be accounted for in a principled or predictable manner. The inconsistent co-occurrences are deviations from the serialization of the preposition and the nominal modifiers but all these deviations do also arise from prepositional languages placing lighter constituents to the left of the head, and heavier ones to the right of the head, with the differences among (25b)–(25f) depending on where languages actually draw the line between heavier and lighter constituents. Thus in (25d) the Dem, and the Num are taken to be lighter as opposed to the rest of the nominal modifiers, in (25e) the dividing line falls in between the A and the G, and in (25g) the positioning of all the nominal modifiers is at odds with the Pr (see below for discussion as to how the frequency of exemplifying languages decreases as one moves from (25a) to (25g), and as to how this phenomenon can be explained by means of distributional universals).

In postpositional languages, however, the HSP alone cannot explain the distribution of the nominal modifiers as it has done with prepositional languages in (25). There are certain co-occurrences of nominal modifiers in postpositional languages which do militate against the HSP although they are captured by Hawkins's universals. The universals in question all involve postpositions as the antecedent property ('∨' means 'or'):

(27)   a.   Po ⊃ (AN ⊃ GN)
        b.   Po ⊃ (DemN ⊃ GN)
        c.   Po ⊃ (NumN ⊃ GN)
        d.   Po ⊃ ((AN ∨ NA) & (RelN ∨ NRel))

The first three implicational statements in (27) are formulated to predict non-occurrence of the co-occurrence patterns in (28) (note that $p \supset (q \supset r)$ allows p & q & r, p & $-q$ & r and p & $-q$ & $-r$, but disallows p & q & $-r$; the asterisk preceding the word order co-occurrences below means 'unattested').

(28)   a.   *Po & AN & NG
       b.   *Po & DemN & NG
       c.   *Po & NumN & NG

The co-occurrences in (28) are also well within the predictions of the HSP; the lighter constituents, the A, Dem and Num, all appear to the left, or before the head N, whereas the heavier one, the G, is placed to the right, or after the head N. There are no languages exemplifying the co-occurrences in (28) in Greenberg's or Hawkins's data.

Moreover, the implicational universals in (27) also predict the co-occurrence patterns in (29) (because $p \supset (q \supset r)$ allows p & $-q$ & r in addition to p & q & r, and p & $-q$ & $-r$).

(29)   a.   Po & NA & GN
       b.   Po & NDem & GN
       c.   Po & NNum & GN
       d.   Po & NA & RelN

The co-occurrences in (29), however, all go against the predictions of the HSP; for instance, in (29a) the lighter constituent, the A, occurs to the right (of the head N), whereas the heavier constituent, the G, occurs to the left (of the head N). The violation is most dramatic in (29d), wherein the heaviest constituent, the Rel, is pushed to the left, and the lighter constituent, the A, to the right. In order to explain the existence of these apparent exceptions to the HSP Hawkins (1983: 93) invokes the MP, which claims that the Dem, the Num and the A are more mobile than the G and the Rel, and thus are able to move around their heads more easily.

(30)   *Mobility Principle (MP)*
       {A, Dem, Num} $\geq_M$ {Rel, G}
       where '$\geq_M$' means 'exhibits greater or equal mobility away from the adposition + NP serialization'

In consistent prepositional languages – consistent in the sense of Vennemann's PNS – all nominal modifiers are placed to the right of the head (i.e. NDem, NNum, NA, NG and NRel as in (25a)). When modifiers move around their heads according to the MP, they will move in the direction also predicted by the HSP, i.e. lighter constituents to the left. In consistent postpositional languages, on the other hand, all nominal modifiers are already placed to the left of the head (i.e. DemN, NumN, AN, GN and RelN). When modifiers deviate from their 'ideally serialized' positions, they can only move to the right. But this is contrary to what is predicted by the HSP insofar as lighter constituents are concerned. In general, however, the MP takes priority over the HSP (with a possible exception of Rel), thereby explaining the co-occurrences in (29).[9] It is indeed the lighter and more mobile constituents, the Dem, the Num and the A, in (29) that have shifted from their ideally serialized positions, whereas the heavier, and less mobile ones, the G and the Rel, remain in the position to the left of the head N.

As briefly discussed in 2.2.1, Greenberg (1963b) appeals to the notions of dominance and harmony in an attempt to make sense of the observed word order correlations. These two interact with each other to the effect that a dominant order may always occur whereas the recessive order occurs only in conjunction with the harmonic order. Thus the Po, which is recessive as opposed to the dominant Pr, is found in SOV, not VSO languages. In a way, this is a fine example of how two conflicting motivations for basic word order are resolved (Croft 1995: 100). Equally important is the fact that Greenberg (1963b) makes reference to more than one principle. As can be recalled from 2.2.2, this is not the case of W.P. Lehmann's and Vennemann's research, in which a single principle, the FPP or the PNS, is proposed at the expense of Greenberg's empirical base. In this sense Hawkins's (1983) work on word order typology is a move back towards Greenberg's original insight. He invokes at least three independent principles, the HSP, the MP and also *the Mobility and Heaviness Interaction Principle* (MHIP), which is designed specifically to resolve the potential conflict between the first two principles (see note 9; also see below for one additional principle; but see Hawkins 1994 and 2.5). Incidentally, Croft (1995: 101) likens Hawkins's notion of heaviness to Greenberg's notion of dominance but this does not seem appropriate because heaviness is inherently relative or continuous, whereas dominance clearly is not – an order is either dominant or recessive.

As the reader may already have realized, all the universal statements cited in this sub-section involve either prepositions or postpositions as the (initial) antecedent property; they all begin with either the Pr or the Po as the implicans. This is not a pure coincidence. As discussed in 2.2.2, Hawkins (1983) abandons the verb-based word order typology, implicit in Greenberg's work but expounded in W. P. Lehmann's and Vennemann's work, albeit in more abstract form. His reason for the disregard of the verb position is due largely to his own belief in the typological ambivalence of SVO. Hawkins (1983: 116) is driven to adopt prepositions and postpositions as much better predictors of other word order properties, or as what he calls 'type indicators'. He thus speaks of two major word order types: prepositional and post-positional languages.

Hawkins's approach to word order universals is, as he (1983: 163) calls it, a two-tier approach: implicational and distributional. As has been discussed, the former type of universal is formulated to define all and only the attested co-occurrence of word order properties. On the other hand, the latter is appropriate for defining relative language frequencies, or quantities of these co-occurrences. Greenberg's statistical universal statements can in principle also capture relative language frequencies. Take his Universals 1, 3 and 4, renumbered as (31), (32) and (33), respectively.

(31)   *UNIVERSAL 1*
       In declarative sentences with nominal subject and object, the dominant order is almost always one in which the subject precedes the object.

(32)   *UNIVERSAL 3*
       Languages with dominant VSO order are always prepositional.

(33)   *UNIVERSAL 4*
       With overwhelmingly greater than chance frequency, languages with normal SOV order are postpositional.

The use of expressions such as 'always', 'almost always' and 'with over-whelmingly greater than chance frequency' is meant to distinguish different levels of language frequency, albeit in a primitive way. But, needless to say, these expressions of frequency are hopelessly difficult to quantify and are susceptible to subjective interpretations. Hawkins (1983: 162–3) is thus correct to say that such statistical universals 'could only be set up for values of p & q that had a very high frequency of occurrence where $*p$ & $-q$ had a very low frequency of occurrence'. In other words, the number of exceptions that statistical universals can accommodate must be severely limited; other-wise, the meaning of 'statistical' as understood in statistical universals will be rendered vacuous. In order to quantify language frequencies more object-ively, and accurately Hawkins (1983: chapter 4; 1980: 210–33) puts forward *the Principle of Cross-Category Harmony* (PCCH):

(34)   *Principle of Cross-Category Harmony (PCCH)*
       The more similar the position of operands relative to their operators across different operand categories considered pairwise (verb in relation to adposition order, noun in relation to adposition order, verb in relation to noun order), the greater the percentage numbers of exemplifying languages.

Hawkins (1983: 134, 157–61) is at pains to explain that the PCCH is dis-tinct from Vennemann's PNS although like the latter the former hinges on the conceptual distinction between operators (or dependents) and operands (or heads) (see Mallinson and Blake (1981: 415–17)). The main difference between the PCCH and the PNS is claimed to be that, whereas the PNS is

Table 2.7:   *Distribution of clausal word orders, Pr/Po, NA/AN and NG/GN*

<1>	SOV & Po & AN & GN	28 (47.4%)	96 (59.3%)
<2>	SOV & Po & NA & GN	24 (40.7%)	55 (33.9%)
<3>	SOV & Po & NA & NG	7 (11.9%)	11 (6.8%)
<4>	VSO & Pr & NA & NG	19 (76.0%)	38 (73.1%)
<5>	VSO & Pr & AN & NG	5 (20.0%)	13 (25.0%)
<6>	VSO & Pr & AN & GN	1 (4.0%)	1 (1.9%)
<7>	SVO & Pr & NA & NG	21 (65.6%)	56 (70.0%)
<8>	SVO & Pr & AN & NG	8 (25.0%)	17 (21.2%)
<9>	SVO & Pr & AN & GN	3 (9.4%)	7 (8.8%)

(Adapted from Hawkins 1983: 135)

based crucially on the consistent serialization of all operators (or operands) in one direction or the other, the PCCH is intended to capture an 'ordering balance across phrasal categories, regardless of where [the] operators are positioned relative to their operands'. Said differently, it aims to produce an overall profile of the ordering of all operators and operands. To see how this principle actually works, consider the frequency distribution of the four word order properties, clausal word order (SOV, VSO and SVO), Pr/Po, NA/AN and NG/GN, as in Table 2.7 (the language quantities and percentage numbers of Greenberg's (1963b) Appendix II in the second column, and those of Hawkins's (1983) Expanded Sample in the third column).[10]

If in a given co-occurrence all operators are consistently serialized in one direction, then that co-occurrence is represented by more languages than any other co-occurrences which deviate in one or more respects from the serialized ordering: the fewer deviations, the more exemplifying languages. Take SOV & Po-sequences in the top section of Table 2.7, for example. The co-occurrence in <1>, which has no inconsistency, is the most frequent, represented by the largest number of languages in the database, followed by <2>, which has one inconsistency (or NA), and then <3>, which with two inconsistencies (NA and NG) is the least favoured co-occurrence (represented by the smallest number of languages in the database).[11] A similar comment can also be made of the VSO & Pr- and SVO & Pr-sequences. Clearly, as the conflict in the ordering of the operands and operators across the different word order co-occurrences increases, the number of exemplifying languages decreases. This distributional fact is exactly what the PCCH is designed to predict.

Hawkins (1983: 98–122) claims that the HSP has a psycholinguistic or processing explanation (cf. e.g. Moore 1972; Fodor, Bever and Garrett 1974;

Clark and Clark 1977) and that the MP embodies a grammatically based phenomenon which is enmeshed in language change. First, the HSP is built on the leftward–rightward asymmetry: there is a linguistic preference for light modifiers to be positioned to the left and heavy ones to the right. This positioning preference is believed to be motivated by ease of processing. For instance, Hawkins interprets the results of Moore's (1972) experiments – subjects were asked to make grammaticality judgements which involved violation of subcategorizations or selectional restrictions, and the reaction time in recognizing violations was measured – to suggest that early head recognition is crucial for early recognition of the whole basic clause structure. This is claimed to be also true of the NP and its modifiers. Since speech is processed from left to right, comprehension decisions must be made on each constituent of the NP as to whether or not it is the head. If there are modifiers to the left of the head, recognition of the head will be delayed until all the modifiers are processed. This head recognition delay is also bound to place much burden on short-term memory because, until the head is processed, all its dependents will have to be held in short-term memory instead of being integrated directly into the overall syntax and semantics of the NP. In the case of an NP with postnominal modifiers, on the other hand, the head will immediately be identified, with the following modifiers integrated into the syntax and semantics of the NP as they come through. In other words, this early head recognition obviates the need to make decisions on head status for each of the modifiers. This also means far less burden on short-term memory because postnominal modifiers are not put on hold in short-term memory. Thus 'all things being equal, the earlier the head appears within the NP, the better from the perspective of processing load' (Hawkins 1983: 99). This then explains the workings of the HSP, heavy modifiers being shifted to the right so that the head can quickly be recognized. Light modifiers, on the other hand, may be allowed to occur to the left since due to their lightness they do not interfere with fast, quick recognition of the head to the extent that heavy modifiers do. In this context recall that the HSP overrides the MP only if the postposed modifier is the Rel, which is the heaviest of all the nominal modifiers (Hawkins 1983: 100). This explains why Po & DemN & NRel and Po & NumN & NRel are 'productively occurring' in Hawkins's expanded sample (see note 9). As will be revisited in 2.5, this processing explanation is further refined and developed in the later work by Hawkins (1990, 1994) (cf. Dryer 1992) – the three principles, the HSP, the MP and the MHIP, reduced into a single one – with a view to making sense of various word order patterns.

The MP is also based on a kind of syntactic asymmetry between the Dem, the Num, the A, on the one hand, and the G and the Rel on the other. The first or more mobile group involves non-branching constituents dominating single terminal nodes, whereas the second or less mobile group includes branching constituents dominating a set of both terminal and non-terminal nodes (cf. Dryer 1992, who develops an explanatory theory of word order correlations based on the distinction between branching and non-branching constituents; see 2.4). Put differently, the more mobile constituents have less syntactically complex structure than the less mobile counterparts. This difference in syntactic complexity is claimed to have different historical consequences in that the more mobile ones are more prone to undergo changes in positioning than the less mobile ones and thus are more likely to move away from the ideal operator–operand serialization. If a language makes a change in operator–operand ordering, then the less syntactically complex constituents will be affected before the more syntactically complex ones. Hence the ranking of the MP.

Finally, although it can take adequate account of a number of distributional facts pertaining to various word order co-occurrences, there is something that the PCCH cannot explain. For instance, the PCCH predicts that Pr & V1 & N1 (N1 = noun-initial, that is the N preceding all modifiers) will have as many exemplifying languages as Po & V3 & N3 (N3 = noun-final, that is N following all modifiers) because both are equally maximally harmonic across the phrasal categories concerned. But this is not empirically borne out in either Greenberg's or Hawkins's data. In fact, Pr & V1 & N1 has fewer representations than less harmonic Pr & V2 & N1. As Hawkins points out, however, this discrepancy between the PCCH and the data has to do with the fact that there simply are far fewer V1 – VSO and VOS – languages in the world (see 2.3). Why this is so, of course, does not fall out from the PCCH. To deal with this apparent anomaly Hawkins (1983: 156–7) appeals to a somewhat vague principle called *the Subjects Front Principle*, which is proposed by Keenan (1979): subjects move to the initial position due probably to their topical nature (cf. Mallinson and Blake (1981: 151)). The principle, however, does not explain much, if at all. In fact, as Manning and Parker (1989: 47) put it, it 'comes to little more than [a] basic observation, still to be explained'. This is the very issue that Tomlin (1986) addresses in his work on basic word order.

2.3   Explaining the distribution of the basic clausal word orders

Tomlin (1986) is a major work on basic word order, a very focused one in that it only deals with basic word order at the clausal level. The aim of this work is to determine the frequency of occurrence of each of the six basic clausal word orders in the languages of the world and to provide an explanation of the relative frequencies of these word orders. It is based on a large sample of 402 languages derived from a database of 1,063 languages (see 1.5.3 for discussion of Tomlin's (1986) sampling technique; also see below).

Table 2.8: *Distribution of the six basic clausal word orders in Tomlin (1986)*

Word order	Number	%
SOV	180	44.78
SVO	168	41.79
VSO	37	9.20
VOS	12	2.99
OVS	5	1.24
OSV	0	0.00
Total	402	100.00

(Adapted from Tomlin 1986: 22)

Table 2.9: *Basic clausal word order frequencies in previous works*

Word order	Ultan (1969)	Ruhlen (1975)	Hawkins (1983)	Mallinson & Blake (1981)
SOV	44%	51.0%	51.8%	41.0%
SVO	34.6%	35.6%	32.4%	35.0%
VSO	18.6%	10.8%	13.4%	9.0%
VOS	2.6%	1.8%	2.4%	2.0%
OVS	–	0.5%	–	1.0%
OSV	–	0.2%	–	1.0%
Unclassified	–	–	–	11.0%

Tomlin first establishes the frequencies of the six clausal word orders, as in Table 2.8.

Tomlin's results do not deviate much from previous studies on clausal word order, some of which are presented in Table 2.9 with their word order percentage figures for the sake of comparison.

Apart from non-representation of O-initial languages in Ultan (1969) and Hawkins (1983) (but see Pullum (1981) and Derbyshire and Pullum (1981) for attested O-initial languages such as Hixkaryana, Hianacoto-Umaua, Panare, Apuriña, Urubú, Nadëb, etc., all from the Amazon basin), there is a great deal of uniformity among these studies including Tomlin's. First, there is a skewed distribution in favour of S-initial languages. In fact, the preponderance of S-initial languages ranges from 76 per cent to 86.6 per cent. Second, O-initial languages are definitely a minority, if they are attested at all (nil–2 per cent). Third, all across these studies there seems to be a marked drop in frequency by an average of 9.8 per cent as one moves down from VSO to VOS (or from the S-before-O orders to the O-before-S orders, irrespective of the verb position). Thus, quite remarkably, the same frequency hierarchy in the form of (35) can be set up for all of these studies, insofar as the percentage numbers are taken into account (where '>' means 'more frequent than').

(35)   SOV > SVO > VSO > VOS > OVS > OSV

Unlike the previous researchers, however, Tomlin (1986: 22, 128–9) applies the chi-square statistic to determine whether there is any statistical significance between the frequencies of the six word orders. This leads him to recognize no statistical significance in the difference between SOV and SVO: it is attributed to chance. The difference between VOS and OVS, on the other hand, is significant at the 0.05 level but, since his sample only contains a very small number of these languages (i.e. twelve VOS languages and five OVS languages), and since there is uncertainty about the status of the reported OVS languages (cf. Polinskaja 1989), Tomlin dismisses the statistical significance in question. He thus offers a rather different frequency hierarchy of his own:

(36)   SOV = SVO > VSO > VOS = OVS > OSV

Then Tomlin (1986) puts forth three functional principles to account for the relative frequencies of the six basic word orders: the Theme First Principle (TFP), the Animated First Principle (AFP) and the Verb-Object Bonding Principle (VOB).

The TFP is based on the notion of thematic information. By thematic information Tomlin (1986: 37–41) means that 'information in an expression is thematic to the extent that the speaker assumes the hearer attends to the referent of the expression'. In other words, thematic information represents information on which the focus of attention is placed during discourse production and comprehension. The TFP is thus designed to capture the tendency that (Tomlin 1986: 48):

(37)   in clauses information that is relatively more thematic precedes information that is less so.

In support of the TFP Tomlin (1986: 41–70) provides not only psycho-linguistic (Tomlin and Kellogg 1986) and textual evidence (Tomlin 1983) but also cross-linguistic data ranging from constraints on movement rules – e.g. definite NPs (more thematic), and indefinite (less thematic) NPs shifted leftward, and rightward, respectively – to the position of independent pronominal (thematic) elements – e.g. the tendency for pronominal elements to take an earlier position in a sentence than nominal NPs (cf. Greenberg's Universal 25 (in (11)). Based on Keenan's (1976) work Tomlin (1986: 38, 71) assumes further that thematic information and subject correlate with each other in basic sentences.

The AFP, which is presented in (38), subsumes two basic hierarchies: animacy and semantic roles, in (39) (Tomlin 1986: 102–10); see 3.3.1 and 3.8 for detailed discussion of the animacy hierarchy).

(38)   in simple basic transitive clauses the NP which is more animated will precede NPs which are less animated.

(39)   a.   *Animacy Hierarchy*
             human > other animate > inanimate
             more animate ————→ less animate
        b.   *Semantic Roles Hierarchy*
             Agent > Instrumental > Benefactive/Dative > Patient

Thus one NP may be regarded as more 'animated' than another if the referent of the former is more animate than that of the latter in terms of the hierarchies in (39). Where in conflict, the semantic roles hierarchy takes precedence over the animacy hierarchy (Tomlin 1986: 106–7). The most animated NP in a basic transitive clause is identified with the subject of that clause (Tomlin 1986: 119). Tomlin's evidence in support of the AFP comes mainly from (i) resolution of potential ambiguity in favour of earlier NPs being interpreted as more animated than later NPs and (ii) cross-linguistic preference of more animated NPs preceding less animated NPs.

The VOB, in (40), is built on the observation that there is a stronger degree of syntactic and semantic cohesiveness between the object and the verb than between the subject and the verb (cf. Behaghel's First Law). Incidentally, the VOB is reminiscent of Lehmann's FPP, which ensures that the complex of the verb and the object be kept intact from other linguistic elements.

(40)   the object of a transitive verb is more tightly bonded to the verb than is its subject.

Tomlin (1986) adduces cross-linguistic evidence in support of the VOB: (i) noun incorporation (e.g. the object, not the subject, incorporated into the verb or incorporation of the subject implying incorporation of the object, not *vice versa*); (ii) prohibition of question particles, negatives, adverbials, modals, etc., occurring between the object and the verb; and (iii) higher frequency of idioms and compounds modelled on the verb and object than of those built on the verb and the subject (cf. Song (1994) for extension of the VOB to pronominal morphology).

Table 2.10:   *Realization of the Functional Principles for the six basic clausal word orders*

Word order	%	TFP	AFP	VOB	Score
SOV	44.78%	+	+	+	3
SVO	41.79%	+	+	+	3
VSO	9.20%	+	+	−	2
VOS	2.99%	−	−	+	1
OVS	1.24%	−	−	+	1
OSV	0.00%	−	−	−	0

SOV = SVO > VSO > VOS = OVS > OSV

Tomlin (1986: 122–9) argues that the more of the three principles are realized in a given word order, the more frequent among the languages of the world that word order will be. The patterns of realization of the principles can be presented as in Table 2.10. The *plus* sign represents realization of the principle in question, whereas the *minus* sign represents non-realization thereof.

As the reader can easily verify, there is a perfect correlation between the frequencies of the basic word orders and the number of the principles realized as is illustrated in the score column on the far right (i.e. value of one per each realization). Both SOV and SVO, which are the two most frequent word order types in the languages of the world, have a total score of 3, with all the three principles realized. For instance, in SOV and SVO, the TFP and the AFP are realized because S (more thematic and more animated) precedes O (less thematic and less animated) in both types; the VOB is also realized because V and O are immediately adjacent to each other. But OSV scores nil because O precedes S, thereby blocking realization of both the TFP and the AFP, and also because S intervenes between V and O, preventing the VOB from being realized. The relative frequencies of the six word orders are remarkably well matched by the extent to which the three functional principles are realized.

There are at least three critical comments that can be made about Tomlin's work. First, as discussed at length in 1.5.3, there is a great deal of risk involved in drawing inferences about linguistic preferences, or tendencies in basic word order from the actual frequency of the word order types. This is because one cannot expect to count languages and at the same time to be able to minimize what Dryer (1988: 206) calls 'the effect of various non-linguistic factors'. Tomlin's word order data in Table 2.8 are, therefore, susceptible to such a risk. Indeed by using his sampling technique based on the concepts of large *linguistic areas* and genera (see 1.5.3 for detailed discussion), Dryer (1989: 269–71) demonstrates that there is, contrary to Tomlin's

claim, a clear linguistic preference of SOV over SVO in the languages of the
world as presented in (41) (N.B.: Afr = Africa, Eura = Eurasia, A-NG =
Australia-New Guinea, NAm = North America, SAm = South America).

(41)

	Afr	Eura	A-NG	NAm	SAm	Total
SOV	[22]	[26]	[19]	[26]	[18]	111
SVO	21	19	6	6	5	57

In (41) SOV outnumbers SVO by five areas to nil, thereby confirming that
there is indeed a linguistic preference of SOV over SVO. Furthermore, in
each of the five areas the number of genera containing SOV languages is
greater than the number of genera containing SVO languages although the
difference in Africa is far from huge. Dryer (1989: 260, 270) also points out
that the lack of a statistical difference between the frequency of SOV and that
of SVO in Tomlin's investigation is caused mainly by over-representation of
the SVO languages from Niger-Congo and from Austronesian. Needless
to say, this preference of SOV over SVO plays havoc with Tomlin's claim
for the equal distribution of SOV and SVO (SOV = SVO in (36)) in the
languages of the world, and, consequently, his explanation thereof.

Tomlin (1986) seems to treat the three principles as equivalent since, for
instance, he calculates the total score for SOV and VSO at 3 and 2, respectively. As a matter of fact, he (1986: 122) states that:

> [t]he TFP is realized if it is the case that the S precedes the O. The TFP
> is not realized if the O precedes the S. The AFP is also realized if the S
> precedes the O. It is not realized if the O precedes the S.

This means that it does not matter whether V precedes or follows S. The
relative position of S with respect to V does not have any bearing on the
value assigned to the realization of the TFP or of the AFP. It is the relative
position of S in opposition to O that counts in Tomlin's calculation. Though
in this way one can account for the relative frequency of each and every
word order in comparison with one another, one cannot explain the substantial difference that exists in the frequencies of the S-initial word orders,
SOV and SVO, and of the rest (see Hawkins (1994: 337–8) for a similar
point). What is being suggested here is that the realization of both the TFP
and the AFP carries far more weight in SOV and SVO – that is, when S
precedes *both* V and O – than in VSO, in which S precedes *only* O. Otherwise one cannot explicitly explain the substantial difference between the two
S-initial word orders and the four non-S-initial word orders. In Table 2.8,
for instance, the total of the percentages of the two S-initial word orders is
almost 6.5 times larger than that of the four non-S-initial word orders, or a
huge difference of 73.14 per cent. Table 2.11 is the re-working of Table
2.10 along the lines suggested here (cf. Song (1991a)). Arbitrary as it may
be, the realization of either the TFP or the AFP will be given the value of 2
instead of 1 only when S is placed initially in the clause pattern (indicated by

Table 2.11: *Weighted realization of the Functional Principles for the six basic clausal word orders*

Word order	TFP	AFP	VOB	Score
SOV	++	++	+	5
SVO	++	++	+	5
VSO	+	+	–	2
VOS	–	–	+	1
OVS	–	–	+	1
OSV	–	–	–	0

the double *plus* sign). Otherwise the realization will only carry the usual value of 1 (indicated by the single *plus* sign).

The last point to be raised here is no less critical of Tomlin's work than the foregoing two points. The TFP and the AFP are inherently semantically and/or pragmatically based. The first thus pertains largely to 'the selective focus of attention on information during discourse production and comprehension' (Tomlin 1986: 40), whereas the second arises from animacy and semantic roles (Tomlin 1986: 103–9). These semantic/pragmatic principles are in turn reflected syntactically by more thematic and/or more animated NPs preceding less thematic and/or less animated NPs – S before O in Tomlin's work. In contrast, the VOB, as is formulated by Tomlin (1986: 74), is largely a grammatical one, representing the formal bondedness of V and O, in opposition to S. To put it differently, this particular principle may potentially be motivated by a (number of) independent semantic and/or pragmatic principle(s). In fact, Tomlin (1986: 135–6) refers to Keenan (1984), who explores the special relationship between the verb and the object from a much wider perspective. Keenan (1984) explores a number of such semantic–pragmatic principles that may underlie the VOB: e.g. existence dependency, sense dependency, specific selectional restrictions and the like. For instance, the referent of the object NP – also that of the intransitive subject NP for that matter but not that of the transitive subject NP – often comes into existence as a direct result of the activity expressed by the predicate (or verb); in *The woman built a shed in the garden*, the shed, unlike the woman, does not exist independently of the activity of building. Hence, the existence dependency relation between the verb and the object NP.[12] Thus the VOB itself may only be a syntactic reflection of multiple semantic–pragmatic principles. To wit, there is a conceptual disparity between the TFP and the AFP on the one hand, and the VOB on the other. For the sake of argument, suppose the VOB can ultimately be replaced by two such semantic–pragmatic principles, say, X and Y, just as the S-before-O order arises out of the TFP and also out of the AFP. In this interpretation, then,

Table 2.12: *Realization of the non-grammatically based Functional Principles*

Word order	TFP	AFP	X (>VOB)	Y (>VOB)	Score
SOV	+	+	+	+	4
SVO	+	+	+	+	4
VSO	+	+	–	–	2
VOS	–	–	+	+	2
OVS	–	–	+	+	2
OSV	–	–	–	–	0

the scoreboard of the six word orders will have to be changed. For the sake of simplicity, Tomlin's original scoring system is used below as the model – the weighted scoring system in Table 2.11 has no bearing on the point being raised here.

The four principles predict that there will be no (statistical) distributional difference between VSO, VOS and OVS in the languages of the world. A look at Tomlin's actual frequency data in Table 2.8 and at the others' in Table 2.9 clearly disconfirms this prediction. Therefore, if the VOB is replaced (ultimately) by more than one independent semantic–pragmatic principle, then Tomlin's functional explanation for the distribution of the six word orders will run into serious difficulty. One can turn this argument around by claiming that the TFP and the AFP are subsumed by a single grammatical principle, e.g. Keenan's (1979) *Subjects Front Principle*, just as the VOB is a single grammatical principle reflecting two independent semantic–pragmatic principles. There is no need to produce another similar table here but it will give rise to a similar problem. This, in fact, raises a more general problem with any attempt to account for the relative word order frequencies as a result of the possible interaction of a number of principles. It may not be possible to claim that the distribution of the six basic word orders can be explained in the manner in which it has been in Tomlin's work unless *all* motivating principles have already been identified. There may still be unknown principles other than the ones that Tomlin has identified – which, once discovered, are likely to modify Tomlin's scoreboard in Table 2.10 yet again.

2.4   Back to the OV–VO typology: the Branching Direction Theory

Dryer (1992) is perhaps the most comprehensive empirical study of basic word order correlations that has ever appeared (cf. Hawkins (1994: 258)).

Its comprehensiveness does not only lie in the range of word order correlations examined but also in the use of a very large language sample. In this work the correlation between the order of twenty-four pairs of elements, and the order of verb and object is tested on the basis of a database of 625 languages, with most of his data derived from a 543-language subset of that database (Dryer 1992: 83) – incidentally, Dryer's (1992) language sample is the largest one utilized in linguistic typology. In conjunction with his ongoing research on word order typology Dryer has over the years been developing a sophisticated sampling technique that may successfully alleviate, if not overcome, major problems with which previous language sampling approaches are beset. This is the technique being employed in the work in question. As discussed in 1.5.3, he determines the distribution of a given property in the six – five in Dryer (1989) – large *linguistic areas* by counting genera, not individual languages with a view to sifting linguistic preferences from the effect of genetic relatedness and areal diffusion.[13] Dryer's work is, in this respect alone, an outstanding example of how the validity and reliability of linguistic typology can be enhanced by a sound sampling technique (but cf. 1.5.3).

Dryer's work on basic word order is best characterized as a return to the OV–VO typology, which was promoted in the earlier work of W.P. Lehmann (1973, 1978b, 1978c), and Vennemann (1974a) but which was subsequently abandoned by Hawkins (1983) in favour of adpositions as the best predictor of word order properties. Dryer (1992: 82–7) thus takes the order of verb and object to be the basic predictor of various other word order properties – evidence in support of the OV–VO typology has already been presented in 2.2.2, based on his earlier work (1991). He has two primary aims: (i) to identify the pairs of elements whose order correlates with that of verb and object; (ii) to explain why such correlations exist. In the process he also demonstrates the inadequacy of *the Head-Dependent Theory* (or HDT), which captures the very – if not the most – popular view that there is a linguistic preference for dependents to be placed consistently on one side of heads, that is, either before or after heads. W.P. Lehmann (1973, 1978b, 1978c), Vennemann (1974a) and Hawkins (1983), as has already been shown, appeal to principles similar to the HDT, differences in detail notwithstanding. For instance, Hawkins (1983) invokes the PCCH in order to predict the frequency of word order co-occurrences in the languages of the world: in general languages that are consistently head-initial or head-final will have the highest frequency of occurrence.

Dryer (1992) argues, however, that, although the HDT adequately accounts for six pairs of elements including the order of noun and genitive, and that of verb and manner adverb, there are certain pairs of elements which do not at all correlate with the order of verb and object contrary to what the HDT predicts, and that for some other pairs of elements what the HDT predicts is the opposite of what is actually found in the data. He also points out that different (theoretical) approaches often disagree on which element is to be taken as the head or the dependent. In what follows an example of each of these three problematic cases will be provided. In common with Dryer (1992: 82) it is assumed here that if in a given pair of elements X and Y, X tends to precede Y (statistically) significantly more frequently in VO languages than in OV languages, then <X, Y> is a correlation pair, with X being a verb patterner and Y an object patterner with respect to that correlation pair.

First, Dryer (1988) demonstrates convincingly that the order of noun and adjective does not correlate with that of verb and object – contrary to the widely held view (e.g. W.P. Lehmann 1973, 1978b, 1978c and Vennemann 1974a): OV and VO languages tend to be AN and NA, respectively (also see 1.5.3). This non-correlation is confirmed again by Dryer (1992: 95) on the basis of a much larger sample. In fact, the average proportion of genera for the AN order is higher among VO languages than OV languages (0.47 vs. 0.39)! This completely contradicts what the HDT predicts about the order of adjective and noun, and that of verb and object.

Under the HDT – and indeed under the standard view, too – articles are taken to be a type of modifier (i.e. dependent) of the noun, which is in turn assumed to be a head. The order of noun and article is thus predicted to correlate with that of verb and object. But this is not the case as clearly is illustrated in Table 2.13.

Although the correlation is not so strong as others, e.g. the order of verb and adposition (see Table 2.5), Table 2.13 shows that, whereas it is more common among OV languages in only two areas (Eurasia and South America), the ArtN order is far more common among VO languages in as many as five areas – incidentally, this suggests that the NArt order may be an areal feature of Africa. This predominance of the ArtN order among VO languages is further substantiated by the higher average proportion of genera figure of NArt among OV languages than among VO languages in all six areas

Table 2.13: *Distribution of NArt/ArtN in OV and VO languages*

	Afr	Eura	SEAsia&Oc	A-NG	NAm	SAm	Total
OV&NArt	[5]	2	[2]	[4]	4	2	19
OV&ArtN	1	[3]	0	2	4	[3]	13
Proportion NArt	0.83	0.40	1.00	0.67	0.50	0.40	Avg. = 0.63
VO&NArt	[9]	0	3	0	3	0	15
VO&ArtN	2	[6]	[7]	[1]	[17]	[4]	37
Proportion NArt	0.82	0.00	0.30	0.00	0.15	0.00	Avg. = 0.21

(Dryer 1992: 104)

Table 2.14: *Distribution of VAux/AuxV in OV and VO languages*

	Afr	Eura	SEAsia&Oc	A-NG	NAm	SAm	Total
OV&VAux	[5]	[12]	[2]	[8]	[1]	[8]	36
OV&AuxV	3	0	0	0	0	0	3
VO&VAux	1	1	0	[1]	0	1	4
VO&AuxV	[15]	[5]	[3]	0	[4]	1	28

(Dryer 1992: 100)

although this is trivial in Africa. In the correlation pair of noun and article, therefore, the Art is a verb patterner, whereas the N that it combines with is an object patterner (also see Dryer (1989)). This is the converse of what is predicted by the HDT.[14]

The correlation pair of auxiliary verb and content (or main) verb illustrates that the HDT may make correct or incorrect predictions depending on which element of the pair is taken to be a head or a dependent. In traditional, and early generative grammar (e.g. Chomsky (1970: 52), Lightfoot (1982: 60–1)) the content verb is the head with the auxiliary verb being the dependent. In the alternative view (Vennemann (1973: 43), Pullum and Wilson (1977), Schachter (1983), Gazdar *et al.* (1982)), on the other hand, the auxiliary verb is the head, with the content verb being the dependent. The actual data provided by Dryer (1992: 100) indicate unquestionably that the auxiliary is a verb patterner (or head), and the content verb an object patterner (or dependent). This correlation is strong enough to make it unnecessary to provide the (average) figures of proportions of genera.

Note that it is only under the assumption that the auxiliary verb is the head that the HDT will make the correct prediction about the correlation pair in question although that assumption is – needless to say – highly theory-internal.

Dryer (1992: 105) concludes, therefore, that there is enough evidence to reject the HDT as an explanation of the word order correlations. What can then be an alternative explanation? He first observes that, although they are both adjunct dependents of the noun, relative clauses are object patterners, and adjectives are not. He suggests that the contrast between these two – also between intensifiers and standards of comparison (both dependents of the adjective), between negative particles and adpositional phrases (both dependents of the verb), etc. – is attributable to the fact that relative clauses (standards of comparison and adpositional phrases) are phrasal, whereas adjectives (intensifiers and negative particles) are non-phrasal. This leads him (1992: 108–18) to put forth what he calls *the Branching Direction Theory*

(BDT), which is based on the consistent ordering of branching (or phrasal) and non-branching (or non-phrasal) categories.

(42) *Branching Direction Theory (BDT)*
      Verb patterners are non-phrasal (non-branching, lexical) categories
      and object patterners are phrasal (branching) categories. That is,
      a pair of elements X and Y will employ the order XY significantly
      more often among VO languages than among OV languages if
      and only if X is a nonphrasal category and Y is a phrasal category.

What the BDT predicts is this: languages tend towards right-branching in which phrasal categories follow non-phrasal categories, or towards left-branching in which phrasal categories precede non-phrasal categories. Thus the fundamental distinction between VO and OV languages is their opposite branching direction: right branching and left branching, respectively. As a brief illustration of how this works, compare English, a VO language, and Korean, an OV language. Note that for the sake of convenience a triangle is used to represent a constituent structure involving branching or phrasal categories. For example, the NP, *the girl*, in (43a) 'branches' into two constituents, the article *the*, and the noun (or, more accurately, N', as will presently be shown) *girl*.

(43) English

a.

```
              VP
           /      \
          V         NP
          |        /△\
        kissed   the  girl
```

b.

```
           NP
          /    \
         N        G
         |       /△\
      friends   of  Mary
```

c.

```
           NP
          /    \
         N        Rel
         |       /    \
       girls   who are singing in the room
```

(44)   Korean

a.

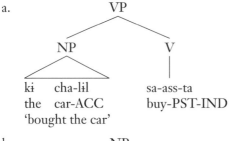

```
ki    cha-lil      sa-ass-ta
the   car-ACC      buy-PST-IND
'bought the car'
```

b.

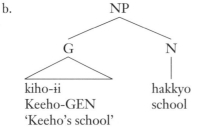

```
kiho-ii           hakkyo
Keeho-GEN         school
'Keeho's school'
```

c.

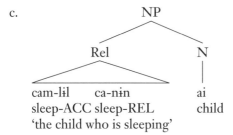

```
cam-lil    ca-nin         ai
sleep-ACC sleep-REL       child
'the child who is sleeping'
```

In English all the phrasal categories, the NP, the G and the Rel (represented by triangles) follow the non-phrasal categories, the V, the N and the N (represented by straight vertical lines) in (43a), (43b) and (43c), respectively. In Korean, on the other hand, the ordering of the phrasal and non-phrasal categories is the converse, with the phrasal categories preceding the non-phrasal categories in (44).

Returning to the correlation pairs problematic for the HDT, the pair of article and noun, and that of auxiliary verb and content verb can now be accounted for by the BDT. In VO languages there is a preference of ArtN, whereas in OV languages there is a tendency towards NArt (see Table 2.13); articles are verb patterners, and nouns with which they combine object patterners. To put it in terms of the BDT, the ArtN order is predominant in VO languages because in these languages non-phrasal categories (e.g. V, Art, etc.) precede phrasal categories (e.g. O, N, etc.), whereas in OV languages the N precedes the Art because the preferred branching direction of these languages is phrasal categories before non-phrasal categories. A similar comment can also be made with respect to the correlation pair of auxiliary and content verb. Being 'a [non-phrasal] verb that is subcategorized to take a VP complement [that is, phrasal]' (Dryer 1992: 115), the auxiliary verb is predicted to precede the content verb (or VP) in VO languages, and the opposite ordering of these two is predicted for OV languages. These predictions are indeed borne out by the data in Table 2.14.

The reason why the order of adjective, and noun is not a correlation pair with respect to the order of verb and object is, according to Dryer (1992: 110–12), that both adjectives and nouns that they combine with are non-phrasal categories. For pairs like this the BDT makes no predictions (cf. (42)). But the non-phrasal status of adjectives (or As) may strike one as questionable especially because adjectives can be modified by intensifiers or degree words such as *very, extremely*, etc., thereby clearly forming adjective phrases (i.e. phrasal and branching). Moreover, if nouns that adjectives combine with are non-phrasal (e.g. *very tall girls*), why is it that nouns are regarded as phrasal when they combine with articles (e.g. *the girls*)? Dryer explains that, although they may be phrasal, modifying adjectives are not fully recursive in that they rarely involve other major phrasal categories such as NPs, PPs or **S**s. [Note that in the text **S** for sentence appears in bold face in opposition to plain S, which represents subject.] The use of intensifiers is also very limited or restricted, with only a handful of them taking part in the forming of adjective phrases such as *very tall*. In other words, recursiveness must also be taken into account in distinguishing verb patterners from object patterners or *vice versa*: verb patterners are either non-phrasal categories or phrasal categories that are not fully recursive (e.g. adjectives), whereas object patterners are fully recursive phrasal categories (see (50)). Moreover, articles do not simply combine with nouns to form NPs, but rather they join together with constituents larger than nouns, or N′ (or N-bar) potentially consisting of adjectives and nouns. Put in a different way, articles form NPs with the fully recursive phrasal or branching category of N′ (cf. *tall girls, tall girls [with long hair]* (with PPs), *tall girls [who are talking at the table]* (with **S**s)). The BDT thus assumes the constituent structure of NPs in (45), not that in (46).[15]

(45)

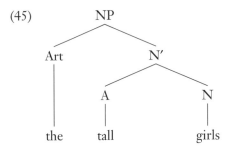

(46)

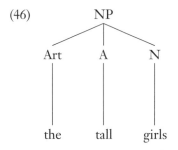

As can clearly be seen in (45), the Art, which is a non-phrasal category, combines with the fully recursive phrasal or branching category N', whereas the A, which is not a fully recursive phrasal category, only combines with the non-phrasal or non-branching category N (or *girls*). This explains why articles, and nouns form a correlation pair, whereas adjectives and nouns do not.

The foregoing discussion also throws some interesting light on the different orderings of adjectives and adjective phrase modifiers in languages such as English. In English, adjectives can combine with other major phrasal categories to form adjective phrases (or APs), as in *a country rich in natural resources*.[16] While the single adjective precedes the noun in *a rich country*, the adjective phrase follows the noun in *a country rich in natural resources*. Within the BDT this difference in ordering is claimed to be due to the fact that the sequence of *rich in natural resources* is phrasal since the adjective, *rich*, does contain a major phrasal category or PP, *in natural resources*. In right-branching languages such as English, phrasal categories follow non-phrasal categories. The AP, *rich in natural resources*, thus comes after the non-phrasal N, *country*. This is exactly what is predicted by the BDT. Indeed Whaley (1997: 93) claims that one of the 'advantages [of Dryer's BDT] over the proposals of Vennemann and Hawkins' is this ability to differentiate between adjectives and adjective phrases in terms of positioning. But this is not entirely accurate insofar as Hawkins (1983) is concerned. First, the BDT has nothing to say about why the adjective should appear before the noun in *a rich country* because in this NP the adjective is not a fully recursive phrasal category, and the noun is a non-phrasal category as has been discussed in relation to (45). Conversely, the BDT cannot explain why in English the opposite order of the adjective and noun – *a country rich*, which should be logically possible within the BDT – does not occur at least equally frequently. As the reader recalls from 2.2.3, Hawkins (1983) does propose the HSP, which embodies the rightward preference of heavy constituents, and the leftward preference of light ones. Since the AP *rich in natural resources* is a very much heavier constituent than the A *rich*, the HSP predicts correctly that the AP and the A – relative to each other – will occur to the right and the left, respectively (Hawkins 1983: 91, 111–12). Thus Whaley's appraisal of the BDT should only apply in relation to Vennemann's work.

The assumption of the constituent structure in (45) and not that in (46) raises a more general question about the role of constituent structure within the BDT as Dryer (1992: 109–10) himself acknowledges. Recall that auxiliary verbs are taken to be subcategorized for VP complements. This, in fact, calls for an additional assumption that they are also heads of the higher VP node as in (47).

(47)

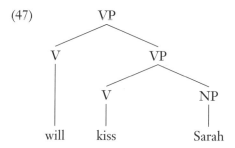

In (47) the auxiliary verb *will* is the head of the higher VP, with the lower VP functioning as its complement (or, broadly speaking, a dependent). This VP structure does not seem different at all from the VP structure posited for the sequence of the non-verbal tense/aspect (T/A) particle and content verb in (48); in fact, they are almost identical in terms of constituent structure.

(48)

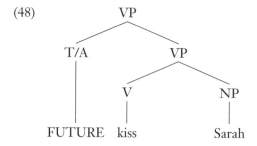

But in (48), as opposed to (47), the future tense particle is only a modifier of the lower VP, that is to say the lower VP itself is the head of the higher VP. This distinction between the auxiliary verb and the non-verbal tense/aspect particle in terms of head and dependent is crucial for the BDT to make correct predictions because, unlike the auxiliary verb, the tense/aspect particle is not a verb patterner, thereby failing to form a correlation pair with the verb.

Dryer (1992: 112–15) also invokes the distinction between major and minor constituents for the purposes of the BDT. If a constituent is immediately dominated by a node of the same category, then that constituent is a 'minor' constituent. Those which are not minor constituents are 'major'

constituents by default. Major, not minor, constituents are considered by the
BDT. This may mean that the lower VPs in both (47) and (48) are minor
constituents for the purposes of the BDT. But actually only the lower VP in
(48) should be regarded as a minor constituent, the reason being that 'minor
constituents are defined not only as constituents immediately dominated
by a node of the same category but also as the HEADS of the higher node
[emphasis original]' (Dryer 1992: 115). Elimination of the minor constituent, or the lower VP node from (48) gives rise to (49), whereas no such
elimination takes place for (47) because in (47) the auxiliary verb, not the
lower VP, is the head of the higher VP.

(49)

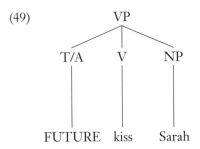

Dryer (1992: 114) thus offers a revised version of the BDT, which ex-
cludes such minor constituents from consideration.

(50)   *Branching Direction Theory* (revised)
       Verb patterners are nonphrasal categories or phrasal categories that
       are not fully recursive, and object patterners are fully recursive
       phrasal categories in the major constituent tree. That is, a pair of
       elements X and Y will employ the order XY significantly more often
       among VO languages than among OV languages if and only if X is
       not a fully recursive phrasal category in the major constituent tree
       and Y is a fully recursive phrasal category in the major constituent
       tree.

But what ultimately distinguishes (47) from (48) for the purposes of the
BDT is not really the distinction between major and minor constituents
but the distinction between head and dependent. Without knowing which
element is the head in (47) and (48), it will never be possible to decide when
minor constituents are to be retained for or eliminated from consideration.
For this reason, Dryer (1992: 116) also provides an alternate version of the
BDT, wherein direct reference is made to the distinction between heads
and (fully) recursive dependents in lieu of that between major and minor
constituents.

(51) *Branching Direction Theory* (alternate version)
Verb patterners are heads and object patterners are fully recursive phrasal dependents – i.e. a pair of elements X and Y will employ the order XY significantly more often among VO languages than among OV languages if and only if X is a head and Y is a phrasal dependent of X.

This alternate version of the BDT now makes predictions only about the ordering of heads and fully recursive dependents. In (47) the auxiliary verb is a head and the lower VP a fully recursive phrasal dependent. Thus the BDT correctly predicts the AuxV order in VO languages and the VAux order in OV languages. In (48), on the other hand, both the head (*kiss*) and the dependent (*FUTURE*) are non-phrasal. The BDT does not make any predictions because they do not form a correlation pair.

Dryer (1992: 116) does not take a stand on which of the two versions of the BDT, (50) or (51), is correct although he (1992: 116) says that, while the revised version does not depend on the distinction between head and dependent, 'the alternate version . . . has the advantage of being more elegant [or simpler]' because it makes no reference to the distinction between major and minor constituents.[17] Perhaps what will decide between the two versions of the BDT may depend on which of the two theoretical assumptions, head vs. dependent or major vs. minor constituents, is required more frequently in explication of other parts of (universal) grammar. At any rate, the point still remains that in order to ensure that the lower VP in (48) as a minor constituent be 'invisible' to the BDT, it is still necessary to determine first which element is the head of the higher VP in (48). This means at least that, although it is put forward as an alternative to the HDT, the BDT cannot completely obviate the distinction between head and dependent.

Dryer (1992: 128–32) thinks that the BDT may be underlain by the nature of human parsers. In other words, languages tend towards one of the two ideals, right-branching languages or left-branching languages, because consistent direction of branching may not cause processing difficulty associated with the combination of right- and left-branching structure (see Kuno 1974, Frazier 1979, 1985; Mallinson and Blake 1981: 300–11, 387; Hawkins 1990, 1994; and also 2.5). For instance, he demonstrates on the basis of Kuno (1974) that in a prepositional language, prepositional phrase (or PP) modifiers will be postnominal, not prenominal, because prenominal PPs will cause a great deal of processing difficulty. That is, PP modifiers will be placed after, not before, modified NPs. This can be illustrated by means of the following two possible constituent structures of a phrase meaning *the size of the tv on the table in the lounge*; (52a) for postnominal PPs and (52b) for prenominal PPs (for the sake of simplicity, the articles have been removed from the tree diagrams below).

(52)   a.

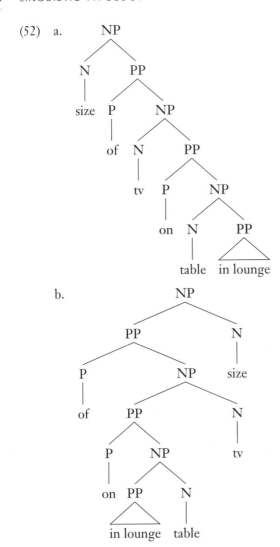

b.

The structure in (52a) is consistently right-branching, whereas that in (52b) is characterized by the alternating of left-branching and right-branching. Dryer (1992: 129) likens the difficulty in processing structures with mixed right- and left-branching as in (52b) to that associated with centre-embedding as in (53).

(53)   The cheese [that the rat [that the cat chased] ate] was rotten.

Consistent direction of branching also seems to have implications for short-term memory (cf. Hawkins 1983: 98–122, and 2.2.3). By comparison with (52a) (52b) will require much burden on short-term memory since, for instance, the preposition *of* has to be put on hold in short-term memory until the material intervening between it and the NP *the tv* that it combines with has all been processed. The same is true of the preposition *on*, and *the table*. The issue of burden on short-term memory will be revisited in Chapter 4, especially with respect to the position of the restricting clause as opposed to the head noun in the relative clause construction.

Finally, Dryer (1992) raises a few issues which may also have wider ramifications for word order typology and also for linguistic typology in general. First, he (1992: 118–22) notes that numerals and demonstratives – both are regarded as dependents of nouns in traditional grammar – do not behave the way that the HDT predicts. If anything, numerals behave more like verb patterners; but Dryer (1992: 119) is ambivalent on the pair of numeral and noun to the extent that he leaves it unclassified. As Dryer (1992: 96–7) discovers, demonstratives do not form a correlation pair with nouns at all although they are normally lumped together with articles into the category 'determiner'. Thus Dryer suggests that (i) languages may vary as to whether or not the numeral is a head; and (ii) that in many languages – probably a majority of the languages of the world – the category of determiners which includes both articles and demonstratives may not exist. It follows from (i) that the standard practice in (word order) typology to identify grammatical categories largely on a semantic basis (cf. 1.5.1) may prevent one from studying (language-)specific grammatical properties that otherwise help bring certain patterns or regularities to light. Clearly, languages which treat the numeral as the head must be distinguished from those which do not. In view of this the point in (ii) also bears a similar comment. Dryer (1992: 122) makes a sobering point that 'it is difficult to distinguish these two [different types of language] on the basis of superficial data [alone]'. This can be taken to suggest that (word order) typology may sometimes need to go beyond 'the simpler question about what the order is of the demonstrative and noun' into in-depth investigation of specific grammatical properties of these elements, which cannot be gleaned from most descriptive grammars.

Second, as Greenberg (1963b) suggests (cf. his Universal 27 in 2.2.1), there is a distinct possibility of affix position correlating with other word order properties, e.g. adpositions. Dryer (1992: 125–8), however, acknowledges that, if there is such a correlation, his BDT is unable to account for it simply because neither stems nor affixes are (fully recursive) phrasal categories – the HDT, on the other hand, may be able to explain such a correlation, provided that affixes are heads (cf. Hawkins and Cutler 1988: 289–90; cf. 2.6). But, when he examines the distribution of tense/aspect affixes and of possessive affixes, he discovers that tense/aspect affixes at least tentatively correlate with verbs, whereas there is no such correlation for possessive affixes – in fact, three of the six areas favour possessive prefixes and the other three possessive suffixes. This leads Dryer (1992: 127) to suggest that in studying the correlation between affix position and other word order properties different types of affix first be distinguished (also see Croft (1995: 104–5)). But why this difference between the two types of affix? Dryer is of the opinion that it may have a diachronic explanation (for a similar view see Bybee (1988) and Bybee, Pagliuca and Perkins (1990)). That is, the different behaviour of these affixes may be due to the sources which they are derived historically from, e.g., Givón (1971a, 1975, 1984); but cf. Comrie (1980). Tense/aspect affixes are known to derive diachronically from auxiliary verbs, and possessive affixes from possessive pronouns. Dryer points out that this explains at least why tense/aspect affixes are verb patterners although such a diachronic explanation is unavailable for possessive affixes because they do not form a correlation pair with verbs. This immediately raises the question as to whether other word correlations may also be explained in a similar way. Croft (1995: 103–4) thinks so although he believes that not all word order correlations may be susceptible to such a diachronic explanation: '[t]he introduction of variables based on the grammatical strategy used to express a word order relation will probably lead to significant advances in word order explanations' (see Bybee (1988) for a most forceful argument in support of this view). For instance, Mandarin Chinese has circumpositions for the expressing of spatial relations, which are really prepositions derived from a VO serial verb construction and postpositions derived from GN genitive constructions. More generally, adpositions are known to arise historically out of genitive phrases – for example, PPs in English such as *inside the house* and *outside the house* from *inside of the house*, and *outside of the house*, respectively, following disappearance of the preposition *of* (cf. Greenberg 1963b: 99; Vennemann 1973: 32; Mallinson and Blake 1981: 387–90, Bybee 1988: 353–4; but cf. Dryer 1992: 128).

Dryer (1992: 122–4) also points out that being object patterners manner adverbs form a correlation pair with verbs. But, as he himself notes, this creates a problem for the BDT because manner adverbs are a non-phrasal or non-branching category. He suggests that perhaps the correlation between manner adverbs and verbs is indirect, with adpositional phrases being an intermediary (cf. Prior 1985). In other words, adpositional phrases correlate with manner adverbs and adpositional phrases in turn with verbs. By transitivity manner adverbs form a correlation pair with verbs. This prompts Croft (1995: 102–3) to point to the possibility that this kind of indirect correlation may also be extended to all other word order correlations that Dryer has discovered. To put it differently, Croft is putting forward an argument in favour of multiple or local explanations for word order correlations. He refers to Justeson and Stephens (1990), who carry out a log-linear analysis on a number of word order correlations based on a 147-language sample derived from Hawkins (1983), thereby arriving at a best-fit model that calls for two-way interactions, rather than n-way interactions. Note that n-way interactions will be required of, for instance, the OV–VO typology. Thus Croft interprets Justeson and Stephens's conclusion to suggest that there may not be a need for global explanations such as the BDT but that word order correlations may 'require explanations in terms of local interactions between pairs of variables'. This is an intriguing suggestion as is perhaps reflected no less clearly in Greenberg's (1963b) original atomistic universal statements than anywhere else. But it is not clear whether it will really turn out to be an attractive – even if worthwhile – option for typological research because in theory building, all other things being equal, a global explanation that accounts for multiple phenomena should be preferred to a multiplicity of basic explanations that deal with the same set of phenomena. Indeed experience shows that it has never been an attractive option for the theoretically minded (e.g. W.P. Lehmann 1973, 1978b, 1978c, Vennemann 1974a, and Hawkins 1983, 1994).

2.5   Seeking a global explanation: the Early Immediate Constituents Theory

As the reader recalls from 2.2.3, Hawkins (1983) proposes three basic principles – HSP, MP and MHIP – in order to account for various word order correlations. He also appeals to Keenan's (1979) *Subjects Front Principle* (SFP) to explain the paucity of verb-initial languages in the world. Among these principles, at least the HSP is taken to be motivated by processing ease: heavy modifiers occur to the right and light ones to the left so that the head can be recognized quickly and efficiently. Early head recognition is in turn claimed to facilitate early recognition at the clausal level. Moreover, early head recognition is claimed to have implications for short-term (or working) memory because, if the head is recognized late, modifiers will have to be put on hold in short-term memory. Hawkins (1983) also puts forward the PCCH in order to explain the distributional universals that he deduces from Greenberg's original database and his own expanded sample.

In his recent work (1994) Hawkins again pursues a processing explanation of word order correlations – in fact, of word order in general – and distributional universals but to the extent that they can all be accounted for by a remarkably simple principle of processing, or what he refers to as *the Principle of Early Immediate Constituents* (PEIC). To put it differently, word order correlations – and word order in general – are claimed to reflect the way languages respond to the demands of rapid and efficient processing in real time. As has been noted at the end of 2.4, all other things being equal, a single global explanation that accounts for multiple phenomena should be preferred to a multiplicity of explanations that deal with the same set of phenomena. In this respect the PEIC is claimed to be superior to a set of different principles such as the HSP, the MP, the MHIP and the SFP.

The PEIC is built upon the basic assumption that words or constituents occur in the orders that they do so that their internal syntactic structures or immediate constituents (ICs) can be recognized (and produced) in language performance as rapidly and efficiently as possible (Hawkins 1994: 57). This means that different permutations of constituents may give rise to different levels of structural complexity, which in turn have a bearing on the rapidity with which recognition of ICs is carried out in real time. Basic word order is then looked upon as conventionalization, or grammaticalization of the most optimal order in performance, that is the order that maximizes efficiency and speed in processing.

There are a few additional assumptions that the PEIC makes in the explaining of basic word order and word order correlations. These assumptions including the PEIC itself can easily be explicated by examining a set of English sentences which contain a verb particle *up*.

(54)   a.   Jessica rang up the boy.
     b.   Jessica rang the boy up.
     c.   Jessica rang the boy in the class up.
     d.   Jessica rang the boy whom she met in the class up.

Leaving the (invariable) subject NP aside, the Verb Phrase (VP) in (54) is a constituent which is in turn made up of three separate ICs, i.e. V, the (object) NP and the verb particle. It is well-known that the further the particle is moved from the verb, the less acceptable the sentence becomes and the less frequent in occurrence it is (e.g. Hunter and Prideaux 1983). Hawkins explains this by claiming that the different sentences in (54) present different degrees of structural complexity. For instance, (54d) is more difficult to process than (54a) because the former has a higher degree of structural complexity than the latter. To demonstrate this he (1994: 58–60) invokes the concept of *the Constituent Recognition Domain* (CRD). This is in effect intended to narrow down on the minimum number of terminal and non-terminal nodes that must be taken into account for purposes of constructing the syntactic structure of a given constituent. Thus the CRD is defined as:

(55)   *Constituent Recognition Domain (CRD)*
     The CRD for a phrasal mother node M consists of the set of terminal and non-terminal nodes that must be parsed in order to recognize M and all ICs of M, proceeding from the terminal node in the parse string that constructs the first IC on the left, to the terminal node that constructs the last IC on the right, and including all intervening terminal nodes and the non-terminal nodes that they construct.

In this context Hawkins's (1994: 62) notion of mother-node-constructing categories (MNCCs) is also crucial. MNCCs are those categories that uniquely determine the mother node of a constituent. For instance, the V is the MNCC of the VP; once the V *rang* in (54) is parsed, it immediately identifies the VP as the mother node of the V. The MNCC of the NP, on the other hand, is either the Det or the N, with either of these two included in the CRD of the NP. For example, the (object) NP in (54) can be uniquely determined by the Det alone since processing is carried out from left to right – in N-initial (or N-Det) languages the N will function as the MNCC of the NP. This concept of MNCCs is very important for Hawkins's processing theory of word order because the PEIC assumes that '[a] mother node must be constructed when a syntactic category is recognized that uniquely determines the higher node [so that o]ther ICs will be attached as rapidly as possible to this higher node, thereby making parsing decisions about sisterhood and groupings proceed as fast and efficiently as possible' (Hawkins 1994: 62). Thus not all terminal and non-terminal nodes in a constituent need to be parsed in order to arrive at the overall syntactic structure of that constituent. Once all ICs are recognized the constructing of the overall syntactic structure comes to completion, as it were, regardless of how many words there may be left in the last IC yet to be processed.

With these background assumptions in mind consider (54a) and (54c) again. These sentences have the following constituent (or tree) structures in (56a) and (56b), respectively.

(56) a.

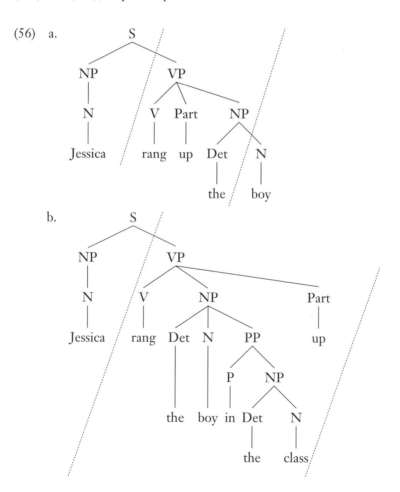

The two broken lines drawn at a slant are meant to enclose the VP CRD in each of (56a) and (56b). In (56a) the VP CRD covers from the first IC, or the V – which constructs the mother node of the VP – to the MNCC of the last IC of the NP, or the Det, whereas in (56b) the CRD stretches from the first IC, or the V all the way to *up*, dominated by the last IC, or the Part. In order to measure syntactic complexity Hawkins (1994: 76) proposes a very simple metric based on the IC-to-non-IC ratio, which is derived by dividing the number of ICs in a CRD by the total number of non-ICs in that CRD (cf. Miller and Chomsky 1963, Frazier 1985). This ratio is converted into a percentage. The ratio for a whole sentence is then calculated by averaging out the percentages of all CRDs contained in that sentence. In (56) the subject NP can be left out of consideration for the sake of convenience since it is invariable throughout. As a shorthand for the IC-to-non-IC ratio, the number of ICs in a CRD is often divided by the total number of words in that CRD. This is referred to as an IC-to-word ratio.[18] The higher the IC-to non-IC (or -word) ratio for a CRD is, the more rapid and efficient the processing of a mother node and its ICs is claimed to be. Said differently, processing efficiency is optimized if and when all ICs are recognized on the basis of a minimum number of non-ICs (or words). In (56a) there are three ICs for the VP CRD, namely, the V, the NP and the Part, and four non-ICs in that CRD, namely, *rang*, *up*, the Det and *the*. This gives rise to 3/4 or 75 per cent. In (56b) the ratio is down to 3/14 or 21.4 per cent – fourteen non-ICs for the same three ICs. The substantial difference in these EIC ratios is then taken to be responsible for the relative difference between (54a) and (54c) in terms of processing ease or efficiency. The IC-to-word ratios for (56a) and (56b) depict the same situation: 3/3 or 100 per cent for (56a), and 3/7 or 42.9 per cent for (56b). Note that it is not the absolute percentage but the relative ranking of IC-to-non-IC (or -word) ratios that counts for the PEIC.

The processing efficiency of (54c) can, however, be improved dramatically if the particle *up* is shifted immediately to the right of the verb or to the left of the object NP, as in (57):

(57)   Jessica rang up the boy in the class.

The reason for this positive change in processing efficiency is due mainly to the fact that the movement of the particle reduces the size of the VP CRD to a considerable extent. This is again illustrated in terms of a tree structure in (58).

(58)

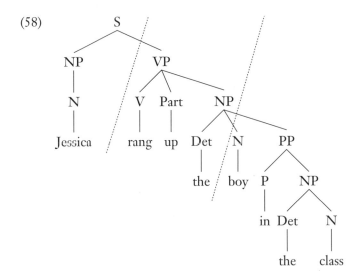

As can be seen in (58), the CRD starts off from the V and ends on *the*, thereby resulting in an improved IC-to-non-IC ratio of 3/4 or 75 per cent, or an IC-to-word ratio of 3/3 or 100 per cent. These ratios are, in fact, identical to those for (56a), which has the most optimal ratio.

The sentence in (54b) has a slightly worse IC-to-non-IC (or -word) ratio than (54a) because the position of the object NP *the boy* increases the size of the VP CRD: an IC-to-non-IC ratio of 3/6 or 50 per cent, or an IC-to-word ratio of 3/4 or 75 per cent. The IC-to-non-IC (or -word) ratio for (54d) is the worst because the intervening object NP contains an embedded relative clause, thereby contributing even further to the distance between the first IC and the last IC of the VP.

From this kind of observation Hawkins (1994: 77) draws the following conclusion:

(59)   *Principle of Early Immediate Constituents (PEIC)*
        The human parser prefers linear orders that maximize the IC-to-non-IC ratios of constituent recognition domains (CRDs).

It also follows that basic word order reflects the most optimal EIC ratio in a conventionalized manner (Hawkins 1994: 95–102, chapter 5). Those linear orders that give rise to more rapid and more efficient structural recognition in processing are (more likely to be) grammaticalized as basic word orders across languages. Moreover, word order property X may co-occur with word order property Y, not Z, because of the processing or performance motivation for optimizing EIC ratios across these word order properties. The PEIC is thus claimed to underlie not only basic word order (e.g. Tomlin 1986) but also various word order correlations (e.g. Dryer 1992).

Table 2.15:   *The verb position, the adpositional phrase position and the adposition types*

Order		Dryer in Hawkins (1994)	Hawkins (1983)
<1>	[V [P NP]]	161 (41.4%)	136 (40.5%)
<2>	[[NP P] V]	204 (52.4%)	162 (48.2%)
<3>	[V [NP P]]	18 (4.6%)	26 (7.7%)
<4>	[[P NP] V]	6 (1.5%)	12 (3.6%)
Totals		389	336

(Adapted from Hawkins 1994: 257)

As the reader recalls from 2.2.2, Dryer (1991: 452) provides ample evidence in support of the correlation between OV and postpositions, and of that between VO and prepositions (see Table 2.5). Dryer (1992: 92–3) amplifies these correlations by observing that the position of the adpositional phrase (AdpP) coincides with that of O: the adpositional phrase before V in OV languages (i.e. 63/72 of his genera), and after V in VO languages (i.e. 59/60 of his genera). In fact, he (1992: 92) reports that the pair of V and AdpP is the strongest correlation of any pair considered in his work. These two separate observations lead to the inference that OV may co-occur with preverbal NPo, and VO with postverbal PrN. This, however, cannot be tested directly on the basis of Dryer's (1992) data, which do not specify individual language quantities for the two adposition orders. Nonetheless the correlation between the position of V, the position of the AdpP and the distribution of adpositions is at least confirmed by the data from Hawkins's (1983) expanded sample and also by the additional information provided by Dryer to Hawkins (1994) as in Table 2.15.

Hawkins (1994: 96–7, 255–9) explains this three-way correlation by arguing that in OV languages the preverbal postpositional phrase (PoP) gives rise to the most optimal EIC ratio for the VP, whereas in VO languages the postverbal prepositional phrase (PrP) does so. To understand this reconsider in terms of EIC the four orderings of verb and adpositional phrase in Table 2.15, slightly differently formulated in (60); (60a) involves a postverbal prepositional phrase, (60b) a preverbal postpositional phrase, (60c) a postverbal postpositional phrase and (60d) a preverbal prepositional phrase.

(60) a. $_{VP}[V\ _{PrP}[Pr\ NP]]$
      b. $VP[_{PoP}[NP\ Po]\ V]$
      c. $_{VP}[V\ _{PoP}[NP\ Po]]$
      d. $_{VP}[_{PrP}[Pr\ NP]\ V]$

Suppose one word is assigned to the V and the P each, which is not an unreasonable assumption. For the sake of simplicity one word is also

Table 2.16: *Distribution of GN/NG in OV and VO languages*

	Afr	Eura	SEAsia&Oc	A-NG	NAm	SAm	Total
OV&GN	[17]	[21]	[5]	[16]	[30]	[23]	112
OV&NG	6	3	1	2	0	0	12
Proportion GN	0.74	0.88	0.83	0.89	1.00	1.00	Avg. = 0.89
VO&GN	5	4	4	[6]	6	[5]	30
VO&NG	[22]	[5]	[12]	0	[21]	3	63
Proportion GN	0.19	0.44	0.25	1.00	0.22	0.63	Avg. = 0.45

(Dryer 1992: 91)

assigned to the NP; this single word is immediately dominated by a non-terminal node N. The size of the NP does not have any direct bearing on the point to be made here. The IC-to-word ratios for (60a) and (60b) are then the most optimal, that is 2/2 or 100 per cent. In (60a) and (60b) the ICs are the V and the AdpP (i.e. PrP or PoP), and these two are recognized on the basis of two adjacent words dominated by the V and the Pr or the Po – the Pr or the Po is the MNCC for the AdpP. In (60c) the MNCC of the AdpP can be parsed only after the associated NP has been parsed, and in (60d) the NP will also delay processing of the V. Thus the size of the VP CRD is increased, whereby processing efficiency is reduced. For both (60c) and (60d) the IC-to-word ratio is 2/3 or 66.7 per cent, well below the optimal ratio for the other two orderings. Note that any increase of the NP in weight or length will further deteriorate the already non-optimal EIC ratio of (60c) and (60d). The observation that Dryer has made about the pair of verb and adpositional phrase can thus be explained by the PEIC.

Moreover, the PEIC can also make a finer discrimination between (60c) and (60d) although both carry the same EIC ratio of 66.7 per cent. This is achieved by counting the ICs in a CRD from left to right, and then counting the non-ICs – or, again, words as a convenient shorthand – in that CRD (Hawkins 1994: 82–3). This is known as a left-to-right EIC ratio and is used in order to distinguish two equally EIC optimal orderings based on IC-to-non-IC (or -word) ratios. This is meant to give a higher EIC ratio to an ordering in which shorter elements occur to the left and longer ones to the right because in this way (more) ICs will be recognized sooner than later. This supplementary metric of complexity shows that (60c) is more optimal than (60d) because in the former the shorter IC or the V occurs to the left of the longer IC or the PoP, whereas in the latter the ordering is the converse, longer before shorter. Indeed this additional prediction is confirmed by both Hawkins's (1983) data and Dryer's (1992) as can be seen in Table 2.15, i.e. 7.7 per cent (or 4.6 per cent) vs 3.6 per cent (or 1.5 per cent).

Another correlation pair reported in Dryer (1992: 91) is between OV/VO and GN/NG. The relevant data are provided in Table 2.16.

Although GN order is more common among VO languages in Australia-New Guinea than NG order, the differences in proportions in the other five *linguistic areas* are considerably larger and, moreover, the difference in the average of proportions is also reasonably large by 2 to 1 (0.89 vs. 0.45). This leads Dryer (1992: 91) to conclude that noun and genitive form a correlation pair. Hawkins (1994: 259–62) reformulates OV/VO and GN/NG into four possible orderings as in (61). Note that G is interpreted below to be PossP (or possessive phrase) because it can potentially contain a fully nominal possessor phrase (e.g. *the student's career* vs. *her career*).

(61)   a. $_{VP}[V _{NP}[N \; PossP]]$
       b. $_{VP}[_{NP}[PossP \; N] \; V]$
       c. $VP[V \; NP[PossP \; N]]$
       d. $VP[NP[N \; PossP] \; V]$

The structures in (61a) and (61b) are represented by 63/217 (29 per cent) and 112/217 (51.6 per cent) of Dryer's (1992) genera, respectively. The other two structures in (61c) and (61d) are represented by far fewer genera, 30/217 (13.8 per cent) and 12/217 (5.5 per cent), respectively. Hawkins explains this distribution in the following way. Within the N-PossP or PossP-N structure the N is the MNCC, which can uniquely determine the mother node NP. (Note that it is assumed for the sake of simplicity that each category dominates a single word.) Then the ordering in (61a) has an IC-to-word ratio of 2/2 or 100 per cent because the two ICs of the VP, i.e. the V and the NP, are recognized on the basis of two words, the one dominated by the V and the other by the N. The same ratio is applicable to (61b). The orderings in (61c) and (61d), on the other hand, have a much lower IC-to-word ratio of 2/3 or 66.7 per cent. Between (61c) and (61d) the former is slightly better than the latter by the left-to-right IC-to word metric because in the former, not the latter, the shorter element V and the longer element NP appear to the left and the right, respectively, much the same way as the V and the AdpP do in (60c), and (60d). The most optimal orderings in (61a) and (61b) together account for 80.6 per cent of Dryer's genera, whereas the non-optimal orderings in (61c) and (61d) are represented by the remaining genera. Moreover, within these two non-optimal orderings (61c) is more frequent than (61d) by 2.5 to 1 as is correctly predicted by the PEIC.

Hawkins (1994: 328–39) claims that the PEIC can also account for the distribution of basic word order at the clausal level. Recall that Tomlin (1986) provides the following frequency hierarchy of the six clausal word orders:

(62)   SOV = SVO > VSO > VOS = OVS > OSV

As has been discussed in 2.3, there are at least two main points about (62) that must be explained: the relative frequencies of occurrence itself and the

Table 2.17:   *Distribution of the six basic clausal word orders in Tomlin (1986)*

Word order	Number	%
SOV	180	44.78
SVO	168	41.79
VSO	37	9.20
VOS	12	2.99
OVS	5	1.24
OSV	0	0.00
Total	402	100.00

(Adapted from Tomlin 1986: 22)

sheer preponderance of S-initial (SOV and SVO) languages in opposition to non-S-initial languages. These are clearly indicated in Tomlin's (1986) data reproduced in Table 2.17.

Hawkins explains the dominance of S-initial languages by claiming that [NP VP] is preferred to [VP NP] – where NP represents S – because of the former's higher EIC ratio. The VP may contain at least the (direct object) NP and possibly also the indirect and/or oblique NPs, adverbial phrases, etc. In head-initial languages (e.g. **SVO**, as in (63a)) ICs are recognized at the left periphery; for instance, the VP is recognized by the V, which appears at the left periphery of the VP, whereas the NP is recognized by the Det, which also occupies a left-peripheral position. In head-final languages (e.g. **SOV**, as in (63b)), on the other hand, ICs are recognized by right-peripheral constructing categories; for example, S is recognized by right-peripheral nominative case marking, whereas the VP is constructed by accusative case marking, which also occurs at the right periphery of the NP (or O).

(63)   a.   English
$_S$[$_{NP}$[The girl] $_{VP}$[$_V$[saw] $_{NP}$[the cat]]]
       b.   Japanese
$_S$[$_{NP}$[Taroo ga] $_{VP}$[$_{NP}$[inu o] $_V$[mita]]]
             Taroo NOM   dog ACC   saw
             'Taroo saw the dog.'

Thus the EIC ratio is the most optimal if the subject NP precedes the VP. If not, the EIC ratio will go down. It will take more time and effort to recognize and construct the whole structure of [VP NP]. The aggregate EIC ratio of (63a) or SVO is 83.4 per cent (66.7 per cent for the **S** CRD and 100 per cent for the VP CRD), and that of (63b) or SOV is also 83.4 per

Table 2.18:   *EIC and the six basic clausal word orders*

	With a VP	Without a VP
SVO	[84%]	75%
VSO	[75%]	[75%]
VOS	[70%]	60%
SOV	[84%]	75%
OVS	[70%]	60%
OSV	45%	[60%]

EIC ranking (Best scores in square brackets):

  84%   > 75% > 70%   > 60%

SVO = SOV > VSO > VOS = OVS > OSV

(Adapted from Hawkins 1994: 338)

cent (66.7 per cent for the **S** CRD and 100 per cent for the VP CRD) – the case markers are treated as separate words (Hawkins 1994: 144). If the VP precedes the subject NP in (63a) (that is, **VOS**), the EIC ratio will by one calculation drop to 75 per cent (50 per cent for the **S** CRD and 100 per cent for the VP CRD), and in (63b) the preposing of the VP (or **OVS**) will also result in the same EIC ratio of 75 per cent (50 per cent for the **S** CRD and 100 per cent for the VP CRD). In the case of the other two non-S-initial orders, OSV and VSO, there is the additional question of whether or not they have a VP mainly because of non-adjacency of the V and O. But, as will be shown below, they are also claimed to have a lower EIC ratio, VP or no VP. Thus this EIC differential is taken to be responsible for the preference of S-initial languages over non-S-initial ones.

In order to explain the relative frequencies of occurrence of the six word orders in Table 2.17, Hawkins (1994) makes two assumptions. First, in VO languages MNCCs are left-peripheral and in OV languages they are right-peripheral as has already been demonstrated for (63). Second, on the basis of the text analysis of a few languages he argues that in OV languages S is heavier or longer than O, whereas in VO languages O is heavier or longer than S. In his EIC predictions Hawkins thus assigns one more word to S than to O in OV languages, but to O than to S in VO languages. This gives rise to the following IC-to-word ratios for the six basic word orders with or without a VP. In Table 2.18 three words are assigned to S and two to O in OV languages, whereas two words are assigned to S and three to O in VO languages; one word is given to V in both OV and VO.

With the highest possible scores taken into account the EIC ratios of the six orders fit in perfectly with Tomlin's relative frequencies of occurrence.

SVO and SOV rank the highest (i.e. 84 per cent) on the EIC scoreboard; they are indeed the most frequent orders in Tomlin's data. VOS and OVS score the same EIC ratio of 70 per cent as is also reflected in Tomlin's frequency hierarchy. With an EIC ratio of 75 per cent VSO is intermediate between the grouping of SVO and SOV, and that of VOS and OVS in both Tomlin's and Hawkins's ranking. The least frequent word order of OSV achieves the lowest EIC ratio of 60 per cent.[19]

In explaining the relative frequencies of occurrence in (62) Hawkins (1994: 337) argues that his EIC theory is superior to Tomlin's functional principles – TFP, AFP and VOB – because the latter three principles can all be replaced by the PEIC. Attractive as this may sound, there are some potential problems with some of Hawkins's assumptions that merit discussion.

First, Hawkins does not question Tomlin's (1986) claim that there is no statistical difference between the frequency of SOV and that of SVO. Their EIC ratios are indistinguishable from each other. But there is Dryer's (1989) strong evidence in support of the preference of SOV over SVO. Thus this is as much a problem for Hawkins's EIC explanation as for Tomlin's functional explanation (see 2.3).

Second, Hawkins claims that ICs in VO languages are constructed on the left. For instance, NPs are constructed by the left-peripheral Det. Presumably both articles (Art) and demonstratives (Dem) are subsumed under the category of the Det in Hawkins's theory. Not many languages have the category of Art, however. In fact, only 84 out of Dryer's (1992) 252 genera exhibit the presence of the Art. By contrast the Dem is attested in as many as 207 genera. Therefore, the Dem, not the Art, is more likely to be an MNCC of NPs in a majority of the languages of the world. But, as has been discussed in 2.4, the Dem and the N do not form a correlation pair (Dryer 1992: 108). There is, in fact, a general linguistic preference for DemN order irrespective of the verb position. In other words, the Dem tends to appear at the left periphery of NPs regardless of whether VO or OV. There is thus a strong likelihood that the Dem may function as the MNCC of NPs in OV languages as well. If the Dem is also taken to be an MNCC of NPs in OV languages by virtue of its appearance on the left of NPs, OVS, for instance, poses an interesting problem for the PEIC. Hawkins (1994: 338) gives it an EIC ratio of 70 per cent with a VP, or 60 per cent without a VP, the second worst on the EIC ranking in Table 2.18. Suppose that a typical OVS sentence will be something like (64):

(64)   s[vp[np[that cat] v[saw]] np[this big girl]]
         'This big girl saw that cat.'

With the Dem taken as an MNCC of NPs, the EIC ratio for the **S** CRD will now increase to 2/2 or 100 per cent because the two ICs, the VP and the S NP, are recognized and constructed on the basis of two adjacent words, *saw* and *this*.[20] The EIC ratio of the VP CRD will be 2/3 or 66.7 per cent because the two ICs, the O NP and the V, are constructed on the basis of *that*, *cat* and *saw*. This will result in an aggregate EIC ratio of 83.4 per cent (or roughly 84 per cent), the same as that of SVO! There is no reason why ICs in OVS, a head-final language, should not be recognized on the left instead of the right with a view to optimizing EIC efficiency when the universally preferred position of the Dem is left-peripheral. This point also raises the question of whether or not ICs should always be recognized and constructed consistently on the left or on the right as is assumed in Hawkins's EIC theory.

Third, the different weight distribution of S and O claimed to exist between OV and VO languages is open to question. Hawkins's evidence for this difference all comes from the text analysis of a few languages such as English, German, Hungarian, Japanese, Korean and Polish. Apart from the fact that this is in much need of confirmation based on data from a considerably wider range of languages, Japanese, Korean and Polish are all known to drop S or O very frequently especially in natural discourse. In other words, S or O tends to be covert in these languages when its referent is known, previously mentioned or predictable. But in Hawkins (1994) such covert S and O are precluded from the calculation of the overall weight distribution of S and O. The question thus arises as to why this should be the case especially when the relative weight difference between S and O ultimately determines the EIC ratios of the six basic word orders in Table 2.18 – presumably covert S and O will be assigned zero weight. In fact, this question points to a more general problem with Hawkins (1994). His many claims including the different weight distribution of S and O are based mainly on written corpora. But, as Berg (1996: 1253) points out, one cannot rule out the strong possibility that written texts are the product of careful editing. They may not realistically reflect processing or parsing decisions that are constantly made on-line in spontaneous speech. Hawkins's performance theory of word order is, therefore, somewhat at odds with the data on which it is built and tested.

Despite these potential problems, both specific and general, Hawkins's EIC theory makes a number of interesting predictions which have not been achieved by previous theories of word order. The EIC theory will thus play an important role in future development of word order typology much the same way that Dryer (1992) has formed the solid empirical basis for word-order research. In the rest of the present section some of these predictions arising from Hawkins (1994) will be critically discussed.

As has already been pointed out, Hawkins's theory is claimed to be superior to previous studies on word order (e.g. Hawkins 1983, Tomlin 1986) because it is based on a single principle, not on a multiplicity of principles. In his earlier work (1983), for instance, Hawkins invokes the MP in order to account for the co-occurrences in (29) renumbered as (65), all of which are counterexamples to predictions of the HSP.

(65)   a.   Po & NA & GN
         b.   Po & NDem & GN
         c.   Po & NNum & GN
         d.   Po & NA & RelN

Recall that the HSP predicts basically that heavy modifiers occur to the right
and light ones to the left. In the four co-occurrences in (65), however, this is
not the case. For instance, in (65d) the A is placed to the right, whereas the
Rel is to the left. This is in complete violation of the HSP. These 'deviations' are taken care of by the MP, which stipulates that the A, being more
mobile than the Rel, is able to move around its head more easily. In consistent postpositional languages, in which modifiers are serialized to the left of
the head, mobile modifiers have no choice but move to the right of the head.
In (65d) thus the mobile A occurs to the right, whereas the immobile Rel
remains in a position to the left of the head where modifiers in consistent
postpositional languages are placed. The same comment can be made *mutatis
mutandis* of the other three co-occurrences in (65).

The co-occurrences in (66), on the other hand, are all unattested at least
in Hawkins's database, and yet they are all predicted or positively sanctioned
by the HSP.

(66)   a.   *Po & AN & NG
         b.   *Po & DemN & NG
         c.   *Po & NumN & NG

The Dem, Num and A occur to the left, and the G to the right, the former
being lighter than the latter. In consistent postpositional languages heads are
serialized to the right and modifiers to the left. In (66) the position of the G
is postnominal, not prenominal, whereas modifiers lighter than the G, namely,
Dem, Num and A, are all prenominal in line with the adpositional order. In
other words, the position of the G alone deviates from the leftward position
of modifiers in ideal postpositional languages. This, however, is rejected by
the MP, whereby mobile modifiers (i.e. Dem, Num and A) are permitted to
move around the head easily but immobile ones (i.e. G and Rel) are not.
Incidentally, the co-occurrence of Po & AN & NRel (cf. (65d)) is predicted
by the HSP, but militates against the MP but it does anyway occur productively because the HSP overrides the MP only when the heavier noun modifier
is the Rel. This interaction between the HSP and the MP is captured by *the
Mobility and Heaviness Interaction Principle* (MHIP) in Hawkins (1983) (see
note 9 for further discussion). Hawkins (1983), therefore, makes use of two
– or three principles if the MHIP is also included – to account for the
various attested or unattested word order co-occurrences in (65) and (66).

In Hawkins (1994), on the other hand, (65) and (66) are all claimed to
be explained in terms of the PEIC alone. First, assume Dem, Num, A and

Table 2.19:   *EIC and attested Po & NP word order properties*

	Structure	IC-to-word ratio (PoP)
a.	Po & NA & GN	
	$_{PoP}[_{NP}[$N A$]$ Po$]$	2/3 (66.7%)
	$_{PoP}[_{NP}[$G N$]$ Po$]$	2/2 (100%)
b.	Po & NDem & GN	
	$_{PoP}[_{NP}[$N Dem$]$ Po$]$	2/2 (100%)
	$_{PoP}[_{NP}[$G N$]$ Po$]$	2/2 (100%)
c.	Po & NNum & GN	
	$_{PoP}[_{NP}[$N Num$]$ Po$]$	2/3 (66.7%)
	$_{PoP}[_{NP}[$G N$]$ Po$]$	2/2 (100%)
d.	Po & NA & RelN	
	$_{PoP}[_{NP}[$N A$]$ Po$]$	2/3 (66.7%)
	$_{PoP}[_{NP}[$Rel N$]$ Po$]$	2/2 (100%)

N = one word, G = two words and Rel = four words, with G consisting of the demonstrative or article and the possessor. With this assumption in place the IC-to-word ratios for the attested co-occurrences in (65) can be computed as in Table 2.19. There are two ICs to be constructed, namely NP and Po, for the constructing of the PoP. These ICs are recognized by two or three adjacent words, thereby achieving an EIC ratio of 100 per cent, or 66.7 per cent. (Note that the Dem is taken here to be the MNCC of the NP, hence the maximum EIC ratio for $_{PoP}[_{NP}[$N Dem$]$ Po$]$.)

These good EIC ratios are possible in the attested co-occurrences in (65) because only single-word constituents are permitted to occur in between the N and the Po, and because constituents larger than a single word, i.e. the G and the Rel, are placed strictly to the left of the N so that the two words that must be minimally processed to construct the PoP, i.e. those words dominated by the N and the Po, can be immediately adjacent to each other. The point is that the best possible EIC ratio is obtained by the way that these constituents are linearized relative to one another.

Now, compare the EIC ratios of the attested co-occurrences in (65) with the unattested ones in (66), whose EIC ratios are presented in Table 2.20. The same number of words is assumed for each of the Dem, the Num, the A, the N and the G – one word for the first four, and two for the last.

Where Table 2.20 is conspicuously different from Table 2.19 is the fact that the unattested co-occurrences have the G, a two-word constituent, in

Table 2.20: *EIC and unattested Po & NP word order properties*

	Structure	IC-to-word ratio (PoP)
a.	*Po & DemN & NG	
	$_{PoP}[_{NP}[\text{Dem N}] \text{ Po}]$	2/2 (100%)
	$_{PoP}[_{NP}[\text{N G}] \text{ Po}]$	2/4 (50%)
b.	*Po & NumN & NG	
	$_{PoP}[_{NP}[\text{Num N}] \text{ Po}]$	2/2 (100%)
	$_{PoP}[_{NP}[\text{N G}] \text{ Po}]$	2/4 (50%)
c.	*Po & AN & NG	
	$_{PoP}[_{NP}[\text{A N}] \text{ Po}]$	2/2 (100%)
	$_{PoP}[_{NP}[\text{N G}] \text{ Po}]$	2/4 (50%)

between the N and the Po, whereas the single-word constituents, i.e. the Dem, the Num and the A, are all placed outside the sequence of the N and the Po. In terms of EIC this means that the intermediate position of the G inevitably increases the size of the PoP CRD because the two words that make up the G must both be counted in EIC calculation – as opposed to none if the G appeared to the left of the N. This positioning of the G thus makes no EIC sense because the G is placed between the two words that must be minimally processed to construct the PoP when even the single-word constituents are all placed to the left of the sequence of the N and the Po. Note that, even if these single-word constituents were placed in between the N and Po, the resulting EIC ratio would be comparable to the similar permutations in the attested co-occurrences in Table 2.19, i.e. 66.7 per cent. Thus there is far less – if any at all – processing motivation for positioning the G between the N and the Po. To sum up, the EIC theory explains both the attested co-occurrences of (65) and the unattested co-occurrences of (66) in terms of a single principle of processing, thereby obviating the need for the multiplicity of principles such as the HSP, the MP and the MHIP.

One apparent problem with Hawkins's (1983) HSP that should also be mentioned at this juncture is that in languages like Japanese the sentential object NP, despite its heaviness, is preposed, not postposed, for performance reasons (cf. Dryer 1980). This is illustrated in (67) (Hawkins 1994: 80–1).

(67) Japanese
    a. $_{s1}[_{NP}[\text{Hanako-ga}] \, _{VP}[_{S'}[_{s2}[\text{kinoo Taroo-ga kekkonsi-ta }] \text{ to}] \text{ it-ta}]]$
    b. $_{s1}[_{S'}[_{s2}[\text{Kinoo Taroo-ga kekkonsi-ta}] \text{ to}] \, _{NP}[\text{Hanako-ga}] \, _{VP}[\text{it-ta}]]$
       'Hanako said that Taro got married yesterday.'

The HSP claims that heavy elements are placed to the right, and light ones to the left. But performance evidence in Japanese displays the opposite tendency in favour of (67b) over (67a). The preposing of the sentential object NP in Japanese thus flies right in the face of the HSP. The EIC theory, however, is not beset with this problem because generally in OV languages such as Japanese as opposed to VO languages – e.g. so-called Heavy NP shift to the right in English – the preposing of heavy constituents like the sentential object NP can be shown to increase EIC efficiency. By one calculation (which assumes the presence of the VP in Japanese), (67a) has an aggregate EIC ratio of 66.7 per cent, whereas (67b) has an aggregate EIC ratio of 83.4 per cent. Since the preposing of the sentential object NP increases EIC efficiency, (67b) is expected to be more frequent in Japanese performance data, and it is indeed. Thus 'ICs are preposed to the left with a frequency that matches the EIC preferences' (Hawkins 1994: 67, 137–54). This example illustrates clearly that it is not simply the weight of a given element that determines whether it will be positioned to the right or to the left but the amount of processing efficiency and rapidity that it contributes to the overall processing of sentences. This is captured in the PEIC, but not in the HSP.

In fact, this preposing of heavy ICs to the left in OV languages as opposed to the right in VO languages reflects the different ways in which OV and VO languages respond to the fundamental fact that 'language is produced and comprehended in an item-by-item manner from left to right, i.e. in a temporal sequence' (Hawkins 1994: 321). This disparity can be observed most clearly in what Hawkins (1994) calls 'left-right asymmetries', not least in the area of basic word order. For instance, Dryer (1992: 101–2) observes that, while both initial and final complementizers (Comp) are found in OV languages, final Comp is unattested in VO languages. In other words, (68c) is non-occurring, whereas (68a), (68b) and (68d) are all attested.

(68) a. $[V_{S'}[\text{Comp } \textbf{S}]]$
      b. $[_{S'}[\textbf{S} \text{ Comp}] V]$
      c. $*[V_{S'}[\textbf{S} \text{ Comp}]]$
      d. $[_{S'}[\text{Comp } \textbf{S}] V]$

The left-right asymmetry in question is thus: why is it that Comp-initial **S** is used in both VO and OV languages, while Comp-final **S** is found only in OV languages? The structure in (68a) is the ideal one for head-initial languages in terms of EIC because the two ICs, V and **S′**, are recognized by two adjacent words. By the same token, the structure in (68b) is the most optimal for head-final languages. Why is (68d) then permitted in head-final languages at all, whereas its mirror image in (68c) is unattested in head-initial languages? This is, according to Hawkins (1994: 323–8), because immediate recognition of subordinate-versus-main-clause status is also crucial to efficient processing (cf. Antinucci, Duranti and Gebert 1979). For instance, Comp *that* cannot be deleted from the sentential subject in English because it will be interpreted as a main clause, not as a subordinate clause:

(69) a. That Jacqui was popular amazed her parents.
     b. *Jacqui was popular amazed her parents.

Clearly, the initial positioning of the Comp contributes a great deal to immediate recognition of subordinate-versus-main-clause status in (69a). For head-final languages, however, this option is not available because the Comp is placed after or to the right of the subordinate clause or **S** as in (68b). The subordinate clause in head-final languages may not immediately be under-stood as what it actually is. In fact, there is a great risk of misinterpreting it as the main clause. There is thus a different kind of processing motivation for avoiding this problem of misinterpretation in head-final languages in spite of the fact that the preferred structure in (68b) has a perfect EIC ratio of 100 per cent. Some languages may choose to do nothing about it in favour of the perfect EIC ratio but there may be other languages which deal with the problem by switching the order of **S** and the Comp within **S′**, as in (68d), so that the onset of the subordinate clause can be immediately and clearly flagged. Head-initial languages, on the other hand, do not have any inherent problems with immediate recognition of subordinate-versus-main-clause status owing to the initial positioning of the Comp within **S′** as in (68a). This explains the non-occurrence of (68c), or the leftward skewing evident in the distribution of the Comp in OV and VO languages (see 2.6 for an instance of rightward skewing).

   What most clearly distinguishes Hawkins's (1994) EIC theory from previous studies of word order is that it is (far more) capable of – or at least seriously concerned with – accounting for the sequencing of multiple cat-egories (but cf. Greenberg 1963b: 87). By contrast, W.P. Lehmann (1973, 1978b, 1978c), Vennemann (1974a), Hawkins (1983) (but cf. 1983: 116–25), and, to a less extent, Dryer (1988, 1992) are all limited to the sequencing of only two categories at a time, usually one modifier and one non-modifier (i.e. head) (e.g. GN/NG, NA/AN, NRel/RelN, NPo/PrN, etc.). In Hawkins (1983: 75), for instance, (70) is identified as one of the seven attested co-occurrences of five nominal modifiers in prepositional languages (cf. (25)).

(70) NDem & NNum & NA & NG & NRel

But it says very little as to how all these modifiers will actually be ordered relative to the head N within the same NP. Similarly, in Dryer (1992) the orders of the Art and the N, of the A and the N, of the N and the Rel, etc. are examined separately from, or independently of, one another in relation to the order of V and O. Thus the relative ordering of multiple modifiers generally falls outside the purview of the word order studies with the exception of Hawkins (1994), who, on the other hand, makes a break with this tradition of word order typology by proposing a theory that provides a much wider perspective on word order typology.

It must be noted, however, that a number of inferences can be drawn from Dryer (1992) as to how multiple categories will be linearized within the same syntactic domain. For instance, given the observation that the order of the N and the G correlates to a statistical significance with the order of V and O, one can make a second-order prediction that in VO languages it will be $_{VP}[[V \ _{NP}[N \ G]]$, whereas in OV languages it will be $_{VP}[_{NP}[G \ N] \ V]$ (note G = PossP in (61)). Indeed, as has been shown, Dryer (1992: 116; see note 17) entertains in passing the possibility of using the BDT to account for the sequencing of multiple categories. The BDT thus predicts that N-A-Rel (and Rel-A-N) will occur whereas N-Rel-A (and A-Rel-N) will not. These predictions are indeed confirmed by available data (e.g. C. Lehmann 1984): in N-A-Rel the ordering of the categories is consistently non-phrasal before phrasal categories (the N before the Rel, and also the A before the Rel), whereas in N-Rel-A there is inconsistency or incongruity between the ordering of the N and the Rel (non-phrasal categories before phrasal categories) on the one hand, and that of the Rel and the A (phrasal categories before non-phrasal categories) on the other. Note that this is exactly what PEIC also predicts about the sequences in question. In the attested N-A-Rel the three ICs are recognized and constructed by three words (only one word, i.e. the Comp for the Rel because Rel = [Comp **S**]). In the unattested N-Rel-A the CRD must include not only the N and the A, but also the intervening Rel as a whole (i.e. [Comp **S**]), thereby delaying the IC recognition to a considerable extent. In a way it does not come as a surprise that the BDT is as good as the EIC theory at making such predictions because the concept of syntactic weight is normally implicit in the concepts of phrasal vs. non-phrasal categories. Phrasal categories are likely to be longer or heavier than non-phrasal ones, which by definition dominate single words.

There are, however, at least two ways in which the EIC theory seems to be in a better position than the BDT. First, the BDT makes somewhat limited predictions about the ordering of categories which are all either phrasal or non-phrasal. The ordering of multiple phrasal categories within the same syntactic domain is a case in point. Given V (non-phrasal), NP (phrasal) and AdpP (phrasal), the BDT predicts the relative position of either the NP or the AdpP relative to the V but that is as far as it can go. It cannot make further predictions about the ordering of the NP and the AdpP because they are both phrasal categories. The EIC theory, on the other hand, makes predictions about not only the ordering of V on the one hand and the NP or the AdpP on the other, but also the relative ordering of the NP and the AdpP. Thus in VO languages the EIC optimal order will be [V

Table 2.21:   *Complex NP word order properties, EIC, BDT inconsistencies and frequencies of occurrence*

	Structure	Left-to-Right EIC Ratio (aggregates)	Number of BDT inconsistencies	Attested languages
<1>	[N A $_{S'}$[Comp **S**]]	100%	–	Extensive
<2>	[A N $_{S'}$[Comp **S**]]	100%	–	Extensive
<3>	[$_{S'}$[**S** Comp] N A]	100%	–	Extensive
<4>	[$_{S'}$[**S** Comp] A N]	100%	–	Extensive
<5>	[N A $_{S'}$[**S** Comp]]	83%	2	Attested
<6>	[A N $_{S'}$[**S** Comp]]	83%	2	Attested
<7>	[N $_{S'}$[Comp **S**] A]	63%	1	None
<8>	[A $_{S'}$[Comp **S**] N]	63%	1	None
<9>	[N $_{S'}$[**S** Comp] A]	63%	1	None
<10>	[A $_{S'}$[**S** Comp] N]	63%	1	Only as marked variant
<11>	[$_{S'}$[Comp **S**] N A]	38%	2	None
<12>	[$_{S'}$[Comp **S**] A N]	38%	2	None

(Adapted from Hawkins 1994: 272)

NP PrP], whereas in OV languages it will be [PoP NP V] (i.e. AdpP = PoP in OV, and AdpP = PreP in VO). IC recognition is far less optimal in, for instance, [V PrP NP] or [NP PoP V] because the intervening heavy PrP or PoP will delay IC recognition. These predictions seem to be generally borne out by available data from English, Japanese, Korean and Turkish (Hawkins 1994: 274–81) although, needless to say, this needs to be tested on the basis of 'more grammatically fine-tuned typological data' (Hawkins 1994: 280).

Second, unlike the BDT the EIC theory is better equipped to handle what Hawkins refers to as distributional universals in his earlier work (1983), i.e. relative frequencies of occurrence among different ordering possibilities. This can be illustrated by the sequencing of the A, the Rel and the N, which has already been mentioned in passing (cf. note 17). There are twelve logically possible orders of these three categories as enumerated in Table 2.21 along with their left-to-right IC-to-word EIC ratios and very rough relative frequencies of occurrence (Hawkins 1994: 271–3). Assume N = one word, A = one word, Comp = one word, **S** = three words and **S′** = four words.

The BDT makes the general prediction about the twelve logically possible orderings in Table 2.21: all those orderings which exhibit a consistent direction of branching (that is, consistently non-phrasal before phrasal, or *vice versa*) will occur at least very frequently, whereas those which do not will be unattested or at least very infrequent. In Dryer (1992) the BDT is not originally designed to predict quantitative differences among possible orderings but it can be reworked to make such quantitative predictions so that it can be compared with the EIC theory. Thus inconsistencies in terms of direction of branching are counted for each of the twelve orderings as has been done in the third column in Table 2.21. Note that the internal ordering of the **S′** is taken here to be the basic one with which the other orderings are compared. The orderings in <1>, <2>, <3> and <4> are all consistent. The remaining possibilities, however, are inconsistent in one or two ways. The orderings in <5> and <6> are inconsistent in two respects. The ordering of the **S** and the Comp is phrasal before non-phrasal but this is at odds with the ordering of the **S′** and the N, and also with the ordering of the **S′** and the A. A similar situation occurs with respect to <11> and <12>: one inconsistency each between the ordering of the Comp and the **S** on the one hand, and that of the **S′** and the N, or that of the **S′** and the A on the other. As for <7>, <8>, <9> and <10>, there is only one inconsistency between the internal ordering of the **S′** and the ordering of the **S′** and either the A or the N. Alternatively, the ordering of the whole **S′**, and either the N or the A can instead be taken to be basic but it will have no bearing on the general point being made here except that those with two inconsistencies will have only one inconsistency, whereas those with one inconsistency will end up with one or two inconsistencies – depending on which of two, the N or the A, forms the basic template with the **S′**. (The N and the A are both non-phrasal; the BDT has nothing to say about their relative ordering (see 2.4).) The frequencies of occurrence in the last column in Table 2.21 indicate that the BDT does not make good quantitative predictions about the ordering possibilities, particularly the last eight. For instance, the orderings in <5> and <6> each have two inconsistencies as opposed to the ones in <7> to <10>, which have only one inconsistency each. But the latter group is non-occurring with the marginal exception of <10>, whereas the former group is attested. The BDT also fails to make a correct distinction between the orderings in <5> and <6>, and the ones in <11> and <12>. Both groups are characterized by two inconsistencies but there is a marked distributional difference between them. The EIC theory, on the other hand, can make correct predictions about the relative frequencies of the twelve orderings as can be seen from comparison of the second and last columns in Table 2.21. With the possible exception of <10>, which is reported to be only attested as a marked variant in languages such as Lahu and Chinese, the EIC ratios correlate remarkably well with the reported frequencies of occurrence. This clearly is one of the advantages that the EIC theory has over previous studies of word order: the ability to make predictions about relative frequencies of occurrence among different ordering possibilities.

Finally, the EIC theory is grounded firmly in performance: it is a performance-based theory of word order. Within this theory the fewer elements a given CRD contains, the more rapid and efficient processing becomes. In other words, smaller CRDs mean less load or pressure on short-term memory because only a small number of elements will be held in short-term memory; smaller CRDs also mean a smaller number of nodes which must be computed or processed simultaneously (Hawkins 1994: 60). In this respect Hawkins's (1994) explanation for the EIC theory is essentially not so different from that of Dryer (1992).

2.6   From word order to morpheme order: the suffixing preference

In the previous section left-right asymmetries were exemplified with special reference to the distribution of the complementizer: the leftward skewing in the positioning of the complementizer. It is not just at the syntactic level that such left-right asymmetries exist but they are also found at the morphological level. One such morphological asymmetry concerns the suffixing preference: the preponderance of suffixes over prefixes and infixes in the languages of the world. Building on Sapir's (1921: 67) earlier observation to that effect, Greenberg (1957b) was the first to make an attempt to explain the suffixing preference – albeit in a programmatic manner – by appealing to psycholinguistic and diachronic factors. Greenberg's initiative has been taken up by other linguists who have not only strengthened the empirical basis for the suffixing preference but have also refined the psycholinguistic and/or diachronic explanations of it.

There are two main avenues of explanation of the suffixing preference as was foreshadowed by Greenberg (1957b). The psycholinguistic approach is adopted by Hawkins and his associates (e.g. Cutler, Hawkins and Gilligan 1985, Hawkins and Cutler 1988 and Hawkins and Gilligan 1988) and the diachronic one by Bybee and her associates (e.g. Bybee, Pagliuca and Perkins 1990) (but cf. Hall 1988 for an attempt to integrate these two approaches; also see Givón 1971a, 1979, and Dryer 1992: 127 in 2.4). These two approaches will in turn be discussed and compared in this section.

The major pattern of occurrence that Hawkins and Gilligan (1988) discover on the basis of about 200 languages – drawn from three or four separate samples – is that languages with VO and/or PrN orders have both prefixes and/or suffixes in their morphology, whereas there is a strong tendency for languages with OV and/or NPo orders to possess only suffixes. This can be most clearly observed when languages with exclusive suffixing or prefixing are considered: if a language has exclusive prefixing, it almost always has PrN and VO orders, not NPo and OV orders, or if a language has NPo and/or OV order, it has exclusive suffixing, not exclusive prefixing. The data in support are presented in Table 2.22.

Table 2.22: *Distribution of prefixing and suffixing in different samples*

	Exclusive Prefixing (%)	Exclusive Suffixing (%)
% of VO languages		
Greenberg sample	5	11
Stassen sample	8	44
Perkins-Bybee sample	18	0
Gilligan sample	10	13
	Avg. 10	Avg. 17
% of PrN		
Greenberg sample	6	0
Stassen sample	8	46
Gilligan sample	7	17
	Avg. 7	Avg. 21
% of OV languages		
Greenberg sample	0	91
Stassen sample	0	61
Perkins-Bybee sample	0	39
Gilligan sample	0	58
	Avg. 0	Avg. 62
% of NPo		
Greenberg sample	0	86
Stassen sample	2	60
Gilligan sample	0	50
	Avg. 0.7	Avg. 65

(Hawkins and Gilligan 1988: 228)

This pattern of distribution can succinctly be presented in the form of a tetrachoric table:

(71)   *Prefixes*   *Suffixes*
    PrN/VO   Yes   Yes
    NPo/OV   (almost) No   Yes

Further evidence in support comes from the aggregate proportions of prefixing to suffixing in all the languages of Hawkins and Gilligan's (1988) samples: the average ratio of prefixing to suffixing in languages with PrN/VO orders is approximately about 50 per cent to 50 per cent, whereas languages with NPo/OV orders display a 4-to-1 to 7-to-1 skewing in favour of suffixes, depending on different grammatical categories. The data clearly point to left-right asymmetry in morphology: in head-initial (PrN/VO) languages the position of the affix is on either the left or the right side of the host, whereas in head-final (NPo/OV) languages there is a strong preference for the affix to be positioned to the right of the host. There is, therefore, an overall skewing in favour of suffixes.

Hawkins and Gilligan (1988) (also Hawkins and Cutler 1988) argue that the suffixing preference, or the rightward skewing in affixation can be explained by means of what they call *the Head Ordering Principle* (HOP) and a number of counterprinciples to the HOP. Hawkins and Gilligan (1988: 227) take affixes to be the heads of their respective lexical categories because 'the categorial status of a word containing affixes can regularly be computed from the affix, whereas non-affixes or stems will very often have their categorial status changed through the addition of a (derivational) affix'.

(72)   *The Head Ordering Principle (HOP)*
       The affixal head of a word is ordered on the same side of its
       subcategorized modifier(s) as P is ordered relative to NP within PP,
       and as V is ordered relative to a direct object NP.

Thus the HOP predicts that PrN and VO languages co-occur with prefixes, and NPo and OV languages with suffixes.

This principle alone, however, is not sufficient to make all necessary predictions because PrN and VO languages do have suffixes as well as prefixes as has been shown in Table 2.22. Hawkins and Gilligan (1988: 231–7) are thus led to put forward a number of – mostly statistical – implicational universals which are specified explicitly in terms of the categorial statuses of the relevant affixes as in (73), for example.

(73)   If a language has NPo, GENDER affixes on N (if any) are suffixed.

These implicational universals are then converted into counterprinciples to the HOP as in (74).

(74)   GENDER affixes (on N) are suffixed.

The domain-specific counterprinciples counteract or reinforce predictions of the HOP in head-initial or head-final languages, respectively. For instance, the HOP predicts that GENDER affixes will be suffixed in head-final languages. The same prediction is made by the counterprinciple in (74). In head-initial languages, on the other hand, the HOP and the counterprinciple will make totally opposite predictions, the former for prefixes and the latter for suffixes. In one of the samples utilized in Hawkins and Gilligan (1988), for example, the average ratio of prefixing to suffixing for GENDER affixes in head-initial languages is 40 per cent to 60 per cent, whereas that for head-final languages is 0 per cent to 100 per cent. To put it differently, in head-initial languages the counterprinciple in (74) militates against the HOP 60 per cent of the time while the HOP succeeds 40 per cent of the time; in head-final languages the HOP and the counterprinciple 'cooperate' with each other, thereby giving rise to complete suffixation. This interaction between the HOP and the counterprinciples can thus explain why there is an overall skewing towards suffixation in the languages of the world.

The HOP shares the same conceptual basis with the PCCH, which Hawkins (1983) proposes in order to make predictions about the frequency distribution of various word order properties (or with Vennemann's PNS for that matter): the consistent serialization of modifiers on either side of heads. The difference between them lies in the grammatical levels at which they apply, i.e. morphology vs. syntax. But what is the nature of the counter-principles, all of which are disposed to suffixation? Hawkins and Cutler (1988) argue that processing efficiency is optimized if lexical–semantic information conveyed by stems is processed as early as possible, that is before syntactic or grammatical information expressed by affixes is encountered.[21] There are at least two psycholinguistic factors whereby they arrive at this conclusion. First, there is ample experimental evidence that speakers and listeners pay most attention to the beginnings of words, less attention to the endings and least attention to the middles. For instance, beginning portions of words are shown to be the most effective cues for successful recall or recognition of words; the effects on recognition performance of distorting the beginnings of words are much more pronounced negatively than the effects of distortions at the end of words. Second, there are psycholinguistic studies of affixation which suggest that stems and affixes are processed separately at some level. For instance, it is found that in a lexical decision task it takes longer to reject non-words if they contain real affixes. Hawkins and Gilligan (1988) conclude, therefore, that stems favour the most salient or initial position in the word and affixes a less salient or the final position in the word because the former (imbued with lexical–semantic information) have 'computational priority' over the latter (loaded with syntactic information) (also see 2.2.3).[22] This processing consideration is then thought to encourage the overall rightward skewing in affixation. Moreover, dispreference of infixes also falls out from the same explanation because, although less informative than stems, affixes are too informative to be allocated the least salient or middle position in the word. Moreover, Hawkins and Cutler (1988: 309) point to a general processing consideration that languages avoid breaking up structural units, morphemic or otherwise. Being inserted into the middle position of the word, infixes inevitably do just that. Hence the lowest frequency of infixes.

As Hall (1988: 326) points out correctly, however, one must also understand the way affixes come into existence in the first place in order to explain the distribution of affixes fully. In Hawkins and Cutler's processing account affixes are treated as if they had started out as an independent category *par excellence*, that is as nothing more or less than affixes. Thus the positioning of affixes is determined axiomatically by the HOP in consort with the processor-driven, domain-specific suffixing preferences. But, as has been well documented by Givón (1971a and b, 1979), C. Lehmann (1982), Heine and Reh (1984), Heine, Claudi and Hünnemeyer (1991), Hopper and Traugott (1993), *inter alia*, affixal material tends to retain the position of the lexical material from which it evolved. For instance, Givón (1971a) claims that the differential positioning of prefixal modality markers and suffixal verb-derivational markers on Bantu verbs is due to the different dominant word orders at the time of their respective development into affixes. Verb-derivational suffixes emerged out of the main verb when it was preceded by the verb of the sentential complement (schematized in (75a)), whereas modality prefixes arose out of the main verb when it was followed by the verb of the sentential complement (schematized in (75b)).

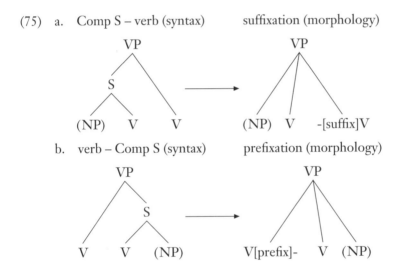

(75)   a.   Comp S – verb (syntax)   suffixation (morphology)

       b.   verb – Comp S (syntax)   prefixation (morphology)

'Thus to study the problem of the position of affixes, [one] must also study the position of non-affixal material' (Bybee, Pagliuca and Perkins 1990: 2) because it is possible that the suffixing preference or the rightward skewing in affixation documented in Table 2.22 may very well be the outcome of the overall grammaticalization process whereby lexical material gradually evolves semantically and phonologically into affixes.

   This is the possibility which Bybee, Pagliuca and Perkins (1990) look into carefully although they (1990: 4) confine their investigation to verbal grammatical categories. Based on detailed data from a sample of randomly selected 71 languages (cf. Perkins 1980, 1989) they argue that 'grammatical material develops in whatever position it happens to be in when grammaticalization occurs' (Bybee *et al.* 1990: 19). They thus call Hawkins and Cutler's psycho-linguistic explanation into question. As evidence in support they document a number of instances in which the position of affixes can be traced back directly to the position of their lexical ancestors. In V-final languages, for instance, person/number suffixes may derive historically from postverbal unstressed and out-of-focus pronouns as in, for example, Mongolian languages (cf. Comrie 1980) or from postverbal auxiliaries which are inflected for person and number as in, for example, Baluchi. In V-medial languages the second verb of the serial or compound verb construction may grammaticalize into a tense or aspect marker, and eventually into a tense or aspect suffix as in, for example, Ewe, Bari, etc. (cf. C. Lehmann 1982, Heine and Reh 1984, Heine and Claudi 1986).

Bybee *et al.* (1990: 4) concur with previous scholars that suffixes are more common or frequent than prefixes; in their sample suffixes indeed outnumber prefixes at a ratio of almost three to one (i.e. 1236 suffixes vs. 426 prefixes). But they do not believe that there is evidence in support of Hawkins and Cutler's claim that processing considerations motivate the preference of suffixation over prefixation. They instead ascribe the suffixing predomin-ance to the fact that there are more V-final languages than V-initial, and also to the fact that grammatical material is postposed consistently in V-final languages.

Consider Bybee *et al.*'s (1990) data, as presented in Table 2.23 (raw num-bers of instances in parentheses, following percentages). Note that the group-ing of the languages is done by the position of the verb: V-initial, V-medial and V-final. In the sample V-final and V-medial languages are more or less equally represented (32 vs. 31), with the remaining eight languages being V-initial. 'Preposed' means grammatical – bound or otherwise – morphemes which are placed before lexical hosts, whereas 'postposed' stands for those which are positioned after lexical hosts. There are a number of descriptive observations that can be drawn from Table 2.23. First, V-final languages are disposed heavily to postposing and to suffixation. Second, V-initial languages have a slight propensity towards postposing, and preposed material in these languages is very likely to be prefixed. Third, V-medial languages exhibit an undeniable tendency not to affix preposed material although they prefer preposing to postposing.

The data in Table 2.23 are further scrutinized in order to arrive at a more accurate picture of the situation (Bybee *et al.* 1990: 7–19). In the sample there are eight V-final languages which are not predominantly suffixing. With these 'exceptional' languages excluded from consideration the postposing tendency of 'typical' V-final languages proves to be much stronger (i.e. from 82 per cent to 93 per cent). So does the suffixing tendency of V-final lan-guages (i.e. from 80 per cent to 90 per cent). Three of the eight languages alone account for 7.5 per cent of the prefixes counted for V-final languages;

Table 2.23: *Position relative to verb by boundness for the three word order types*

V-initial (n = 8)

	Non-bound	Bound	All
Preposed	16% (13)	84% (68)	42% (81)
Postposed	26% (29)	74% (82)	58% (111)
All	22% (42)	78% (150)	

V-medial (n = 31)

	Non-bound	Bound	All
Preposed	60% (298)	40% (200)	54% (498)
Postposed	19% (82)	81% (341)	46% (423)
All	41% (380)	59% (541)	

V-final (n = 32)

	Non-bound	Bound	All
Preposed	32% (75)	68% (158)	18% (233)
Postposed	20% (205)	80% (813)	82% (1018)
All	22% (280)	78% (971)	

(Adapted from Bybee *et al.* 1990: 6)

almost 50 per cent of the non-bound postpositions in the V-final languages also come from three other languages of the eight exceptional ones. The slight postposing tendency of V-initial languages, on the other hand, is due mainly to the general preference for person/number markers to be postposed irrespective of the verb position. With these postposed person/number markers ignored, therefore, V-initial languages do not exhibit the postposing tendency at all (i.e. from 58 per cent down to 47 per cent). Moreover, there is no suffixing preference, either, although the tendency for postposed grammatical material to be suffixed is nearly as strong as that for preposed material to be prefixed (73 per cent vs. 81 per cent). Finally, the preposing tendency of V-medial languages is understated by the presence of a large number of postposed person/number markers. Thus V-medial languages are otherwise far more preposing than postposing (57 per cent vs. 43 per cent). More importantly, they actually display a much stronger prefixing dispreference than they do in Table 2.23; preposed grammatical morphemes are more likely – by almost three to one – to be non-bound than bound (73 per cent vs. 27 per cent). But the tendency to affix postposed grammatical material remains very strong although less so than when post-posed person/number markers were also taken into consideration (i.e. from 81 per cent to 74 per cent).

Then how do Bybee *et al.* (1990) take account of all these observations? They (1990: 30–4) argue that grammatical material grows increasingly more dependent on adjacent material as it develops into affixes. In V-final languages grammatical material can only 'lean' to the left as it typically follows the verb in clause-final position; there is nothing to fuse with to the right, apart from the abstract clause boundary. The situation in V-initial languages is the mirror image of that in V-final languages. Grammatical material occurs between the clause boundary and the verb since it tends to precede the verb. When it fuses with the verb, therefore, grammatical material in V-final languages will suffix to the verb, whereas that in V-initial languages will prefix to the verb. This explains at least the suffixing preference in V-final languages. Bybee *et al.* (1990: 33) reserve their judgement about V-initial languages; as opposed to V-final languages V-initial languages do not form 'a coherent type' because their grammatical material is highly likely to be not only postposed but also bound. The state of affairs in V-medial languages is very different in that preposed grammatical material will be placed between the subject and the verb, and postposed material between the verb and the object. Bybee *et al.* (1990: 31) claim that, because it abuts on other material on either of its sides grammatical material in V-medial languages will maintain its 'phonological integrity' for a longer time and thus affix to the verb very slowly, if ever. The basis of this claim is that, whereas grammatical material in V-final or -initial languages has no other alternatives but to affix to the verb, that in V-medial languages has the option of going one or the other way, as it were. It can attach itself to the verb or to other adjacent material, e.g. pronouns, or it may even continue without ever affixing to the verb. The distinct dispreference of prefixation in V-medial languages can thus be accounted for precisely because preposed material in these languages falls in between the verb and other grammatical material, not between the verb and the clause boundary (see below for discussion of postposed grammatical material in V-medial languages).

They also suggest that where grammatical material has alternatives other than fusion with the verb, the semantic factor of 'relevance' may exert influence on the distribution of affixes to the effect that the more highly relevant to a host grammatical material is, the more readily it becomes an affix. In her earlier work (1985a) Bybee demonstrates convincingly that some grammatical categories are more relevant to the meaning of verbs than others. For instance, aspect is more relevant to the verb than is mood. This is because the former modifies the temporal dimension of the event denoted by the verb, whereas the latter describes the speaker's position, or attitude towards the whole situation, or proposition. The hierarchy of verbal categories in terms of relevance may thus be:

Table 2.24: *Percentage of bound and non-bound preposed material in V-medial languages*

	Non-bound	Bound
valence/voice	27% (7)	73% (19)
aspect	59% (39)	41% (27)
tense	77% (53)	23% (16)
mood/modality	90% (89)	10% (10)

(Bybee *et al.* 1990: 31)

(76) valence > voice > aspect > tense > mood/modality
    > = 'more relevant to the verb than'

If it does affix to the verb, preposed material in V-medial languages is then only predicted to do so in proportion to the extent to which it is semantically relevant to the verb. This seems to be the case in Bybee *et al.*'s (1990) sample. Note that in Table 2.24 valence and voice are lumped together.

As the degree of relevance decreases from valence/voice to mood/modality, the percentages of non-bound grammatical material increase, whereas those of bound or affixed grammatical material decrease. Thus there is a direct correlation between relevance and affixation. The same comment can be made of preposed grammatical material in V-final languages based on similar data in support, which will not be presented here in the interests of space.

The behaviour of postposed grammatical material in V-medial languages, however, proves to be highly problematic for Bybee *et al.*'s (1990) hypothesis. In V-medial languages postposed grammatical material should not be expected to be different in terms of affixation from preposed grammatical material because it likewise appears between the verb and other material. But, when the distribution of postposed grammatical material in V-medial languages is analysed similarly in terms of the hierarchy of verbal categories in (76), its behaviour could not be more 'aberrant' as can be seen in Table 2.25.

There are two points to be noted about the data in Table 2.25. First, there is a very strong suffixing preference here – in most cases by a great margin – (Bybee *et al.* 1990: 16) despite the fact that postposed grammatical material is not adjacent immediately to the clause boundary. This immediately calls into serious question Bybee *et al.*'s (1990) claim that grammatical material has a much stronger affixing propensity when it occurs between the verb and the clause boundary than it does between the verb and other grammatical material. By the same token the relatively strong tendency

Table 2.25: *Percentage of bound and non-bound postposed material in V-medial languages*

	Non-bound	Bound
valence/voice	6% (1)	94% (16)
aspect	41% (7)	59% (10)
tense	20% (2)	80% (8)
mood/modality	25% (4)	75% (12)

(Adapted from Bybee *et al.* 1990: 33)

towards suffixation of postposed grammatical material in V-initial languages is also problematic for Bybee *et al.*'s position. Second, contrary to their prediction, tense and mood/modality markers show a stronger tendency to affix to the verb than do aspect markers. The latter category appears much further to the left on the hierarchy in (76) than the former categories. In full awareness of this 'anomaly' Bybee *et al.* (1990: 33–4) suggest that a detailed investigation of these aberrant suffixes be carried out in order to determine their exact sources and reasons for suffixation. But this could also very well mean that there are additional factors which have a bearing on the distribution of affixes. If so, it may perhaps be premature to reject Hawkins and Cutler's psycholinguistic explanation outright because processing preference may possibly be one such factor which competes with the syntactic and semantic factors to which Bybee *et al.* (1990) make exclusive reference (but cf. Bybee *et al.* 1990: 35).

Siewierska and Bakker (1996: 139–49) pursue a similar study but focus their attention on the formal realization of subject and object agreement markers, i.e. prefixes, suffixes, both or something else. Thus their work is much narrower in scope than Hawkins and Gilligan (1988), Hawkins and Cutler (1988) and Bybee *et al.* (1990). One of the aims of Siewierska and Bakker's work is to evaluate the two main avenues of explanation featured in the preceding discussion – the HOP hypothesis and the diachronic hypothesis – in conjunction with the suffixing preference (captured in Hawkins and Gilligan's (1988) multiple counterprinciples to the HOP). With the exception of subject agreement prefixes in V-medial languages these two hypotheses make opposite predictions about the formal realization of subject and object agreement markers depending on the word order types. In the HOP hypothesis the position of affix, taken to be the head, is defined in line with the position of the verb in basic word order. In V-final languages, for instance, the verb (or the head) comes last, after the dependents, in basic word order. This means that V-final languages opt for suffixes, not prefixes. In V-initial and V-medial languages the prefix is the preferred choice. In

Table 2.26: *Predictions of the HOP and the diachronic hypotheses with respect to the formal realization of subject and object markers*

	HOP	DIACHRONIC
V-final		
subject	suffix	prefix
object	suffix	prefix
V-medial		
subject	prefix	prefix
object	prefix	suffix
V-initial		
subject	prefix	suffix
object	prefix	suffix

the diachronic hypothesis the dependent comes before or after the head depending on the position of the verb, and it will grammaticalize as prefixes or suffixes to the verb, respectively. This means that in V-final languages both the subject and object agreement markers will preferably appear in the form of prefixes to the verb. In V-medial languages the subject agreement marker will preferably be a prefix, and the object agreement marker a suffix. In V-initial languages both the subject and the object agreement markers will appear as suffixes to the verb. These predictions are summarized in Table 2.26.

Siewierska and Bakker then set out to test the predictions in Table 2.26 against their own data (presented in Table 2.27), collected from a sample of 237 languages – which is set up according to Rijkhoff *et al.*'s (1993) sampling methodology in conjunction with Ruhlen's (1987) classification of the languages of the world. They (1996: 142–3) break the data in Table 2.27 down further into the six *linguistic areas* in the sense of Dryer (1991) with a view to detecting geographical effect but in the present section reference will only be made to the data in Table 2.27 for the sake of easy exposition since this has no serious bearing on the main points to be discussed here. (Note that, although reference will only be made here to the subject marker as a whole, Siewierska and Bakker (1996) also make an additional distinction between intransitive subject (or subject$_i$) and transitive subject (or subject$_t$) for other purposes – for further discussion see 3.14.)

In V-final languages there is a clear tendency for the subject marker to be realized by a suffix rather than by a prefix. In V-medial languages the prefix is clearly the choice for the subject marker. In V-initial languages the suffix

Table 2.27: *The formal realization of subject and object agreement relative to verb position*

agreement	suffix	prefix	both	detached
V-final				
subject$_i$	43 (51%)	27 (32%)	10 (12%)	4 (5%)
subject$_t$	45 (54%)	23 (28%)	11 (13%)	4 (5%)
object	22 (38%)	28 (48%)	3 (4%)	5 (6%)
V-medial				
subject$_i$	11 (25%)	21 (48%)	6 (14%)	6 (14%)
subject$_t$	12 (27%)	23 (51%)	4 (9%)	6 (13%)
object	15 (54%)	9 (32%)	1 (4%)	3 (20%)
V-initial				
subject$_i$	7 (28%)	6 (24%)	2 (8%)	10 (40%)
subject$_t$	8 (31%)	7 (27%)	2 (8%)	9 (35%)
object	8 (50%)	4 (25%)	0 (0%)	4 (25%)

(Adapted from Siewierska and Bakker 1996: 140)

only has the edge over the prefix with respect to the subject marker. As for the object marker, the preference is more pronounced for each of the word order types: for the V-final word order prefixes predominate over suffixes, whereas for both the V-medial and V-initial word orders the converse is the case. Moreover, in V-initial languages the detached marking – clitics or particles – is the most common realization of the subject marker.

First, take the HOP hypothesis. It makes incorrect predictions about the formal realization of the object marker in V-medial and V-initial languages: in Siewierska and Bakker's data the suffix is favoured by the object marker in these two word order types, contrary to the preference for the prefix predicted by the HOP hypothesis. For V-final word order type the HOP points to the suffix for both the subject and object markers but in Siewierska and Bakker's data the subject, not the object marker prefers the suffix.

In the diachronic hypothesis V-medial languages are predicted to favour the prefix and the suffix for the subject and object marker, respectively. This is indeed the case in Siewierska and Bakker's data. As for V-initial languages, the diachronic hypothesis, unlike the HOP hypothesis, only fails to make a correct prediction about the subject marker, which exhibits a strong preference for the detached marking, and only a weak preference for the suffix over the prefix. It correctly predicts, however, that the object marker favours the suffix in V-initial languages. In the case of V-final languages the diachronic hypothesis correctly identifies the prefix as being the preferred choice for the object marker although it runs up against the preference for the suffix of the subject marker. However, Siewierska and Bakker (1996: 148) point to Givón's earlier work (1976b), which attempts to explain this problematic presence of subject agreement suffixes in V-final languages by postulating that these suffixes were originally prefixes attached to a finite verb in a complex construction, and they subsequently fused with the preceding non-finite verb. If Givón's diachronic scenario is correct, then, the existence of subject agreement suffixes in V-final languages may perhaps not be much of a conundrum for the diachronic hypothesis. This leaves only the predomin-ance of the detached marking for the subject marker in V-initial languages, a serious anomaly for the diachronic hypothesis, compared to the incorrect predictions of the HOP hypothesis for the formal realization of the object marker in each of the three word order types. This leads Siewierska and Bakker (1996: 149) to conclude that the diachronic hypothesis accounts for their data better than the HOP hypothesis although both hypotheses are not without problems in their own ways.

Siewierska and Bakker (1996: 147, 149) are also of the view that the diachronic hypothesis, not the HOP hypothesis, is consistent with the fact that there are more subject agreement (i.e. $43 + 45 = 88$ languages) than object agreement (i.e. 22 languages) suffixes in V-final languages, and more subject agreement (i.e. $6 + 7 = 13$ languages) than object agreement (i.e. 4 languages) prefixes in V-initial languages (see Table 2.27). They (1996: 147) point out that, provided that agreement markers derive historically from unstressed pronouns (e.g. Givón 1976a, Mallinson and Blake 1981: 155), subject is more susceptible to the pressure of pragmatic or processing factors than object, which is known to be more bonded syntactically to the verb than is subject (cf. Tomlin's (1986) Verb-Object Bonding principle; see 2.3). Thus subject agreement markers are more prone than object agreement markers to move out of the positions which nominal or stressed pronominal NPs normally occupy. As indicated by the data just mentioned, such devia-tions are indeed far more frequent in subject than object markers. The HOP hypothesis, on the other hand, does not tie in conceptually well with, for instance, the fact that V-initial languages with subject prefixes exceed those with object prefixes by over 3 to 1 in number because it makes a prediction in favour of a uniform prefixing preference for the subject and object markers in V-initial languages.

Finally, Greenberg (1963b) addresses ordering of multiple affixes by reporting that, when both number and case occur on the same side of the noun base, number almost always comes between the noun base and case. Number is thus placed much closer physically to the noun base than is case. However, not so much has been written about this issue as about the distri-bution of affixes itself. It falls outside the purview of, for instance, Hawkins and Cutler (1988: 306) as their processing theory 'is neutral with respect to ordering of affixes in multiply affixed items.' Bybee (1985a: 33–5), on the other hand, argues that the notion of relevance makes it possible to predict how ordering of multiple affixes will be sorted out: the more highly relevant a given affix is to the stem or root, the closer to the latter the former is found to occur. Put differently, there is an iconic relation between the meanings and their expressions (Bybee 1985a: 35; cf. Haiman 1985a, Foley and Van Valin 1984: 225–34 *inter alia*). For instance, number has a direct bearing on the entity or entities referred to by the noun; case, on the other hand, specifies the relation to the other elements in the clause of the entity or entities referred to by the noun (Bybee 1985a: 34). Thus number is more relevant to the noun than is case, whereby the expression of the former is found to be closer to the noun than that of the latter. Testable predictions can also be produced as to relative ordering of other grammatical affixes. Recall the hierarchy of verbal categories in (76). The categories to the left on the hierarchy are more relevant to the verb than the ones to the right. This leads to the prediction that the categories to the left on the hierarchy will be placed closer to the verb stem than those to the right. Bybee (1985a) tests this based on a sample of fifty languages – the sample is put together by utilizing Perkins's (1980) sampling technique. The prediction is borne out with few exceptions. For example, aspect markers are predicted to be closer to the verb stem than tense markers. Indeed the opposite order is reported not to occur in the sample. Aspect markers are also predicted to occur closer to the stem than mood markers. There is no language in the sample in which mood markers are found to be closer to the stem than aspect markers, whereas the predicted order is found in ten out of a total of twenty-three languages with both aspect and mood markers (but cf. Table 2.25). Tense markers are in turn predicted to occur closer to the stem than mood markers as they do so in eight languages out of twenty that have both tense and mood markers. The hierarchy in (76) can thus in effect be interpreted to reflect the relative ordering of the relevant affixes. Moreover, it is a widely known fact that derivational morphemes occur closer to the base than do inflectional ones – unless they appear on the different sides of the base. This is also accounted for similarly in terms of relevance. For one thing, derivational morphemes tend to alter the meaning of the base, more often than not, drastically, whereas inflectional morphemes do not do so but only add a grammatical dimension to the meaning of the base. Needless to say, Bybee's (1985a) sample is far too small to draw any firm conclusions as to ordering of affixes in multiply affixed items. But the hierarchy of categories based on the notion of relevance seems to provide a very promising theoretical basis for further investigation (for one such piece of research with positive evidence see Song (1994), in which the same notion of relevance is applied with respect to the relative propinquity to the verb of subject and object referential pronouns).

2.7   Closing remarks

Far more frequently than not the fact that Greenberg's (1963b) pioneering work had been based on a very small, genetically and areally unrepresentative sample was not borne in mind by some researchers who followed in his footsteps to work on word order properties. His 'universal' statements were thus taken unjustifiably to be much more than he had originally intended them to be: tentative or preliminary generalizations. W.P. Lehmann (1973, 1978b, 1978c) and Vennemann (1974a), for instance, went so far as to draw sweeping generalizations and unwarranted inferences directly from some of Greenberg's 'universal' statements. Hawkins (1983), on the other hand, recognized the need to ground such generalizations on a much firmer empirical footing with a view to 'fine-tuning' them into exceptionless universals. He was thus led to make use of not just Greenberg's original database but also his own much expanded sample. But, somewhat ironically but understandably, his work also suffered from empirical inadequacy since his database was far from genetically and areally representative of the languages of the world. As a consequence, many of his generalizations have already been called into question or invalidated (e.g. Campbell, Bubenik and Saxon 1988, Dryer 1988, 1991, 1992).[23]

This lack of empirical validity is more or less characteristic of early studies in word order typology. But, as has amply been demonstrated in 1.5.3, the validity and reliability of work in linguistic typology can greatly be enhanced by using good sampling methods or techniques. Thus it does not come as a surprise that recent years have seen the development of sampling techniques, and the wide use of them, especially in the area of word order typology. In particular, Dryer (1989) has not only developed a reliable sampling technique of his own but he (1988, 1991, 1992) has also set out to (dis)confirm or to (re)discover a large number of observations, or facts about word order properties. No doubt his work will – very much in the tradition of Greenberg's seminal work – give a strong impulse to further theorizing in word order typology and also provide a solid empirical base for subsequent research on basic word order.

Most word order studies have of late revealed a strong inclination towards processing as a major avenue of explanation. This is evident particularly in the works by Dryer (1992) and, to a greater extent, Hawkins (1994). The thrust of their positions is that processing efficiency is optimized if direction of branching is consistent across all different syntactic categories (Dryer 1992), or if a maximum number of ICs are recognized on the basis of a minimum number of non-ICs or words (Hawkins 1994). To wit, basic word order is in principle conceived of as a reflection of the way languages respond to processing demands (cf. Hawkins 1994: 321). Needless to say, these processing theories of word order are in their infancy. It is envisaged, however, that future word order research will increasingly be processing-based very much along the lines of Dryer (1992) and Hawkins (1994). Hopefully, it will also be fully supported by non-internal or extra-linguistic evidence as the time has come for evidence in word order typology to be independently verifiable (cf. Song 1991a).

Notes

1. Word order is a misnomer because what is being referred to by this term actually is constituent order. For example, S or O may be phrases, consisting of more than one word. But the term word order will be retained in this book since it is well established in linguistic typology.
2. Greenberg (1963b) provides further basic word order information on an expanded list of languages.
3. Linguistic typology lost much ground between the rise of the Neogrammarian school in the 1870s and the 1950s (when Greenberg's (1954) paper on the reworking of Sapir's (1921) classification scheme appeared). The following comment by Martinet (1962: 66) is a clear reflection of the prevailing attitude to linguistic typology in the period in question:

   What contemporary linguists somewhat pompously call 'typology' is not basically different from what a long line of thinkers have attempted to do when they classified languages, not according to their antecedents and genealogy, but with respect to their directly observable characteristics. It is not difficult to understand why so little has been achieved along these lines to date ... We need not go too far back in time to find and, as far as I am concerned, to remember a period when attempts to classify languages on any other basis than genetic relationship were frowned upon as a sheer waste of time and energy ... Our fundamental objection to previous [typological] classification is, of course, that they were bound to be random and intuitive, since so little was really known about the languages which we so glibly labelled isolating, agglutinative, or inflexional ... If so little has been done about typology during the last decades, it is because no one knows how to establish a hierarchy among the various items isolated by linguistic analysis.

   He (1962: 67, 94) then brands Sapir's (1921) morphological classification, or typology as 'a nearly tragic illustration of the pitfalls of psychologism', and Greenberg's (1954) quantitative rendition of the morphological typology as a translation of 'Sapir's scheme into currently fashionable jargon'. In fairness to Martinet, however, it must be emphasized that his comment is directed at morphological typology, and holistic typology in particular (e.g. Martinet 1962: 69; see section 1.6).
4. It is not possible to determine exactly how many languages are included in Greenberg's Appendix II because he often speaks of X languages, Y group, many Z languages, etc. But with slight modification and correction Hawkins puts the total number of the languages in Appendix II at 142.

5. In fact, Dryer (1988: 190–1) demonstrates that, except for Eurasia (see 1.5.3), OV languages do prefer NA to AN more than either SVO or V-initial languages.

6. Vennemann's conversion into bilateral ones of Greenberg's unilateral universal statements also results in a considerable number of counterexamples to the PNS because the bilateral implicational statement of $p \supset q$ disallows two co-occurrence types (i.e. p & $-q$, and $-p$ & q) as opposed to only one in the unilateral implicational statement (i.e. p & $-q$), and because the co-occurrence type of $-p$ & q is well represented in the languages of the world (Hawkins 1983: 35–6). Thus under Vennemann's scheme it is not possible to distinguish $-p$ & q from p & $-q$.

7. Dryer (1991: 443–4) does not make a distinction between the two types of V-initial languages, i.e. VSO and VOS, because 'there is no evidence that VSO languages behave differently from other V-initial languages, either VOS languages or V-initial languages which are neither clearly VSO nor clearly VOS' (Dryer 1988: 190).

8. Hawkins (1983: 66–7) actually replaces the statistical universal in (22a) with an exceptionless one by incorporating the feature of [–SVO] into the universal since there is only one counterexample to (22a) in Greenberg's expanded list (or four in Hawkins's own expanded sample), which is (or are) SVO. Thus (22a) has a non-statistical counterpart in the form of:

(i)   Pr & –SVO $\supset$ (NA $\supset$ NG)

9. For instance, Hawkins (1983: 95) notes that the productively attested co-occurrences of Po & DemN & NRel and Po & NumN & NRel are predicted by the HSP, but not by the MP. The HSP makes a prediction that the Rel, not the Dem, will occur to the right because the former is much heavier than the latter. The MP, on the other hand, makes a contradictory prediction that the Dem, not the Rel, will move around the head, or to the right in this case because the former is more mobile than the latter. As has been noted in the main text, it is generally the case that the MP overrides the HSP. But, since the difference in heaviness between the Dem and the Rel is substantial enough, the HSP will take precedence over the MP. Hence (DemN $\vee$ NumN) & NRel. Hawkins (1983: 94) proposes *the Mobility and Heaviness Interaction Principle* to resolve the present case of conflict between the HSP and the MP.

10. Note that the subject is regarded as an operator in Hawkins (1983: 136–7). For example, the sequence in <7> in Table 2.7 has one inconsistency, S before V, with the rest being consistently serialized as operand before operator.

11. As has been pointed out, Hawkins (1983) takes adposition order to be the type predictor. This also means that it is the operator–operand serialization in the adpositional phrase that the operator–operand orderings in the verb phrase and in the noun phrase are measured against in order to calculate the number of operator–operand ordering deviations (if any) in a given co-occurrence type. Thus '[t]he more the ratio of operator preposing or postposing in the verb phrase and the noun phrase departs from the

operator–operand serialization in the adpositional phrase, the fewer languages there are' (Hawkins 1983: 160).

12. Sense dependency can be illustrated by the tendency for the sense of a predicate to vary with the semantic nature of the referent of the object NP (again, also of the intransitive subject). For example, the meaning of the verb *cut* in the following examples depends on the meaning of the object NP (Keenan 1984: 201).

    (i)   John cut his arm/his foot.
    (ii)   John cut his nails/his hair/the lawn.
    (iii) John cut the cake/the roast.
    (iv)   John cut a path (through the field)/a tunnel (through the mountain).
    (v)   John cuts his whisky with water/his marijuana with tea.
    (vi)   The company cut production quotas/prices.
    (vii) The rock band, *Mahth*, cut twenty singles in 1999.

    Predicates may also impose specific selectional restrictions on the object NP (and also on the intransitive subject) but weak and general restrictions such as humanness, animacy or concreteness on the transitive subject NP.

13. Unlike Hawkins (1983) Dryer (1992) is not concerned with finding exceptionless language universals but rather with statistical universals, or linguistic preferences. In a way this is dictated by his sampling decision to count genera, rather than individual languages. Exceptionless universals must by definition be absolute, admitting of not a single counterexample. But by counting genera, not languages, Dryer (1992) has no way of telling whether or not a given universal is exceptionless since genera are genetic groups of languages.

14. Under the so-called DP Hypothesis in generative grammar, on the other hand, the determiner is taken to be the head of the noun phrase (cf. Dryer 1992: 104).

15. The structure in (46) is what was assumed in pre-generative and earlier generative approaches, whereas that in (45) is the one favoured in later generative approach.

16. Dryer (1992: 111), however, observes that many languages do not seem to permit fully recursive adjective phrases.

17. Dryer (1992: 116) points out that the revised version has an advantage over the alternate version in that it cannot only make predictions about the ordering of heads and dependents but also about the ordering of multiple dependents relative to one another. For instance, it predicts that only N-A-Rel and Rel-A-N will be attested, whereas N-Rel-A and A-Rel-N will not be attested. Dryer's database contains only seventeen languages which can shed light on this but his data are consistent with these predictions. C. Lehmann (1984: 201) provides similar evidence in support. In N-A-Rel the ordering of the N and the Rel is that of a non-phrasal category before a phrasal category, and the ordering of the A and the Rel is likewise. A similar comment applies *mutatis mutandis* to Rel-A-N. In N-Rel-A, on the other hand, there is inconsistency between the ordering of

the N and the Rel (a non-phrasal category before a phrasal category), and that of the Rel and the A (a phrasal category before a non-phrasal category). A similar comment can also be made *mutatis mutandis* of A-Rel-N. But see 2.5 for further discussion of the sequencing of multiple categories.

18. One practical advantage of using the IC-to-word ratio is that one does not have to worry about low-level internal constituent structure, which may vary from one theoretical framework to another (Hawkins 1994: 74–6).

19. Hawkins (1994: 336) thinks that the lower EIC ratio of OSV with a VP as opposed to without a VP is a motivation for that word order not to have a VP, or that at least if OSV is a basic word order, it will occur in languages without a VP.

20. Note that in (64) the subject NP is allocated three words as has been done in Hawkins (1994) for OV languages. Moreover, the EIC ratio for the **S** CRD in (64) has been calculated only on the basis of the two words, the V and the Dem of the subject NP. This does contrast with Hawkins (1994: 335), who arrives at the EIC ratio for the **S** CRD in OVS languages by taking into account not only the V (one word) and the S NP (three words), but also the right-peripheral MNCC of the O NP (one word) (i.e. 2/5 or 40 per cent). This, however, does not seem to be consistent with his calculation of the EIC ratio for SVO, for which only the subject NP (two words) and the V (one word) are taken into consideration (i.e. 2/3 or 67 per cent).

21. It is, however, a matter of dispute in psycholinguistics whether or not lexical processing indeed precedes syntactic processing.

22. Recall that Hawkins (1983) argues for early head recognition, whereby heads must be processed as early as possible or before their modifiers. This position does not go well with Hawkins and Cutler's (1988) claim that stems have computational priority over affixes, in spite of the fact that affixes are regarded as heads.

23. In the words of Campbell, Bubenik and Saxon (1988: 215), 'proposed universals are only as good as the sample upon which they are based'.

3

Case marking

3.1 Introduction

In Chapter 2 various studies of the basic word order at the clause level were surveyed and discussed. Though it was not explicitly mentioned there, one of the major functions of the basic word order at that level is to indicate 'who is doing X to whom', as it were. This can easily be demonstrated by comparing the following two English sentences. Note that the roles of the NPs *the girl*, and *the boy* in (1) are different from those of the same NPs in (2) despite the fact that these two sentences contain exactly the same (number of) words and constituents. By roles is meant the relationship that holds between the NPs and the verb, and also between the NPs themselves. In (1) *the girl* is the 'kicker' and *the boy* is the 'kickee'. In (2) the roles of these NPs are reversed, with *the boy* being the 'kicker' and *the girl* being the 'kickee'.

(1) The girl kicked the boy.

(2) The boy kicked the girl.

This difference in the roles of the NPs in the English sentences in (1) and (2) is, of course, signalled directly by the difference in the relative position-ing of the NPs. The preverbal NP is interpreted to be the one who carried out the act of kicking, whereas the postverbal NP is understood to be the one who 'suffered' the kicker's action. Neither the NPs, nor other elements in the sentence – the verb in this case – bear any marking whatsoever that may represent the semantic relationship in question.

In languages such as English the clausal basic word order is relatively fixed (hence English as a fixed word order language) and exploited to a great extent for the purpose of indicating 'who is doing X to whom'. In many other languages, however, there are other grammatical or formal mechanisms in use for marking such roles as reflected in (1) and (2). These mechanisms may involve morphological forms (e.g. affixes) or function words (e.g. adpositions) which express the semantic roles or grammatical relations of the NPs in the clause. This type of explicit marking is referred to broadly as case marking in the literature. Nichols (1986) offers a typological parameter that is useful for discussion of case marking: head marking vs. dependent marking (cf. 3.13). Morphological marking of semantic roles or grammatical relations may appear directly on the head or on the dependent of the constituent (or even on both). At the clausal level the predicate or the verb is the head, whereas the argument(s) is (are) the dependent(s). If the marking of 'who is doing X to whom' is represented on the verb, it will be called head marking. If, on the other hand, the marking is borne by the dependent (i.e. the argument NP), it is known as dependent marking. Languages such as Tzutujil are characterized as exhibiting head marking since case marking appears directly on the verb (Dayley 1985: 417).

(3)   Tzutujil
       x-Ø-kee-tij   tzyaq ch'ooyaa7
       ASP-3SG-3PL-ate clothes rats
       'Rats ate the clothes.'

Note that the prefixes on the head of the clause or the verb, i.e. -Ø- and -kee in (3) represent the grammatical or semantic relations between the verb and the full NPs by registering the person and number properties of those NPs. The Japanese sentence in (4), on the other hand, is a good example of dependent marking (Kuno 1973: 129).

(4)   Japanese
       boku ga   tomodati ni   hana   o   ageta
       I   NOM friend   DAT flowers ACC gave
       'I gave flowers to my friend.'

The postpositions *ga*, *ni* and *o* bear information about the relationships between the verb and the NPs. Associated structurally with the NPs the postpositions in question are instances of dependent marking. Dependent marking may also be inflectional as in (5) (Roth 1897, Blake 1977: 19).

(5)   Pitta-Pitta
       kaṇa-lu   matjumpa-ṇa piṭi-ka
       man-ERG roo-ACC   kill-PST
       'The man killed the kangaroo.'

There may be other minor mechanisms of indicating 'who is doing X to whom' in the languages of the world – e.g. relator nouns and possessive adjectives as has been discussed in Blake (1994: 16–18). But, apart from the basic word order at the clausal level, case marking is the major means of expressing 'who is doing X to whom'. The present chapter is thus concerned mainly with core case marking, with one of its main objectives being to survey how what Nichols (1992: 8; cf. Plank 1979: 4) calls the 'clause alignment' or simply alignment is actually carried out: how is core case marking (differently) structured in the languages of the world? For instance, languages may vary from one another in terms of organizing such core grammatical relations or semantic roles as exemplified in (1) and (2) especially relative to the single core argument of the intransitive clause. (Non-core case marking, i.e. adjuncts, will not be dealt with in the present chapter with the marginal exception of case marking of oblique NPs in basic, as opposed to non-basic or altered, constructions (cf. 3.11); refer to Blake (1994) for discussion of non-core case marking.) Discussion will thus be developed as to the different types of case marking system and their distribution, and also as to possible (uniform) explanations of them. Building on the understanding of these theories, the minor types of case marking system including split-ergative, active-stative and direct-inverse marking systems will be taken account of. Case marking in the context of 'altered' or 'non-neutral' constructions will also be examined. Furthermore, it will be investigated to what extent the major types of case marking – particularly the ergative-absolutive and nominative-accusative systems – find a parallel in the realms of syntax. Finally, discussion will be provided concerning a possible correlation between case marking type and word order type.

3.2   A, *S* and P, and types of case marking

In discussion of case marking within linguistic typology it has become a very useful convention to make reference to three grammatical–semantic primitives, A, *S* and P (e.g. Comrie 1978, 1989, Dixon 1979, 1994, Mallinson and Blake 1981; but cf. Harris 1997: 366–8).[1] (Note that the grammatical–semantic primitive *S* is printed in italics so as to distinguish it from **S** (sentence) and S (subject).) A stands for agent or, more accurately, the logical subject of the transitive clause. P represents patient or, more accurately, the logical object of the transitive clause. *S* is the sole argument NP – i.e. the logical subject – of the intransitive clause. Thus in (6) *the girl* is A, whereas *the boy* is P; in (7) *the girl* is S.

(6)   The girl pinched the boy.

(7)   The girl ran.

The main advantage of using these primitives is that they can also be extended easily to non-prototypical transitive clauses, e.g. those with verbs of

Figure 3.1: *Five logically possible combinations of A, S and P*

a. Nominative-accusative

b. Ergative-absolutive

c. Tripartite

d. AP/S

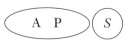

e. Neutral

perception, impression, emotion, etc. (or *verba sentiendi*) as opposed to verbs of action. In (8), for instance, the NP *the girl* is the perceiver and the other NP *the boy* is the object of perception or the perceivee.

(8)   The girl heard the boy.

The sentence in (8), however, contains two core arguments just as does (6). Despite the fact that these NPs have different semantic roles, *the girl* (perceiver) and *the boy* (perceivee) in (8) behave grammatically just like *the girl* (agent) and *the boy* (patient) in (6), respectively. In (8) as well, therefore, *the girl* is taken to be in A function and *the boy* in P function. The principle used here is that in a clause with two core arguments the one which is 'most likely to be relevant to the success of the activity will be identified as A' (Dixon 1994: 8), with the other core argument put into P function by default (cf. Foley and Van Valin 1984: 59). In the intransitive clause there is only one core argument, which will go into S function.

Given the three primitives, A, S and P, there are five logical possibilities of grouping them for purposes of case marking (e.g. Comrie 1978: 331; 1989: 125). These are represented in Figure 3.1.

In what follows these five logically possible organizations of the three primitives will first be exemplified and then discussed.

3.2.1   Nominative-accusative system

In the system of (a) in Figure 3.1 case marking is organized on an AS/P basis as is evident in languages such as English, Swahili, etc. As has already been pointed out, there is no case marking in English that indicates the relationship that the NPs in (6) or (7) bear to the verb. Word order instead does the work. However, there are some vestiges of case marking in English personal pronouns. With the NPs replaced with appropriate pronouns, (6) and (7) will come out as (9) and (10), respectively.

(9)   She pinched him.

(10)   She ran.

Note that the same form *she* is used for both A and S functions. If, however, this pronoun were in P function, it would have to take a different form, namely *her* as in (11) (cf. (2)).

(11)   The boy kicked her.

Thus, insofar as pronominal case marking (or dependent marking) is concerned, English treats A and S alike (i.e. *she*) in opposition to P (i.e. *her*). The case label for the grouping of A and S is referred to traditionally as *nominative* as opposed to *accusative* for P. The case marking system schematized in (a) in Figure 3.1 is thus known as the nominative-accusative system.

   This type of case marking is observed also in head marking. Consider the following Swahili examples (Vitale 1981: 24, 35).

(12)   Swahili
        Ahmed a-li-m-piga   Badru
        Ahmed he-PST-him-hit Badru
        'Ahmed hit Badru.'

(13)   Swahili
        Fatuma a-li-anguka
        Fatuma she-PST-fall
        'Fatuma fell.'

In (12) the NP in A function is represented by the verbal prefix *a-*, whereas the NP in P function is signalled by the verbal prefix *m-*. The NP in S function is also marked on the verb by the prefix *a-* as in (13). Thus A and S are marked alike, whereas P is marked differently from both A and S.[2]

   Languages such as Latin have both head marking and dependent marking on the nominative-accusative basis.

(14) Latin
      puer labora-t
      boy work-3SG
      'The boy is working.'

(15) Latin
      puer magistr-um   lauda-t
      boy teacher-ACC praise-3SG
      'The boy praises the teacher.'

(16) Latin
      magister puer-um   lauda-t
      teacher boy-ACC praise-3SG
      'The teacher praises the boy.'

(17) Latin
      magistrī puer-um   lauda-nt
      teachers boy-ACC praise-3PL
      'The teachers praise the boy.'

The NP in *S* function is represented on the verb by the suffix *-t* in (14). There are, in fact, no other NPs present in the sentence with which the verb can possibly agree. In (15) and (16) there are two core NPs, both of which are third person singular but it is A, not P, that the verb agrees with. This is evidenced by (17), in which the verb bears a third person plural suffix in agreement with the NP in A function – the NP in P function is singular. Thus the verb in Latin agrees with A or *S* to the exclusion of P. The same nominative-accusative system is at work in Latin dependent marking since the NP in A or *S* function is unmarked, whereas the NP in P function is marked by the accusative suffix, *-um*. The nominative-accusative case marking system is the most common type of case marking system in the languages of the world (see 3.4 for statistical evidence in support).

3.2.2   Ergative-absolutive system

The case marking alignment of (b) in Figure 3.1 is referred to as the ergative-absolutive system. In this system the case label, *ergative*, is reserved for A with the other case label, *absolutive*, covering both *S* and P. To put it differently, *S* and P are treated alike as opposed to A. According to one informal count (Dixon 1994: 2) the ergative-absolutive system occurs in about a quarter of the languages of the world (but see 3.4 for statistical data). This is thus also a fairly common type of case marking system albeit far less common than the nominative-accusative system. Yalarnnga is a fine example of the ergative-absolutive system (Blake 1977: 8, and personal communication).

(18) Yalarnnga
kupi waya kunhu-ŋka
fish that water-LOC
'That fish is in the water.'

(19) Yalarnnga
kupi-ŋku milŋa taca-mu
fish-ERG fly   bite-PST
'A fish bit a fly.'

(20) Yalarnnga
ŋia waka-mu
I   fall-PST
'I fell.'

(21) Yalarnnga
ŋa-ṯu   kupi waḷa-mu
I-ERG fish kill-PST
'I killed a fish.'

(22) Yalarnnga
kupi-ŋku ŋia taca-mu
fish-ERG me bite-PST
'A fish bit me.'

The NP in A function is marked by the ergative suffix *-ŋku* or *-ṯu*, with the NPs in S or P function unmarked or marked differently from A.

The ergative-absolutive system is also found in head marking. For instance, in Tzotzil A is marked by a set of verbal affixes, or what Mayanists call Set A, whereas S or P is marked by a different set of verbal affixes, or Set B. Note that Tzotzil lacks dependent marking (Aissen 1987: 1–2).

(23) Tzotzil
l-i-tal-otik
CMP-1ABS-come-1PL.INC
'We (inclusive) came.'

(24) Tzotzil
l-i-s-pet-otik
CMP-1ABS-3ERG-carry-1PL.INC
'He carried us (inclusive).'

(25) Tzotzil
7i-j-pet-tik   lok'el ti   vinik-e
CMP-1ERG-carry-1PL.INC away the man-CLT
'We (inclusive) carried away the man.'

(26) Tzotzil
      7i-tal
      CMP-come
      'He/she/it/they came.'

When in A function, the first person plural inclusive is marked by a Set A affix, *-j-* . . . *-tik* (i.e. (25)). But, when in S or P function, it bears a Set B affix, *-i-* . . . *-otik* (i.e. (23) and (24)). As for the third person singular NP, it is unmarked for S or P function (i.e. (25), and (26)) but, when in A function, it is represented on the verb by a Set A affix, *-s-* (i.e. (24)).

Though very uncommon (Mallinson and Blake 1981: 72), languages which have both head marking and dependent marking on the ergative-absolutive basis do exist. A good example comes from Avar (Ebeling 1966: 77 cited in Blake 1994: 122).

(27) Avar
      w-as   w-ekér-ula
      M-child.NOM M-run-PRS
      'The boy runs.'

(28) Avar
      inssu-cca   j-as   j-écc-ula
      (M) father-ERG F-child.NOM F-praise-PRS
      'Father praises the girl.'

In (27) the NP in S function is head-marked by the pronominal prefix *w-* (masculine), whereas in (28) the NP in P function is represented on the verb by the pronominal prefix *j-* (feminine). But note that the NP in A function in (28) is not represented at all on the verb. Thus the head marking for case in Avar operates on the ergative-absolutive basis. As for the dependent marking, the NP in A function in (28) *inssu-* is marked by *-cca*, with the NP in S or P function unmarked. The dependent marking in Avar is thus also based on the ergative-absolutive alignment.

3.2.3   Tripartite system

The tripartite system of (c) in Figure 3.1 is understood to be very rare. The Australian Aboriginal language Wangkumara is often cited to be an example of this uncommon type of case marking (e.g. Mallinson and Blake 1981: 50–1, Comrie 1989: 125, Dixon 1994: 41).

(29) Wangkumara
      kaṇa-ulu   kalka-ŋa ṭiṭi-ṇaṇa
      man-ERG hit-PST dog-F:ACC
      'The man hit the bitch.'

(30)   Wangkumara
       kaṇa-ia   palu-ŋa
       man-NOM die-PST
       'The man died.'

In (29) and (30) the NPs in A, *S* and P function are marked differently from
one another. Dixon (1994: 41) mentions a group of Australian Aboriginal
languages spoken in south-east Queensland which make three-way distinctions for A, *S* and P across all NPs. It is interesting to note that Wangkumara
comes from this group. Yazgulyam, a south-east Iranian language, is also
reported to be of this rare type of case marking system but its tripartite case
marking system is operative only in past tense.

3.2.4   AP/*S* system

The AP/*S* case marking system in Figure 3.1 is reported to be extremely
rare. Probably it may only exist as a system in transition from one system to
another. For instance, Comrie (1989: 125) makes reference to certain Iranian
languages, e.g. Rushan, which are developing a nominative-accusative system
out of an earlier ergative-absolutive system (also see Dixon 1994: 202–3).
Moreover, in these languages the transitional system does not work across
the board, only operating for certain types of noun phrase. Proto-Pamir,
which Rushan has historically derived from, had only two cases, direct and
oblique. These cases were initially organized in different ways, depending
on the tense in use, present or past. In present tense they operated on the
A*S*/P basis (i.e. nominative-accusative), whereas in past tense they were aligned
on the A/*S*P basis (i.e. ergative-absolutive) (see 3.3.1 for further discussion
of such a mixed case marking system). In Rushan the oblique, which appeared
on P in present tense, was then generalized to mark P in past tense. As a
consequence, A and P are now marked identically in the past, with *S* treated
differently from A and P. This language thus evinces the case marking
system in (d) (Dixon 1994: 202–3).

3.2.5   Neutral system

The last logical possibility of (e) in Figure 3.1, or the neutral system is
totally irrelevant to case marking *per se* since there are no case marking
distinctions between A, *S* and P. This is, in fact, evident in the absence
of case marking in English full (i.e. non-pronominal) NPs as has been discussed with respect to (1) and (2). Even if non-zero marking is adopted in
this type of system, it will not do much in terms of differentiating A, *S* and
P. Languages of this type may need to rely on other grammatical means of
indicating 'who is doing X to whom', for instance word order.

3.3   More types of case marking

There are case marking systems other than the five logically possible simple organizations of the three grammatical-semantic primitives, A, S and P. These additional case marking systems can perhaps be regarded as more complicated or less straightforward than the ones that have been surveyed in 3.2 in (i) that they may involve a mixture of two (or more) of the five case marking systems represented in Figure 3.1 (i.e. the split-ergative system), (ii) that complexity is added to one of the three grammatical–semantic primitives (i.e. S in the active-stative system) or (iii) that it is not the alignment of the three primitives but person and/or discourse salience that ultimately determine(s) the marking of 'who is doing X to whom' (i.e. the direct-inverse system).

3.3.1   Split-ergative system

In a number of languages both the nominative-accusative and ergative-absolutive case marking systems are in active service. This type of mixed case marking system is known as the split-ergative system. Dyirbal is probably the best known language of this type. Consider the following data from the Australian Aboriginal language (Dixon 1994: 10, 14).

(31)   Dyirbal
        ŋuma-Ø   yabu-ŋgu   bura-n
        father-ABS mother-ERG see-NFUT
        'The mother saw the father.'

(32)   Dyirbal
        ŋuma-Ø   banaga-n^{y}u
        father-ABS return-NFUT
        'The father returned.'

(33)   Dyirbal
        ŋana-Ø   n^{y}urra-na   bura-n
        we.all-NOM you.all-ACC see-NFUT
        'We saw you all.'

(34)   Dyirbal
        nyurra-Ø   banaga-n^{y}u
        you.all-NOM return-NFUT
        'You all returned.'

In (31) and (32) the NP in S or P function is unmarked (i.e. the zero absolutive case), whereas the NP in A function is marked by the ergative suffix -*ŋgu*. In (33) it is the NP in P function that is marked by the accusative

Figure 3.2: *The Nominal Hierarchy*

> 1st person, 2nd person
> 3rd person
> personal name/kin term
> human
> animate
> inanimate

suffix -*na*, thereby differentiating itself from the unmarked NP in A (i.e. the zero nominative case), and in (34) the NP in S function is also unmarked (i.e. the zero nominative case). Dyirbal thus relies not only upon the ergative-absolutive system but also upon the nominative-accusative system.

What is most intriguing about the split-ergative system is that the division of labour between the nominative-accusative and ergative-absolutive systems is far from random but regular or systematic. Consider Dyirbal again. In this Australian Aboriginal language the pronouns – actually the first and second person – operate on the nominative-accusative basis, with nouns (and the third person pronouns) inflecting on the ergative-absolutive basis as can be verified by looking at the examples in (31) to (34). In fact, in most known cases of the split-ergative system the division of labour is conditioned by the referential/semantic nature or the inherent lexical content of NPs. In Dyirbal the dividing line exists between the first and second person pronouns (i.e. the speech act participants) on the one hand, and the third person pronouns and nouns (i.e. non-speech act participants) on the other. In other languages the dividing line may be drawn differently. For instance, in languages such as Nhanda the nominative-accusative system may spread on to not only personal pronouns but also personal names and kin terms. In the Australian Aboriginal language Mangarayi the division is located between inanimates and the rest (i.e. the pronouns and all non-inanimate nouns), whereby the former category is taken care of by the ergative-absolutive system, and the latter by the nominative-accusative system (Blake 1994: 193). There are also languages where these two different systems overlap, thereby giving rise to the tripartite system for some types of NP, e.g. in Yidin[y] the deictics with human reference (Dixon 1994: 87). Indeed this distribution of the split-ergative system is systematic and regular to the extent that the converse situation does not exist. No languages with the split-ergative system are known to organize pronouns on the ergative-absolutive basis and nouns on the nominative-accusative basis, for instance. This particular observation leads to the formulation of the hierarchy in Figure 3.2 – or something akin to it (Silverstein 1976). In the present book it will be referred to as *the Nominal Hierarchy*, following Dixon (1994: 85).[3]

The referential or semantic nature of NPs is not the only factor that is known to have a bearing on use of the split-ergative case marking system.

Tense and aspect also play a role in some languages with this system. In Georgian, for instance, the ergative-absolutive system is employed in aorist (or, broadly speaking, past) tense and the nominative-accusative system in present tense. Consider (Comrie 1978: 351–2):

(35) Georgian
      sṭudenṭ-i   midis
      student-NOM goes
      'The student goes.'

(36) Georgian
      sṭudenṭ-i   ceril-s   cers
      student-NOM letter-ACC writes
      'The student writes the letter.'

(37) Georgian
      sṭudenṭ-i   mivida
      student-ABS went
      'The student went.'

(38) Georgian
      sṭudenṭ-ma   ceril-i   dacera
      student-ERG letter-ABS wrote
      'The student wrote the letter.'

The sentences in (35) and (36) being in the present tense, the suffix -*i* is used to mark S and A, respectively. The NP in P function in (36) is marked differently by the suffix -*s*. The aorist tense of the sentences in (37) and (38), on the other hand, is responsible for use of the ergative-absolutive system, whereby A is marked differently from S and P (-*ma* vs. -*i*). A similar situation is reported to be common in many Indo-Iranian languages and also in a number of Mayan languages (see Comrie 1978: 351, Dixon 1994: 100–1). Dixon (1994: 101) also describes a variation on tense/aspect-conditioned split-ergativity. In Newari, for instance, the tense/aspect split further interacts with mood: the imperative mood in nominative-accusative, and all other moods in ergative-absolutive. He reports that Sumerian and Päri are similar to Newari in this respect.

In some languages split-ergativity is motivated by the difference between main and subordinate clauses. In Shokleng main clauses may be in either the ergative-absolutive or the nominative-accusative system but in subordinate clauses the case marking (head marking) system is consistently on the ergative-absolutive basis (Dixon 1994: 101). Jacaltec is another such language wherein main clauses operate on the ergative-absolutive basis, whereas certain types of subordinate clauses are in the nominative-accusative system (Craig 1976).

Harris (1997: 364) also makes reference to one more possible factor that may have a bearing on the split-ergative system: finiteness of the verb. In Thangu, for instance, the tripartite system is used in conjunction with finite verbs but in nominalization the ergative-absolutive system must come into play. Chinook is another such language that Harris mentions: the ergative-absolutive system with finite verbs, and the nominative-accusative system with (some) non-finite verbs. But whether or not this can be regarded as a genuine example of the split-ergative system may possibly be open to question because nominalizations may be taken to be derived or non-basic (Harris 1997: 366).

Lastly, languages may combine head marking and dependent marking in the split-ergative system. It has been pointed out that in such languages the nominative-accusative system is in the form of head marking, and the ergative-absolutive system in the form of dependent marking. The converse situation, however, is claimed not to exist in the languages of the world (e.g. Comrie 1978: 340, Mallinson and Blake 1981: 70–2, Dixon 1994: 95–7 and Harris 1997: 372; cf. 3.10).

3.3.2   Active-stative system

This is the case marking system which goes by a host of other names in the literature, e.g. split-intransitive, active-inactive, active-static, active-neutral, stative-active, agentive-patientive, split-S (plus fluid-S), etc. (Mithun 1991: 511). In this system the case marking of S depends basically on the semantic nature of the intransitive verb. For instance, if the verb refers to an activity which is likely to be under the control of S, the latter will bear the same case marking as A. If not (that is, if it refers to a state or non-controlled activity), it will be marked in the same way as P. In other words, S is divided between A and P in terms of case marking. This alignment of A, S and P is represented schematically in Figure 3.3 (but cf. Mithun 1991: 542, Harris 1997: 367; also see note 8).

It seems that there are two variations on the basic criterion whereby S is split between A and P. First, the semantics of a particular instance or context of use is what really counts for the actual case marking of S in some languages with the active-stative marking system (Dixon 1994: 71). Thus the actual context for which each intransitive verb is used must be assessed in terms of whether the activity referred to by that verb qualifies as a controlled activity or as a state or non-controlled activity. Potentially, then, each intransitive verb has the ability of assigning A- or P-marking to S. Some verbs may always be interpreted as referring to controlled activities, and others as

Figure 3.3: *Active-stative system*

referring to non-controlled activities or states. But there will be a number of verbs which can denote either controlled activities or non-controlled activities or states. For these verbs *S* may be marked either as A or as P. This type of active-stative marking is called the fluid-*S* system by Dixon (1994: 78–83). Batsbi (or Tsova-Tush) is a language with the fluid-*S* system (Comrie 1978: 366–7).

(39) Batsbi
      tχo   naizdraχ   qitra
      we-ABS to-the-ground fell
      'We fell to the ground (unintentionally, not our fault).'

(40) Batsbi
      atχo   naizdraχ   qitra
      we-ERG to-the-ground fell
      'We fell to the ground (intentionally, through our own carelessness).'

Other languages with the fluid-*S* system include: Tonkawa, (Spoken) Tibetan, Eastern Pomo and Pomoan languages (Dixon 1994: 78–83, Mithun 1991: 542).

In the other type of active-stative marking system intransitive verbs are categorized more or less consistently into two groups: those which mark *S* in the same way as A, and those which mark *S* in the same way as P. Thus each intransitive verb belongs to either of the two categories: those which assign A-marking to *S*, and those which assign P-marking to *S*. For this reason this type of active-stative marking system is referred to as the split-*S* system by Dixon (1994: 78). Among the languages with the split-*S* system that Dixon (1994: 71–8) mentions are Cocho, Dakota, Guaraní, Ikan, Ioway-Oto, Ket, Laz and Onondaga. The split-*S* system is exemplified here by Laz (Harris 1985: 52ff).

(41) Laz
      bere-k   imgars
      child-ERG 3SG.cry
      'The child cries.'

(42) Laz
      bere-Ø   oxori-s   doskidu
      child-NOM house-DAT 3SG.stay
      'The child stayed in the house.'

(43) Laz
      baba-k   mečaps   skiri-s   cxeni-Ø
      father-ERG 3SG.give.3SG.3SG child-DAT horse-NOM
      'The father gives a horse to his child.'

The NP in *S* function in (41) is marked differently from the NP in *S* function in (42). In fact, the former is marked in the same way as the NP in A function in (43), whereas the latter is unmarked just as the NP in P function in (43). There seem to be far more split-*S* languages than fluid-*S* languages (Mithun 1991: 542).

Though the examples given so far of the active-stative marking system all exhibit dependent marking, it must be pointed out that head marking is, in fact, a far more frequent realization of this type of case marking system.[4] Nichols (1992) and Siewierska (1996), for instance, both find that the active-stative marking system is far more likely to be found on heads (or verbs) than on dependents (on NPs). There is a distinct skewing for head marking in this system (see Tables 3.1 and 3.2 below). Dixon (1994: 90) puts forward an interesting explanation as to why this may be the case. The split of *S* in the active-stative marking system is conditioned by the semantic nature of the verb. This makes the verb a more compatible host for the active-stative marking than the noun (for a similar view also see Mithun 1991: 540). Lakhota, exemplified below (Mithun 1991: 514), is thus more representative cross-linguistically of the active-stative marking system than are Batsbi and Laz (Dixon 1994: 77).

(44) Lakhota
      a.   **wa**psíča   'I jumped.'
      b.   **ma**xwá   'I'm sleepy.'

(45) Lakhota
      waktékte   'I'll kill him.'

(46) Lakhota
      maktékte   'He'll kill me.'

In (45) the NP in A function is represented by the prefix *wa-* on the verb. Similarly, the intransitive verb in (44a) is marked by the prefix *wa-* for the NP in *S* function. But in (44b) the intransitive verb is marked by a different prefix *ma-* for the NP in *S* function. This prefix is used to mark the NP in P function in (46). Thus the marking of *S* is split between A and P. Lakhota is thus a language with active-stative head marking.

Mithun's (1991) detailed study adds much to the understanding of the active-stative system. She argues that there are, in fact, a number of semantic features that may have a bearing on the split of *S* between A and P: lexical aspect (Aktionsart), agency, control and affectedness. In Colloquial Guaraní, for instance, the split is based primarily on a distinction of lexical aspect, i.e. events vs. states. In Lakhota, however, some verbs denoting events co-occur with P-marking, whereas some verbs denoting states co-occur with A-marking. The distinction in this language is not based on lexical aspect but rather on the parameter of agency, which is equated with the ability to perform, effect, instigate or control the situation denoted by the predicate (Mithun 1991: 516). Central Pomo generally behaves like Lakhota but it has a further complication in that control is sometimes taken out of the notion of agency as ultimately conditioning the split of S between A and P. Moreover, in Central Pomo not all out-of-control participants are conceived of as patients. In fact, the notion of patient in this language must also involve significant affectedness. For example, basic adjectives, which denote inherent properties or states, require A-marking, whereas inchoative counterparts, which denote temporary conditions or states, call for P marking. In Mithun's (1991: 521) words '[t]he coming into being of a state is viewed as affecting a participant more than simply being in a state'.

Mithun (1991: 537–40) also points out that the active-stative system has a general semantic basis but that such a semantic basis may over time be obscured or obliterated to an extent by a number of processes including shifts in conditioning semantic features (e.g. in Iroquoian agency was reinterpreted as lexical aspect probably due to use of third-person pronominal prefixes referring to non-humans as well as humans), grammaticalization (e.g. in Mohawk all arguments of intransitive verbs in the perfect aspect are marked systematically as P irrespective of their affectedness because the perfect aspect describes a state resulting from an earlier event) and lexicalization (e.g. the original semantic motivation of the Mohawk verb meaning 'yell, scream, etc.' – containing the causative suffix, it may once have meant 'it makes me yell, scream, etc.' – has now been lost, and the verb is learned and used as a separate lexical unit but the P-marking associated with it remains unaltered or has become fossilized). Dixon (1994: 74) also appeals to cultural differences: for example, 'in some societies vomiting plays a social role and is habitually induced, while in other societies it is generally involuntary'.

3.3.3   Direct-inverse system

The last type of case marking to be surveyed in the present section is what is known as the direct-inverse marking system. This is not common in the languages of the world but is prevalent in the Algonquian languages and also attested in Australian languages, Tibeto-Burman and Nootkan (DeLancey 1981: 641). The way that this case marking system operates is conditioned strictly by the Nominal Hierarchy in Figure 3.2. Basically, when the higher being (i.e. higher on the Nominal Hierarchy) acts or impinges on the lower being (i.e. lower on the Nominal Hierarchy), one set of verbal marking – called direct marking – is used. But if, on the other hand, the lower being acts on the higher being, a different set of verbal marking – called inverse marking – must be employed. Plains Cree is often cited as a typical direct-inverse marking language (Wolfart 1973, Foley and Van Valin 1985: 297–9, Blake 1994: 130–1).

(47)   Plains Cree
       ki-tasam-i-n
       2-feed-DR-1
       'You feed me.'

(48)   Plains Cree
       ki-tasam-iti-n
       2-feed-INV-1
       'I feed you.'

Note that in both (47) and (48) – regardless of their semantic roles or grammatical functions – the second person pronominal element appears on the verb as a prefix, whereas the first person element is represented on the verb as a suffix. (Note that in Plains Cree second person outranks first person in 'animacy'.) Which of the two, the first person or the second person, is A or P is indicated by the presence of the direct or inverse marker. In (47) a direct marking suffix is used on the verb, thereby identifying the situation described by (47) as one wherein the higher being acts on the lower being (i.e. second person → first person, where → indicates the direction of action). In (48), the situation is reversed, that is, first person → second person; accordingly, an inverse suffix is selected to signal this change in the direction of action. Plains Cree also makes a finer distinction between two different types of third person, namely proximate, and obviative. The choice between these two depends on a number of factors, one of which is topicality, or discourse salience (Foley and Van Valin 1985: 298). Compare:

(49)   Plains Cree
       asam-ē-w napew-Ø   atim-wa
       feed-DR-3 man-PROX dog-OBV
       'The man feeds the dog.'

(50)   Plains Cree
       asam-ekw-w napew-wa atim-Ø
       feed-INV-3 man-OBV dog-PROX
       'The man feeds the dog.'

In (49) the NP *napew* is the argument that is established as given (or topical), whereas the other NP *atim* is not given (or not topical). The former is in A function, whereby the direct marking on the verb is selected. The situation is reversed in terms of topicality in (50), triggering use of the inverse marking on the verb. It is interesting to note that the proximate or more topical NP is unmarked, whereas the obviative or less topical NP is signalled by non-zero marking (cf. 3.9).

Table 3.1: *Frequencies of case marking systems in Nichols (1992)*

	Pronoun	Noun	Verb	Total
Nominative-accusative	65	45	88	198
Ergative-absolutive	11	29	15	55
Active-stative	0	0	22	22
Direct-inverse	0	0	8	8
Tripartite	4	0	1	5

(Adapted from Nichols 1992: 90)

3.4   Distribution of the case marking systems

In contrast to word order studies few studies have been carried out to determine the (statistical) distribution of the case marking systems in the languages of the world. Most studies on case marking operate with informal or impressionistic estimates of the distribution of the case marking systems (e.g. Comrie 1978, Blake 1994, Dixon 1994 *inter alia*) and, far more frequently than not, they have little to say about the distribution of the case marking systems other than qualifying it by such expressions as 'common', 'very rare', etc. Nichols (1992), and Siewierska (1996), however, provide statistically viable data on the distribution of the case marking systems, albeit on a smaller scale than some of the word order studies discussed in Chapter 2.[5] Based on a sample of 155 languages, Nichols (1992: 90) sets out to determine the frequencies of the case marking systems across three different grammatical categories, i.e. pronouns, nouns and verbs – the first two dependent marking, and the last head marking.[6] Her results are summarized in Table 3.1.

It is clear from Table 3.1 that the nominative-accusative system is the most frequently employed case marking system irrespective of whether it is dependent or head marking. The ergative-absolutive system is overall the second most common case marking system, albeit not when head marking is concerned. The tripartite system is overall the most infrequent type of case marking. The other two case marking systems, active-stative and direct-inverse, are confined to verbs (that is, head marking).

Siewierska (1996) is another detailed study of the frequencies of the case marking systems. Her work is based on a sample of 237 languages, set up according to the sampling technique of Rijkhoff *et al.* (1993) (see 1.5.4 for discussion of this sampling technique). Her results generally confirm Nichols's as can readily be seen in Table 3.2.[7]

Also in Table 3.2 the most frequent type is the nominative-accusative system, followed by the ergative-absolutive system. The direct-inverse marking

Table 3.2: *Frequencies of case marking systems in Siewierska (1996)*

	Pronoun	Noun	Verb	Total
Nominative-accusative	82	63	131	276
Ergative-absolutive	28	41	15	84
Active-stative	1	0	13	14
Direct-inverse	0	0	4	4
Tripartite	6	4	0	10

(Adapted from Siewierska 1996: 155)

system is the most infrequent in the aggregate (but cf. Table 3.1). Note that, although it is far more likely to be found on verbs, the active-stative marking system is also attested on pronouns at least in one instance, whereas in Nichols's (1992) data it is only used in conjunction with verbs. Thus Siewierska's (1996: 153) data suggest that only the direct-inverse marking system is restricted to verbs (also see Mithun 1991: 540, 542, and Dixon 1994: 90). Also worthwhile noting in Tables 3.1 and 3.2 is the fact that pronouns, nouns and verbs do not pattern likewise with respect to the case marking systems (Siewierska 1996: 156). This is due to the fact that not all languages employ a single case marking system across the board, like Avar or Latin, for instance – the head marking and dependent marking in Avar operate consistently on the ergative-absolutive basis, and those in Latin on the nominative-accusative basis. In fact, Siewierska (1996: 156) points out that consistent use of a single case marking system for pronouns, nouns and verbs may be the exception rather than the norm in the languages of the world. In her sample the number of languages which exhibit a single case marking system for all the three syntactic categories is 139 – 112 for the nominative-accusative, 18 for the ergative-absolutive and 9 for the active-stative. With the neutral system taken into account the number of languages like Avar or Latin goes down to 60.

3.5   The discriminatory view of case marking

In this section an attempt will be made to make sense of the distribution of at least the five alignment possibilities of A, *S* and P, as presented in Figure 3.1, in the languages of the world: the nominative-accusative, the ergative-absolutive, the neutral, the tripartite and the AP/*S* system. The other 'less straightforward' types of case marking system, i.e. split-ergative, active-stative and direct-inverse, will be discussed in due course. In both Nichols (1992), and Siewierska (1996) the nominative-accusative is no doubt the most widely

attested type of case marking. The ergative-absolutive is the second most common type. The tripartite is extremely infrequent relative to the nominative-
accusative and the ergative-absolutive system, whereas the AP/S system is
not represented at all in Nichols's (1992) and Siewierska's (1996) sample.
In the present discussion the neutral system is regarded as irrelevant to case
marking *per se* since there are no case marking distinctions inherent in this
system.

Now the question immediately arises as to why these four different case
marking systems – nominative-accusative, ergative-absolutive, tripartite, AP/
S – are distributed the way they are in the languages of the world. One
prominent view is that the major function of case marking is to distinguish
'who' from 'whom' in 'who is doing X to whom'. In other words, case
marking is used primarily to distinguish A from P. There is no functional
need to distinguish S from either A or P because S occurs alone in the
intransitive clause. On the other hand, A and P co-occur in the transitive
clause. Hence the need to distinguish them. This is known as the discriminatory view of case marking, associated largely with Comrie (1978, 1989) and
Dixon (1979, 1994). Under this view, then, both the nominative-accusative
system and the ergative-absolutive system make functional sense because
in both these systems A is distinguished from P with S aligning itself with
either A or P. If S is treated in the same way as A, it is the nominative-
accusative system. If, on the other hand, S is treated in the same way as P,
it is the ergative-absolutive system. This view may also explain why the
tripartite system is very rarely found in the languages of the world when
compared with the nominative-accusative and ergative-absolutive systems.
This system is simply overly functional or uneconomical because S does not
need to be distinguished from the other two and yet S bears case marking
distinct from both A and P. Now the AP/S system, on the other hand, is
completely dysfunctional in that, although they co-occur in the same clause
type, A and P are not marked differently from each other but they are
distinguished from S, with which they never co-occur. This may perhaps
explain why this system is extremely rare and also why it perhaps exists only
as a transitional system or as a kind of historical accident, as it were.

Proponents of the discriminatory view also point to the fact that most
frequently the nominative is realized by zero (or at least a zero allomorph),
whereas the accusative has non-zero realization, and that it is almost always
the case that the ergative is marked by a non-zero element, whereas the
absolutive is marked by zero (Comrie 1989: 126–7, Dixon 1994: 11). This is,
in fact, captured in Greenberg's (1963b: 112) Universal 38: where there is a
case system, the only case which ever has only zero allomorphs is the one
which includes among its meanings that of the subject of the intransitive verb
(i.e. S). This makes sense if, as proponents of the discriminatory view claim,
it is S, not A or P, that does not need to be distinguished from the other
primitives by the very virtue of occurring alone in the intransitive clause.

This motivates S to receive zero marking. In the nominative-accusative system S is aligned with A, whereby the latter also has zero realization; in order to distinguish itself from zero-marked A, P will have to be marked by a non-zero element. In the ergative-absolutive system it is P that S is aligned with, whereby the former is also marked by zero. This leaves A to have non-zero realization in order to distinguish itself from the zero-marked P.

Another argument – perhaps weaker than the foregoing – in support of the discriminatory view is that in some languages with the nominative-accusative system the non-zero marking of P is dispensed with in the 'absence' of A, whereas in some languages with the ergative-absolutive system A appears without its non-zero marking provided that there is no room for misunderstanding or ambiguity concerning A and P. In Finnish, for instance, the NP in P function normally receives the accusative (or genitive) ending. But in the first or second person imperative construction or the impersonal construction, where A is not expressed overtly, P loses its usual accusative (or genitive) marking (Mallinson and Blake 1981: 92).

(51) Finnish
      Maija söl kala-n
      Maija ate fish-ACC
      'Maija ate the fish.'

(52) Finnish
      Syö   kala-Ø
      eat-IMP fish-Ø
      'Eat the fish.'

In Hua the ergative has non-zero realization in the form of *-bamu'*, whereas the absolutive is zero-marked (Haiman 1980 cited in Comrie 1978: 384–5).

(53) Hua
      Busa' rmie
      Busa' he-went-down
      'Busa' went down.'

(54) Hua
      Busa'-bamu' egbie
      Busa'-ERG   he-hit-him
      'Busa' hit him.'

However, the ergative suffix can optionally be omitted if there is no confusion as to 'who is doing X to whom'. Dixon (1994: 58–9) also reports a similar situation for Motu, Murin^ypata and a number of Papuan languages including Hua.

The discriminatory view thus explains the distribution of the case marking systems in Figure 3.1 very well. But there are a few issues that it does not seem to be able to deal with, at least not as well as the simple distribution of the four case marking systems. These issues relate to the other case marking systems: active-stative, direct-inverse, and split-ergative. Brief discussion of the problems associated with the first two systems is presented below with that of the last system deferred to 3.8.

First, in the active-stative system some Ss are marked like As, and others like Ps. This is singularly problematic for the discriminatory view, which claims that S does not need to be distinguished from either A or P.[8] Clearly, the function of this distinction in S is not to distinguish argument NPs because S is the sole argument in the intransitive clause. The fact that S is sometimes marked in the same way as A, and sometimes as P may suggest that some Ss behave semantically as A, and others as P. Indeed, as Mithun's (1991) study reveals, in active-stative-type languages S is characterized as representing either 'the participant who performs, effects, instigates or controls the situation denoted by the predicate' (i.e. A), or 'the participant who does not perform, initiate or control any situation but rather is affected by it in some way' (i.e. P). It thus seems that, insofar as the active-stative system is concerned, the function of case marking is that of characterization or indexing (see below for further discussion), not of discrimination. Of course, proponents of the discriminatory view may be quick to point to the low frequency of the active-stative system itself being strong evidence in support of their position (Mallinson and Blake 1981: 97).

Second, the direct-inverse system does not seem to involve the function of distinguishing A from P at all. This system instead registers the relative positions of A and P on the Nominal Hierarchy. In other words, the whole situation involving both A and P – which, A or P, is ranked higher on the Nominal Hierarchy? – is taken to be the basis for the choice between direct and inverse marking (see 3.9 for further discussion). The direct-inverse system thus also poses a problem for the discriminatory view of case marking. But then proponents of this view can again argue that this may perhaps explain why there are only a small number of languages with this particular type of case marking system.

3.6 The indexing view of case marking

Based on the observation that confusability at the clausal level between A and P can readily be tolerated in many languages Hopper and Thompson (1980: 291) point out that the distinguishing function of case marking has been overemphasized to the exclusion of the characterizing or indexing function of case marking (also see Wierzbicka 1980, 1981).[9] To put it differently,

Figure 3.4: *Parameters of transitivity*

		High	*Low*
a.	PARTICIPANTS	2 or more participants	1 participant
b.	KINESIS	action	non-action
c.	ASPECT	telic	atelic
d.	PUNCTUALITY	punctual	non-punctual
e.	VOLITIONALITY	volitional	non-volitional
f.	AFFIRMATION	affirmative	negative
g.	MODE	realis	irrealis
h.	AGENCY	A high in potency	A low in potency
i.	AFFECTEDNESS OF P	P totally affected	P not affected
j.	INDIVIDUATION OF P	P highly individuated	P non-individuated

(NB Hopper and Thompson 1980 adopt O instead of P, following Dixon 1979.)

the function of the marking on the NP in A function is to index the A-ness of that NP, whereas the function of the marking on the NP in P function is to index the P-ness of that NP. This view can immediately explain the existence of the active-stative system without much difficulty, for instance: S is sometimes marked in the same way as A and at other times as P because S is similar in some ways to A, and in other ways to P (also see Dixon 1994: 40 for the same position).

Hopper and Thompson's argument is based on the notion of transitivity, which 'is traditionally understood as a global property of an entire clause, such that an activity is "carried-over" or "transferred" from an agent to a patient' (Hopper and Thompson 1980: 251). They identify a number of parameters of transitivity as listed in Figure 3.4.

Each of these parameters constitutes a scale along which clauses can be ranked or compared. For instance, a clause with two participants is more transitive than a clause with a single participant because no transfer of an activity can occur unless there are at least two participants involved in the situation. Also take affectedness of P – which was briefly discussed earlier in relation to the active-stative marking. A clause with a completely affected P is more transitive than a clause with a partially affected P. Thus the transfer of an action is carried out more effectively in (55) than in (56).

(55)   I ate up the cake.

(56)   I ate some of the cake.

The more features a clause has in the high columns in the parameters from (a) to (j) in Figure 3.4, the more transitive it is. Conversely, the more features a clause has in the low columns in the parameters from (a) to (j), the

less transitive it is. Transitivity can be seen to be a cluster of these parameters. Thus a natural consequence of this conception of transitivity is that
some Ps have more P-ness or are more P-like than other Ps. The parameters
that pertain most to the present discussion of the indexing view of case
marking are: individuation of P, affectedness of P, aspect and affirmation.

Hopper and Thompson (1980: 253) argue that an action can be more
effectively transferred from an agent to a patient which is individuated than
to a patient which is not. Properties associated with an individuated patient
include among others: human, animate and referential/definite. A non-individuated patient, on the other hand, is inanimate and/or non-referential. The
more individuated the referent of a noun is, the more P-ness it has, as it
were.[10] They (1980: 255–9) adduce a fair amount of evidence in support of
this position. For instance, it is widely known (e.g. Comrie 1977, Mallinson
and Blake 1981: 48) that in many languages P-marking does not apply across
the board. That is, P-marking tends to be found on definite NPs or on
human or animate NPs. In Modern Hebrew, for instance, indefinite Ps are
unmarked, whereas definite Ps must be preceded by the 'object-marker' *et*
(Berman 1978: 123 cited in Hopper and Thompson 1980: 256).

(57) Hebrew
      David natan matana lərina
      David gave present to Rina
      'David gave a present to Rina.'

(58) Hebrew
      David natan et   ha-matana   lərina
      David gave OBJ DEF-present to Rina
      'David gave the present to Rina.'

Similarly, in Russian there is an alternation for a number of verbs between
the accusative case and the genitive case, whereby the former case relates to
the definite P, and the latter to the indefinite P (Wierzbicka 1981: 56).

(59) Russian
      Ivan ždet   tramvaj
      Ivan is.waiting.for tram-ACC
      'Ivan is waiting for the tram.'

(60) Russian
      Ivan ždet   tramvaja
      Ivan is.waiting.for tram-GEN
      'Ivan is waiting for a tram.'

In Persian the accusative suffix *-rā* must be used only if P is referential as in
(61) and (63). If not, P-marking is not used at all as in (62) (Comrie 1989:
132–5).

(61)   Persian
    Hasan ketāb-rā   did
    Hasan book-ACC saw
    'Hasan saw the book.'

(62)   Persian
    Hasan yek ketāb did
    Hasan a   book saw
    'Hasan saw a book.' [non-referential]

(63)   Persian
    Hasan yek ketāb-rā   did
    Hasan a   book-ACC saw
    'Hasan saw a book.' [referential]

The NP *ketāb* in both (62) and (63) is indefinite as indicated by the preceding indefinite article *yek*. But there is an important difference between the two in terms of reference. The NP in (62) is non-referential; that is, it does not refer to any specific book. In (63), the reference of the NP is to a specific book, which is identifiable by the speaker and/or determinable by the hearer. Thus the use of the accusative suffix *-rā* in (63) is justified. Turkish is another language which restricts its P-marking to referential Ps (Comrie 1989: 132–5). Spanish is also known to restrict its P-marking *a* to human or human-like and referential Ps (Hopper and Thompson 1980: 256, Mallinson and Blake 1981: 95).

There are also languages in which the distinction between a totally affected P and a partially affected P is reflected in P-marking. This phenomenon is very commonly found in languages of eastern and northeastern Europe, e.g. Latvian, Lithuanian, Polish, Russian, Finnish, Estonian and Hungarian (Mallinson and Blake 1981: 65). In Hungarian it is reflected in the alternation between the accusative case (for a totally affected P), and the partitive case (for a partially affected P) (Moravcsik 1978: 261–2).

(64)   Hungarian
    olvasta   a   könyvet
    read.s/he.it the book-ACC
    'He read the book.'

(65)   Hungarian
    olvasott   a   könyvböl
    read.s/he the book-PRTV
    'He read some of the book.'

In some languages the genitive case instead is employed to mark a partially affected P as opposed to the accusative case, e.g. Russian and Polish (cf. Moravcsik 1978: 266; Blake 1994: 153).

(66)   Russian
        peredajte me xleb
        pass   me bread-ACC
        'Pass me the bread.'

(67)   Russian
        peredajte me xleba
        pass   me bread-GEN
        'Pass me some bread.'

In Finnish the alternation between the accusative case (for a totally affected P) and the partitive case (for a partially affected P) interacts further with aspect (Hopper and Thompson 1980: 262). Thus use of the accusative case gives the clause in (68) a perfective or telic interpretation of the clause, whereas use of the partitive case gives the clause in (69) an imperfective or atelic interpretation.

(68)   Finnish
        Liikemies   kirjoitti kirjeen   valiokunnalle
        businessman wrote   letter (ACC) committee-to
        'The businessman wrote a letter to the committee.'

(69)   Finnish
        Liikemies   kirjoitti kirjettä   valiokunnalle
        businessman wrote   letter (PRTV) committee-to
        'The businessman was writing a letter to the committee.'

As a matter of fact, this aspectual distinction ties in conceptually well with the difference between a totally affected P and a partially affected P in that a completed activity is one in which that activity is transferred in entirety from an agent to a patient, whereas this is not true of a non-completed or ongoing activity. Also related to the use of the partitive for the marking of a partially affected P are the parameters of affirmation and mode. In Finnish and Estonian, for instance, the partitive case, not the accusative case, must be used for the P of a negated clause (Hopper and Thompson 1980: 277).

Hopper and Thompson's indexing view of case marking also extends to A. As with P-marking the function of A-marking is also to characterize A. Thus A in a clause of reduced transitivity may not be marked in the same way as A in a clause of full transitivity. This also leads them to interpret the fact that S is marked in the same way as P in the ergative-absolutive system as 'a signal of the REDUCED TRANSITIVITY' of the intransitive clause, which by definition lacks a P (Hopper and Thompson 1980: 254). Evidence in support of the indexing view of A-marking is not very difficult to find. In Bzhedukh the alternation between the ergative case and the absolutive case depends on whether the activity denoted by the predicate is carried out successfully, completely or conclusively (Hopper and Thompson 1980: 268–9; also Anderson 1976).

(70)   Bzhedukh
       č''aaλa-m č'əg°-ər   ya-ź°a
       boy-ERG field-ABS 3SG(-3SG)-plough
       'The boy is ploughing the field.'

(71)   Bzhedukh
       č''aaλa-r č'əg°-əm   ya-ź°a
       boy-ABS field-OBL 3SG(-3SG)-plough
       'The boy is trying to plough the field.' *or*
       'The boy is doing some ploughing in the field.'

The ergative case is used to mark the NP in A function in (70), whereas in (71) the same NP bears the absolutive case, the same case used for the marking of P in (70). In (70) the agent is carrying out the activity of ploughing, thereby affecting the patient, whereas in (71) the agent is merely involved in the activity of ploughing or just ploughing away at the field – that is, the focus is not so much on the field as on the boy. This difference in case marking of the agent then signals the difference in A-ness of the same NP in (70) and (71). Also note that the marking of P changes accordingly from the absolutive case in (70) to the oblique case in (71).

   Further support for this indexing view of A comes from the so-called 'dative-subject' construction, commonly found in languages of Europe, the Caucasus, South Asia and North America (Croft 1995: 115). In these languages, when the predicate of experience or cognition – low kinesis or no action – is involved, what is expressed as the subject in English is marked by the dative subject (Blake 1990: 46, Masica 1976: 163).

(72)   Georgian
       Gelas   uqvars   Nino-Ø
       Gela-DAT love.he.her Nino-NOM
       'Gela loves Nino.'

(73)   Spanish
       Me   gusta la   comida china
       1.DAT like   the food   Chinese
       'I like Chinese food.'

(74)   Malayalam
       enikku raamane   ariññilla
       1-DAT Raman-ACC knew-not
       'I didn't know Raman.'

The semantic nature of the predicate of experience or cognition does not involve the prototypical transferral of an activity from an agent to a patient. Rather, it denotes a certain physical, emotional or cognitive condition or state of the participant. As such, the clause which is built on such a verb is not characterized as transitive (enough). This is reflected in the case marking of the experiencer or cognizer in languages such as Georgian, Spanish and Malayalam. It is thus not marked in the same way as the prototypical A is. (For further examples in support of this indexing view of A marking, see 3.11, in which case marking is discussed in relation to different types of non-neutral construction.)

3.7 The discriminatory view vs. the indexing view

The indexing view can better explain the active-stative system, the dative-subject construction and the alternation between the accusative case and the genitive or partitive case, conditioned primarily by the features of transitivity such as aspect, affectedness, affirmation, etc., than does the discriminatory view. It may be argued, however, that at least the fact that in some languages P-marking is restricted to definite/referential, human/animate Ps can also be understood in terms of the latter view (Comrie 1977; but cf. Hopper and Thompson 1980: 291). A tends to be animate and definite/referential, whereas P tends to be inanimate and indefinite/non-referential (cf. Tomlin's discussion in 2.3). Thus P does not need to be marked as such because there is no room for confusion between A and P. But when P is also animate and definite/referential, it will be in competition with A, as it were, whereby P must now be marked as a P. Wierzbicka (1981: 56) points out, however, that in Russian the definite P is marked by the accusative case, whereas the indefinite P is marked by the genitive case (see (59) and (60) for exemplification). This turns out to be problematic for the discriminatory view because the accusative case that the definite P tends to receive has the same form as the nominative case for A, and because the genitive case which marks the indefinite P is different formally from the nominative case. Thus if, as the discriminatory view claims, the function of case marking is to distinguish A from P, the definite P should be marked by the genitive case, not by the accusative case in Russian.

Moreover, Hopper and Thompson (1980: 280–8) argue that the features of transitivity correlate strongly with textual foregrounding and backgrounding – the former represents the linguistic material that 'supplies the main points of the discourse', whereas the latter 'does not immediately and crucially contribute to the speaker's goal, but . . . merely assists, amplifies, or comments on it'. Thus actual sequential events are encoded in foregrounded clauses, and scene-setting and evaluative commentaries in backgrounded clauses.

Based on their analysis of three narrative texts they go on to suggest that foregrounded clauses are more transitive than backgrounded clauses because the former contain far more transitivity features than the latter. If so, the P in foregrounded clauses, not that in backgrounded clauses, is a real P. When Ps in foregrounding are examined, they indeed tend to have properties of animacy and referentiality/definiteness. To put it differently, 'definite/animate [Ps] may be MORE, not LESS, natural [Ps] than indefinite/inanimate ones [emphasis original]' (Hopper and Thompson 1980: 291). Thus definite/animate Ps are marked as such because of their high degree of P-ness (cf. Chapter 5 for discussion of case marking of the causee NP in the light of the indexing view).

The discriminatory view of case marking, on the other hand, can take better account of the rarity of, for instance, the AP/S system and also the tripartite system. Recall that Hopper and Thompson's (1980: 291) observation that confusability at the clausal level between A and P is tolerated in many languages. If so, it rather comes as a surprise that the AP/S system is not more frequent in the languages of the world than it actually is (e.g. due to randomness). It does only exist as a transitional system in few languages. Moreover, it is also a bit of a conundrum why the tripartite system is not as common as the ergative-absolutive system, if not the nominative-accusative system. Though S is similar to A in some ways, and to P in other ways (e.g. Dixon 1994: 40), by virtue of appearing alone in the intransitive clause S should at least be characterized differently from A and P – both of which occur in the transitive clause. Last but not least, it is also the discriminatory view, not the indexing view, that makes much sense of Greenberg's (1963b) Universal 38, discussed in 3.5: in a case system the only case which ever has only zero realization is S. This leads to the conclusion that, rather than being competing views of case marking, both the discriminatory and the indexing view complement each other in the overall understanding of case marking (cf. Mallinson and Blake 1981: 114–15, and Du Bois 1987: 849).

There are still two other types of case marking system that remain to be taken account of: the direct-inverse system and the split-ergative system. As has already been pointed out, the former operates on a quite different basis from the other case marking systems. The function of this system does not seem to be either to distinguish A from P, or to index A, S and P, but rather to indicate whether the action is transferred from a higher being to a lower being, or *vice versa* (see 3.9 for a possible explanation). Thus this system has a totally different conceptual basis. The split-ergative system, on the other hand, can perhaps be taken to be a mixture of the nominative-accusative and the ergative-absolutive system. Interpreted in this way this system as a whole can be explained by the discriminatory view. But what it fails to explain is the fact that the nominative-accusative system and the ergative-absolutive system work from the top and the bottom of the Nominal Hierarchy, respectively, not the other way around (cf. Blake 1994: 138). Though it may take account of the two systems individually, Hopper and Thompson's (1980) indexing view may also find it difficult to explain why the distribution of the nominative-accusative and the ergative-absolutive system within the split-ergative system is the way it is (but cf. Wierzbicka 1981). For one thing, it is not entirely clear why the nominative-marked A should in terms of A-ness be different from the ergative-marked A and, if so, how – also why the accusative-marked P should in terms of P-ness be different from the absolutive-marked P (cf. Du Bois 1987: 833–4, and 3.10).

3.8   The Nominal Hierarchy and the split-ergative system

Silverstein (1976) is the first to address the nature of the split-ergative system with a view to providing an answer to the very question raised at the end of the last section: the distribution of the nominative-accusative system and the ergative-absolutive system. His theory is based largely on the inherent lexical/referential content, or the semantic nature of NPs being the conditioning factor for the choice between the two case marking systems (also see Dixon 1979, 1994).[11] The inherent lexical content of NPs relates to agency (or agentivity), which he organizes into a hierarchy of binary features. This hierarchy is later revised into a single multi-valued one by Dixon (1979) as represented in somewhat different form in Figure 3.2. Silverstein's hierarchy is often referred to alternatively as the Agency Hierarchy (e.g. Dixon 1979), the Animacy Hierarchy (e.g. Comrie 1978, 1989), the Person/Animacy Hierarchy (e.g. Blake 1994) or, rather neutrally, the Nominal Hierarchy (e.g. Dixon 1994). For reasons to be explained shortly the Nominal Hierarchy is chosen in the present book to refer to Silverstein's hierarchy.

Silverstein (1976: 113) claims that the Nominal Hierarchy represents 'the semantic naturalness for a lexically specified NP to function as agent of a true transitive verb, and inversely the naturalness of functioning as patient of such'. In other words, some NPs are inherently more likely to be As than Ps, whereas other NPs are more likely to be Ps than As. In many situations, for instance, humans are indeed more likely to be As than Ps, while inanimate entities are more likely to be Ps than As. A much stronger restatement of this claim may be that it is 'natural' for a higher being to act or impinge on a lower being but it is 'unnatural' for a lower being to act or impinge on a higher being (e.g. Comrie 1989: 127–9, Dixon 1994: 84–5). If so, the nominative-accusative system and the ergative-absolutive system work continuously from the top and the bottom of the hierarchy, respectively, precisely because in this way NPs will be unmarked when they are in their natural functions but will be marked when in their unnatural functions or 'unaccustomed roles' (Dixon 1994: 85). Thus human NPs will be unmarked when in A function but will be marked when in P function; conversely, inanimate NPs will be unmarked when in P function but will be marked

Table 3.3: *The core case marking of Dyirbal based on Dixon (1972)*

	Nominative-accusative	Ergative-absolutive
A	-ø	-ŋgu
S	-ø	-ø
P	-na	-ø

in A function. This indeed is a very functional explanation. To give a brief mundane analogy, consider the function of the stop light on the back of a vehicle, based on a similar principle. The natural function of a vehicle is to move from point A to point B. Thus, when the vehicle is moving or in its natural function, the stop light is off (or it is unmarked). But, as the vehicle comes to a halt, or comes into its unnatural function, the stop light is activated (or it is marked). If the vehicle does not work this way, it will be taken off the road by the police! As the reader recalls from 3.5, the nominative is most frequently realized by zero (or at least a zero allomorph), whereas the accusative has non-zero realization, and also that it is almost always the case that the ergative is marked by a non-zero element, whereas the absolutive is marked by a zero element (or at least a zero allomorph) (e.g. Comrie 1989: 126–7, Dixon 1994: 11 *inter alia*). In conjunction with this observation it becomes very clear why the nominative-accusative system covers a continuous segment from the top of the Nominal Hierarchy, and the ergative-absolutive system from the bottom of the Nominal Hierarchy, and never the other way around. This is because in this way NPs higher on the hierarchy will be unmarked when in A function – the nominative has zero realization. But, when they are in P function, they will be marked by the non-zero accusative case. Conversely, NPs lower on the hierarchy will be unmarked when in P function – the absolutive case is realized by zero. But, when they are in A function, they will be marked by the non-zero ergative case.

To see how this principle works in an actual language with the split-ergative system, consider Dyirbal, perhaps the most famous language in this regard (Dixon 1972). The case marking of this Australian language is presented in Table 3.3.

For Dyirbal the point where the nominative-accusative system and the ergative-absolutive system meet in the hierarchy is located between the first and second person pronouns, and the third person pronouns (cf. (31) to (34) in 3.3.1) (Dixon 1972).

(75) Dyirbal
       nʸurra-Ø   bayi-Ø yaṛa-Ø   balga-n
       you.all-NOM M-ABS man-ABS hit-NFUT
       'you all hit the man.'

(76) Dyirbal
      nʸurra-na   baŋgul   yaṛa-ŋgu   balga-n
      you.all-ACC M-ERG man-ERG hit-NFUT
      'The man hit you all.'

In terms of the Nominal Hierarchy the referent of the second person plural pronoun is much higher than that of the common noun. Thus in (75), wherein the referent of the second person plural pronoun acted on that of the common noun, both NPs are unmarked, or they do not receive any case forms. In (76), on the other hand, the situation is reversed, whereby the two NPs in question are marked by non-zero case forms. The situation denoted in (75) has two participants in their natural functions, whereas in (76) these participants occur in their unnatural functions. This difference is reflected in the choice between the nominative-accusative and the ergative-absolutive system, and ultimately in the difference between zero and non-zero marking.

   This certainly has implications for both the speaker and the hearer. By marking or not marking the NPs in the clause (or the participants in the situation) the speaker can signal to the hearer that the state of affairs denoted by the clause is a natural or unnatural one. Thus the functional principle underlying the presence or absence of marking seems to be very straightforward or economical: mark only if it is unnatural. This principle may not come as a surprise at all when other types or forms of human behaviour are taken into consideration (e.g. the stop light of a vehicle devised and operated by humans).

   The foregoing explanation of the split-ergative system is based crucially on the Nominal Hierarchy being interpreted in terms of agency and animacy: e.g. a human (or more animate) entity is likely to be more agentive than an inanimate entity. But upon closer inspection the parameters of agency and animacy clearly cannot account for the whole spectrum of the hierarchy. For instance, though humans (or non-human animate entities) are more agentive than inanimate entities, it is implausible to suggest that first person is some-how more agentive than third person or other humans. The same comment can be made of animacy. It simply does not make much sense to claim that first person is more animate than other human beings, and so on. They are all equally animate and human![12] For these reasons the neutral label of the Nominal Hierarchy has been selected in the present book to refer to Silverstein's hierarchy. In fact, if the Nominal Hierarchy were only based on the parameters of agency and animacy, one would expect the split 'to occur more commonly between human and non-human, or between animate and inanimate NPs' as is correctly pointed out by DeLancey (1981: 645). But, while the split can potentially occur at any point in the hierarchy, the general tendency is actually for first and second person pronouns to opt out of the ergative-absolutive system in favour of the nominative-accusative system, thereby giving rise to the split between first and second person pronouns and the rest (Mallinson and Blake 1981: 104, DeLancey 1981: 645). As a result, third person pronouns tend to receive ergative case marking much more often than do first and second person pronouns (Wierzbicka 1981: 51). Also widespread is the split between pronouns and full NPs but other splits are reported to be rare occurrences (DeLancey 1981: 645).[13] Why is it, then, that first and second person pronouns tend to outrank the other nouns and/or third person pronouns on the hierarchy? Equally importantly, the agency/animacy-based interpretation of the Nominal Hierarchy seems unable to take account of the tense/aspect-conditioned split-ergative system (see 3.3.1). As has already been discussed, the nominative-accusative system is used in non-past tense or imperfective aspect, whereas the ergative-absolutive system is employed in past tense or perfective aspect. It is not clear how this correlation can – if at all – be explained in terms of the Nominal Hierarchy alone; it has nothing to do with the 'nominal' nature of the hierarchy.

3.9   Towards a unified explanation: attention flow and viewpoint

Mallinson and Blake (1981: 86) point out that the reason why first and second person pronouns opt out of the ergative-absolutive system is that these pronouns encode the speech act participants, i.e. the speaker and the hearer (cf. Blake (1977); also see Wierzbicka (1981: 67) for a similar view). The speech act participants are more topical than other NPs. They are 'more interesting to talk about than other people [or other things]' (Wierzbicka 1981: 64). Thus the Nominal Hierarchy 'represents a relative centre of interest' to the effect that 'events tend to be seen from the point of view of the speech act participants' (Blake 1994: 139). This interpretation can also be applied to entities further down the hierarchy: that is, human is more topical than animate, and animate in turn more topical than inanimate because humans have less and less in common with non-human entities as one goes down the hierarchy. The Nominal Hierarchy can thus be conceived of as a hierarchy of topicality.

There is an abundance of evidence from areas other than case marking that supports this topicality-based interpretation of the Nominal Hierarchy, particularly the special topical status of the speech act participants. For instance, Mallinson and Blake (1981) and Wierzbicka (1981) demonstrate that first and second person pronouns (or personal pronouns in general) receive special treatment over other NPs in the realms of ordering, agreement, number marking, advancement, etc. In Gunwiⁿygu, for instance, first or second person pronominal elements must always precede third person pronominal elements regardless of their grammatical relations (Blake 1994:

139). A similar comment can be made of Spanish, French, Pashto, Yukulta and Warlmanpa (Wierzbicka 1981: 62): first and second person clitics tend to appear before third person clitics. In Dargwa, if first or second person is in P function while third person is in A function, the verb must agree with P, not with A. In the reverse situation (that is, with first or second person in A function, and third person in P function), it is A that the verb must agree with; in Maasai the verb agrees with P if first or second person is in P function although in sentences with third person in both A and P functions the verb agrees only with A (Wierzbicka 1981: 62). In many languages number marking tends to be found on pronouns but not on nouns. In Chinese pronouns are marked for plurality, whereas no plural marking is used on nouns – save for human nouns with polysyllabic stems (Li and Thompson 1989: 11–12, 40–1); in many Australian languages pronouns bear singular vs. plural distinctions, often with dual, less often trial distinctions as well, but nouns – with the exception of kinship terms – are normally not subject to number marking (Comrie 1989: 190).

Proponents of the topicality-based view of the Nominal Hierarchy (e.g. Mallinson and Blake 1981, Wierzbicka 1981, Blake 1994) are of the opinion that, the speaker and hearer being inherently topical, their viewpoint is the natural viewpoint from which events are described or encoded. The speech act participants' viewpoint being natural (i.e. unmarked), first and second person pronouns in turn do not receive ergative marking. Third person pronouns and other NPs, on the other hand, do attract ergative marking because non-speech act participants' viewpoint is not natural (i.e. marked) (Wierzbicka 1981: 66–9; also see Du Bois 1987: 843–6). If neither of the speech act participants is involved in the event depicted, then it is more natural to describe the situation from the viewpoint of human beings in-volved in that situation – humans close and/or known to the speech act participants in preference to those who are not – than from the viewpoint of non-human animate or inanimate entities involved because the speech act participants relate to, or empathize with, human beings better than animals or inanimates (DeLancey 1981: 645). This explains why in some languages the split may occur much lower than first and second person pronouns. In Nhanda, for instance, not only pronouns but also personal names and kin terms opt out of the ergative-absolutive system in favour of the nominative-accusative system (Blake 1994: 138).

The foregoing discussion suggests that the Nominal Hierarchy can now be conceived of as a set of concentric circles of what DeLancey (1981: 645) calls 'egocentrism' as presented in Figure 3.5.

As one moves outwards from the centre of the circles (i.e. first and second person), the speech act participants' empathy with other entities on the hierarchy decreases. Conversely, as one moves inwards to the centre of the circles, the speech act participants' empathy with others on the hierarchy increases.

Figure 3.5: *The concentric circles of egocentrism*

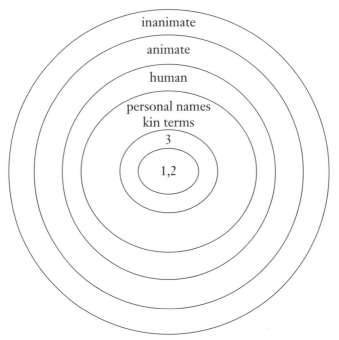

It is DeLancey (1981) who further develops this topicality-based theory with a view to putting forth a unified explanation of not only the Nominal-Hierarchy-based split-ergative system but also other case marking patterns including aspect-conditioned split-ergativity. He introduces two fundamentally psychological notions: attention flow and viewpoint. The order of NP constituents in a clause reflects attention flow, which is the order in which the speaker expects the hearer to attend to them (DeLancey 1981: 626). Events have an inherent natural attention flow, which is the flow of attention in witnessing how events actually unfold spatially and/or temporally (DeLancey 1981: 632–3). In a typical transitive situation the natural attention flow is from the agent to the patient (cf. Hopper and Thompson 1980, Comrie 1989: 128). In other words, linguistic structure (i.e. linear order) recapitulates cognitive/perceptual structure (i.e. spatial-temporal order) (DeLancey 1981: 634). Furthermore, events can be seen or reported from a number of possible viewpoints. The natural viewpoint, however, is that of the speech act participants as has already been explained in relation to the topicality-based interpretation of the Nominal Hierarchy: the speech act participants are located at the deictic centre of the speech act, thereby constituting natural viewpoint loci (DeLancey 1981: 639–40).

Figure 3.6:   *Schematization of the Nominal-Hierarchy-based split-ergativity*

   (A)   2   3

   (B)   2   3

Attention flow and viewpoint sometimes coincide, while at other times they may not do so. According to DeLancey (1981), then, the split-ergative system represents a resolution of conflicts between the natural viewpoint and attention-flow assignments. If attention flow agrees with viewpoint or *vice versa*, what is being described is a natural event in the universe of discourse. If, on the other hand, they do not agree with each other, what is being encoded is not a natural event in the universe of discourse. The difference between these two scenarios is in turn reflected directly in the case marking of the participants in the event. Consider the examples from Dyirbal again, repeated here.

(75)   Dyirbal
      n^{y}urra-Ø   bayi-Ø yaṛa-Ø   balga-n
      you.all-NOM M-ABS man-ABS hit-NFUT
      'you all hit the man.'

(76)   Dyirbal
      n^{y}urra-na   baŋgul yaṛa-ŋgu balga-n
      you.all-ACC M-ERG man-ERG hit-NFUT
      'The man hit you all.'

In (75) attention flow and viewpoint do coincide with each other. Thus both NPs are unmarked, thereby indicating that the situation described is a natural one. In (76), on the other hand, the two parameters do not coincide, whereby the NPs are marked for case. The use of non-zero marking indicates that the situation depicted in (76) is an unnatural one. The difference between (75) and (76) can be schematized as in Figure 3.6. Recall that in the case of the Nominal-Hierarchy-based split-ergativity the direction of the natural viewpoint is determined ultimately by the concentric circles of egocentrism in Figure 3.5. (Note that attention flow is represented by thick arrows, and natural viewpoint by thin arrows.)

In Figure 3.6 the numerals 2 and 3 stand for second and third person, respectively. In the diagram of (A) (= (75)) the two arrows are pointed in the identical direction, whereas that is not the case of (B) (= (76)). The NPs in (76) (= (B)) are both marked because there is a conflict between attention flow and viewpoint. The NPs in (75) (= (A)), on the other hand, are un-marked because there is no such conflict.

The theoretical advantage of DeLancey (1981) is that the same resolution of conflicts between the natural viewpoint and attention-flow assignments is also taken to be the basis of the aspect-conditioned split-ergative system, the active-stative system and the direct-inverse system. As with the Nominal-Hierarchy-based split-ergative system, the natural situation (i.e. when attention flow and viewpoint coincide) is indicated by zero marking, whereas the unnatural situation (i.e. when attention flow and viewpoint do not agree) is signalled by non-zero marking.

First, take tense/aspect-conditioned split-ergativity. In this type of case marking the tendency is for the nominative-accusative system and the ergative-absolutive system to co-occur with non-past tense or imperfective aspect, and with past tense or perfective aspect, respectively. Transitive events are taken 'to originate with the agent [or A] at one point in time, and terminate at the patient [or P] at a later point' (DeLancey 1981: 647; cf. Dixon 1979: 94–5, 1994: 97–9, Wierzbicka 1981: 67). Non-past tense or imperfective aspect is related to A because the event has not yet terminated as it is still emanating from A, as it were. Thus in non-past tense or imperfective aspect the natural viewpoint is with the starting point, i.e. A. In past tense or perfective aspect the event has come to an end, whereby the natural view-point is assigned to the terminal point, i.e. P. With this in mind consider the following sentences from Gujarati.

(77)   Gujarati
       ramesh pen khərid-t-o   hə-t-o
       Ramesh pen buy-IPFV-M AUX-IPFV-M
       'Ramesh was buying the pen.'

(78)   Gujarati
       ramesh-e   pen khərid-y-i
       Ramesh-ERG pen buy-PFV-F
       'Ramesh bought the pen.'

In this Northern Indian language the nominative-accusative system and the ergative-absolutive system are used in imperfective aspect and perfective aspect, respectively. The viewpoint is assigned to A in (77) and to P in (78). The attention flow is from A to P in both (77) and (78). In (77) attention flow and viewpoint coincide, whereas in (78) they disagree with each other. Thus the A in (78) is marked for case (i.e. the ergative case -e), signalling that it is not the natural viewpoint. In (77) the A is not marked for case because it is the natural viewpoint. Schematically, the situations in (77) (= (C)) and (78) (= (D)) are represented in Figure 3.7. (Again, attention flow is represented by thick arrows and natural viewpoint by thin arrows.)

Figure 3.7: *Schematization of tense/aspect conditioned split-ergativity*

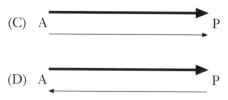

Note that in the aspect-conditioned split-ergativity – unlike in the Nominal Hierarchy-based split-ergativity, for which the viewpoint is with the speech act participants – 'viewpoint is assigned with respect to the actual point of view of a participant [i.e. A or P] in the event' (DeLancey 1981: 653).

The direct-inverse system is also explained in a similar fashion. As with the Nominal Hierarchy-based split-ergative system viewpoint is assigned more or less on the basis of the concentric circles of egocentrism in Figure 3.5. The natural viewpoint is thus with the speech act participants. In this system the verb in the transitive clause bears non-zero inverse marking when P is a speech act participant and A is not. Conversely, when A is a speech act participant and P is not, the verb bears zero direct marking – in some languages, however, both direct and inverse marking have non-zero realization. Moreover, in languages with this type of case marking it is usual to find a further distinction within the category of the speech act participants. In some languages (e.g. Jyarong, Nocte) first person outranks second person, while in others (e.g. Plains Cree, Potawatomi and other Algonquian languages) the latter outranks the former. The following examples come from Jyarong (DeLancey 1981: 642).

(79) Jyarong
     nga mə nasno-ng
     I   he scold-1
     'I will scold him.'

(80) Jyarong
     mə-kə   nga u-nasno-ng
     he-ERG I   INV-scold-1
     'He will scold me.'

In (79) attention flow and viewpoint coincide with the effect that the verb is unmarked. But in (80) these two come into conflict, whereby the verb is marked with the inverse prefix *u-*. Note also that this presence or absence of the non-zero inverse marking finds an exact parallel in the appearance of ergative marking *-kə* on the NP in A function in (80) as opposed to (79).

Figure 3.8: *Schematization of the direct-inverse system*

Again, the difference between (79) (= (E)) and (80) (= (F)) is schematized in Figure 3.8.

Finally, the active-stative system can similarly be understood in terms of the presence or absence of the conflict between attention flow and viewpoint. Recall that in this system some *S*s are treated in the same way as A and others as P. Consider the data from Eastern Pomo (DeLancey 1981: 651).

(81)   Eastern Pomo
    mí˙p'-Ø mí˙p-al šá˙k'a
    he-NOM he-ACC killed
    'He killed him.'

(82)   Eastern Pomo
    mí˙p'-Ø káluhuya
    he-NOM went.home
    'He went home.'

(83)   Eastern Pomo
    mí˙p-al xá   ba˙kú˙ma
    he-ACC water fell
    'He fell in the water.'

In (82) the referent of the NP in *S* function has volition in his action (i.e. going home), whereas in (83) the referent of the NP in *S* function lacks such volition. '[T]he onset point of the event . . . [in (82)] is with the actor at the point in time when he first intends the act, rather than the point at which he initiates the action' (DeLancey 1981: 652); otherwise the action will be non-volitional. In (83), on the other hand, the 'event originates somewhere other than with a decision on the part of the actor' (DeLancey 1981: 652). To put it differently, while in both (82) and (83) viewpoint is assigned to the actor, attention flow starts from different sources, i.e. the actor in (82) and someone or something other than the actor in (83). Thus there is a conflict between attention flow and viewpoint in (83) (= (H)) but not in (82) (= (G)). As a result, the NP referring to the actor in (83) is marked for case, whereas the same NP is not in (82). Again, this difference

Figure 3.9: *Schematization of the active-stative system*

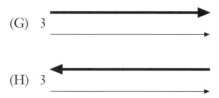

can be clearly represented in schematized form in Figure 3.9. (The terminal point in (G) or the onset point in (H) is absent in the diagrams because the event is an intransitive one.)

DeLancey's theory based on attention flow and viewpoint provides an insightful unified account of the split-ergative (Nominal-Hierarchy-based or aspect-conditioned), the direct-inverse and the active-stative systems. This certainly is a huge theoretical improvement over previous accounts in that it has detected the same conceptual basis for a number of seemingly disparate case marking systems. It has been pointed out (e.g. Croft 1995: 121), however, that DeLancey's theory cannot take account of animacy effects other than those associated with the speech act participants. This claim, however, is far from warranted because, as DeLancey (1981: 645) suggests, the scale of 'empathy' (Kuno and Kaburaki 1977) can be invoked with the effect that, being animate and human, the speaker is understood to empathize more with other human beings than with animals, and more with animals than with inanimates. This is, in fact, precisely what underlies the concentric circles of egocentrism in Figure 3.5.

It has so far been assumed that the speech act participants constitute a single category in the Nominal Hierarchy. But, as has been shown in relation to the split-ergative and direct-inverse systems, first person (i.e. the speaker) outranks second person (i.e. hearer) in some languages, and in others the reverse ranking is observed. Even within the same genetic group the ranking of these two speech act participants may vary from one language to another. For instance, in the direct-inverse system of Plains Cree second person is treated as higher than first person on the hierarchy (cf. (47) and (48)). In Blackfoot, on the other hand, second person → first person is marked as inverse, and first person → second person as direct (DeLancey 1981: 643–4). But perhaps it is not unreasonable to treat the speech act participants as a single universal category in the Nominal Hierarchy with possible cross-linguistic variations of first person → second person, and second person → first person although Dixon (1994: 88–90) is of the opinion that there may still be a distinction between first person and second person on the Nominal Hierarchy. As evidence in support he points to the fact that in the majority of languages in which there is such a distinction it is first person that is located in a higher position than second person.

3.10   Ergativity from discourse to grammar

Whether in the discriminatory view or the indexing view case marking is interpreted to be operative at the clausal level: the marking of arguments within the clause. In DeLancey's (1981) unified theory case marking is also regarded basically as a clausal phenomenon; both attention flow and viewpoint take scope over the situation denoted by the clause. There is, however, an attempt to examine ergativity – and also accusativity for that matter – from the perspective of information distribution among argument positions in spoken discourse. In his insightful study Du Bois (1987) sets out to determine whether or not it is possible to find the basis for the ergative-absolutive system outside the domain of grammar, i.e. discourse or management of information distribution. By analysing a set of narratives in Sacapultec Maya about the so-called 'Pear Film' (Chafe 1980) Du Bois finds that there is a very strong preference in discourse for full, lexical (i.e. not pronominal) NPs to be in either *S* or *P* function. Conversely, there is only a very limited use of lexical NPs for A function, frequently realized by unstressed pronouns or pronominal affixes. Moreover, he discovers that a fairly large portion of all the new mentions – whereby new participants are introduced into the discourse – also appear in *S* or *P* function, with only a small portion in A function. This correlation between lexical NPs (i.e. grammar) and new mentions (i.e. discourse) in *S* or *P* function – conversely, the correlation between non-lexical NPs and old mentions in A function – makes much sense because new mentions tend to be realized linguistically by lexical NPs, whereas old information is likely to be expressed by 'an attenuated form', e.g. unstressed pronouns or pronominal affixes, or even zero anaphora. This is demonstrated typically by the following two clauses spoken in succession by the same speaker of Sacapultec Maya.

(84)   Sacapultec Maya
    a.   š-e:-pe: e: išeb' al"ʔ-o:m,
         CMP-3PL.ABS-come PL three boy-PL
         'Three boys came,'
    b.   . . . š-Ø-a:-ki=-siky'-aʔ   l   pe:ra
         CMP-3.ABS-MVT-3PL.ERG-pick.up-MVT the pear
         '(they came) and picked up the pears.'

In (84a) *three boys* is introduced as a new participant into the discourse. It is thus expressed by a new lexical argument mention in the *S* role of an intransitive verb *-pe:* 'come'. In (84b), on the other hand, the reference to *three boys* is expressed by the pronominal prefix on the verb, and it occurs in A function. Another new participant *the pears* is realized by a new lexical mention in P function. Clearly, in Sacapultec Maya the ergative pattern in grammar finds an exact parallel in the recurrent patterns in discourse or language use.

Du Bois (1987: 829) argues that this correlation between grammar and discourse is due ultimately to the role of topic continuity. Human participants tend to play a central role in narrative discourse and are thus normally maintained as topic. Moreover, human participants are more likely to perform, initiate and control situations than, for instance, inanimate entities, which are more likely to be affected by such situations. This suggests that human participants are likely to be agents, and inanimate entities patients (cf. 3.8). Thus topical human participants tend to occur in A function, in the form of unstressed pronouns, pronominal affixes or zero anaphora, rather than full lexical NPs. Non-topical inanimate entities, on the other hand, tend to assume P function, thereby 'rarely persisting through more than a few successive clauses' (Du Bois 1987: 829). Consequently, the frequent change of patient referents gives rise to the tendency for P to be filled with new lexical mentions or NPs. But why is it that so many new mentions should also occur in S function when in common with mentions in A function they are also very likely to refer to human participants? Du Bois (1987: 830–2) points out that in Sacapultec Mayan discourse intransitive verbs are, in fact, more frequently than not used in order to introduce new human participants. These intransitive verbs thus include: a semantically empty verb – e.g. *k'o:(l)*- 'there is', or neutral verbs like 'come', 'arrive', 'appear' and the like. He also observes that narrators do not use transitive clauses when introducing new human participants as agents of actions. Rather, expression of the transitively coded activities is delayed for the space of one clause (Du Bois 1987: 830–1); typically, new participants are introduced by means of intransitive clauses and they are taken up as topical agents in subsequent transitive clauses. This discourse strategy is, in fact, clearly evident from (84) – *Three boys came . . . and they* [i.e. expressed by a pronominal prefix] *picked up the pears* vs. *Three boys picked up the pears.*

If, as Du Bois (1987) suggests, the appearance of new and lexical mentions in S or P function but not in A function is related to information flow in discourse, it should not be limited to Sacapultec Maya, or to languages with the ergative-absolutive system but should also be found in languages with different case marking systems. Du Bois (1987: 837) adduces a fairly large amount of evidence in support not only from languages with the ergative-absolutive system, e.g. Mam (England 1986) but also from those with other case marking systems including the nominative-accusative and active-stative systems, e.g. Rama (Craig 1987), Quechua (Stewart 1984), Chamorro (Scancarelli 1985), Achenese (Durie 1988), Hebrew (Smith 1987), Japanese (Downing 1985), etc. (for additional evidence see Dixon (1994: 210–11)). This, however, immediately raises the question of why all the languages of the world are not ergative (Du Bois 1987: 839–43). It is, according to Du Bois (1987: 839), because there is a universal counterbalancing motivation that links A and S, as opposed to P. That is, A and S are typically associated with human, agentive and topical participants. This factor is thus also 'type-independent' – that is, it is not only found in languages with the ergative-absolutive system but also those with other case marking systems. As evidence in support he (1987: 842) points to the fact that even in Sacapultec Maya – a language with a solid ergative-absolutive system – anaphoric links across adjacent clauses revolve around A and S, not S and P. In other words, a mention of a referent appears in S function in the nth clause, and the next mention of that referent in A function in the succeeding ($n + 1$) clause. This is an instance of the interclause anaphoric link between A and S. But if a mention of a referent appears in S function in the nth clause, and the next mention of it in P function in the succeeding ($n + 1$) clause, this is an instance of the interclause anaphoric link between S and P. Du Bois (1987: 842) finds that in Sacapultec Maya discourse topic continuity favours the S/A anaphoric link over the S/P anaphoric link by four to one (see (84) for a typical example; *three boys* (S), and *they* (A)). Thus even in languages with a strong ergative-absolutive case marking system 'the topic continuity dimension can be shown to define a nominative/accusative {S, A} alignment' (Du Bois 1987: 843). In a typical language with the nominative-accusative system the discourse pressure to ergativity is 'latent', having lost to the topic continuity factor; there are no grammaticalized ergative patterns as such although there may still be a tendency for new mentions to be in S or P, and old mentions in A in discourse. In languages like Sacapultec Maya, on the other hand, the propensity towards ergativity strongly permeates grammar (i.e. case marking, and also some other aspects of syntax), with the topic continuity pressure to accusativity confined to discourse.

Du Bois (1987: 843–6) also takes this interaction of the two pressures to be accountable for the way the split-ergative system works. In this system the nominative-accusative system operates from the top of the Nominal Hierarchy, and the ergative-absolutive system from the bottom of the Nominal Hierarchy. Personal pronouns – also personal names and/or kin terms – 'are based on their relatively high propensities for a consistently given information status, rather than on a lexical "agency potential"' (Du Bois 1987: 845). In other words, personal pronouns by definition always represent given, not new information, thereby realized linguistically by old non-lexical mentions, not by new lexical mentions. This means that the given/new-based pressure to ergativity in personal pronouns is extremely weak or even absent, thereby giving way to the topic continuity pressure to accusativity. Therefore, personal pronouns are susceptible to the nominative-accusative alignment. As for the bottom of the Nominal Hierarchy, taken care of by the ergative-nominative system, the given/new-based pressure to ergativity persists, thereby suppressing the topic continuity pressure to accusativity. But in some languages (e.g. Nhanda in 3.3.1) the split does take place much lower on the Nominal Hierarchy than personal pronouns vs. the rest. The existence of such languages could potentially be embarrassing for Du Bois's explanation, as pointed out by Croft (1990: 197), but can probably also be dealt with by reference to the scale of 'empathy' as suggested by DeLancey (1981: 645) (cf. the concentric circles of egocentrism in 3.9).

Finally, there are two potential problems with Du Bois's theory of the discourse basis of ergativity. First, the topic continuity pressure to accusativity links A and S in opposition to P. Thus A and S are topical or unmarked, whereas P is non-topical or marked. Indeed this difference in topicality between A and S on the one hand, and P on the other is nicely reflected in actual case marking itself because, as has already been noted in 3.5, the nominative is most frequently realized by zero (or at least a zero allomorph), whereas the accusative has non-zero realization. What about the given/ new-based pressure to ergativity? Du Bois (1987: 817, 845) points out correctly that given status – as opposed to new status – is the norm for nominal reference with the effect that given information is more common than new in the domain of nominal reference. This is, in fact, totally expected because narratives generally revolve around certain selected participants and around what actions or activities they carried out or did not carry out. Given information, which is realized by old non-lexical mentions in A function, is unmarked, and new information, which is realized by new lexical mentions in S and P functions, is marked. But recall that it is almost always the case that the ergative is marked by a non-zero element, whereas the absolutive is marked by zero. Thus there seems to be a mismatch between functional and formal markedness, something that is baffling for Du Bois's interpretation of the given/new-based pressure to ergativity. Second, it is not clear how the ergative-absolutive system actually arises out of the given/new-based pressure to ergativity. To put it differently, what is (are) the mechanism(s) through which the ergative discourse pattern becomes grammaticalized into the ergative-absolutive case marking system (cf. Du Bois 1987: 851)? For instance, how does the non-zero ergative case marker get to be assigned to the NP in A function?

3.11   Case marking in altered or non-basic constructions

In the present chapter case marking in basic transitive and intransitive clauses – i.e. with verbs in simple active declarative form – has so far been examined. But languages are also known to have the option of altering basic clausal patterns for grammatical, semantic or discourse purposes. When the basic clausal pattern undergoes such alteration, so does case marking. In the present section two major types of change in clausal patterns – demotion and promotion – will be discussed. In the former basic transitive clauses are converted into intransitive ones through demotion to peripheral argument status (or optional loss) of one of the core argument NPs. In the latter non-core or peripheral argument NPs are promoted to core argument NP status. Both demotion and promotion may be involved in a single instance of alteration of clausal patterns. There are four important devices of clausal alteration in the languages of the world: passive, antipassive, noun incorporation and advancement of non-core arguments. Each of these will be examined in turn here.

3.11.1   Passive

The passive is typically found in languages with the nominative-accusative system. In the passive clause the A of the active transitive clause is demoted to an adjunct (agent) phrase – very frequently marked by an oblique adposition or case – and the P of the active transitive clause is promoted to the S, with the effect that the total number of core argument NPs is reduced from two in the original active transitive clause to one in the corresponding passive clause.[14] The reduction in the number of core argument NPs is signalled on the verb either by a verbal affix or by a periphrastic element in the verb phrase. In many languages with the passive it is also possible to omit or suppress the adjunct (agent) phrase completely (cf. Dixon 1994: 152). K'ekchi provides a good example of the passive (Berinstein 1990; also Whaley 1997: 186).

(85)   K'ekchi
    x-at-in-bok   (lian)
    TNS-2-1-call (I)
    'I called you.'

(86)   K'ekchi
    x-at-bok-e'   (laat) (in-ban)
    TNS-2-call-PASS (you) (I-by)
    'You were called by me.'

Note that the active verb in (85) carries verbal prefixes for both A and P (i.e. core argument NPs) but the verb in the passive in (86) only registers the presence of S (corresponding to the P of the active clause in (85)) since the A of the basic transitive clause is now demoted to a peripheral NP, clearly marked by an oblique case suffix *-ban*. In many languages the adjunct (agent) phrase is omitted by preference as in Turkish (Perlmutter and Postal 1983: 4–5) and K'ekchi, or obligatorily as in Ulcha (Nichols 1979b, Foley and Van Valin 1984: 155).

(87)   Turkish
    Hasan-Ø bavul-u   açtı
    Hasan   suitcase-ACC open-PST
    'Hasan opened the suitcase.'

(88) Turkish
      bavul-Ø   (Hasan tarafından) açıldı
      suitcase-NOM (Hasan by)   open-PASS.PST
      'The suitcase was opened by Hasan.'

(89) Ulcha
      ti   dūse-we   hōn-da ta-wuri
      DEM tiger-ACC how-Q do-PASS
      'What's to be done about that tiger?'

Note that in Turkish the *S* of the passive is marked by the nominative case
just as is the A of the active clause, and that the A of the active is marked by
an oblique postposition in the passive should it ever appear on the surface at
all. Ulcha also illustrates a variation on the passive in that in some languages
– e.g. Nanai, Finnish and Ute – the passive involves only demotion of the
A of the active transitive clause with the P remaining intact. Thus in (89)
the NP *ti dūse* is still marked by the accusative case, which is used for the
marking of P. Note that the verb is suffixed with the passive -*wuri*; it is now
intransitive.

   One of the major functions of the choice between the active and the
passive seems to be maintenance of discourse cohesion as is most evident
in NP ellipsis under coreference in conjoined or coordinated clauses. This
is demonstrated by the following German data taken from Foley and Van
Valin's (1984: 150–1) discussion, based on Zubin (1979).

(90) German
      Der   Junge hat   das   Butterbrot gegessen
      the-NOM boy   have-3SG the-ACC sandwich   eat-PST.PART
      und dann Ø ist   ins Kino gegangen
      and then   be-3SG into movie go-PST.PART
      'The boy ate the sandwich and then went to the movie.'

(91) German
      Er   wurde   zusammengeschlagen und
      3SG-NOM became-3SG beat.up-PST.PART   and
      Ø dann ging   ins Krankenhaus
        then went-3SG into hospital
      'He was beaten up and then went to the hospital.'

The zero symbol (Ø) indicates ellipsis in the second conjunct clause of NPs
under coreference with A or S. Note that it is either A or S, not P, that is
either the controller or target of NP ellipsis in German (that is, A = S in
(90), or S = S in (91); see below for the NP ellipsis under coreference in the
antipassive in 3.11.2); in (91) the *S = S* coreference is achieved only by means

of passivization of the first conjunct clause. Often, the passive is also used to highlight 'the result of an activity on the patient [or the undergoer]' (Dixon 1994: 148) rather than the activity itself. (Also see Chapter 4 for a different grammatical role of passivization in relativization.)

3.11.2   Antipassive

The antipassive is sometimes regarded as the counterpart of the passive in languages with the ergative-absolutive system (e.g. Palmer 1994: 18). But it should not be inferred from this that the passive is never found in languages with the ergative-absolutive system. In fact, as Dixon (1994: 17) notes, both the passive and the antipassive occur in the same language. For instance, Mam, a language with the ergative-absolutive system, has one antipassive construction and also at least four different types of passive. Eskimo and Basque are akin to Mam in this regard (Dixon 1994: 149–50). In the antipassive the A of the active clause appears as S, marked by the absolutive case, with the P of the basic transitive clause demoted to peripheral status. Moreover, just as the adjunct (agent) phrase is optionally or obligatorily eliminated from the passive clause, the demoted P of the basic transitive clause in the antipassive can optionally be omitted or must be suppressed completely from the clause. When present in the antipassive, however, the demoted P of the active clause is accordingly marked by a non-core or oblique case. This suggests that the antipassive is as much intransitive or detransitivized as is the passive. Note also that the verb in the antipassive also bears an affix as a signal of detransitivization. Dyirbal provides a good example of the antipassive (Dixon 1972). Note that in this Australian language the P of the basic transitive clause is marked by the dative case -gu in the corresponding antipassive clause, with the verb suffixed with -ŋa-y (Dixon 1972: 65–6).

(92)   Dyirbal
       balan dʸugumbil baŋgul yaṛa-ŋgu balga-n
       F-ABS woman-ABS M-ERG man-ERG hit-NFUT
       'The man is hitting the woman.'

(93)   Dyirbal
       bayi   yaṛa   bagun   dʸugumbil-gu balgal-ŋa-nʸu
       M-ABS man-ABS F-DAT woman-DAT hit-APASS-NFUT
       'The man is hitting the woman.'

A similar situation is found in Greenlandic Eskimo (Woodbury 1977). In this language, as with Dyirbal, A is case-marked as ergative and P as absolutive in the basic transitive clause. In the antipassive the original A is case-marked as absolutive, with the original P demoted to peripheral status, marked by the instrumental case. The verb accordingly registers a change of transitivity by means of the antipassive suffix -*NNig* (cited in Foley and Van Valin 1984: 171).

(94) Greenlandic Eskimo
      arna-p   niqi-Ø   niri-vaa
      woman-ERG meat-ABS eat-IND.3SG
      'The woman ate the meat.'

(95) Greenlandic Eskimo
      arnaq-Ø   niqi-mik   niri-NNig-puq
      woman-ABS meat-INST eat-APASS-IND.3SG
      'The woman ate some of the meat.'

In some languages the demoted original P of the basic transitive clause must be completely eliminated from the antipassive clause as the demoted original A may be in some languages with the passive. A case in point comes from Bandjalang (Crowley 1978 cited in Foley and Van Valin 1984: 172).

(96) Bandjalang
      mali-yu   ḍa:ḍam-bu mala-Ø   bulan-Ø   ḍa-ila
      that-ERG child-ERG that-ABS meat-ABS eat-PRS
      'The child is eating the meat.'

(97) Bandjalang
      mala-Ø   ḍa:ḍam-Ø   ḍa-le-ila
      that-ABS child-ABS eat-APASS-PRS
      'The child is eating.'

As with the passive the antipassive is sometimes also exploited for maintenance of discourse cohesion, i.e. NP ellipsis under coreference in conjoined clauses (cf. discussion of German above). A detailed examination of this phenomenon will be carried out in the next section on syntactic ergativity but a brief description of how this works may be appropriate and useful at this juncture. Again, the data come from Dyirbal (Dixon 1972, Foley and Van Valin 1985: 336).

(98) Dyirbal
      bayi   yaṛa   bani-nʸu   bagun   dʸugumbil-gu
      M-ABS man-ABS come-NFUT F-DAT woman-DAT
      buṛal-ŋa-nʸu
      see-APASS-NFUT
      'The man came and saw the woman.'

(99) Dyirbal
      bayi   yaṛa   bagun   dᵞugumbil-gu buṛal-ŋa-nᵞu
      M-ABS man-ABS F-DAT woman-DAT see-APASS-NFUT
      waynᵞdyi-n
      go.uphill-NFUT
      'The man saw the woman and went uphill.'

In (98) the NP in *S* function in the first conjunct clause is the controller of
NP ellipsis, with the target of NP ellipsis in the second conjunct clause also
in *S* function. But note that the second conjunct clause is antipassivized with
the effect that the A of the basic transitive clause, if explicitly expressed,
would now be marked as *S* by the absolutive. In other words, the NP ellipsis
under coreference in (98) does not involve the NP in A function. Similarly,
in (99) the controller of NP ellipsis in the first conjunct clause is placed in *S*
function by way of antipassivization so that the coreferential NP, which is in
S function, can be deleted from the second conjunct clause. The point is that
the two Dyirbal sentences will be ungrammatical without antipassivization of
the second conjunct clause in (98) or the first conjunct clause in (99) because
NP ellipsis under coreference will otherwise be between *S* and A in (98),
or between A and *S* in (99). In Dyirbal NP ellipsis under coreference in
conjoined clauses – and also other grammatical operations – is based on
S = *S* – as will be shown in 3.12, also on *S* = P or P = *S* – not on *S* = A, or
A = *S*. This thus contrasts starkly with the NP ellipsis under coreference in
German, which is based on A = *S*, or *S* = A to the exclusion of P. In German
in the case of A = P, or P = A, the passive comes into play in order to
promote P to *S* so that NP ellipsis under coreference can be executed on
the basis of A = *S*, or *S* = A. It is in this respect that the antipassive and
the passive are sometimes thought of as 'functionally parallel constructions'
(Foley and Van Valin 1984: 170). (Also see Chapter 5 for a different grammatical role of antipassivization in causativization.)

   In addition to the role that it plays in NP ellipsis under coreference in
conjoined clauses the antipassive has a semantic function, 'indicating un-
completed or habitual activity or a nonspecific patient [or P]' (Mallinson and
Blake 1981: 75; also see Comrie 1978: 359–60, Foley and Van Valin 1984:
175–6). In Kabardian, for instance, the antipassive is used to express incom-
pleteness of the action and thus a partially affected P (Catford 1976).

(100) Kabardian
       ħe-m   qʷɨpŝħe-r je-dzaq'e
       dog-ERG bone-ABS bite
       'The dog bites the bone (through to the marrow).'

(101) Kabardian
       ħe-r   qʷɨpŝħe-m je-w-dzaq'e
       dog-ABS bone-ERG APASS-bite
       'The dog is gnawing the bone.'

Based on Kibrik (1990) Dixon (1994: 149) also mentions Bezhta, in which the antipassive is used to express the meaning of potential mood, in contrast with the basic transitive clause. Cooreman (1994) provides a useful overview of semantic/pragmatic functions of the antipassive based on a sample of nineteen 'ergative' languages. She (1994: 51, 81) also makes an attempt to offer a general definition of the various semantic/pragmatic functions by reference to difficulty with which P of a proposition is or can be clearly and uniquely identified.

3.11.3   Noun incorporation

Noun incorporation is another type of device of clausal alteration found in many languages of the world, whereby one of the arguments of the clause is incorporated into the verb, thus losing its syntactic status as an argument of the clause. The passive is normally found in languages with the nominative-accusative system, whereas the antipassive tends to be associated with languages which are organized on the ergative-absolutive basis not just in case marking but also possibly in other grammatical areas (Mallinson and Blake 1981: 74, Dixon 1994: 147). Noun incorporation, however, has not been correlated strongly with any particular type of case marking system. For instance, Mithun (1984: 874) points out that noun incorporation 'operates equally in nominative/accusative, ergative/absolutive and agent/patient [active-stative] systems' although Palmer (1994: 191) suggests that it is 'a feature found mostly with ergative systems'.

When one of the arguments of the clause is incorporated into the verb, the resulting larger derived verb stem may function as a single word, undergoing all word-internal phonological processes. In Chukchi (Comrie 1973: 243–4; also Hopper and Thompson 1980: 257, and Mithun 1984: 875), for instance, vowels of incorporated nouns must participate in word-internal vowel harmony in conjunction with host verbs.

(102)   Chukchi
       tumg-e   na-ntəwat-ən kupre-n
       friends-ERG set-TR   net-ABS
       'The friends set the net.'

(103)   Chukchi
       tumg-ət   kopra-ntəwat-gʔat
       friend-NOM net-set-INTR
       'The friends set nets.'

Note that with the P incorporated into the verb the A of the basic transitive clause in (102) loses its ergative marking and is instead marked in (103) by the nominative case (i.e. S). In Chukchi the incorporation also motivates the verb to shed its transitive marking in favour of the intransitive marking.

Alternatively, the incorporated noun and the verb may simply be juxtaposed to form a syntactic unit, within which they remain separate words phonologically but, grammatically, they still behave as a tightly bonded unit. This simple juxtaposition of the incorporated noun and the verb is found very commonly in Oceanic languages. In Kusaiean (Sugita 1973, Lee 1975), for instance, the completive aspect suffix -læ must immediately follow the verb in the basic transitive clause but in the case of noun incorporation it follows the entire noun-incorporated verb complex (Sugita 1973: 399).

(104)   Kusaiean
        nga ɔl-læ   nuknuk ɛ
        I   wash-CMP clothes the
        'I finished washing the clothes.'

(105)   Kusaiean
        nga owo nuknuk læ
        I   wash clothes CMP
        'I finished washing clothes.'

Whether the noun is fully incorporated into the verb morphophonologically or simply is juxtaposed next to the verb, the noun-incorporated verb unit functions as an intransitive verb due to the incorporated noun abdicating its independent status as an argument of the clause.

However, noun incorporation does not necessarily give rise to detransitivization of the basic transitive clause as in the case of the passive and antipassive. There is, in fact, an interesting variation on noun incorporation with the effect that, when one of the arguments of the basic clause is incorporated into the verb, the case position vacated by that argument may then be usurped by a non-core or oblique argument, e.g. instrument, location or possessor (Mithun 1984: 856–9). In Tupinambá the possessor can be promoted to the direct object position (i.e. P) when the possessed noun is incorporated into the verb. Compare (106), and (107) (Mithun 1984: 857).

(106)   Tupinambá
        s-oβá   a-yos-éy
        his-face I-it-wash
        'I washed his face.'

(107)   Tupinambá
        a-s-oβá-éy
        I-him-face-wash
        'I face-washed him.'

In (107) the possessor or the 'derived P' is represented on the verb by the prefix s-, whereas in (106), without noun incorporation, the P is s-oβá 'his face', and it is thus registered on the verb by the prefix *yos-*. In Yucatec Mayan the case position vacated by the incorporated P is taken up by the locative NP (Bricker 1978, Mithun 1984: 858).

(108)   Yucatec Mayan
      k-in-č'ak-Ø-k   čeʼ ičil in-kool
      INCMP-I-chop-it-IPFV tree in my-cornfield
      'I chop the tree in my cornfield.'

(109)   Yucatec Mayan
      k-in-č'ak-čeʼ-t-ik   in-kool
      INCMP-I-chop-tree-TR-IPFV my-cornfield
      'I clear my cornfield.'

In some languages with noun incorporation a relatively general noun stem is incorporated into the verb, and at the same time an additional, more specific, external NP is used to 'identif[y] the argument implied by the [incorporated noun]' (Mithun 1984: 863). In Gunwin^ygu, for instance, a general noun stem *dulg* 'tree' is incorporated into the verb, with a more specific external NP *mangaralaljmayn* 'cashew nut' occurring in P function (Oates 1964, Mithun 1984: 867).

(110)   Gunwin^ygu
      ... bene-dulg-naŋ   mangaralaljmayn
         they.two-tree-saw cashew.nut
      '... They saw a cashew tree.'

Incorporated Ps tend to be non-referential, inanimate and thus non-individuated (Hopper and Thompson 1980; see 3.6). This is evident from (103) and (105), for example. Thus, when non-individuated Ps are incorporated into the verb, the derived construction is 'generally used to describe activities or events whose patients are neither specific nor countable, e.g. habitual, ongoing or projected activities; those done by several people together; or those directed at non-specific [unspecified] part of a mass' (Mithun 1984: 850). This is why the noun-incorporated verb compound tends to denote the name of institutionalized activity or state (Mithun 1984: 856). Compare (111), and (112).

(111)   John was out deer-hunting.

(112)   John hunted deer.

In some languages noun incorporation further plays an important role in management of information distribution. Thus it is also 'used to background known [old] or incidental information within portions of discourse' (Mithun 1984: 859). This type of function is associated typically with polysynthetic languages, wherein the verb carries most of the information in conjunction with obligatory pronominal affixes. Separate NPs will 'sidetrack the attention of the listener' when they do not represent informationally significant new participants (Mithun 1984: 859). In such cases noun incorporation is called for with the effect that nouns encoding old or incidental information are incorporated into the verb. (Also refer to Chapter 5 for discussion of a different grammatical role of noun incorporation in causativization.)

It has also been observed (e.g. McKay 1976: 503, Comrie 1978: 337, Mallinson and Blake 1981: 76–7, Mithun 1984: 875) that between A, S and P it is P that is most likely to be incorporated into the verb, and that, if a language incorporates one argument in addition to P, then it will be S, not A. Thus A is reported to be most resistant to noun incorporation. This tendency seems to be true of noun-incorporating languages with all types of case marking systems.

3.11.4   Advancement of obliques to P

While discussing a special type of noun incorporation in 3.11.3 reference has been made to those languages in which the case position vacated by the incorporated P is taken over by a non-core or peripheral argument such as instrument, location or possessor (e.g. Tupinambá and Yucatec Mayan). This is clearly an instance of non-core arguments being promoted to core-argument status, i.e. P. In this section languages in which non-core arguments are promoted to core-argument status in a different way will be briefly discussed and exemplified. In these languages there is a systematic, productive syntactic operation whereby peripheral or oblique arguments such as recipient, beneficiary, instrument, location, etc. can be promoted to P. In order to signal the promotion or advancement the verb is also normally marked by an affix, or what is known in the literature as the applicative affix. This type of promotion has important grammatical consequences because, when promoted to P, erstwhile oblique arguments can further be potentially promoted to S by way of, for instance, passivization (e.g. Mallinson and Blake 1981: 78, Palmer 1994: 161). (Also see Chapter 4 for further discussion of such grammatical consequences for relativization.)

In Kinyarwanda, for instance, instrumental NPs can be optionally promoted to P. Compare the following two sentences (Kimenyi 1980: 79).

(113)   Kinyarwanda
        úmwáalímu a-ra-andik-a   íbárúwa n'ííkárámu
        teacher   he-PRS-write-ASP letter   with-pen
        'The teacher is writing a letter with the pen.'

(114)   Kinyarwanda
       úmwáalímu a-ra-andik-iish-a   íbárúwa íkárámu
       teacher   he-PRS-write-INST-ASP letter   pen
       'The teacher is writing a letter with the pen.'

The instrumental NP in (113) is promoted to P in (114), evidence for which can be adduced from the fact that the instrumental NP, which is marked by the instrumental case prefix in (113), appears with no marking in (114). Moreover, this advancement must also be registered on the verb by the instrumental suffix -*iish* as in (114). In Kinyarwanda other oblique nominals such as locatives and benefactives can also be similarly promoted to P, albeit with some complication in the case of locative advancement. This type of advancement is, in fact, very common in Bantu languages (see Baker 1988, Bresnan and Moshi 1990 and Palmer 1994: 166). Note that both the promoted instrumental NP and the postverbal NP in (114) can be further promoted to S via passivization, whereas in (113) only the postverbal NP *íbárúwa* 'letter' can be promoted to S via passivization.

Advancement of oblique NPs to P is not confined to transitive verbs but also occurs in the context of intransitive verbs as can be seen in the following examples from Kalkatungu (Blake 1990: 63), and Indonesian (Blake 1990: 7).

(115)   Kalkatungu
       kalpin nuu-mi irratyi-thi
       man   lie-FUT girl-LOC
       'The man will lie with the girl.'

(116)   Kalkatungu
       kalpin-tu nuu-nti-mi   irratyi-Ø
       man-ERG lie-LOC-FUT girl-ABS
       'The man will lay the girl.'

(117)   Indonesian
       Ali duduk diatas bangku itu
       Ali sit   on   bench   that
       'Ali sits on the bench.'

(118)   Indonesian
       Ali men-duduk-i bangku itu
       Ali TR-sit-LOC bench   that
       'Ali occupies the bench.'

In (116) what is a locative-case-marked nominal in (115) is promoted to P, which is, in fact, indicated by the fact that the verb is now marked by the locative suffix -*nti*-, and also by the fact that the NP in S function and the locative-case-marked NP in (115) are now marked by the ergative case (i.e.

A) and the absolute case (i.e. P), respectively, in (116). To put it differently, the advancement of the locative (or comitative) NP to core-argument status has resulted in transitivization of the original intransitive verb in (115) or in valence increasing. A similar comment can be made of the Indonesian pair of sentences in (117) and (118). The locative NP in (117) is preceded by the locative preposition but when it is promoted to P in (118) it rids itself of the locative preposition and this advancement is reflected on the verb by the locative suffix -*i*. In addition, the fact that the verb in (118) is now associated grammatically with two core arguments is signalled by the transitive marker *men-* prefixed to the verb.

In the standard analysis of advancement that has so far been presented in the present section the following Indonesian sentences illustrate a straightforward advancement of the beneficiary NP (e.g. Mallinson and Blake 1981: 78, Palmer 1994: 162). The beneficiary NP *guru* in (119) is promoted to P in (120), whereby it loses its benefactive preposition *untuk* and accordingly the verb is marked by the benefactive suffix -*kan*. Moreover, the promoted beneficiary NP is placed immediately to the right of the verb in (120), with the erstwhile P *pintu* removed further away from the verb.

(119)   Indonesian
        Ali mem-buka pintu untuk guru
        Ali TR-open door for   teacher
        'Ali opens the door for the teacher.'

(120)   Indonesian
        Ali mem-buka-kan guru   pintu
        Ali TR-open-BEN teacher door
        'Ali opens the door for the teacher.'

Dryer (1986), on the other hand, treats (120) as the basic or unaltered clause and (119) as an altered version of (120). His argument is based crucially on the observation that in contrast to the widely known distinction between direct object and indirect object the recipient or beneficiary NP of the ditransitive clause in many languages behaves grammatically like the direct object NP of the monotransitive clause. For instance, the verb must agree with the recipient or the beneficiary NP, not with the direct object NP in the ditransitive clause, whereas it agrees with the direct object NP in the monotransitive clause. For example, in Palauan (Josephs 1975: 96, 347) the verbal suffix -*terir* stands for the direct object NP in the monotransitive clause in (121) but for the recipient NP in the ditransitive clause in (122).

(121)   Palauan
        a   Droteo a   cholębędę-tęrir a   rę-ngalęk
        DET Droteo DET hit-3PL   DET   PL-child
        'Droteo is going to hit the children.'

(122) Palauan
    ak m-il-s-tẹrir   a   rẹ-sẹchẹl-ik   a   hong
    I   V-PST-give-3PL DET PL-friend-my DET book
    'I gave my friends a book.'

Dryer (1986: 815–18) cites a number of unrelated languages which behave like Palauan in this respect, e.g. Huichol, Khasi, Lahu and Nez Perce. In these languages the recipient or beneficiary NP of the ditransitive clause behaves like the direct object NP of the monotransitive clause but these two in turn behave differently from the direct object NP of the ditransitive clause. Dryer refers to the grouping of the first two as the primary object, and the direct object NP of the ditransitive clause as the secondary object. This can be schematized in Figure 3.10.

Figure 3.10: *Primary object vs. secondary object based on Dryer (1986)*

DITRANSITIVE:	Direct object	Recipient/Beneficiary
MONOTRANSITIVE:	Direct object	

Primary object   =
Secondary object =

In other words, the Indonesian example in (120) contains the sequence of the primary object (i.e. *guru*) and the secondary object (i.e. *pintu*) in that order, whereas in the example in (119) the secondary object (i.e. *pintu*) is promoted to primary object status, displacing the original primary object – into what relational grammarians (e.g. Perlmutter and Postal 1983) call chômeur status.

Dryer's innovative distinction between primary object and secondary object has interesting implications for a general theory of grammatical relations. First, within the traditional distinction between direct object and indirect object, the indirect object NP indeed is not like the direct object of the monotransitive clause but is treated like an oblique NP. As has been shown, however, this does not seem to be appropriate for languages such as Palauan, Huichol, Khasi, etc. in that the recipient or beneficiary NP – which would be treated as indirect object in the standard analysis – does behave like the direct object NP of the monotransitive clause. Thus Dryer (1986: 814) points out that this situation is analogous to the theoretical problem which the grammatical relations of ergative and absolutive pose for the traditional subject/object distinction (see Blake 1976, Dixon 1979, 1994). Second, Dryer (1986: 828) points out that, just as ergativity is not a property of languages but of rules, objectivity also pertains to rules, not to languages. This means that the traditional direct object/indirect object distinction and the new primary object/secondary object distinction may also apply to different rules of the same language. Dryer refers to this phenomenon as *split-objectivity*, analogous to split-ergativity. In Southern Tiwa, for instance, various rules, e.g. passive, verb agreement, etc. are indeed sensitive to the primary object/ secondary object distinction, whereas noun incorporation is based on the direct object/indirect object distinction with the effect that only direct object can incorporate into the verb. Other languages which Dryer (1986: 829–30) thinks exhibit split-objectivity include Mohawk, Tzotzil and Yindjibarndi.

Finally, Blake (1990: 8, 63; cf. Mallinson and Blake 1981: 78) points out that 'advancements to [P] are often associated with the advancee [oblique NPs] acquiring some sense of being more affected'. Thus what is conceptualized as a location in (115) is now effectively regarded as a patient in (116). In other words, the semantic effect of advancement is to emphasize the notion of affectedness. But Mallinson and Blake (1981: 78) observe that when the advancee is a beneficiary or a recipient, as in (119) and (120), 'there does not appear to be any semantic reinterpretation [of the recipient or beneficiary as the patient]'. Dryer (1986: 841), however, makes a convincing suggestion that the primary object/secondary object distinction is based on the discourse/pragmatic function of these grammatical relations: being generally human, definite or individuated in the sense of Hopper and Thompson (1980), and often first or second person, the recipient/beneficiary NP is more topical than the direct object NP, which is generally non-human, indefinite or non-individuated, and 'almost invariably third person' (Dryer 1986: 841). Following Givón (1979), Dryer (1986: 841) argues, therefore, that the recipient/beneficiary NP is a 'secondary clausal topic', after the subject NP (i.e. the principal clausal topic). The direct object/indirect object distinction, on the other hand, is more closely related to semantic roles, with direct object corresponding to theme/patient and indirect object to recipient/ beneficiary. Thus the promotion of the recipient/beneficiary NP to P gives rise to an increment in topicality of that NP. In view of this Dryer (1986: 841–2) explains why in languages such as Palauan (i.e. (121) and (122)) the recipient/beneficiary NP takes priority for verb agreement over the patient/ theme NP in the ditransitive clause: the former, due to its inherent properties, is more topical than the latter.

3.12   Syntactic ergativity

When the ergative-absolutive system was first discovered by linguists it was generally thought that this exotic alignment was only morphological or confined to case marking, whereby S and P are marked in the same way, and A in a different way. But with the appearance of Dixon's (1972) in-depth grammar of Dyirbal this assumption was quickly revealed to be false. The A/SP alignment in the ergative-absolutive case marking system is found to extend to a number of syntactic patterns – though no languages are known to be ergative at the syntactic but not at the morphological level (Dixon 1994: 172). This is referred to generally as *syntactic* or *deep ergativity* in the literature – Dixon (1994) favours 'inter-clausal ergativity' as opposed to 'intra-clausal (i.e. morphological) ergativity'.

In Dyirbal – which is arguably the most studied language in terms of syntactic ergativity – NP ellipsis under coreference in conjoined clauses (cf. 3.11.1 and 3.11.2) is carried out strictly on the A/SP basis. That is, the controller and the target of NP ellipsis must be based on $S = S$, $S = P$, $P = S$ or $P = P$ to the exclusion of $A = P$, $P = A$, $A = S$ or $S = A$. First, consider the following basic clauses (based on Dixon 1994: 10–16).

(123)   Dyirbal
        ŋuma-Ø   banaga-nʸu
        father-ABS return-NFUT
        'Father returned.'

(124)   Dyirbal
        ŋuma-Ø   yabu-ŋgu   bura-n
        father-ABS mother-ERG see-NFUT
        'Mother saw father.'

(125)   Dyirbal
        yabu-Ø   ŋuma-ŋgu   bura-n
        mother-ABS father-ERG see-NFUT
        'Father saw mother.'

When conjoined with each other, (123) and (124) share one NP, *ŋuma*. This particular NP can thus be susceptible to ellipsis under coreference in the second conjunct clause.

(126)   Dyirbal
        ŋuma-Ø   banaga-nʸu   yabu-ŋgu   bura-n
        father-ABS return-NFUT mother-ERG see-NFUT
        'Father returned and mother saw (him).'

The controller NP in the first conjunct clause is in S function and the target of NP ellipsis in the second conjunct clause is in P function. The order of (123) and (124) can be reversed, as in (127).

(127)   Dyirbal
        ŋuma-Ø   yabu-ŋgu   bura-n   banaga-nʸu
        father-ABS mother-ERG see-NFUT return-NFUT
        'Mother saw father and (he) returned.'

In (127), again, the coreference is between the NP in P function in the first conjunct clause and the NP in S function in the second conjunct clause.

But when (123) and (125) are conjoined in either order, the coreference between the NPs across the clauses would only hold on the $S = A$ or $A = S$ basis – e.g. *Father (S) returned and (he = A) saw mother.* The outcome of this potential NP ellipsis is ungrammaticality of the conjoined clauses. This is where the antipassive comes into play and contributes to maintenance of the ergativity constraint on NP ellipsis under coreference in Dyirbal. Thus (123) and (125) can successfully be conjoined with NP ellipsis in full force owing to the antipassive.

(128)   Dyirbal
    ŋuma-Ø   banaga-n^{y}u   bural-ŋa-n^{y}u   yabu-gu
    father-ABS return-NFUT see-APASS-NFUT mother-DAT
    'Father returned and (he) saw mother.'

(129)   Dyirbal
    ŋuma-Ø   bural-ŋa-n^{y}u   yabu-gu   banaga-n^{y}u
    father-ABS see-APASS-NFUT mother-DAT return-NFUT
    'Father saw mother and (he) returned.'

In (128) the controller NP in the first conjunct clause is in S function and the target NP (or the omitted NP) in the second clause is also in S function only because the latter NP has been changed from its original A function through antipassivization of the second clause. In (129) the NP *ŋuma* in the first clause is also converted from A to S via antipassivization so that it can function as the controller of the omitted coreferential NP in the second clause, which is in S function. The antipassive thus ensures that NP ellipsis under coreference be confined to NPs in S or P function to the exclusion of NPs in A function. Other syntactic patterns that also operate on the ergative-absolutive basis in Dyirbal are relativization and purposive-type conjoined clauses (see Dixon 1994: 168–72 for further discussion). This ergative-absolutive basis in Dyirbal syntax contrasts clearly with the nominative-accusative basis in German syntax, as illustrated in 3.11.1 (i.e. (90) and (91)).

Syntactic ergativity in, for instance, conjoined clauses in Dyirbal cuts across morphological ergativity. That is, NP ellipsis under coreference does not pay heed to the actual case marking of coreferential NPs but operates strictly on the A/SP basis (Dixon 1994: 161). Recall that the first and second person pronouns in Dyirbal are based on the nominative-accusative system. Consider (Dixon 1994: 164):

(130)   Dyirbal
    ŋana-Ø   banagu-n^{y}u   bural-ŋa-n^{y}u   n^{y}urra-ngu
    we.all-NOM return-NFUT see-APASS-NFUT you.all-DAT
    'We returned and (we) saw you all.'

(131)   Dyirbal
       ŋana-na   jaja-ŋgu   ŋamba-n   bural-ŋa-nʸu
       we.all-ACC child-ERG hear-NFUT see-APASS-NFUT
       nʸurra-ngu
       you.all.DAT
       'The child heard us and (we) saw you all.'

Dixon (1994: 178–9) reports that other Pama-Nyungan languages and Mayan languages also show syntactic ergativity. The Mayan languages, for instance, operate a number of syntactic rules on the A/SP basis; thus, only NPs in S or P function can be relativized, focused, negated or questioned, with NPs in A function first changed to S through antipassivization (Dixon 1994: 178). In Chukchi the antipassive construction is preferred with some verbs for WH-questions on A, whereas WH-questions on P must be formed in ergative clauses (Kozinsky, Nedjalkov and Polinskaja 1988).

Not all languages with the ergative-absolutive case marking system exhibit syntactic ergativity. In fact, only a small portion of these languages are known to do so (Dixon 1994: 172, 175). For instance, languages such as Hindi, Basque, North-east Caucasian languages and Papuan languages are organized completely on the nominative-accusative basis in syntax, their (partial) morphological ergativity notwithstanding. Furthermore, in languages which exhibit syntactic ergativity it is not necessarily the case that all syntactic rules operate on the A/SP basis. In Chukchi (Comrie 1989: 115–16) the infinitive construction is based on the nominative-accusative system with the NP in S or A function omitted in the infinitive clause. But in the negative participial construction NPs in S or P function in the participial clause can be relativized on to the exclusion of those in A function. Similarly, in Quiché reflexivization is organized on the nominative-accusative basis to the effect that only A and S can function as the controller of reflexivization, whereas in relativization the A/SP organization is adopted so that it is S or P, not A, that can be relativized on (Larsen and Norman 1979, Dryer 1986; also see 4.7 and 4.8). Dixon (1994: 176) also reports Yidinʸ and Tongan to be similar to Chukchi and Quiché with some syntactic patterns operating on the nominative-accusative basis, and others on the ergative-absolutive basis.

3.13   Head marking vs. dependent marking

At the beginning of the present chapter a brief reference was made to the typological distinction between head marking and dependent marking, theorized and popularized by Nichols's (1986) work, based on a core sample of sixty languages. Head marking and dependent marking can be observed at the phrasal, clausal and sentential levels. At the phrasal level, for instance, if the morphology of agreement, government, etc. is marked on the head of the possessive phrase (i.e. the possessed or N), it is an instance of head marking; if, on the other hand, such marking is represented on the dependent of the possessive phrase (i.e. the possessor or G), it is dependent marking. This distinction at the phrasal level is exemplified by Chechen (for dependent marking) and Abkhaz (for head marking) (Nichols 1986: 60).

(132)   Chechen
        de:-n   a:xča
        father-GEN money
        'father's money'

(133)   Abkhaz
        à-č'k°'ən yə-y°nә̀
        the-boy   his-house
        'the boy's house'

The same phrase-level distinction between head marking and dependent marking also applies to the adpositional phrase with the adposition as its head. Again, the data come from Chechen (for dependent marking) and Abkhaz (for head marking) (Nichols 1986: 60).

(134)   Chechen
        be:ra-na   t'e
        child-DAT on
        'on the child'

(135)   Abkhaz
        a-jә̀yas   a-q'nә̀
        the-river its-at
        'at the river'

At the sentential level the difference between head marking and dependent marking is exhibited by relativization, for instance. The modified NP in the main clause is the head, whereas the modifying clause is the dependent clause – e.g. *the boy* is the modified NP, and the rest the modifying clause in *the boy who flew out of the window* (cf. Chapter 4). If the relative-clause NP is affected by either deletion or pronominalization (e.g. relative pronouns), while the main clause is not altered at all, it is an example of dependent-marked relativization. If, on the other hand, the locus of such alteration resides within the main clause, not within the relative clause, it is head-marked relativization. An example of dependent-marked relativization comes from Korean, whereas an example of head-marked relativization is provided by Navajo (Platero 1974: 10) – both examples of relativization by way of deletion as indicated by Ø (cf. 4.2).

(136) Korean
kiho-ka   [nε-ka Ø manna-n]   haksεŋ-ita
Keeho-NOM [I-NOM meet-REL] student-is
'Keeho is the student whom I met.'

(137) Navajo
[łééchąą'í maa'iitsoh bishxash-ę́ę]   Ø nahał'in
dog   wolf   3.PFV.3.bitten-REL   IPFV.3.bark
'The dog that was bitten by the wolf is barking.'

Marking of A, S and P is a typical example of head vs. dependent marking at the clausal level. Recall that the verb is the head of the clause, with its arguments being the dependents of that clause. Chechen and Abkhaz provide an example of dependent marking and head marking, respectively, at the clausal level (Nichols 1986: 61).

(138) Chechen
da:-s   woʕa-na urs-Ø   tü:xira
father-ERG son-DAT knife-NOM struck
'The father stabbed the son with a knife.'

(139) Abkhaz
a-xàc'a a-pħ°ǝs   a-š°q°'ǝ Ø-lǝ̀-y-te-yt'
the-man the-woman the-book it-to.her-he-gave-FIN
'The man gave the woman the book.'

There may be two different types of variation on head marking and dependent marking. First, the position of marking may be determined by purely syntactic constraints or rules. The auxiliary verb in many Uto-Aztecan languages, for instance, must generally be placed in sentence-second position. Also subject to syntactic constraints is the so-called phrase-internal linker in Tagalog, which must be attached to whichever comes first within the phrase, be it head or dependent. Nichols (1986: 65) calls this type of marking as 'neutral marking'. Second, grammatical marking can be represented not only on the head but also on the dependent as demonstrated by the following Turkish example. This is referred to as 'double marking' in Nichols (1986: 65).

(140) Turkish
ev-in   kapɨ-sɨ
house-GEN door-3SG
'the door of the house'

Languages such as Aleut, Arabic and Huallaga Quechua also fall into the category of double marking although the tendency is for double marking to be confined to one or a few constituent types (Nichols 1986: 72). Moreover, languages may be characterized as having neither head marking, nor dependent marking. This is often the case with languages with little or no morphology (Nichols 1986: 65).

Languages may be consistently head-marked (e.g. Abkhaz, Blackfoot, Chumash, Cree, Lakhota, Nootka, Shuswap, Tzutujil, Wichita, Wiyot, etc.), or consistently dependent-marked (e.g. Chechen, Batsbi, Dyirbal, German, Greek, Hawaiian, Mongolian, Russian, Samoan, Uradhi, etc.) (Nichols 1986: 71–2). But other languages may be regarded as 'split' with some patterns head-marked and others dependent-marked. Nichols (1986: 72) lists Adyghe, Basque, Finnish, Georgian, Nanai, Squamish, Tongan, Yurok, etc. as 'split-marking' languages. Nichols (1986: 72) also points out that, though many languages are predominantly either head marking or dependent marking, no languages may be exclusively of one or the other type.

More importantly, Nichols (1986) proposes a number of fascinating correlations between the typological parameter of head/dependent marking and other structural properties. For instance, head marking is more favoured at the clausal level than at the phrasal level, and also more at the phrasal level than at the sentential level. Conversely, dependent marking is more likely to be favoured at the sentential level than at the phrasal level, and more so at the phrasal level than at the clausal level (Nichols 1986: 75). Furthermore, person, number and/or gender agreement prefer head marking to dependent marking. So do quantifiers, delimiters, negation, etc., with the head, rather than dependent, of the constituent in their scope (Nichols 1986: 77). Dependent marking, on the other hand, is much favoured by adjuncts or peripheral/oblique NPs – those denoting location, instrument, etc. – in the form of case markers, or adpositions (Nichols 1986: 78–9). Nichols (1992: 100–5) also addresses the interesting question of whether there is a significant correlation between head/dependent marking and different case marking systems or alignments. Her data thus reveal that the nominative-accusative alignment seems to be compatible with both head and dependent marking although the ergative-absolutive alignment prefers dependent-marking morphology. Moreover, the active-stative alignment and the direct-inverse alignment strongly favour head-marking morphology (see 3.4; cf. Mithun 1991: 540; Dixon 1994: 90).

Nichols (1986: 79–83, 104) also perceives correlations between head/dependent marking and word order with the effect that head marking favours V-initial order, whereas dependent marking disfavours it – in fact, dependent marking, split marking and double marking are claimed to favour V-final order.[15] These correlations are upheld in her later work (1992), based on a much larger and better stratified sample of 174 languages:[16] V-initial order – and also unknown order or lack of any basic order pattern – prefers head marking, whereas V-final or V-medial order favours dependent marking.

Siewierska and Bakker (1996: 116), however, point out that Nichols's correlation between head marking and V-initial order 'holds only for the *combined* head marking at clause and NP levels [emphasis added]'. They (1996: 116) also think that it is only at the clausal level that Nichols's data provide evidence for 'merely a weak preference for head marking in [V-initial] languages rather than an actual correlation between the two'. Moreover, they argue that, because Nichols's study does not make a subject/object distinction in head marking at the clausal level (that is, verbal agreement), it is not clear whether V-initial order actually correlates with head marking of subject (i.e. subject agreement) or object (i.e. object agreement), or even with head marking of both. To find this out Siewierska and Bakker (1996) carry out a fine-tuned investigation of Nichols's putative correlation, based on a much larger sample of 237 languages, and reach a number of interesting conclusions. First, head marking of subject and that of object are as likely to be employed in V-final languages as in V-initial languages – in fact, they discern no statistically significant difference between the two orders (see below) – whereas V-medial languages are likely to shun head marking of both subject and object. When these tendencies are re-examined in terms of Dryer's (1991) six *linguistic areas* for possible geographical effect, however, V-initial languages are found to be more likely to exhibit head marking of subject than V-final languages, whereas there is an overall dispreference for head marking of subject in V-medial languages. Thus this particular finding ties in well – at least on areal grounds – with Nichols's (1992) correlation of head marking and V-initial order. Head marking of object, on the other hand, is as prone to occur in V-final languages as in V-initial languages. In other words, there is no clear tendency or preference for head-marked object to occur in V-initial languages, in contrast to head-marked subject. This suggests that Nichols's correlation between head marking and V-initial order does not extend to head marking of object.

Finally, Nichols (1986, 1992) advances an intriguing functional explanation for the putative correlation of head marking and V-initial order and that of dependent marking and V-final order. With the verb coming first in head-marking languages the grammatical relations of the core argument NPs are established at the outset because those grammatical relations are marked on the verb. With the NPs coming first in dependent-marking languages, on the other hand, identification of the grammatical relations of the core argument NPs is also achieved at the outset because those grammatical relations are marked on the NPs. In other words, the correlations in question are claimed to reflect the way in which identification of the grammatical relations of the core argument NPs is facilitated with a view to 'streamlin[ing] the hearer's processing' (Nichols 1986: 82; also 1992: 108–9). As Siewierska and Bakker (1996: 137) point out, however, there is an extremely high proportion of head marking in V-final languages, in fact, to the extent that the difference in the overall distribution of head marking in V-initial and V-final languages is statistically non-significant (Siewierska and Bakker 1996: 137) – i.e. 84 per cent in V-final languages vs. 88 per cent in V-initial languages in Siewierska and Bakker's sample but 86 per cent in V-final languages vs. 95 per cent in V-initial languages in Nichols's (1992) sample (Siewierska and Bakker 1996: 130). In view of Nichols's functional explanation there is no reason why the occurrence of head marking in V-final languages should be as frequent as it is in both her own sample and Siewierska and Bakker's. In an effort to resolve this apparent problem Siewierska and Bakker (1996: 138) entertain the possibility that it is the absence, rather than the presence, of head marking that is functionally motivated in the way the Nichols claims. This means that the absence of head marking is 'a good predictor of the presence of dependent marking, but the presence of dependent marking does not entail the absence of [head marking]' (Siewierska and Bakker 1996: 138). For instance, in their sample only two of the seventeen V-final languages which lack head marking also have no dependent marking, nominal and/or pronominal; of the seventy V-final languages with nominal and/or pronominal dependent marking, on the other hand, as many as fifty-five display head marking. This alternative interpretation also seems to explain that only one of the four V-initial languages without head marking also lacks dependent marking, whereas fifteen of the seventeen V-initial languages with dependent marking also have head marking (Siewierska and Bakker 1996: 138). It has to be borne in mind, however, that the number of the V-initial languages which exhibit the absence of head marking is too small to draw firm conclusions. Moreover, take neat account of the data on hand as Siewierska and Bakker's alternative approach may, there still remains the fundamental question of why the presence of dependent marking, which is claimed to be functionally motivated by the absence of head marking, does not in turn obviate reliance on head marking.

3.14   Case marking type and word order type

In his pioneering paper Greenberg (1963b: 96) observes that, if in a language the verb follows both the nominal subject and nominal object as the dominant order, the language almost always has a case system (i.e. his Universal 41). Thus Greenberg detects a possible correlation between the presence of case marking and SOV order though it has long been assumed that word order is an alternative to case marking for purposes of indicating 'who is doing X to whom'. There has indeed been much – perhaps often casual – interest in the relationship between case marking type, and word order type among linguistic typologists. But it is fair to say that this question has never received so much attention as the frequencies of the basic word orders as has been surveyed in Chapter 2. As a matter of fact, as Siewierska

Table 3.4: *Case marking and word order based on Mallinson and Blake (1981)*

	VSO	SVO	SOV
[+case]	3	9	34
[−case]	6	26	7
Total	9	35	41

Table 3.5: *Dominant alignment and word order in Nichols (1992)*

Alignment	V-initial	V-medial/final	Total	
Accusative	10	64	74	
Ergative+Stative–Active	9	26	35	
Total	19	90	109	$(p \approx 0.10)$

(Adapted from Nichols 1992: 113)

(1996: 161) puts it, '[t]he relationship between the various non-neutral align-ments and word order type has aroused little curiosity'. Indeed no serious work on the frequencies of case marking systems had been undertaken, at least not until very recently.

Apart from occasional impressionistic statements (e.g. Vennemann 1974a, W.P. Lehmann 1978b), Mallinson and Blake (1981: 179) may probably be one of the first few typological works to address the issue in question in a statistical sense, based on a sample of 100 languages (cf. Steele 1978). Their findings are presented in Table 3.4 (also Blake 1994: 15).

It is glaringly obvious from Table 3.4 that SOV tends to employ case marking, whereas SVO tends to lack case marking. There are too few VSO languages to make any comment about VSO and case marking.

But contrary to Mallinson and Blake's (1981) results, and also to the widely held assumption Nichols (1992: 112–13) argues that there are no significant correlations between word order type and alignment (or case marking) type, perhaps except for the possible correlation between non-nominative-accusative case marking, and V-initial word order as can be gleaned from Table 3.5.

But even this 'correlation' is eventually dismissed owing to the possibility of it being 'an accident of geography' – V-initial order and non-nominative-accusative case marking are relatively frequent in the New World, consisting of three large areas, namely North America, Mesoamerica and South America (Nichols 1992: 113).

Siewierska (1996), however, points to the fact that in Nichols's (1992) work only dominant alignment is taken into account relative to word order type, with the dominant alignment type identified in terms of the following criteria – which are, by the way, applied in the order given below (Nichols 1992: 92):

- the alignment in the majority of parts of speech
- the sole non-neutral type
- the alignment of nouns rather than pronouns
- in the case of tripartite splits, the most semantic of the types involved, in the following order: direct-inverse > active-stative > tripartite > ergative-absolutive > nominative-accusative

Thus whether or not lack of the correlation between word order type and dominant alignment type is also true of the alignments of each of the three different categories, i.e. nouns, pronouns and verbs, remains to be seen (Siewierska 1996: 149).[17] This is the very question that Siewierska (1996) makes an attempt to answer by carrying out a detailed and sophisticated investigation, based on a sample of 237 languages (cf. Siewierska and Bakker 1996) – these languages are selected by employing Rijkhoff *et al.*'s (1993) sampling technique in conjunction with Ruhlen's (1987) genetic classification of the languages of the world, and also by making use of Dryer's (1991) six *linguistic areas* for purposes of areal comparison (for detailed discussion of Rijkhoff *et al.* 1993 and Dryer 1991 see 1.5.3 and 1.5.4). Siewierska (1996) addresses at least three different types of potential correlation: (i) the correlation between word order type and the occurrence of neutral as opposed to non-neutral alignment; (ii) the correlation between word order type and different types of non-neutral alignment; and (iii) the correlation between word order type and dominant alignment, in direct comparison with Nichols's (1992) work.

First, Siewierska (1996: 158–60) discerns a significant correlation between word order type and occurrence of neutral vs. non-neutral alignment with nouns, pronouns and verbs – albeit with V-medial and V-initial languages exhibiting more neutral alignment than V-final languages for each of the three categories. She (1996: 160) points out, however, that the 'correlation' between word order type and neutral/non-neutral alignment in verbs 'is heavily dependent on geography', due to the minimal presence of neutral alignment in verbs in both North America and Eurasia (5 per cent and 7 per cent, respectively) – as opposed to Africa, and South-East Asia & Oceania, where neutral alignment in verbs is relatively frequent, i.e. both 41 per cent. To put it differently, it is possible to predict within the realms of statistical significance whether or not the verb in a given language will exhibit neutral or non-neutral alignment if and when that language comes from any one of the four *linguistic areas* in question.

Second, Siewierska (1996: 160–8) suggests that, though there is no significant correlation between word order type and non-neutral alignment in verbs, in the case of nouns and pronouns non-nominative-accusative alignment is found to be more common in OV languages than in VO languages. (Note that she makes use of the OV–VO typology here instead of the verb position for purposes of adequate statistical testing – for instance, the low frequencies of free and split word order languages in her sample preclude the administering of significance tests on the data.) The essence of Siewierska's statistical data on nouns is captured in Table 3.6.

However, Siewierska (1996: 167) notes that there are a number of factors which vitiate the putative correlation between non-nominative-accusative alignment and OV order. First, though there are no large *linguistic areas* in which OV languages do not exhibit non-nominative-accusative alignment, there is not a single representative or language with both non-nominative-accusative alignment and VO order in at least one *linguistic area*, i.e. Africa. Second, in VO languages the predominance of non-nominative-accusative alignment over nominative-accusative is confined to Australia-New Guinea and South America. To wit, the effect of geography seems to be more pronounced in VO languages than in OV languages. One may thus be tempted to suggest on the strength of this observation that the correlation of non-nominative-accusative and OV order is not entirely without substance. But Siewierska (1996: 167) is prudent enough to point out that, though in OV languages non-nominative-accusative is more common or equal to nominative-accusative in four of the six *linguistic areas*, the proportion of nominative-accusative as compared to non-nominative-accusative in OV languages in two of the three *linguistic areas* which display the predominance of the latter alignment – Australia-New Guinea (22 per cent vs. 41 per cent) and South America (20 per cent vs. 33 per cent), in contrast to South East Asia & Oceania (13 per cent vs. 75 per cent) – is too low to support the putative correlation of non-nominative-accusative and OV order. What, then, about the obverse possibility, a possible correlation between nominative-accusative and VO order? Siewierska reasons that this also cannot be justified because it is only in two of the six *linguistic areas* that the percentage of nominative-accusative in VO languages exceeds that in OV languages. Conversely, in four of the six *linguistic areas* the occurrence of nominative-accusative is more frequent in OV languages than in VO! Admittedly, the number of *linguistic areas* with the higher percentage of nominative-accusative in VO languages than in OV languages would go up from two to four only if neutral alignment were completely left out of consideration. But Siewierska (1996: 167) is cautiously doubtful whether this increase will 'constitute sufficient justification for positing a correlation between [nominative-accusative] and VO order.' In sum, there is no clear correlation between

Table 3.6: *Nominative-accusative/non-nominative-accusative in nouns and OV/VO typology in Siewierska (1996)*

Alignment/Linguistic area	OV	VO
EURASIA		
nominative-accusative	37%	67%
non-nominative-accusative	37%	11%
SOUTH-EAST ASIA & OCEANIA		
nominative-accusative	13%	26%
non-nominative-accusative	75%	7%
AUSTRALIA-NEW GUINEA		
nominative-accusative	22%	8%
non-nominative-accusative	41%	42%
AFRICA		
nominative-accusative	77%	20%
non-nominative-accusative	11%	0%
SOUTH AMERICA		
nominative-accusative	20%	0%
non-nominative-accusative	33%	17%
NORTH AMERICA		
nominative-accusative	27%	26%
non-nominative-accusative	18%	5%

N.B.: The percentages are computed relative to the instances of OV and VO order in each of the six *linguistic areas*.

(Adpated from Siewierska 1996: 166)

non-nominative-accusative and OV word order on the one hand, and between nominative-accusative and VO word order on the other. These considerations lead Siewierska to propose a negative – much safer – correlation between non-nominative-accusative and VO order. This correctly predicts, for instance, the observed infrequency of non-nominative-accusative in VO languages outside Australia-New Guinea, the only *linguistic area* in her sample which does display the predominance of non-nominative-accusative (i.e. 42 per cent) over nominative-accusative (i.e. 8 per cent).

Finally, Siewierska (1996: 168–72) carries out a brief comparison of her work and Nichols's (1992) in terms of dominant alignment. She imputes the discrepancy in the findings of the two works – the presence or absence of correlations – to differences in the genetic and areal make-up of the two samples. For instance, 81 per cent of the V-initial languages in Nichols's sample come from the Americas as compared to 49 per cent in Siewierska's sample (cf. Dryer 1989: 264–6); the American languages with non-nominative-accusative alignment account for 38 per cent of the total V-initial languages in Nichols's sample but 24 per cent in Siewierska's sample. More importantly, Nichols's sample – as is actually acknowledged by her (1992: 112) – contains too few (i.e. four) V-initial languages outside the Americas in contrast to Siewierska's sample, which includes four times more non-American V-initial languages. This is, as the reader will recall, what has eventually led Nichols (1992: 113) to discard the 'correlation' of non-nominative-accusative alignment and V-initial order in the first place. But the main source of the discrepancy seems to arise from the fact that in Nichols's sample 50 per cent of the dominant alignments have only been based on those associated with verbs, whereas in Siewierska's sample only 29 per cent of the dominant alignments are related to verbs (Siewierska 1996: 172) – a clear typological bias. As Siewierska's study shows, however, there is no correlation between alignment of verbs and word order type. It may thus perhaps not come as a great surprise that Nichols (1992) does not discern any correlations between alignment type and word order type on the basis of her sample. These genetic and areal differences of the samples notwithstanding Siewierska (1996: 172) demonstrates convincingly that there are significant correlations between the alignments of nouns and pronouns and word order type, especially between neutral vs. non-neutral alignment and word order type, and also between non-neutral nominal alignment and word order. These significant correlations – positive or negative – may have gone undetected in Nichols's study not least because she takes into account dominant alignment type rather than individual alignments for nouns, pronouns and verbs (Siewierska 1996: 173).

Notes

1. Different linguistic typologists may use different symbols. For instance, Dixon (1979, 1994) adopts O in lieu of P, whereas Mallinson and Blake (1981) make use of S_i in place of S. In the present chapter Comrie's (1989) A, S and P will be adopted (also Blake 1994, Whaley 1997).
2. Grammatical elements like the verbal prefixes in Swahili are referred to in the literature as 'cross-referencing agreement markers' because they agree with, or refer to NPs. In point of fact cross-referenced NPs are normally used only for emphasis, focus or contrast to the effect that they may be taken to be mere adjuncts in apposition with cross-referencing agreement

markers (Blake 1994: 14). In other words, the verb in (12) or (13), with the cross-referenced NP(s) omitted, can actually stand on its own to form a sentence. Thus cross-referencing agreement markers do function like unstressed pronouns. This function of agreement or reference is referred to as 'indexation' by Croft (1990: 14–15). Though indexation may be their primary function, cross-referencing agreement markers can indeed also be looked upon as marking core grammatical relations or semantic roles by means of their 'distinct positions within the verb', and also their 'differences of form' in (12), for instance (Mallinson and Blake 1981: 42; Blake 1994: 14). This is so particularly when the referents of cross-referenced NPs are introduced into the discourse for the first time. Thus it is only fair to say that cross-referencing agreement markers 'serve as an alternative to case [marking] in signalling grammatical relations [or semantic roles]' (Blake 1994: 14). The case-marking function, not the indexation function, of cross-referencing agreement markers is taken into account in the present chapter.

3. Some scholars believe that there is no distinction between first and second person on the hierarchy (e.g. DeLancey 1981, Wierzbicka 1981). But there is a large amount of evidence in support of first person being higher than second person (see Dixon 1994: 88–90). Furthermore, there is variation on the actual form of the hierarchy in the languages of the world. For instance, in Ojibwa and southern Cheyenne, second person outranks first person; in some Australian languages demonstratives (or third person) are outranked by personal names (Dixon 1994: 90). These languages are only a minority, however. The general tendency in the languages of the world is reasonably well represented in the Nominal Hierarchy in Figure 3.2.

4. Nichols (1992: 103) observes that the dependent-marked active-stative system is generally of the fluid-S type. She is also of the opinion that this makes functional sense because the fluid-S type encodes nominal semantic roles rather than verb categorization – as opposed to the split-S type. Borne by dependents (or NPs) of the clause nominal semantic roles are more likely to be signalled on the dependents than on the head (i.e. dependent marking). Verb categorization, on the other hand, is related directly to the verb itself, thereby being represented on the verb (i.e. head marking).

5. Both Nichols (1992) and Siewierska (1996) include the neutral system but in the present discussion it will be ignored for the reason explained earlier.

6. In Nichols's (1992: 90) table of the frequencies of the case marking systems (or what she calls alignment patterns) the sample languages are also counted in terms of dominant alignment patterns. By dominant alignment is meant the pattern that is found in the majority of syntactic categories, or the pattern that is the sole non-neutral type, the nominal rather than pronominal pattern, or the most semantic of the patterns (cf. 3.14). At any rate, in terms of dominant alignment patterns the same frequencies of the case marking systems are observed, that is the nominative-accusative being the most frequent, followed by the ergative-absolutive. The tripartite is

again the most infrequent type of case marking. Note that both the active-
stative and direct-inverse are found only on verbs.

7. As a matter of fact, in Siewierska (1996: 155) the internal splits in alignment
    among pronouns, nouns and verbs are also considered. Thus a variety of
    mixed systems are found to be in use for each of these three categories, e.g.
    nominative-accusative/ergative-absolutive, nominative-accusative/active-
    stative, etc. However, these internal splits have been left out of Table 3.2
    primarily because of their infrequency.

8. Dixon (1994: 77) entertains the possibility of treating the active-stative
    system as a hybrid of the nominative-accusative and ergative-absolutive
    systems (for a similar view see Nichols 1992: 66, 103, 105, who also
    points out that most active-stative languages seem to have a nominative-
    accusative base or slant in that most intransitive subjects are formally
    identical to transitive subjects). Analysed in this way the active-stative
    system may be taken account of by the discriminatory view. Mithun (1991:
    542), however, is firmly of the opinion that the active-stative system is a
    coherent, semantically motivated grammatical system in itself. Indeed the
    active-stative system is very different from the other two systems in that,
    as Harris (1997: 367) points out, in the active-stative system some Ss are
    treated differently from others, while in both the nominative-accusative
    system and the ergative-absolutive system S is treated uniformly.

9. The indexing function of case marking is in the sense of Hopper and
    Thompson (1980). This must not be confused with the indexation func-
    tion of cross-referencing agreement markers (Croft 1990: 14–15), referred
    to earlier in note 2. The indexing function of case marking is alternatively
    known as the characterizing function of case marking (Mallinson and Blake
    1981: 93): the function of case marking is to impute A-ness or P-ness to A
    or to P, respectively.

10. For instance, compare the following two sentences (Hopper and Thompson
    1980: 253).

    (i)   I bumped into my friend in the supermarket.
    (ii) I bumped into the door at school.

    In (i) the effect of the event will be on both participants. The NP *I* is as
    much affected as the NP *my friend*. In (ii), on the other hand, the effect of
    the event is far more on the NP *I* than on the NP *the door*.

11. In fact, Silverstein (1976) is an attempt to provide a theory of case
    marking, in which the various attested configurations of case marking are
    understood to arise out of the interaction of a number of independent
    variables (Silverstein 1981: 228–9). Four such variables are clearly identi-
    fied in Silverstein (1981: 229–30): (i) the inherent referential content of
    NPs, (ii) predicate-argument relationships at the clausal level, (iii) the
    clause-linkage between two (or more) clause-level structures in a complex
    or compound sentence, or in sequential discourse and (iv) the reference-
    maintenance relations of arguments across discourse-level structures. As
    Silverstein (1981: 235; cf. Du Bois 1987: 849) himself notes, however,

most attention has been paid to the inherent referential content of NPs (but see Foley and Van Valin 1984, Van Valin 1993b).

12. In this context note that the Nominal Hierarchy is referred to as the Agency Hierarchy, the Animacy Hierarchy or the Person/Animacy Hierarchy. These labels obviously are attempts at highlighting different parameters prominent in the hierarchy. Croft (1995: 118) also points out that the component of definiteness must also be recognized as being part and parcel of the Nominal Hierarchy because pronouns by definition are inherently definite as opposed to common nouns (covering human, animate and inanimate on the hierarchy). Thus to call the Nominal Hierarchy by one of these names really does not capture what is hidden behind the hierarchy, as it were.

13. There do not seem to be any statistical data to substantiate these observations.

14. The label 'agent phrase' is misleading in that the A of the active clause can bear semantic roles other than agent. But this is the standard term frequently used in the literature.

15. Dryer (1989: 264–6) sounds a warning that Nichols's correlation between head marking and V-initial order remains to be demonstrated primarily because '[t]he thirteen V-initial languages in her sample include four instances of pairs of languages from the same family' (cf. 3.14, and Siewierska 1996).

16. The actual number of the languages in Nichols's (1992) sample fluctuates for different purposes of her study. For instance, when she (1992: 90) compares the distribution of different case marking systems among parts of speech, she has a total of 155 languages, whereas when the dominant case marking systems are examined, only 149 languages are taken into consideration (Nichols 1992: 112).

17. Siewierska (1996: 154) speaks of agreement rather than verbs since she includes under agreement not only verbal affixes but also clitics and particles, which may not necessarily be adjacent to verbs, e.g. second position clitics. But for the sake of convenience reference is made here, in line with Nichols's (1992: 113) usage, to alignment of verbs instead of agreement.

4

Relative clauses

4.1 Introduction

The relative clause (or RC hereafter) – along with basic word order and case marking – occupies a very prominent place in linguistic typology. Keenan and Comrie's (1977) cross-linguistic study, which deals with none other than grammatical constraints on relativization or relative clause formation, is regarded as 'one of the most influential works in the language universals literature' (Fox 1987: 856). The RC construction, as is generally understood, consists of two components: the head noun and the restricting clause. The semantic function of the head noun is to establish a set of entities, which may be called the domain of relativization, following Keenan and Comrie (1977: 63), whereas that of the restricting clause is to identify a subset of the domain – a one-member subset in the case of (1) below – by imposing a semantic condition on the domain of relativization referred to by the head noun. In the following example the head noun is *the girl* and the restricting clause *whom Miss Edge coached*.

(1) The girl whom Miss Edge coached won the game.

In (1), thus, the domain of relativization is denoted by the head noun *the girl*. This domain of relativization is then 'narrowed down', as it were, to the only entity that can satisfy the condition expressed by the restricting clause *whom Miss Edge coached*. It is in this sense that the restricting clause has tradition-ally been understood to modify the head noun, hence the alternative label of the attributive clause.

   In the present chapter a survey of the types of RC found in the languages of the world will first be presented, focusing on the position of the head noun relative to the restricting clause and also on the various ways – referred to as relativization strategies in the literature – in which the role of the head noun is expressed in the restricting clause. Keenan and Comrie's

(1977) hierarchy of grammatical relations, i.e. *the Accessibility Hierarchy*, will then be discussed with a view to identifying constraints that operate cross-linguistically on relativization. Some of the predictions made by the Accessibility Hierarchy will also be shown to be better understood in the light of C. Lehmann's (1986) investigation of correlations between diverse RC-related properties. Moreover, the top end of the Accessibility Hierarchy – subject and direct object – will be re-evaluated in view of Fox's (1987) *Absolutive Hypothesis*, which shares the same conceptual basis with Du Bois's (1987) discourse analysis of ergativity, discussed in 3.10. In the last part of the chapter discussion of the relationship between RC type and word order type will be developed as a prelude to critical examination of processing-based accounts of the distribution of the 'major' RC types. In particular Hawkins's (1994) Early Immediate Constituents (EIC) Theory, which was discussed in great detail with respect to basic word order in Chapter 2, will again be taken into consideration with a view to shedding light not only on the distribution of the types of RC in relation to word order type but also on the Accessibility Hierarchy itself. In so doing other processing-based works on relativization, i.e. Kuno (1974) and Dryer (1992) will also be examined.

4.2   The position of the head noun vis-à-vis the restricting clause

There are two main types of RC, depending on whether the head noun appears outside the restricting clause or inside the restricting clause. The former type is known as the external-headed RC, whereas the latter is referred to as the internal-headed RC. English is an example of the external-headed RC, as illustrated in (1), since the head noun is positioned outside the restricting clause. Malay also exhibits the external-headed RC type (Keenan and Comrie 1977: 71).

(2)   Malay
      Ali bunoh ayam   yang Aminah sedang memakan
      Ali kill   chicken that Aminah PROG eat
      'Ali killed the chicken that Aminah is eating.'

The external-headed RC can further be classified into two types: prenominal (or RelN) and postnominal (or NRel). As the names suggest, these two types are determined on the basis of the position of the head noun relative to the restricting clause. If the restricting clause follows the head noun as in English and Malay, the external-headed RC is postnominal. But if the restricting clause precedes the head noun as in the following Basque and Japanese examples, it is known as prenominal (Keenan and Comrie 1977: 72, Keenan 1985: 143).

(3) Basque
     gizon-a-k   liburu-a eman dio-n   emakume-a
     man-the-SBJ book-the give has-REL woman-the
     'the woman that the man has given the book to'

(4) Japanese
     Yamada-san ga ka't-te   i-ru   sa'ru
     Yamada-Mr SBJ keep-PART be-PRS monkey
     'the monkey which Mr Yamada keeps'

Though it will be discussed in detail (see 4.9), it is worth noting at this juncture that there are more languages which favour postnominal RCs than prenominal RCs. Moreover, in languages with both postnominal and prenominal external-headed RCs it is the postnominal type that is less constrained in application than the prenominal type (see 4.6 for discussion).

The internal-headed RC, which is far less frequent cross-linguistically than the external-headed RC, is found in a handful of languages such as Bambara, Diegueño, Murin^ypata, Navajo, Quechua, Tibetan and Wappo. In this type of RC the head noun normally occupies the same position that it would occupy if the restricting clause were an independent – i.e. main – clause (cf. Comrie 1989: 146). The internal-headed RC in (5) comes from Tibetan (Keenan 1985: 161). Note that in (5) the head noun *thep* 'book' appears within the restricting clause.

(5) Tibetan
     Peem-ε   thep   khii-pa   the   nee   yin
     Peem (ERG) book (ABS) carry-PART the (ABS) I (GEN) be
     'The book Peem carried is mine.'

Murin^ypata also demonstrates clearly that the head noun is located inside the restricting clause (Walsh 1976 cited in Mallinson and Blake 1981: 359).

(6) Murin^ypata
     mut^yiŋga-Ø   paɲanduwi mundakɲayya-ɹe ŋayi panɲibaḍ
     old.woman-ABS arrive   earlier-ERG   me hit
     'The old woman who arrived earlier hit me.'

(7) Murin^ypata
     mut^yiŋga-ɹe   ŋayi panɲibaḍ-Ø paɲanduwi mundakɲayya
     old.woman-ERG me hit-ABS   arrived   earlier
     'The old woman who hit me arrived earlier.'

In (6) the RC as a whole is marked as A by ergative case -ɹe just as the NP *mutʸiŋga* will be without the accompanying restricting clause. In (7), on the other hand, the NP *mutʸiŋga* itself receives ergative marking because it has A function in the restricting clause but with its S function in the main clause the RC as whole is marked by the (zero) absolutive. This difference points clearly to the head noun being embedded within the restricting clause. Also note that, although it may appear to be a subordinate clause, the internal-headed RC is better understood to be an NP as it receives ergative case in (6), for instance.

The head noun in the internal-headed RC is not marked in any distinctive way to indicate its status as the head noun of the RC. This is, in fact, the tendency of languages with the internal-headed RC type although Bambara is reported to be an exception. In this West African language the head noun is signalled inside the restricting clause by a special marker *min*, which is glossed as *REL* in (8) (Keenan 1985: 162).

(8)   Bambara
       tye   ye   ne ye   so   min ye san
       man PST I   PST horse REL see buy
       'The man bought the horse which I saw.'

One of the distinguishing features of the internal-headed RC is that because of the tendency not to mark the head noun as such in the restricting clause there may be much room left for ambiguity especially when there is more than one NP inside the restricting clause. Diegueño is a good case in point. The restricting clause in (9) has at least two full NPs, each of which can potentially function as the head noun for the internal-headed RC (Keenan 1985: 163).

(9)   Diegueño
       xatəkcok-Ø wi:-m   ʔtuc-pu-c   nʸiLʸ
       dog-DO   rock-COM I.hit-DEF-SBJ was.black
       'The rock I hit the dog with was black' *or*
       'The dog I hit with the rock was black.'

In addition to the external- and internal-headed RC types there is the so-called correlative RC type – probably including the so-called adjoined RC, which is referred to briefly in 1.5.1 in relation to cross-linguistic comparability. In this type of RC the main clause and the subordinate (or restricting) clause are loosely joined together. The head noun appears within the subordinate clause and the same head noun is repeated in full form or in some anaphoric form such as pronouns, demonstrative expressions, etc. in the main clause. The head noun in the subordinate clause is more often than not distinctively marked by a special marker as the following example from Hindi demonstrates (Keenan 1985: 164).

(10) Hindi
      jis   a:dmi ka   kutta bema:r hai,
      CREL man GEN dog   sick   is
      us a:dmi ko   mai ne   dekha
      that man DO I   ERG saw
      'I saw the man whose dog is sick.'
      (lit: 'Which man's dog is sick, that man I saw.')

The special correlative marker *jis* – which is specific to the RC in Hindi –
identifies the head noun as such in the subordinate clause. Moreover, the
same noun, *a:dmi*, appears in full form in the immediately following main
clause. Warlpiri, on the other hand, seems to pick up reference to the head
noun in the subordinate clause by means of a demonstrative expression – or
zero anaphora – in the main clause (C. Lehmann 1986: 670).

(11) Warlpiri
      njuntulu-lu kutja-Ø-npa   wawiri   pantu-ṇu,
      you-ERG   SR-AUX-SBJ.2 kangaroo spear-PST
      ṇula kapi-ṇa   pura-mi   ṇatjulu-lu
      DEM FUT-SBJ.1 cook-PRS I-ERG
      'The kangaroo that you speared, I will cook [it].'

In (11) the subordinate clause is clearly marked by the subordinator *kutya* –
which can also function as a temporal subordinator. The head noun is present
in the subordinate clause and it is repeated in demonstrative form in the
main clause. Note that in both Hindi and Warlpiri the subordinate clause
precedes the main clause in the correlative RC construction. This may not
be a coincidence, albeit in need of verification (Keenan 1985: 168).
    Moreover, the correlative type of RC seems to be found in languages
which exhibit the internal-headed RC (Keenan 1985: 165). Bambara, for
instance, has not only the internal-headed RC as in (8) but also the correlative RC as in (12) (Keenan 1985: 165, C. Lehmann 1986: 665 based on Bird
1968: 43).

(12) Bambara
      ne ye   tye min   ye, o   ye   fini   fere
      I PST man CREL see, D.3 PST cloth.DEF sell
      'The man that I saw sold the cloth.'

Note that the special relative marker *min*, which is used to signal the head
noun in (8), is used again in (12). What is important here is that the head
noun in the subordinate clause is picked up by the third person deictic form
o in the main clause. Keenan (1985: 165) proposes on the basis of Downing
(1973, 1978) that the reason why the correlative RC tends to co-occur with

the internal-headed RC in the same language is that both types of RC are used mainly in V-final, especially loosely V-final, languages (see 4.9 for discussion of the possible relationship between RC type and word order type).

4.3   Expression of the head noun

In the previous section it was mentioned *en passant* how the head noun may be expressed in the restricting clause. While discussing the correlative RC it was pointed out that the head noun appears in full form in the subordinate clause, albeit often signalled by a special marker. Also, in the internal-headed RC the head noun is embedded in full form in the restricting clause; the internal-headed RC, as its name clearly indicates, has its head noun inside the restricting clause. Conversely speaking, in the case of the correlative RC the head noun is expressed either in full or anaphoric form in the main clause, whereas in the case of the internal-headed RC it is completely absent from the main clause.

In the external-headed RC type the head noun is located in full form outside the restricting clause. Thus there should be little or no variation in languages of this type as to how the head noun is expressed in the main clause. There is, however, much cross-linguistic variation – in fact, a typologically significant parameter in itself (Comrie 1989: 147) – on the way in which the head noun is expressed in the restricting clause. These different ways are referred to commonly in the literature as relativization strategies (e.g. Keenan and Comrie 1977, Comrie 1989). When the head noun and the restricting clause form the external-headed RC, the role of the head noun in the restricting clause may somehow be marked. In the English example in (1), for instance, the head noun *the girl* has P function in the restricting clause, while A function in the main clause. In (1) the word *whom* encodes the P function borne by the head noun in the restricting clause.

(1)   The girl whom Miss Edge coached won the game.

Languages may differ in representing the role of the head noun in the restricting clause. Keenan and Comrie (1977) identify two major relativization strategies, namely [+case] and [–case]. Basically, the [+case] or case-coding strategy draws upon overt formal devices to indicate the role of the head noun in the restricting clause in one way or another as in the case of *whom* in (1). Compare (1) with (13).

(13)   The girl Miss Edge coached won the game.

The restricting clause in (13), as opposed to in (1), does not explicitly signal the role of the head noun in the restricting clause. In other words, the relativization strategy exhibited in (13) is characterized as [–case] or non-case-coding. Keenan and Comrie's (1977) typology of relativization strategies, i.e. [+case] and [–case], however, is called into question by Maxwell (1979: 361, 364), who points out, among other things, that in the distinction between [+case] and [–case] it is not clear how 'case' is coded, and that the bipartite typology predicts unattested configurations of relativization strategies as possible in human language. Following Maxwell's proposal, Keenan (1985) and Comrie (1989) both recognize that there are at least four different relativization strategies: (i) gapping or obliteration; (ii) pronoun-retention; (iii) relative-pronoun; and (iv) non-reduction. The fourth strategy – i.e. full expression of the head noun in the restricting clause – will not be discussed here; it is confined largely to the internal-headed RC (e.g. Bambara, Diegueño, etc.) and to the correlative RC (Bambara, Hindi, etc.). Each of the remaining three strategies will be discussed below with exemplification.

4.3.1   The obliteration strategy

This type of expression – more accurately non-expression – of the head noun in the restricting clause is associated overwhelmingly with languages with the prenominal RC type although it is not incorrect to say that it is also found in languages with the postnominal RC type (Keenan 1985: 154). Basically, there is no expression whatsoever of the head noun in the restricting clause, hence the alternative name for the strategy, i.e. gapping. The Basque and Japanese RCs in (3) and (4) are good examples of the obliteration strategy. To see clearly how this strategy works, compare the RC in (4), repeated here, with the corresponding independent clause in (14).

(4)   Japanese
       Yamada-san ga ka't-te   i-ru   sa'ru
       Yamada-Mr SBJ keep-PART be-PRS monkey
       'the monkey which Mr Yamada keeps'

(14)   Japanese
       Yamada-san ga sa'ru   o   ka't-te   i-ru
       Yamada-Mr SBJ monkey DO keep-PART be-PRS
       'Mr Yamada keeps the monkey.'

Note that as opposed to (14) the restricting clause, *Yamada-san ga ka't-te i-ru*, in (4) has lost its original direct object NP plus its accusative-case marking, namely *sa'ru o*. In other words, the restricting clause in (4) contains no explicit formal traces of the direct object NP. Compare the English examples in (1) and (13) as well. Turkish is also known to employ the obliteration relativization strategy (C. Lehmann (1986: 666) based on Andrews (1975: 152)).

(15) Turkish
      Orhan-ın   gör-düğ-ü   adam cık-tı
      Orhan-GEN see-NR-POSS.3 man   leave-PST
      'The man Orhan saw left.'

4.3.2   The pronoun-retention strategy

This strategy involves use of a personal pronoun in the restricting clause, which is coreferential with the head noun (but cf. the correlative RC type, in which such a personal pronoun appears in the main clause, not in the restricting clause). In other words, reference to the head noun in the main clause is provided or retained in appropriate personal pronominal form in the restricting clause. Aoban, Arabic, Hebrew, Gilbertese, Kera, Persian, Urhobo, etc. are listed in Keenan and Comrie (1977, 1979) as languages exhibiting this strategy. Examples come from Gilbertese, Persian and Urhobo (Keenan and Comrie 1979: 337, 343, 349).

(16) Gilbertese
      te   mane are oro-ia   te aine
      the man that hit-him the woman
      'the man whom the woman hit'

(17) Persian
      man zan-i   râ   ke John be u   sibe zamini dâd mišenâsam
      I   woman-the DO that John to her potato   gave know
      'I know the woman to whom John gave the potato.'

(18) Urhobo
      John mle aye   l-ǫ   vbere
      John saw woman that-she is.sleeping
      'John saw the woman who is sleeping.'

    The pronoun-retention strategy is confined mainly to the postnominal external-headed RC type. The only languages with the prenominal external-headed RC type that are known to exhibit the pronoun-retention strategy are Chinese and Korean. However, even in these languages use of the strategy is heavily restricted. In Chinese it is generally employed only when the head noun has grammatical relations other than subject and direct object. In Korean it is confined to the restricting clause in which the head noun has the role of possessor and even in this case it is not always used for unknown reasons (see Song 1991b for discussion). It must also be borne in mind that the pronoun-retention strategy involves grammatical use of personal pronouns in the context of the RC construction. If personal pronouns are also in obligatory use elsewhere, the use of such personal pronouns in the RC construction should not be regarded as the pronoun-retention strategy. Rumanian, for instance, makes use of the relative-pronoun relativization strategy to be discussed in the next section. When the head noun has direct or indirect object relation in the restricting clause, a personal pronoun agreeing with that head noun must appear immediately after the relative pronoun. But Rumanian also employs personal pronouns for preverbal full direct object or indirect object NPs in simple clauses, anyway. Thus this Romance language cannot be said to use the pronoun-retention strategy but only the relative-pronoun strategy (Keenan and Comrie 1979: 344).

4.3.3 The relative-pronoun strategy

In this relativization strategy special pronouns – which generally are formally related to demonstrative expressions and/or interrogative pronouns – are used to represent the role of the head noun in the restricting clause. The relative-pronoun strategy is reported to be most frequently found in European languages and, in fact, is not very widespread cross-linguistically (Comrie 1989: 149). The English example in (1) demonstrates the use of such a special pronoun in the restricting clause. The relative pronoun *whom*, which happens to function also as an interrogative pronoun, expresses the grammatical relation of the head noun *the girl* – direct object – in the restricting clause. German, Modern Greek and Russian provide additional examples of the relative-pronoun strategy (Keenan 1985: 149, Keenan and Comrie 1979: 338, 344).

(19) German
     der Mann, den   Marie liebt
     the man   who (M.SG.ACC) Mary loves
     'the man whom Mary loves'

(20) Modern Greek
     ksero ti yineka stin opia eðose o Yanis to vivlio
     I-know the woman to whom gave the John the book
     'I know the woman to whom John gave the book.'

(21) Russian
     Ivan videl devušku, kotoruju Petr ljubit
     Ivan saw   the girl who (DO) Peter loves
     'Ivan saw the girl whom Peter loves.'

Non-European languages with the relative-pronoun strategy are Classical Nahuatl and Luganda.

What is intriguing about the relative-pronoun strategy is that there is a very strong tendency for the relative pronoun to occur leftmost in the restricting clause. This can easily be verified by looking at the examples in (19–21) – in Modern Greek the preposition is, strictly speaking, placed immediately to the left of the relative pronoun. Keenan (1985: 151) points out that Luganda may be an exception to this generalization in that in this Bantu language the relative pronoun does not appear clause-initially but is rather prefixed to the verb of the restricting clause, as in (22), although he takes special note of Givón's (1973) observation that in several other Bantu languages relativization on the direct object NP gives rise to the postposing of the subject NP in the restricting clause, thereby placing the relative pronoun clause-initially.

(22)   Luganda
       omusajja omukazi gwe-ya-kuba
       man   woman   RPRO-she-hit
       'the man who the woman hit'

As with the pronoun-retention strategy, the relative-pronoun strategy is also used mainly in conjunction with the postnominal external-headed RC type as opposed to the prenominal external-headed RC type. This may not come as a total surprise because the personal pronoun and the relative pronoun both belong to the syntactic category of pronouns, having referential function (cf. 4.6). This may perhaps also explain why some languages exhibit not only the pronoun-retention strategy but also the relative-pronoun strategy, e.g. Modern Czech, Modern Greek, Slovenian, etc. (Maxwell 1979: 367, Keenan 1985: 151). For example, the Greek sentence in (20) can alternatively be expressed by (23), using the pronoun-retention strategy (Keenan and Comrie 1979: 338).

(23)   Modern Greek
       ksero   ti yineka pu   tis   eðose o   Yanis to vivlio
       I-know the woman COMP to.her gave the John the book
       'I know the woman to whom John gave the book.'

Note, however, that in (23) the position of the personal pronoun is immediately to the right of the invariant complementizer, thus virtually clause initial.

4.3.4   Language-internal distribution of the relativization strategies

Languages may also combine different relativization strategies. For instance, in English varieties which make a distinction between the two relative pronouns *who* and *whom*, the grammatical relation of the head noun in the restricting clause is signalled by the choice between these two relative pronouns – *who* for subject (24) and *whom* for direct object (25).

(24)   the girl who won the game

(25)   the girl whom Miss Edge coached

But, when the head noun has direct object relation in the restricting clause as in (25), the relative pronoun is optional, thereby giving rise to (26).

(26)   the girl Miss Edge coached

The RC in (26) is an example of the obliteration strategy because there is no explicit or overt formal trace or signal of the role of the head noun *the girl* in the restricting clause. German is akin to English in this respect: both the obliteration strategy and the relative-pronoun strategy are employed for relativization although the former strategy produces the prenominal RC type, and the latter the postnominal RC type (cf. Maxwell 1979: 356–7).

Similarly, the obliteration strategy may also be used in conjunction with the pronoun-retention strategy as in Arabic, Chinese, Hebrew, Korean, Persian, etc. In Arabic the obliteration strategy is used for the head noun with subject relation in the restricting clause. For other grammatical relations including direct object the personal pronoun must be retained in the restricting clause for the head noun. In Chinese the obliteration strategy is normal for the head noun with subject relation in the restricting clause but the pronoun-retention strategy is used optionally for direct object, and obligatorily for other grammatical relations. In Korean the obliteration strategy is the primary relativization strategy but the pronoun-retention strategy is employed – albeit with certain poorly understood restrictions – for the head noun bearing possessor role in the restricting clause. Similar comments can be made of Hebrew and Persian.

The relative-pronoun strategy is generally not found to be used in conjunction with the pronoun-retention strategy. But the use of personal pronouns (i.e. the pronoun-retention strategy) in association with the invariant complementizer in Modern Greek, which also relies upon the relative-pronoun strategy, may come close to this configuration (see (23)). Recall, however, that the retained personal pronoun is placed immediately to the right of the invariant complementizer *pu* in (23), thereby 'mimicking' the clause-initial position of the relative pronoun. Hebrew is another similar language. This language employs the pronoun-retention strategy optionally for direct object, and obligatorily for grammatical relations other than subject but the retained pronoun may alternatively be shifted from its usual position as in (27) immediately to the right of the invariant complementizer as in (28). This particular juxtaposition of the complementizer and the personal pronoun, *she-otam*, may perhaps be analysed as a relative pronoun (Keenan 1985: 152).

(27) Hebrew
      ha-sarim   she-ha-nasi   shalax otam la-mistraim
      the-ministers COMP-the-President sent   them to Egypt
      'the ministers that the President sent to Egypt'

(28) Hebrew
      ha-sarim   she-otam   ha-nasi   shalax la-mistraim
      the ministers COMP-them the-President sent   to Egypt
      'the ministers that the President sent to Egypt'

A similar situation has been reported for Modern Czech, Slovenian and also for Bantu languages as mentioned briefly in 4.3.3.

While examining languages which combine different relativization strategies, linguistic typologists (Keenan and Comrie 1977, Keenan 1985, C. Lehmann 1986, Comrie 1989) have observed an intriguing tendency in the distribution of these strategies. Languages such as Arabic, Chinese, Hebrew, Korean and Persian utilize the pronoun-retention strategy as well as the obliteration strategy. In Persian, for example, the pronoun-retention strategy is used obligatorily for relativization of grammatical relations other than subject and direct object, and optionally for relativization of direct object, but the obliteration strategy is the relativization strategy for subject (Comrie 1989: 147–8). Thus the tendency is for the obliteration strategy to be employed for relativization of grammatical relations like subject, and for the pronoun-retention strategy to be applied to grammatical relations like oblique. What is unattested in the languages of the world is, for instance, a situation in which the obliteration strategy is applied to oblique relation and the pronoun-retention strategy to subject relation. Similarly, in Modern Czech and Slovenian the relative-pronoun strategy takes care of all grammatical relations but in the case of the pronoun-retention strategy no personal pronoun (i.e. the obliteration strategy) is used for the head noun with subject relation in the restricting clause (for both Modern Czech and Slovenian), and also for the non-masculine and inanimate head noun with direct object relation in the restricting clause (only for Modern Czech). Again, the converse situation is unattested. Intriguing as this may be, proper discussion of this phenomenon has to be deferred to the end of 4.4.

4.4   Accessibility Hierarchy: accessibility to relativization

The main objective of Keenan and Comrie's (1977; originally Keenan and Comrie 1972) celebrated investigation is to examine formal constraints on relativization. They focus on the grammatical relation of the head noun in the restricting clause (also Comrie 1989: 147) because, as will be shown in

4.7, the grammatical relation of the head noun in the main clause turns out to be typologically far less interesting. (In the present section, therefore, grammatical relation refers to that borne by the head noun in the restricting clause, not in the main clause.) Based on a sample of about fifty languages Keenan and Comrie (1977) discover that, although they vary with respect to which grammatical relations can or cannot be relativized on, languages may not do so randomly. There are regular patterns in the cross-linguistic variation. For instance, there are no languages in their sample that cannot relativize on subject although there are languages which can relativize only on subject. In other words, all languages must have at least one relativization strategy whereby subjects are relativized on. This relativization strategy is referred to by Keenan and Comrie (1977: 68) as the 'primary strategy'. There is also a very strong tendency – possibly a language universal – for relativization strategies to apply to a continuous segment of a hierarchy of grammatical relations, or of what Keenan and Comrie (1977) refer to as the Accessibility Hierarchy (or AH hereafter), defined in (29).

(29)   SBJ > DO > IO > OBL > GEN > OCOMP
       N.B.: '>' = 'is more accessible to relativization than'; SBJ = subject,
       DO = direct object; IO = indirect object; OBL = oblique;
       GEN = genitive; and OCOMP = object of comparison

The primary strategy, which must by definition apply to subject relation, may also continue to apply down to 'lower' relations on the AH and, at the point where it ceases to apply, other relativization strategies may or may not take over and apply to a continuous segment of the AH. English is one of the rare languages which can almost freely relativize on all the grammatical relations on the AH. This language thus serves as a good example by which the AH can be illustrated with respect to relativization. Consider:

(30)   the girl who swam the Straits of Dover [*SBJ*]

(31)   the girl whom the boy loved with all his heart [*DO*]

(32)   the girl to whom the boy gave a rose [*IO*]

(33)   the girl with whom the boy danced [*OBL*]

(34)   the girl whose car the lady bought for her son [*GEN*]

(35)   the girl who the boy is taller than [*OCOMP*]

The majority of the languages of the world, however, are not so generous as English in their relativizing possibilities. In fact, the very nature of the

AH is grounded on the observation that there are more languages which can – whether by primary or non-primary relativization strategies – relativize on subject than languages which can also relativize on direct object, on direct object than also on indirect object, on indirect object than also on oblique, and so forth. This suggests strongly that 'the further we descend the AH the harder it is to relativize' (Keenan and Comrie 1977: 68) – with the AH perhaps reflecting 'the psychological ease of comprehension' (Keenan and Comrie 1977: 88); see 4.10 for discussion of processing in relativization).

Two additional but related points follow from the preceding discussion. First, if it applies to a given grammatical relation on the AH, the primary strategy must then apply also to all 'higher' grammatical relations. For example, if the primary strategy in language X is known to relativize on genitive NPs, then a prediction can be made to the effect that it will also be able to relativize on subject, direct object, indirect object and oblique NPs; if the primary strategy in language Y is known to relativize on oblique NPs, then a prediction can be made to the effect that it will also be able to relativize on subject, direct object and indirect object NPs; and so forth. Moreover, all relativization strategies including the primary strategy may 'switch off' at any point on the AH but they should in principle not 'skip' on the AH (but see 4.5).

The validity of the AH can be justified if and when each grammatical relation of the AH proves to be the point at which primary strategies actually cease to apply, and also if non-primary relativization strategies commence to apply at, and to a continuous segment lower than, that point – provided, of course, that there are non-primary relativization strategies in use. As a matter of fact, Keenan and Comrie (1977, 1979) provide much evidence in support of the AH in the manner just described.

In many Western Malayo-Polynesian languages including Javanese, Minang-Kabau, Malagasy and Toba Batak only subjects can be relativized on by the primary strategy. Also worth mentioning is that many European languages, e.g. German, Russian and Polish, have participial relativization strategies which may only relativize on subject relation (Keenan and Comrie 1977: 70). The following examples come from Malagasy, the basic clausal word order of which is VOS (Keenan and Comrie 1977: 70).

(36) Malagasy
      ny mpianatra izay   nahita ny vehivavy
      the student   COMP saw   the woman
      'the student that saw the woman'

(37) Malagasy
      *ny vehivavy izay   nahita ny mpianatra
      the woman   COMP saw   the student
      'the woman that the student saw'

The RC in (37) is totally ungrammatical in the sense that the head noun has direct object relation in the restricting clause; (37) can only be grammatical in the sense that *the woman that saw the student*. The reader may wonder at this point if and how Malagasy and other similar languages may go about expressing RCs formed on grammatical relations other than subject as in languages like English, e.g. *the woman that the student saw* (i.e. DO), *the pen with which the woman wrote a letter* (i.e. OBL), etc. This will be the topic of 4.5.

In (Literary) Welsh the primary strategy applies only to subject and direct object, and so does one of the primary strategies in Finnish. Other grammatical relations are taken care of by different relativization strategies in these languages. In Welsh, for instance, the non-primary relativization strategy expresses the head noun in the restricting clause by means of an anaphoric pronoun (cf. Tallerman 1990 on relativization in Colloquial Welsh) (Keenan and Comrie 1977: 70).

(38)   Welsh
      y   bachgen a   oedd yn darllen
      the boy   who was a' reading
      'the boy who was reading'

(39)   Welsh
      dyma 'r llyfr y   darllenais y   stori ynddo
      here-is the book that I-read   the story in-it
      'Here is the book in which I read the story'

In Basque, Tamil and Roviana the three highest grammatical relations on the AH are relativized on by the primary strategy. In Basque there is a dialectal variation on whether or not other grammatical relations can also be relativized on. If they can, the non-primary pronoun-retention strategy comes into play. In Tamil the primary strategy involves a prenominal restricting clause with its verb in participial form *-a*, whereas the non-primary strategy retains the head noun in full form in the restricting clause as well as in the main clause, viz the correlative RC type (Keenan and Comrie 1977: 72–3).

(40)   Tamil
      Jān pāṭu-kiṟ-a   penmaṇi(y)-ai kaṇ-ṭ-āṇ
      John sing-PRS-PART woman-DO   see-PST-3SG.M
      'John saw the woman who is singing.'

(41)   Tamil
      anta maṇitaṇ aṭi-tt-a   penmaṇi(y)-ai jāṇ   kaṇ-ṭ-āṇ
      that man   hit-PST-PART woman-DO John see-PST-3SG.M
      'John saw the woman that that man hit.'

(42) Tamil
      Jān   puttakatt-ai(k) koti-tt-a   penmani(y)-ai
      John book-DO   give-PST-PART woman-DO
      nān kan-t-ēn
      I   see-PST-1SG
      'I saw the woman to whom John gave the book.'

(43) Tamil
      enna(k) katti(y)-āl kori(y)-ai   anta manitan kolaippi-tt-ān
      which   knife-with chicken-DO that man   kill-PST-3SG.M
      anta katti(y)-ai jān   kan-t-ān
      that knife-DO John see-PST-3SG.M
      'John saw the knife with which the man killed the chicken.'
      (lit. 'With which knife the man killed the chicken, John saw that
      knife.')

Note that, as is normally expected of the correlative RC type, the correlative
marker *enna(k)* appears clause-initially in (43).
      Languages which make use of the primary strategy to relativize from
subjects all the way down to obliques include Catalan and North Frisian
(Fering dialect).[1] Keenan and Comrie (1977: 74) point out that many well-
known European languages, e.g. French, Spanish, German and Rumanian,
relativize on all grammatical relations including GEN but excluding OCOMP
by means of primary strategies. But there are few languages that actually
relativize on all grammatical relations on the AH. English and Urhobo –
incidentally, the latter happens to use the pronoun-retention strategy for all
grammatical relations on the AH – are listed in Keenan and Comrie (1977:
75) as uncommon across-the-board-relativizing languages (cf. (35)).

(44) Urhobo
      oshale na l-i   Mary rho n-o
      man   the that Mary big than-him
      'the man that Mary is bigger than'

      The preceding survey demonstrates that primary strategies apply to sub-
ject relation and also possibly down to the 'lower' grammatical relations on
the AH. Primary strategies may also stop at any point on the AH and, if that
happens, and also if relativization is permitted to take place even further
down the AH, non-primary strategies may take over.
      Keenan and Comrie's (1977) AH makes it possible to make sense of the
cross-linguistic tendency mentioned at the end of 4.3: between the obliteration strategy and the relative-pronoun or pronoun-retention strategy, for
instance, the former covers the higher portion of the AH and the latter the
lower portion of the AH; and between the relative-pronoun and pronoun-

retention strategy, the former takes care of the higher portion of the AH and the latter the lower portion of the AH. The converse situations, however, seem to be virtually unattested in the languages of the world.[2] The three relativization strategies in question can be ranked in terms of explicitness in the encoding of the grammatical relation of the head noun in the restricting clause as follows.

(45)   obliteration > relative-pronoun > pronoun-retention
        (where '>' means 'less explicit than').

The obliteration strategy, as the name suggests, does not mark the grammatical relation of the head noun in the restricting clause. The other two strategies, on the other hand, each retain a pronominal 'copy' of the head noun in the restricting clause, the relative-pronoun strategy being less specific or more abstract and, therefore, less explicit than the pronoun-retention strategy – for example, English relative pronouns *who* and *whom* do not express gender or number, whereas personal pronouns *he*, *she* and *they* encode gender and/or number. Also note that, as has been discussed, the AH reflects the different degrees of accessibility to relativization: higher grammatical relations more accessible than lower ones. In view of this the distribution of different relativization strategies across the AH within individual languages can now be seen to be far from arbitrary or random because more explicit relativization strategies are used for less accessible grammatical relations and less explicit relativization strategies for more accessible grammatical relations (Comrie 1989: 163). The lower the grammatical relation is on the AH (that is, the less accessible to relativization), the more information may be needed of the grammatical relation being relativized on, whereas the higher the grammatical relation is on the AH (that is, the more accessible to relativization), the less information may be required of the grammatical relation being relativized on.

4.5   Conspiracy in relativization

In 4.4 not all languages were shown to be able to relativize on every grammatical relation of the AH. In fact, languages which can relativize over the whole spectrum of the AH are few and far between. No less remarkable are languages in which only subjects can be relativized on, e.g. Malagasy. But does this suggest, for instance, that languages such as Malagasy may be communicatively deficient, if not inferior, in comparison with languages such as English which can very generously relativize on all the grammatical relations on the AH? The answer definitely is no. Heavily constrained as their relativization strategies may be, languages such as Malagasy do have grammatical means to make it possible to relativize ultimately on grammatical relations other than subject. This situation is depicted aptly by Croft (1990: 197) as a 'conspiracy' between accessibility to relativization and other grammatical devices. He thus appeals to the 'communicative motivation' whereby communication of certain concepts or combinations of concepts is made possible by whatever grammatical means available. Indeed languages such as Malagasy make up for the hefty price they pay on subject-only relativization by taking full advantage of the grammatical devices which they already possess. Recall from 3.11 a number of grammatical operations which are designed to alter the basic clause pattern: passive, advancement of obliques to P, etc. In the languages in question these grammatical operations are exploited in order to create grammatical conditions conducive to application of heavily constrained relativization strategies. Take Malagasy, for instance. This language happens to have a very 'rich' voicing (or passive) system whereby not only direct object but also various oblique relations, e.g. benefactive, instrumental, locative, etc., can be promoted to subject, which is relativized on by the primary relativization strategy, anyway. The RC in (37) is taken to be ungrammatical because the head noun *ny vehivavy* bears direct object, not subject relation in the restricting clause. In order for the NP in question to be relativized on the restricting clause must thus first be passivized so that the 'original' direct object can be promoted to subject. This is why the RC in (46) is fully grammatical as opposed to (37) (Keenan and Comrie 1977: 70).

(37)   Malagasy
      *ny vehivavy izay   nahita ny mpianatra
      the woman   COMP saw   the student
      'the woman that the student saw'

(46)   Malagasy
      ny vehivavy izay   nohitan'ny mpianatra
      the woman   COMP seen   the student
      'the woman that was seen by the student'

The RC in (47) involves a head noun which has an instrumental (or oblique) role in the restricting clause, the voice of which has to be passive (Keenan 1985: 158).

(47)   Malagasy
      ny savony izay   anasan-d   Rasoa lamba
      the soap   COMP wash with-by Rasoa clothes
      'the soap that Rasoa is washing clothes with'

What about languages which restrict relativization to subject and direct object relation? In common with other Bantu languages Luganda, for instance, cannot directly relativize on oblique relations such as the instrumental NP *ekiso* 'knife', as in (48), because the primary strategy applies only to subject and direct object (Keenan 1972: 186; 1985: 158–9).

(48) Luganda
      *ekiso John (na)   kye-yatt-a   enkoko (na)
      knife John (with) REL-killed-TA chicken (with)
      'the knife with which John killed the chicken'

But Luganda and other Bantu languages have a highly developed verb-derivational or valence-increasing system whereby various oblique NPs can be promoted to direct objects. Indeed this mechanism is exactly what is pressed into service to make it possible to relativize on the instrument NP in question in (48). Consider (49).

(49) Luganda
      ekiso John kye-yatt-is-a   enkoko
      knife John REL-kill-INST-TA chicken
      'the knife with which John killed the chicken'

Note that the verb in the restricting clause in (49) bears a so-called advancement marker (i.e. *-is*) which indicates that the 'original' instrumental NP has been promoted to direct object status. Equally noteworthy is complete absence from the RC in (49) of the instrumental- or oblique-case marker *na*, which will normally be prefixed to the instrumental NP, as in (50).

(50) Luganda
      John yatt-a   enkonko n'-ekiso
      John kill-TA chicken with-knife
      'John killed the chicken with the knife.'

Comrie (1989: 159–60) also discusses an analogous phenomenon in Kinyarwanda, another Bantu language which directly relativizes only on subject and direct object but indirectly relativizes on oblique relations by means of similar promotion.

  Recall from 3.12 that in Dyirbal NP ellipsis under coreference across clauses is carried out on the A/SP basis. The same syntactic ergativity is also observed in relativization in Dyirbal (Dixon 1972). Thus *S* and P (or, collectively, the absolutive) can be relativized on but A can never directly undergo relativization. In order for A to be relativized on, in fact, the transitive clause which includes the NP in A function must first be antipassivized (or detransitivized) so that the 'original' A can turn up as *S* in the antipassivized clause. As Croft (1990: 197) would put it, antipassivization conspires with the primary relativization strategy in order to relativize on A, which otherwise cannot directly be relativized on. This is illustrated in (51) (Dixon 1972: 101, Keenan and Comrie 1977: 82).

(51) Dyirbal
      bayi   yaṛa   bagal-ŋa-ŋu   bagul   yuṛigu
      M-ABS man-ABS spear-APASS-REL DET-INST kangaroo-INST
      banaga-nʸu
      return-NFUT
      'The man who speared the kangaroo is returning.'

In (51) the grammatical relation of the head noun in the restricting clause is now *S* owing to antipassivization, as a direct result of which it is rendered compatible with the *S* function that it also bears in the main clause. As a matter of fact, this particular grammatical constraint on relativization in Dyirbal may call for re-examination of the AH as formulated by Keenan and Comrie (1977) because absolutive relation covers intransitive subject (*S*) and direct object (P). The relativization constraint in Dyirbal does cut across the traditional notion of subject relation (that is, A and *S*), which occupies the top position on the AH.

Related to the problem in Dyirbal is the apparent exception to the AH of Tongan (Keenan and Comrie 1977: 86–8). In this Polynesian language personal pronouns may – sometimes must – be retained when subjects are relativized on but, when direct objects are relativized on, no personal pronouns can be used in the restricting clause. But, contrary to Keenan and Comrie's (1977) AH theory, personal pronouns must be retained in the restricting clause when indirect object, oblique and genitive NPs are relativized on. In other words, the pronoun-retention strategy skips direct object on the AH. This problem for the AH and also the one raised in relation to the syntactic ergativity in Dyirbal will be discussed in more detail in 4.8.

There are other minor grammatical mechanisms which have been reported in the literature to be used in conspiracy with relativization strategies: the conjunction device and the adverb device. One type of conjunction device used in Korean, for instance, introduces a separate lexical verb which then adopts the unrelativizable oblique NP of the original verb as its direct object NP (Song 1991b: 205–11). The adverb device also found in Korean relativization, on the other hand, draws upon use of adverbial expressions meaning 'together', thereby restoring the meaning of comitative relation which is lost by the primary obliteration strategy (Song 1991b: 212).

Some languages may even leave the domain of grammar in order to find ways to relativize on AH positions which cannot directly be relativized on, whether by primary or non-primary strategies. In these languages pragmatic knowledge of the real world is also taken advantage of to a great extent in relativization. In Korean, for instance, some oblique NPs (or some instances of the same oblique NP type) can directly be relativized on by the primary obliteration strategy without recourse to the conspiratorial devices mentioned above. For instance, the instrumental NP in (52) can straightforwardly be relativized on by the primary obliteration strategy.

(52) Korean
kiho-ka   kɨ kɛ-lɨl   ttɛli-n   maktɛki
Keeho-SBJ the dog-DO beat-PART stick
'the stick with which Keeho beat the dog'

Note that the instrumental-case marker *-lo* has been eliminated from the restricting clause in (52) as opposed to (53), which is a simple non-relative clause involving the same instrumental NP.

(53) Korean
kiho-ka   kɨ kɛ-lɨl   maktɛki-lo ttɛli-əss-ta
Keeho-SBJ the dog-DO stick-INST beat-PST-IND
'Keeho beat the dog with a stick'

Comrie (1989: 145) discusses briefly how the instrumental interpretation associated with (52) can be recovered. He points out correctly that it is common sense – in other words, pragmatics – on the basis of which the 'missing' relation between the actor's action and the instrumental NP is construed: in the real world the most likely relation between the act of someone's hitting a dog and a stick is that of instrument.[3] That pragmatics plays such an important role in recovery of instrumental relation in Korean is very well illustrated by the following RC, which is very similar to (52), except for the relativized instrumental NP being *pɛchu* 'cabbage' instead of *maktɛki* 'stick' (Song 1991b: 214).

(54) Korean
??kiho-ka   kɨ kɛ-lɨl   ttɛli-n   pɛchu
  Keeho-SBJ the dog-DO beat-PART cabbage
'the cabbage with which Keeho beat the dog'

It is extremely difficult to interpret (54) (as indicated by the preceding double question marks) since in the real world people normally do not beat a dog using a head of cabbage. In Korean it is this kind of pragmatic knowledge that ultimately determines whether or not a given oblique NP can directly be relativized on by the obliteration strategy. Thus, when the relationship between the head noun and the action or process denoted by the predicate of the restricting clause can be pragmatically taken for granted, the obliteration strategy can be applied without any complication. When such pragmatic information is not forthcoming or implausible, however, one of the grammatical devices referred to earlier is called into the relativization conspiracy.

In fact, use of pragmatic knowledge is so strong in Korean relativization that it actually is often possible to find 'RCs' as in (55), in which the head noun has no coreferential relationship to any obvious (logical) constituent of the restricting clause (Tagashira 1972: 224–5); in other words, the head noun bears no apparent or real grammatical relation in the restricting clause.

(55)   Korean
        kwika-ka   niccəci-nɨn   kyowoisɛŋhwal
        getting.back.home-SBJ becoming.late-PART suburban.life
        '?the suburban living of which the getting back home becomes late'

Again, the pragmatic knowledge involved in the construal (and also in the generation) of (55) may be that it takes increasingly more time to travel from a downtown workplace to a suburban home than to a downtown home and/or that, having moved out to live in the suburbs, more and more people contribute to traffic congestion between work and home. This extra-linguistic knowledge seems to be sufficient to make up for the lack of a logically coreferential NP in the restricting clause in (55). It remains to be seen, however, whether or not (55) can actually be regarded as a genuine RC though it cannot be denied that the function of the subordinate clause in (55) is none other than that of modification or attribution, very characteristic of RCs. At any rate, what the present discussion has demonstrated is the powerful exploitation of pragmatics in the generation and construal of RCs in Korean (cf. Matsumoto (1997) for an in-depth study of the role of pragmatics in Japanese RCs or what she calls 'noun-modifying' constructions).

4.6   Correlations between RC-related properties

At the end of 4.4 the distribution of the pronoun-retention and the relative-pronoun strategy was discussed with respect to the different grammatical relations on the AH. Use of these two relativization strategies is known to be limited largely to the postnominal external-headed RC type (Keenan 1985: 151; cf. Downing 1978: 392). For instance, Keenan (1985: 148–9) observes that Chinese and Korean may possibly be the only languages which make use of both the pronoun-retention strategy and the prenominal external-headed RC type, and that in no known languages is the relative-pronoun strategy used in conjunction with the prenominal external-headed RC type. Thus both the pronoun-retention and relative-pronoun strategies seem to be highly incompatible with the prenominal external-headed RC type. This is not the only difference in behaviour between the prenominal RC type and the postnominal RC type, however. In languages with both the prenominal and the postnominal RC type, for instance, the former is far more restricted in terms of application than the latter. This actually was briefly mentioned in 4.4 with respect to German, Russian and Polish, the participial relativization strategies of which may apply only to subjects, thereby producing prenominal RCs (Keenan and Comrie 1977: 70). These languages also have other relativization strategies which apply not only to subjects but also further down the AH, thereby resulting in postnominal RCs. In other words, accessibility to relativization is also known to be somehow related to, or dictated by the position of the head noun relative to the restricting clause. Finally, it has also been observed that in the prenominal RC type the verb of the restricting clause is 'almost always in some sort of non-finite form, that is a form different from the one it would have as the main verb of a simple declarative sentence' (Keenan 1985: 160; cf. Downing 1978: 392). This non-finite form of the verb in the restricting clause is characterized by a heavy reduction in tense-aspect marking and in agreement morphology as opposed to finite verb forms of the declarative main clause (e.g. Turkish in (15), and Tamil in (40–2)). The possibly sole exception to this generalization is Japanese (cf. (4)) (Keenan 1985: 161).

To say the least, the preceding observations may strike one as seemingly disparate or unrelated. C. Lehmann (1986), however, puts forth a very insightful theory that may be able to explain these empirical observations in a coherent manner. He (1986: 677) claims that what the grammatical properties in question constitute actually is 'a bundle of correlations', appertaining to relativization. First, he (1986: 672) observes that the degree of nominalization of RCs correlates significantly with the distinction between the prenominal and postnominal RC types on the one hand, and with the degree of accessibility to relativization (that is, in terms of the AH) on the other. He argues that the adjoined (or correlative) RC type exhibits no signs of nominalization as indeed is suggested by the fact that the adjoined RC type can potentially be ambiguous between RC and temporal interpretations. The internal-headed RC and postnominal external-headed RC types tend to be weakly nominalized. The prenominal external-headed RC type, on the other hand, displays the strongest degree of nominalization. This is taken to explain why it is in the prenominal external-headed RC type that the verb of the restricting clause appears in non-finite form, characteristic of nominalization. This in turn is taken to have ramifications for accessibility to relativization. Nominalization tends to give rise to a curtailment in the range of grammatical relations available in the basic or unaltered main clause (cf. Silverstein's 1976, 1980 'normal form'); 'increasing nominalization involves constraints on the expandability of the clause by nominal constituents' (C. Lehmann 1986: 672). For instance, the logical subject of the restricting clause in the Turkish RC in (15), repeated below, turns up in genitive case, that is, as the possessor of the nominalized restricting clause. (Also notice the presence of the nominalizing suffix in the verb of the restricting clause.)

(15)   Turkish
       Orhan-ın   gör-düğ-ü   adam çık-tı
       Orhan-GEN see-NR-POSS.3 man leave-PST
       'The man Orhan saw left.'

This also suggests that the adjoined RC type can relativize on all grammatical relations on the AH, whereas the internal-headed RC and postnominal RC types may be more limited in relativization than the adjoined RC type but far less constrained than the prenominal RC type. C. Lehmann (1986: 672–3) quantifies these claims on the basis of Keenan and Comrie's (1977) data. Because they only provide sufficient data on the prenominal vs. postnominal RC type, he estimates that postnominal RCs can relativize 5.7 AH grammatical relations on average, whereas prenominal RCs can relativize only 3.5 AH grammatical relations on average.

Moreover, the distribution of the pronoun-retention and the relative-pronoun strategy can be re-examined in view of the difference in nominalization between the prenominal vs. postnominal external-headed RC type. Recall that these strategies are found only in, or confined mainly to the postnominal RC type. C. Lehmann (1986: 674) points out that personal pronouns or relative pronouns are basically anaphoric, thereby performing the function of interclausal coreference. This leads to the prediction that the pronoun-retention and the relative-pronoun strategy are more likely to occur in the context of more sentential or less nominalized restricting clauses. In other words, these relativization strategies are more liable to be employed in conjunction with the postnominal, rather than prenominal RC type. As a matter of fact, the prenominal RC type is better taken to be akin to an adjective or a participial attribute by virtue of its heavy nominalization (cf. Mallinson and Blake 1981: 296) and, thus, less susceptible to interclausal coreference. In addition, it is preferable to have the referent (or head noun) before the anaphoric expression, not the anaphoric expression before the referent (or head noun) – 'backwards anaphora is constrained' (C. Lehmann 1986: 676). This means that there is also the precedence preference militating against the use of the pronoun-retention or the relative-pronoun strategy in the prenominal RC type, in which the anaphoric expression – personal or relative – in the restricting clause precedes the referent in the main clause. In fact, C. Lehmann (1986: 676) points out that even in the adjoined RC type the head noun normally is placed in the first clause, and the anaphoric expression in the second clause regardless of whether or not the restricting clause comes first. He (1986: 676) also evaluates this prediction against Keenan and Comrie's (1977) data and concludes that there is no pronominal expression of the head noun in the postnominal restricting clause on the first 1.5 AH grammatical relations on average, whereas there is no pronominal expression of the head noun in the prenominal restricting clause on the first 2.5 AH grammatical relations on average. The difference is not so significant as in the case of the correlation between the prenominal vs. postnominal RC type and accessibility to relativization. Nevertheless it may well be taken to be in support of the claim in question.

The major advantage of C. Lehmann's (1986) theory is that it provides a coherent perspective in which a number of seemingly disparate RC properties can be seen to be very closely interconnected or interwoven though, needless to say, its validity must be tested against far more cross-linguistic data not only from the prenominal and postnominal external headed-RC types but also from both adjoined/correlative RC type and the internal-headed RC type.

Finally, one important point of distinction that C. Lehmann's theory may perhaps inadvertently highlight by making reference to interclausal anaphora in relativization must be mentioned. It is not entirely clear how the net effect brought about by the obliteration strategy in the restricting clause can be distinguished from use of so-called zero anaphora – which happens to be very frequent in languages such as Korean and Japanese. For instance, does the Japanese prenominal RC in (4) involve obliteration of the head noun in the restricting clause, or does it simply contain an instance of zero anaphora? To rephrase the question, is (4) an example of relativization by the obliteration strategy or by the pronoun-retention strategy? Difficult to define as it may be, this point of distinction is relevant to the other studies of RCs, not just to C. Lehmann's (1986).

4.7   The head noun in the main clause

Discussion has so far focused mainly on the grammatical relation of the head noun in the restricting clause. This may raise in the reader's mind an interesting question of whether or not the grammatical relation of the head noun in the main clause will have any bearing on the way in which relativization is carried out in the languages of the world. But, at least intuitively, one expects there to be little cross-linguistic variation on this, let alone relativization constraints induced by the grammatical relation of the head noun in the main clause because by definition the RC is merely an adjunct or optional subordinate clause of modification or attribution. In other words, regardless of whether a given sentence contains an RC or not, the head noun will act as a constituent of that sentence. Thus in (1) the presence or absence of the restricting clause *whom Miss Edge coached* makes no difference to the grammaticality or the structure of the main clause *The girl won the game*.

(1)   The girl whom Miss Edge coached won the game.

Probably this is more or less representative of the majority of the languages of the world. Indeed the intuition is generally borne out by what has been written about the topic in the literature. There are, however, at least three known instances of the role played by the head noun in the main clause in terms of relativization.

First, Comrie (1989: 153–4) makes reference to what is referred to as 'case attraction' in classical grammar of Latin and Greek. In Ancient Greek, for instance, the case of the relative pronoun assimilates into that of the object of a preposition. Thus in (56) the preposition *ek* governs the object NP *tōn póleōn*, which is also the head noun of the postnominal RC. The head noun has direct object relation in the restricting clause, whereby the relative pronoun is expected to be marked by accusative case. But the relative pronoun bears genitive case, the same case that the preposition assigns to its object.

(56)   Ancient Greek
      ek   tōn póleōn   hōn   éxei
      from the cities-GEN RPRO-GEN he-has
      'from the cities which he has'

In addition, Comrie (1989: 154–5) briefly discusses Modern Hebrew, in which the anaphoric pronoun retained in the restricting clause can optionally be deleted along with its governing preposition under identity to the head noun and the same preposition in the main clause. But, as Comrie (1989: 155) himself notes, this may better be treated as a type of the obliteration relativization strategy. But the point remains that the grammatical relation of the head noun and the preposition in the main clause trigger omission of the head noun and the preposition in the restricting clause.

Finally, as has been discussed in 4.5, there may be a few languages wherein the grammatical relation of the head noun in the restricting clause must be compatible with that of the head noun in the main clause. In Dyirbal if the head noun is in S function in the main clause but is in A function in the restricting clause, the latter clause must first be antipassivized so that the head noun can ultimately occur in S function not only in the main clause but also in the restricting clause. Mayan languages are also known to carry out relativization on the same A/SP basis: NPs in A function must be converted into S function via antipassivization prior to undergoing relativization (e.g. Larsen and Norman 1979, Bricker 1978, Larsen 1981, England 1983, Dayley 1978, 1985, Dixon 1994; also see 3.12). Note, however, that such a strict relativization constraint is a rarity in the languages of the world. Strictly speaking, the A/SP organization in relativization evident in Dyirbal and Mayan languages does not illustrate a case wherein the grammatical relation of the head noun in the main clause determines that of the head noun in the restricting clause. What it actually demonstrates is the syntactic constraint whereby the head noun should bear the grammatical relation that is compatible across the main and restricting clause; antipassivization can also take place in the main clause in conformity with the grammatical relation of the head noun in the restricting clause.

4.8 Subject primacy vs. discourse preferences in relativization

The highest position on Keenan and Comrie's (1977) AH is occupied by subject relation. Thus subject is more accessible to relativization than any other grammatical relations. In Dyirbal, however, there is a strict constraint on relativization to the effect that both S and P (or, collectively, absolutive relation) are accessible to relativization, but A is not. This means that the highest position on the AH in Dyirbal is not subject as is traditionally understood (i.e. A and S) but absolutive relation (i.e. S and P) instead. This, in fact, leads Johnson (1974) to redefine the upper segment of the AH for Dyirbal as something like ABS > ERG > IO > OBL, etc. (Keenan and Comrie 1977: 82). Similarly, in Tongan the pronoun-retention strategy applies to indirect object, oblique and genitive NPs as well as some subject NPs but it does bypass direct object relation altogether (see 4.5). By citing a number of 'subject' properties of the absolutive Keenan and Comrie (1977: 84–5) suggest that in Dyirbal the absolutive is perhaps the subject after all. This will certainly preserve the conceptual integrity of the AH as conceived by Keenan and Comrie (1977). Moreover, Keenan and Comrie (1977: 86–8) put forth a diachronic explanation of the apparent anomaly in Tongan relativization. Based on Hohepa (1969) they suggest that the ergative-absolutive system in Tongan may have evolved from an original nominative-accusative system but with the ergative 'subject' still in the process of emerging from an earlier passive agent phrase. Conversely, the absolutive 'direct object' has not yet lost its original subject status. Thus it is still susceptible to the obliteration strategy, not the pronoun-retention strategy, which applies to lower grammatical relations such as indirect object, oblique and genitive NPs.

Note that Keenan and Comrie's (1977) explanations of the 'anomalies' in Dyirbal and Tongan depend crucially on these languages having the ergative-absolutive system whether in fully developed form or not. In other words, P shares the same grammatical primacy with S in relativization because in Dyirbal and Tongan subject relation encompasses S and P to the exclusion of A. Thus they imply that the situations observed in Dyirbal and Tongan relativization can only be found in languages with the ergative-absolutive system, not those with the nominative-accusative system, for instance.

Fox (1987) carries out a statistical analysis of naturally occurring conversations in English – perhaps one of the most nominative/accusative-orientated languages – with a view to re-examining the highest position of Keenan and Comrie's (1977) AH or subject relation. Because of the very nature of her data RCs with non-definite head nouns are investigated in contrast to Keenan and Comrie's (1977) study, in which only RCs with definite head nouns are examined. In so doing Fox (1987) adduces strong

Table 4.1:   *Frequencies of A-, S- and P-RCs*

P-RCs	46	(50%)
Subject-RCs		
S-RCs	36	(39%)
A-RCs	10	(11%)
Total	92	(100%)

(Adapted from Fox 1987: 858)

evidence against the notion of subject primacy embodied in Keenan and Comrie's (1977) theory of relativization: subject relation has some kind of cognitive prominence unattained by the other grammatical relations on the AH. What is crucial for the present discussion is her empirical findings that even in nominative/accusative-orientated languages such as English constraints on introduction into discourse of referents may demand that S and P be treated preferentially in relativization as opposed to A.

First, Fox (1987: 858) takes note of the fact that in her data there is a clear predominance of P- and S-RCs over A-RCs as is presented in Table 4.1 (P–RC = RC with the head noun which has P, or direct object relation in the restricting clause; S–RC = RC with the head noun which has S or intransitive subject relation in the restricting clause; and A–RC = RC with the head noun which has A or transitive subject relation in the restricting clause).

She then sets out to define the role in natural discourse of each of the A-, S- and P-RC. S-RCs tend to have a descriptive function, that is they are employed mainly to characterize entities referred to by head nouns. This probably also explains why 43 per cent (15/36) of the S-RCs have *be* as the main verb in the restricting clause as in (57) (Fox 1987: 859).

(57)   She's married to *this guy who's really quiet.*

She (1987: 859) also finds that with its head noun likely to be non-definite (68 per cent) the S-RC often introduces a new referent into discourse for the first time. On the other hand, there are only ten tokens of the A-RC as Table 4.1 indicates. She explains that the discourse function of these A-RCs is to present the current utterance as being relevant to the preceding discourse by 'using the object of the relative clause as the bridge' as in (58).

(58)   A.   Did they get rid of Kuleznik yet?
       B.   No in fact I know *somebody who has her now.*

Thus the pronoun *her* in the A-RC in (58) refers back to the full NP *Kuleznik* in the preceding utterance. In Fox's data the head nouns of the ten A-RCs divide themselves neatly into non-definites or predicate nominals. Now the P-RC is found to carry out the discourse function of 'anchoring' in the sense of Prince (1981). By anchoring is meant that a discourse entity is linked or anchored to another entity via a third entity or an 'anchor'. Because of their linking function anchoring entities never carry brand-new information (Fox 1987: 859). That P-RCs are indeed used to anchor what is referred to by the head noun to the ongoing discourse is illustrated in (59).

(59)   This man *who I have for linguistics* is really too much.

In (59) the head noun *this man* is anchored by the personal pronoun *I*. Thus by embodying the anchoring NP in question the P-RC effectively contributes to the contextual relevance of the referent of the head noun; 'the reference is carefully formulated to include a display of how the something being referenced is "related to us and what we have been talking about"' (Fox 1987: 860). Fox (1987: 860) also mentions that P-RCs are very likely to take pronominal subjects as in (59), which by their very nature 'claim relevance to something in the immediate context'. They are also found to contain 'a very low-transitivity, semantically bleached verb as the relative verb', e.g. *have*, in 75 per cent of the cases where the head noun is the subject of the main clause but the object of the restricting clause.

The primary discourse functions of the three different types of RC, as has been discussed, boil down to this: RCs are employed to 'situate the referent that is being introduced as a relevant part of the on-going discourse; in a sense, they justify the introduction of the referent in the first place' (Fox 1987: 861). Fox points out that there are two major ways in which RCs serve to situate referents in the ongoing discourse: (i) RCs providing a stative description of some aspect of the referent so that they can be used not only to situate that referent but also to justify its introduction into the discourse; and (ii) RCs signalling the referent as contextually relevant to the ongoing discourse by virtue of containing an anchoring entity that has already been introduced into the discourse. As has already been shown, the discourse strategy in (i) draws heavily on the intransitive clause, which itself explains why the S-RC enjoys a high frequency of occurrence in Fox's data. The discourse strategy in (ii), on the other hand, makes use of the transitive clause because it involves at least two entities, namely the anchor and the anchoree. But why is this discourse strategy associated largely with the P-RC, not with the A-RC? Asked differently, why does the P-RC predominate over the A-RC? The reason for this is that A proves to be a far better anchor than does P. By definition the anchor must be a carrier of given information; otherwise it will not be able to perform its anchoring function. This is in turn due largely to the fact that Ps tend not to bear given information,

Table 4.2: *Distribution of pronominal vs. lexical A and P*

	PRONOUN NP	LEXICAL NP
A	177 (87%)	26 (13%)
P	40 (23%)	136 (77%)

(Adapted from Fox 1987: 863)

thereby failing to 'serve as good anchors to the preceding discourse', whereas As tend to carry given information (Fox 1987: 862). In fact, as the reader will recall from 3.10, this is exactly what Du Bois (1987) has also discovered in his analysis of Sacapultec Mayan narrative discourse. In Sacapultec Maya there is a strong discourse preference for full, lexical – not pronominal – NPs to be in either S or P function. There is, on the other hand, only a very limited use of lexical NPs for A function, which is frequently assumed by unstressed pronouns or pronominal affixes instead. He also finds that a large portion of all new mentions in the discourse appear in either S or P function, whereas old mentions (i.e. given information) tend to be in A function. As further evidence for As being better anchors than Ps Fox (1987: 863) runs a statistical analysis on As and Ps in non-RCs in terms of lexical (new) vs. pronominal (old) mentions. The results of this analysis are presented in Table 4.2.

The figures in Table 4.2 indicate clearly that A is more likely to be a good anchor than P. Thus Fox (1987: 864) comes to the conclusion that, while the grammatical relation of subject may have a privileged status with respect to a number of grammatical operations and thus alleged cognitive prominence as well, it is none other than the discourse roles of RCs that contribute to the predominance of the S- and the P-RC over the A-RC.

In view of Fox's investigation, then, much sense can be made of the relativization constraint evident in Dyirbal. Irrespective of its alignment orientation, if a language is permitted to relativize at all, it must be able to relativize on at least S and P. This interpretation is referred to by Fox (1987: 864) as *the Absolutive Hypothesis*. For nominative-accusative-orientated languages A must also be relativized on because in these languages S is aligned structurally with A. Languages with the ergative-absolutive organization must also be able to relativize on at least S and P. This does not create any particular problem for these languages because S and P are treated alike in opposition to A, anyway. In ergative-absolutive-orientated languages there is also the option of extending relativization to A. But in 'a wonderfully ergative language' like Dyirbal (Fox 1987: 865) – and also Mayan languages – this option is shunned. The anomaly reported in Tongan relativization may be explained in a similar fashion. In this language the discourse preference for S and P, perhaps reinforced by its new ergative-absolutive orientation, may persist to the effect that direct object relation is relativized on by the (primary) obliteration strategy, whereas the lower grammatical relations are taken care of by the (non-primary) pronoun-retention strategy.

Finally, on the strength of her findings Fox (1987: 865) challenges the cognitive prominence associated with Keenan and Comrie's (1977) subject primacy. She suggests that subject primacy may be attributed to the kind of experimental data on which Keenan and Comrie's (1977) study is based – RCs with definite head nouns presented to native speakers. This kind of RC normally is not found in her conversational data, however. Thus she (1987: 865) sounds a warning that '[t]he experimental findings . . . [may] not transfer to the conversational data'. Be that as it may, it remains to be seen whether or not Fox's (1987) discourse-based explanation can also extend to the remaining lower portion of the AH. If not, the kind of cognitive prominence associated with Keenan and Comrie's (1977) AH theory may still turn out to be quite relevant to, or at least a possible avenue of explanation for accessibility to relativization (cf. 4.10). At any rate, Fox's Absolute Hypothesis must first be evaluated on the basis of in-depth analysis of discourse data from a wide range of languages – nominative-accusative or ergative-absolutive orientation – mainly because it draws its empirical support from a single language, viz English.

4.9 RC type and word order type

Greenberg (1963b: 90–1) is – again – the first (linguistic typologist) to discuss the distribution of RC type relative to word order type, albeit not directly. Based on his modest sample of thirty languages he makes at least three interesting observations: (i) that VSO languages have a distinct preference for the postnominal RC type; (ii) that SOV languages display a strong tendency to have the prenominal RC type; and finally (iii) that SVO languages behave exactly like VSO languages. His data are provided in Table 4.3.

Table 4.3: *Distribution of prenominal and postnominal RC types in relation to basic word order*

	VSO	SVO	SOV
prenominal/RelN	0	0	7
postnominal/NRel	6	12	2

(Adapted from Greenberg 1963b: 90)

Mallinson and Blake (1981: 271–85) make use of a 150-language sample to explore further Greenberg's (1963b) preliminary findings about the relationship between RC type and basic word order type. Although their sample is acknowledged to be heavily biased typologically in favour of SVO (Mallinson and Blake 1981: 275), one of Greenberg's (1963b) putative correlations, namely, that between VO (i.e. VSO and SVO) order and NRel seems to be borne out by their data: only six of the eighty-five SVO languages exhibit RelN order, with only one of these six (Palauan) not having NRel order as an alternative, whereas only two out of the twenty-four V-initial languages have RelN order, with both these two (i.e. Kapampangan and Tagalog) also having NRel order as an alternative (Mallinson and Blake 1981: 285).[4] Greenberg's (1963b) putative correlation between OV and RelN order, however, is not well supported because only sixteen out of the forty-one SOV languages have RelN order exclusively, with not only seventeen SOV languages exhibiting NRel order as an alternative but also four SOV languages having only NRel order (Mallinson and Blake 1981: 285; also see 4.10). As has already been pointed out, Mallinson and Blake's (1981) sample has a major sampling flaw: the typological bias in favour of SVO languages. This problem notwithstanding most of their findings seem to be broadly confirmed by subsequent studies.

Without providing any statistical evidence in support or revealing his empirical source Keenan (1985: 144–5, 163, 165) also proposes a number of interesting generalizations about the correlation between RC type and word order type. Unlike Greenberg (1963b) or Mallinson and Blake (1981), he also makes reference to RC types other than the external-headed RC type. First, he takes note of the general cross-linguistic tendency in favour of the postnominal RC type over the prenominal RC type. He (1985: 144) then observes that the postnominal RC type is 'almost the only type attested in [V]-initial languages', whereas in V-medial languages the postnominal RC type clearly is the predominant type. He (1985: 144) also notes that '[c]ompared with [V]-initial languages . . . it is more common in SVO languages to find both prenominal and postnominal RC[s]'. He (1985: 144) claims that it is only in V-final languages that the prenominal RC type is 'the only or most productive form' although V-final languages can also commonly have any of the other RC types as dominant. Thus both the correlative and the internal-headed RC type are found in V-final languages – e.g. Navajo, Quechua, Tibetan, etc. – along with the prenominal RC type. It can thus be extrapolated from this observation that both the correlative and internal-headed RC type are generally associated with V-final languages. Keenan (1985: 163), in fact, points out that 'clear cases of internal[-headed RC type] are present only in languages whose basic word order is SOV'. Lastly, he thinks that, because both the correlative and internal-headed RC type are confined largely to V-final languages, it is not totally surprising to

Table 4.4: *Distribution of word order types and RC types*

	Afr	Eur	SEAsia&Oc	Aus-NG	NAm	SAm	Total
V-final&RelN	5	[11]	2	2	2	3	25
V-final&NRel	[8]	4	2	[4]	[11]	3	32
Proportion RelN	0.38	0.73	0.50	0.33	0.15	0.50	Avg. = 0.43
SVO&RelN	0	0	1	0	0	0	1
SVO&NRel	[19]	[5]	[11]	[3]	[2]	[2]	42
Proportion RelN	0.00	0.00	0.08	0.00	0.00	0.00	Avg. = 0.01
V-initial&RelN	0	0	0	0	0	0	0
V-initial&NRel	[5]	[1]	[3]	0	[9]	[3]	21
Proportion RelN	0.00	0.00	0.00	–	0.00	0.00	Avg. = 0.00

(Dryer 1991: 455)

find V-final languages which exhibit both the two RC types. It should be borne in mind, however, that there is at the moment a dearth of cross-linguistic data on the basis of which to verify his generalizations concerning these 'minor' RC types.

Remarkably enough, though, both Mallinson and Blake's (1981) and Keenan's (1985) generalizations converge on what is essentially embodied in Greenberg's (1963b) correlations between RC type and word order type: V-initial languages definitely favour NRel order or the postnominal RC type; and V-medial languages are more similar to V-initial languages than to V-final languages insofar as RCs are concerned (cf. Dryer 1991). Mallinson and Blake (1981) and Keenan (1985) both portray V-final languages as being more ambivalent towards RC type than V-initial or V-medial languages. In a sense this ambivalence of V-final languages is reflected also in Greenberg's (1963b) data. In Table 4.3 it is only SOV that exhibits both the prenominal and postnominal RC type although the former exceeds the latter in frequency by 3.5 to 1.

Dryer (1991: 455–6) revisits the relationship between RC type and word order type, based on a statistically far more adequate 603-language database (see 1.5.3 for discussion of his insightful sampling methodology). The main objective of his work is to determine the typological behaviour of SVO relative to V-final and V-initial word order. This is why in Table 4.4 only these three word order 'types' are represented (cf. Dryer 1992: 86–7).

From the data in Table 4.4 Dryer (1991: 456) draws the conclusion that V-final languages do not tend to have RelN order or the prenominal RC type. The data, in fact, show that both the prenominal and postnominal RC type are common in V-final languages (cf. Keenan's comment on the ambivalence of V-final languages above). In fact, a random V-final language has only a chance of 43 per cent of being RelN. Moreover, almost half of the aggregate genera with V-final&RelN come from a single *linguistic area*, viz Eurasia. V-initial languages, on the other hand, clearly are NRel. Dryer (1991: 456) points out that in his data there are no instances of V-initial&RelN languages. In other words, a random V-initial language has a likelihood of zero per cent of being RelN. What is equally intriguing in Table 4.4 is that V-medial languages are virtually like V-initial languages and have little resemblance to V-final languages – there is only one instance of V-medial&RelN, viz Chinese (also cf. Greenberg 1963b: 90). To put it differently, the likelihood of a random SVO language being RelN is only one per cent. In fact, as the reader will recall from 2.2.2, one of the arguments that Dryer (1991) provides in support of the OV–VO typology comes precisely from the data in Table 4.4. Moreover, Dryer (1992: 86–7) concludes on the basis of similar data that 'RelN order is more common among OV languages than it is among VO languages and conversely for NRel order'. But it should be remembered that these correlations only emerge when the proportion of genera containing OV languages with RelN is compared with the proportion of genera containing VO languages with RelN. To wit, Dryer's (1991, 1992) findings broadly support the generalizations arrived at in both Mallinson and Blake's (1981) and Keenan's (1985) work although it has more strongly than any other works underlined the behavioural similarity to V-initial languages of V-medial languages.

The reader will also recall from 2.4 that Dryer (1992) develops what is referred to as the Branching Direction Theory (BDT) with a view to explaining a large number of word order correlations including OV&RelN and VO&NRel. The thrust of this theory is that phrasal (or branching) categories follow or precede non-phrasal (or non-branching, lexical) categories consistently across different grammatical levels so that languages may tend towards either right-branching or left-branching, respectively. Thus the correlations of OV&RelN and of VO&NRel can be explained as follows. In the case of OV&RelN, for instance, the RC is placed before the head noun because the former is a phrasal category and the latter a non-phrasal category, thereby patterning with O (a phrasal category) and V (a non-phrasal category), respectively. In the case of VO&NRel, on the other hand, the ordering of the RC and the head noun is reversed, patterning likewise with respect to V and O. This kind of consistent ordering of phrasal and non-phrasal categories is claimed to reflect the nature of human parsers itself (Dryer 1992: 128–32): consistent direction of branching may avoid processing difficulty associated with the combination of right- and left-branching structure. In the next two sections the role of processing will be explored further especially with respect to the distribution of the prenominal and postnominal RC types and also to the AH.

4.10   The role of processing in the distribution of RC types

Probably Kuno (1974) is the first to make a serious attempt to address the possible correlation between SOV/VSO and RelN/NRel order in terms of processing. Speculative as it may be due mainly to lack of cross-linguistic evidence in support, his theory continues to be of relevance to subsequent processing-based studies, which draw upon his insight in one way or another. First, Kuno (1974: 119–21) observes that centre-embedding causes processing difficulties. This is claimed to be why the sentence in (60) is almost incomprehensible, let alone grammatical, compared to (61), which is not only grammatical but also not at all difficult to process.

(60)   *The cheese the rat the cat chased ate was rotten.

(61)   The cat chased the rat that ate the cheese that was rotten.

The sentence in (60) contains two instances of centre-embedding: *the cat chased* is centre-embedded in the subordinate clause *the rat . . . ate*, which is in turn centre-embedded in the main clause *the cheese . . . was rotten*. The sentence in (61), on the other hand, involves no instance of centre-embedding. Kuno (1974: 120) explains that processing difficulties associated with centre-embedding are related ultimately to the human capacity of temporary or short-term memory. That is, having received *the cheese the rat the cat* in (60), the human parser will have to put as many as three NPs on hold or standby in anticipation of three predicates or VPs that follow, and then match them accordingly. Kuno (1974: 119) points out, however, the Japanese equivalent to (60), 'is perfectly comprehensible'.

(62)   Japanese
        neko ga   oikaketa nezumi ga   tabeta chiizu wa   kusatte-ita
        cat   SBJ chased   rat   SBJ ate   cheese SBJ rotten-was
        'The cheese the rat the cat chased ate was rotten.'

The sentence in (62) does not involve a single instance of centre-embedding, with all the restricting clauses left-embedded, or placed to the left of their respective head nouns. Note that in Japanese the restricting clause is placed before the head noun, whereas in English the ordering of these two main constituents is reversed. Thus what Japanese, with its (rigid) SOV basic word order, achieves by having RelN, rather than NRel, order is that it successfully obviates centre-embedding. This observation has implications for the preferred positioning of restricting clauses in SOV vs. VSO languages. The intransitive clause has one core NP (i.e. S in SV), and the transitive clause two core NPs (i.e. both S and O in SOV). Each of these three core NPs can potentially function as the head noun of an RC. This means that, if they have the restricting clause before the head noun (i.e. prenominal RC type), SOV languages will have only one instance of centre-embedding (i.e. in O) but as many as three instances of centre-embedding (i.e. each for intransitive S, transitive S and O) if they place the head noun before the restricting clause (i.e. postnominal RC type). This difference is schematized in (63) and (64) (centre-embedded restricting clauses (i.e. rc) in bold face).

(63)   SOV with prenominal rc
   a.   **rc**-S V
   b.   **rc**-S O V
   c.   S **rc**-O V

(64)   SOV with postnominal rc
   a.   S-**rc** V
   b.   S-**rc** O V
   c.   S O-**rc** V

In VSO languages, on the other hand, RelN order (or the prenominal RC type) will result in the maximum instances of centre-embedding but, when the restricting clause occurs to the right of the head noun (i.e. the postnominal RC type), VSO languages have only one instance of centre-embedding, schematized in (65) and (66).

(65)   VSO with prenominal rc
   a.   V **rc**-S
   b.   V **rc**-S O
   c.   V S **rc**-O

(66)   VSO with postnominal rc
   a.   V S-**rc**
   b.   V S-**rc** O
   c.   V S O-**rc**

To put it differently, SOV and VSO languages should prefer RelN and NRel order, respectively, in order to minimize centre-embedding. Thus Kuno (1974: 120) claims that the correlation between RelN and SOV, and between NRel and VSO can be directly explained in terms of a 'universal' tendency to avoid centre-embedding.

Mallinson and Blake (1981: 309–16) generalize Kuno's processing account to V-initial, V-medial and V-final word orders. They find that V-final and V-initial languages – with V-final word order generalized from SOV, and V-initial from VSO – should prefer RelN and NRel order, respectively.[5] At least the putative correlation between V-initial and NRel is well supported by Dryer's (1991) cross-linguistic data. The correlation between V-final word order and RelN, on the other hand, is not well supported as has already been pointed out in relation to Table 4.4 (cf. Dryer 1992: 86). Mallinson and Blake also note that V-medial order has a maximum of two instances of centre-embedding regardless of whether it co-occurs with RelN or with NRel order, defined in (67) and (68). (Note that S and O are represented simply as NPs since V-medial order covers both SVO and OVS.)

(67)   V-medial with prenominal rc
  a. rc-NP V *or* V **rc**-NP
  b. rc-NP V NP
  c. NP V **rc**-NP

(68)   V-medial postnominal rc
  a. NP-**rc** V *or* V NP-rc
  b. NP-**rc** V NP
  c. NP V NP-rc

Thus V-medial languages can go for either NRel or RelN order without affecting the degree of centre-embedding in relativization more adversely. Mallinson and Blake (1981: 310) point out, however, that verb-medial languages do tend to display NRel order (or the postnominal RC type). Indeed SVO languages actually behave like V-initial languages in the positioning of the restricting clause (Dryer 1992; see Table 4.4). They (1981: 310) suggest that verb-medial languages like English may draw upon extraposition, whereby the centre-embedded restricting clause (italicized) can optionally be shifted to the right end of the sentence as exemplified in (69) and (70).

(69)   Some of the relatives *whom I hadn't seen since my mother passed away* visited me last month.

(70)   Some of the relatives visited me last month *whom I hadn't seen since my mother passed away*.

This device will effectively remove centre-embedding, manifested in (68.a) or (68b). But at the same time Mallinson and Blake (1981: 328–9) draw attention to the fact that not all SVO languages have access to extraposition, and to the fact that 'languages with an antipathy towards [centre]-embedding may simply avoid such perceptually complex structures rather than rescuing them by means of devices like extraposition'.

 In Dryer's (1992: 129–30) BDT centre-embedding can easily be conceived of as alternating left- and right-branching, i.e. multiple nestings of the identical category, as opposed to consistent direction of branching. Kuno's explanation based on centre-embedding can easily be reconciled conceptually with the BDT. Thus the correlation between V-initial word order and NRel order clearly falls out of not only Kuno's (1974) processing explanation but also from Dryer's (1992) BDT because the two V-initial word orders, i.e. VSO and VOS, do both reflect VO. V-medial word order presents an interesting situation because it covers not only SVO but also OVS. While exhibiting the identical position of the verb, SVO and OVS do exhibit VO and OV order, respectively. Kuno (1974) actually does not examine V-medial order with respect to RelN/NRel order but, according to Mallinson and Blake's (1981) generalization, V-medial word order should in principle be ambivalent between NRel and RelN. In point of fact, V-medial word order tends to co-occur with NRel order, not with RelN order. Thus SVO, one of the two V-medial orders, displays a distinct preference for NRel order (Dryer 1991). This can also be explained in terms of the BDT since, just like V-initial order, SVO is also subsumed under VO. But what about the other V-medial order, namely OVS? It is not entirely clear from published sources which of the two, RelN or NRel, OVS actually has a preference for, if at all (cf. Mallinson and Blake 1981: 313–15). In view of the paucity of OVS (and of O-initial languages in general) and the prevalence of SVO in the languages of the world the general correlation of V-medial and NRel order will not be dramatically affected regardless of what the preference of OVS turns out to be. But at least in terms of the BDT OVS is predicted to display a preference for RelN order since it reflects OV order. Lastly, V-final word order – which subsumes both SOV and OSV – can actually be equated to OV order, albeit not conversely. Thus OV order is predicted by the BDT to correlate with RelN order, which is exactly what Dryer (1992: 86) finds in his data.

In general these processing-based theories seem to be able to explain reasonably well the observed correlations between RC type and word order type. There is, however, one striking fact in Table 4.4 which cannot easily be handled by the theories in a similar fashion: while virtually all the genera with VO order (or V-initial) – incorporating SVO – have NRel order, both RelN and NRel order are common in the genera with OV order (or V-final). In other words, while there is a sheer preponderance of NRel order in VO languages, not only RelN but also NRel is commonly found in OV languages, e.g. Persian, Yaqui, etc. (Hawkins 1994: 325). For instance, Persian is predominantly SOV but it displays NRel order. The existence of languages such as Persian is indeed a thorn in the side of the processing-based theories.

(17)   Persian
        man zan-i   râ   ke John be u   sibe zamini dâd   mišenâsam
        I   woman-the DO that John to her potato   gave know
        'I know the woman to whom John gave the potato.'

Hawkins's (1994) EIC theory is also processing-based in that the human parser is predicted to prefer linear orders that maximize the IC-to-non-IC ratios of CRDs or constituent recognition domains (see 2.5). Thus it is interesting to find out whether or not his theory can take care of this problem. As a matter of fact, Hawkins (1994: 264–5) does discuss the distribution of NRel and RelN order relative to the position of the verb. Consider the following four logically possible permutations, for instance (S′ = restricting clause in the present case).

(71) a. [V [N S′]]
      b. [[S′ N] V]
      c. [V [S′ N]]
      d. [[N S′] V]

In terms of EIC ratios (71a) and (71b) are the most optimal, the former representing NRel order or the postnominal RC type in VO languages and the latter RelN or the prenominal RC type in OV languages. The other two permutations, on the other hand, produce poor EIC ratios primarily because of the position of the restricting clause (or S′) in between the two other ICs, V and N. The permutation in (71c) is indeed virtually unattested in VO or V-initial languages – the only exception in Dryer's (1991, 1992) data being Chinese (cf. Mallinson and Blake 1981: 291–2). But, as has more than once been pointed out, the equally non-optimal permutation in (71d) (that is, NRel or the postnominal RC type) is known to be commonly found in OV or V-final languages. Thus the existence of NRel order in OV or V-final languages is as problematic for the EIC theory as for the BDT.

The reader may, however, recall a very similar situation from 2.5: both the initial and final complementizers are found in OV languages, with the final complementizer unattested in VO languages (Dryer 1992: 101–2). This distribution of initial and final complementizers is represented in (72) (Comp = complementizer).

(72) a. [V $_{S′}$[Comp S]]
      b. [$_{S′}$[S Comp] V]
      c. *[V $_{S′}$[S Comp]]
      d. [$_{S′}$[Comp S] V]

The reader will also recall that the distribution in question is one of what Hawkins (1994) refers to as 'left-right asymmetries', caused by the fundamental fact that 'language is produced and comprehended in an item-by-item manner from left to right, i.e. in a temporal sequence' (Hawkins 1994: 321). As was discussed in 2.5, Hawkins explains this particular asymmetry by arguing that the positioning of Comp at the onset of the subordinate clause contributes to immediate recognition of the main clause/

subordinate clause distinction (cf. Frazier 1979, 1985 and Antinucci, Duranti and Gebert 1979).

To resolve the left-right asymmetry evident in the distribution of NRel and RelN order Hawkins (1994: 323) thus puts forward a similar explanation that V-final languages, unlike V-initial languages, have 'regular opportunities for misanalyzing main and subordinate clause arguments as arguments of the same verb'. For example, consider the following sentence with an RC from Japanese, a V-final or SOV language.

(73) Japanese
      zoo-ga   NP[S'[kirin-o   taoshi-ta]   shika-o]   nade-ta
      elephant-SBJ   giraffe-OBJ knock.down-PST deer-OBJ pat-PST
      'The elephant patted the deer that knocked down the giraffe.'

When (73) is processed on-line, the main clause argument *zoo-ga* is associated with the verb of the subordinate clause *taoshi-ta* so that it will initially be interpreted as 'the elephant knocked down the giraffe'. Then, when the rest of the sentence is also subsequently processed, the initial wrong interpretation has to be revised to the correct one (cf. Inoue 1991). Thus in V-final languages there is a real processing need for immediate disambiguation between the main and subordinate clause. Hawkins (1994: 324–8) argues that the human parser may have the option of expediting 'immediate matrix disambiguation' (or hereafter IMD), in the process of which EIC efficiency may be sacrificed for the sake of 'early decision-making' on the main clause/ subordinate clause distinction. It is claimed, therefore, that in some OV or V-final languages this option is actually taken up, whereby the EIC-optimal permutation in (71b) can be optionally rearranged structurally to (71d) – that is, from RelN to NRel order. To put it differently, immediate recognition as a subordinate clause of the restricting clause can be achieved by bringing the head noun forward to the onset of the RC: having processed the arguments of the main clause, the human parser expects to deal with, for instance, the verb of the main clause but when faced with another batch of arguments s/he will take them to be part of the subordinate clause. This is then claimed to be the reason why NRel order is also commonly attested in OV or V-final languages despite the fact that the rearrangement gives rise to a reduction in EIC efficiency – or, in terms of the BDT, to inconsistent direction of branching, with right-branching NRel and left-branching OV. Hawkins (1994: 327) also points out that this rearrangement has an added advantage in that being shifted to the onset of the RC the head noun now 'provides a lexically filled phrase for the on-line interpretation' of the – empty or otherwise – position relativized on in the immediately following restricting clause. In contrast the EIC-optimal permutation in (71a), which is adopted predominantly by VO or V-initial languages, does not suffer from the problem of IMD since the head noun is associated immediately with the right verb.

At this juncture it must be pointed out that, although IMD is proposed in the context of Hawkins's (1994) EIC theory, there is no reason why it should not also be incorporated into the BDT, for instance. That is, it can be said that inconsistent direction of branching is tolerated for the sake of immediate recognition of the main clause/subordinate clause distinction in OV or V-final languages to the effect that these languages may have NRel order as well as RelN order. In other words, the concept of IMD is not inherent in, but is an addendum to the EIC theory.

There is, however, at least one issue that needs to be clarified before Hawkins's explanation of the left-right asymmetry, defined in (71), is accepted as fully valid.[6] If NRel or RelN functions as the subject NP – as opposed to the object NP – of the main clause, IMD may be efficiently achieved with RelN, rather than NRel order in OV or V-final languages. For demonstration of this consider the following Japanese example.

(74)   Japanese
         $_{NP}[_{S'}$[kirin-o   taoshi-ta]   zoo-ga]   shika-o   nade-ta
         giraffe-OBJ knock.down-PST elephant-SBJ deer-OBJ pat-PST
         'The elephant that knocked down the giraffe patted the deer.'

In (74) the subordinate clause is recognized as soon as the verb is processed. This is because the verb of the subordinate clause is a transitive one, thereby requiring two core NPs but there is only one core NP, i.e. direct object, present within the subordinate clause – the direct object status of this NP is clearly signalled by the accusative-case marker -o. Thus absence of the subject NP alerts the parser to the possibility that what has so far been processed may merely be a subordinate clause or a restricting clause. The valency of the verb of the subordinate clause and the absence of the subject NP together enable the parser to identify very quickly and efficiently the subordinate clause as what it is; two major constituents, i.e. the object NP and the verb of the subordinate clause, are what is required for this correct interpretation (see Mallinson and Blake 1981: 330–46 for detailed discussion of the role of case marking, word order and valency in RCs). But, if the restricting clause were shifted to the right of the head noun in (74) (i.e. NRel), there would be a distinct possibility of the head noun and the object NP of the restricting clause being incorrectly interpreted as the subject and object NP of the main clause, respectively, until the real direct object NP of the main clause has begun to be processed. This would indeed be analogous to the indeterminacy evident in Hawkins's Japanese example in (73). Moreover, as opposed to RelN in (74), the hypothetically rearranged NRel order would also require processing of up to four major constituents so as to arrive at the point of proper recognition as a subordinate clause of the restricting clause, i.e. the subject NP, and object NP of the main clause, and the (intervening) object NP and verb of the restricting clause. In view of all this one may suggest that the structural rearrangement that Hawkins (1994: 323–8) claims takes place in certain OV or V-final languages will perhaps apply only to object, not subject relation. Said differently, there should be OV or V-final languages that display NRel order when the head noun has object relation in the main clause but RelN order when the head noun has subject relation in the main clause – provided that the head noun consistently bears subject relation in the restricting clause. There seem to be no detailed published studies or data to verify this, however.

Furthermore, the rearrangement of the head noun and the restricting clause may not be the only solution to the problem of IMD. For instance, consider Yaqui, which is one of the languages that Hawkins (1994: 325) actually names as displaying the rearrangement in question (Keenan 1985: 145).[7] The postnominal RC type in Yaqui, an SOV language, is thus claimed to be motivated by the need to expedite IMD (Hawkins 1994: 323–8).

(75)   Yaqui
       hu   kari   in   acai-ta   hinu-k-aʔu   wece-k
       this house my   father-DEP   buy-PFV-REL   fall-PFV
       'The house which my father bought fell down.'

But, in fact, the subject NP of the restricting clause is signalled by the so-called dependency marker -*ta*, which is reported to be, among other things, characteristic of the subject NP of the subordinate clause in this language; the dependency marker never appears on the subject of the main clause (Lindenfeld 1973: 65, 75, 81–99).[8] This means that in Yaqui there may not be any 'regular opportunities for misanalyzing main and subordinate clause arguments as arguments of the same verb' (Hawkins 1994: 323), with the marker -*ta* warning clearly against such 'regular opportunities'. Thus it is doubtful that this Uto-Aztecan language would suffer from the problem of IMD even if it had RelN order. Nonetheless it does exhibit NRel order, or the postnominal RC type. This suggests strongly that there may possibly be (a) motivating factor(s) for the NRel order in Yaqui, quite different from the resolution of IMD.

Persian is another V-final language which Hawkins (1994: 325) claims deals successfully with the problem of IMD by opting for NRel order. Refer to (17) for exemplification.[9] Mallinson and Blake (1981: 287–8), however, point out on the basis of Kuno (1972, 1974), and Vennemann (1974b: 352–4) that, although it is predominantly SOV, Persian does possess some VO features – for instance, the optional positioning to the right of the verb of the accusative-marked direct object NP (i.e. SVO) and NG order. They (1981: 403, 410) also suggest that the NRel order (and the other VO features) in Persian may be due directly to contact with Classical Arabic, which is a consistent VSO (or VO) language. One may perhaps argue that Persian has adopted NRel order as part of the 'restructuring' of its grammatical profile, that is from OV to VO. There are problems with this view, however.

First, its basic word order is undoubtedly SOV. Second, RelN order, more consistent with SOV, does not exist at all in competition with NRel order. The point being made here is, therefore, that the existence of NRel order in Persian does not seem to be owing to the need to expedite IMD but to language contact. In Hawkins's theory, however, language contact is not considered at all as one of the potential factors that may ultimately motivate languages to adopt one RC type in preference to the other (cf. Mallinson and Blake 1981: 286–91, 398–9, Smith 1981: 51–2 and Campbell 1997; also see Thomason and Kaufman 1988: *passim* for detailed documentation of similar cases). (For a similar example of contact-induced change in violation of Hawkins's theory see note 9.)

4.11   The AH and structural complexity

Hawkins (1994: 37–46) makes an attempt to re-interpret the rankings of the grammatical relations on Keenan and Comrie's (1977) AH in processing terms. He is in full agreement with Keenan and Comrie's (1977: 88) claim that the AH directly reflects 'the psychological ease of comprehension'. But he also argues that Keenan and Comrie (1977) are unable to justify their claim because they lack a structural complexity metric with which to quantify the psychological ease of comprehension. He (1994: 39) proposes that his concept of *Minimal Structural Domain* (or hereafter Min SD) does just that:

(76)   *Minimal Structural Domain*
        The Min SD of a node X in C consists of the smallest set of
        structurally integrating nodes that are grammatically required to
        co-occur with X in C.

Thus the Min SD of the direct object NP properly includes that of the subject NP because the former cannot be constructed without the latter. To put it differently, the Min SD of the direct object NP can be removed from that of the subject Min SD but not *vice versa*. This is demonstrated schematically in (77).

(77)
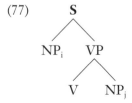

The Min SD of NP$_i$ (or the subject NP) consists of **S** and VP; in other words, **S** and VP define the subject NP structurally. The Min SD of NP$_j$ (or the direct object NP), on the other hand, consists of **S**, NP$_i$, VP and V; in other words, at least four nodes must be counted – as opposed to two in the case of the subject NP – in order to define the structural integration of NP$_j$. Thus the Min SD of NP$_j$ properly includes that of NP$_i$. The thrust of Hawkins's argument is: the more structurally complex a Min SD is, the more difficult it is to process in psychological terms. For instance, the direct object NP is more difficult to process than the subject NP simply because the former involves far more structural nodes to be counted than the latter. Based on this complexity metric Hawkins (1994: 39–41) goes on to demonstrate – limitations of space preclude further detailed discussion – that for each grammatical relation on the AH the Min SD of X$_i$ is always smaller or equal to that of X$_j$ (where X$_i$ is more accessible to relativization than X$_j$), and that for most of the grammatical relations there is, in fact, a relation of (proper) inclusion as in between the subject and direct object NP defined in (77). This is summarized in (78). (Note that Hawkins (1994: 41) does not discuss OCOMP on the AH but examines the genitive of each of the grammatical relations on the AH, not included in (78) for the sake of convenience.)

(78)   a.   Min SD (SBJ) ⊂ Min SD (DO)
       b.   Min SD (SBJ) ⊂ Min SD (IO), Min SD (DO) ⊂ Min SD (IO)
       c.   Min SD (SBJ) ⊂ Min SD (OBL), Min SD (DO) ⊆ Min S (OBL), Min SD (IO) ≤ Min SD (OBL)
       d.   Min SD (SBJ) ⊂ Min SD (GEN), Min SD (DO) < Min SD (GEN), Min SD (IO) ≤ Min SD (GEN), Min SD (OBL) ≤ Min SD (GEN).

Building on Primus's (1987, 1991) work, Hawkins (1994: 29, 42) also extends the same complexity metric to languages with case marking but perhaps without grammatical relations. In languages with nominative-accusative morphology, for instance, the Min SD of accusative includes nominative but that of nominative does not involve accusative, and that of dative involves nominative and accusative, but not *vice versa*, and so forth.

Hawkins's extension to the AH of the complexity metric based on the Min SD is quite intriguing not only because it provides a quantitative method of measuring structural complexity of the grammatical relations but also because it seems to be also able to handle languages for which the status of grammatical relation may be in doubt or dispute. Nevertheless one should at the same time not lose sight of Fox's (1987) hypothesis (see 4.8) that all languages should at least be able to relativize on *S* (or intransitive subject relation) and P (or direct object relation). In her discourse analysis, therefore, it is P that turns out to be more accessible to relativization than A, not *vice versa*. In terms of Hawkins's complexity metric, however, the Min SD of

P must include that of A, but not *vice versa*. What this suggests is that structural complexity may not be the only factor that may have a bearing on accessibility to relativization in the languages of the world, which is the very point brought by Fox (1987) against Keenan and Comrie's (1977) original work. Moreover, though it may be able to quantify Keenan and Comrie's accessibility to relativization, Hawkins's re-interpretation also begs the very question of why, for instance, subject relation should in the first place have a less complex structural domain than direct object relation.

Notes

1. Keenan and Comrie (1977: 74) include Korean in this group of languages but Song (1991b: 196–200) argues that the situation in Korean is more complicated than they claim. For instance, the primary obliteration strategy applies to subject, direct object, indirect object, locative, some other oblique NPs and some genitive NPs. The non-primary pronoun-retention strategy is restricted to genitive NPs in its application.
2. English may be a counterexample to this tendency, because the obliteration strategy can be optionally used for non-subject relation, as in (25) vs. (26), whereas the relative pronoun strategy must be used for subject relation as in (24). But see 4.10 for a possible processing-based explanation of this.
3. This is also possible in English to a marginal extent, e.g. *I've got no place to live* (cf. *I've got no place to live in*) or *Give me wings to fly* (cf. *Give me wings to fly with*). Matsumoto (1989: 233) provides more attested English examples of this kind, e.g. *Here is a snack that you don't have to wash your hands* (cf. *Here's a snack that you don't have to wash your hands in order to eat*).
4. In line with the general conventions in word order typology the prenominal and postnominal RC will hereafter be referred to interchangeably as RelN and NRel, respectively.
5. The other V-final order, namely OSV, also has two NPs before the transitive verb and one NP before the intransitive verb just as does SOV. A similar comment can be made of the other V-initial order, namely VOS (two NPs after the transitive verb and one NP after the intransitive verb as in the case of VSO).
6. Although they originally represent the verb phrase (that is, the verb and NRel or RelN with object relation) in Hawkins's (1994) work, the structures in (71) can all equally apply to the intransitive clause, with NRel or RelN functioning as its sole core NP, i.e. subject.
7. Keenan (1985: 145) incorrectly identifies *-ta* on the NP *in acai-* as a marker of definiteness.
8. Lindenfeld (1973: 71) does not discuss the exact circumstances under which this dependency marker is used to mark the subject of the subordinate or embedded clause. But it is clear from her description at least that it is sometimes used to mark the subject NP of the restricting clause.

9. Note that in Persian RCs the general or invariant subordinator *ke* is placed
   at the onset of the restricting clause. Thus, even if the restricting clause
   were placed before the head noun (that is, RelN), there is no possibility of
   arguments of the main and subordinate clause being misanalysed as arguments of the same verb though the Comp-initial prenominal RC is claimed
   to be unattested (Hawkins 1994: 327). By the way, Hawkins is of the view
   that the Comp-initial prenominal RC is functionally 'pre-empted' by the
   Comp-initial postnominal RC type and the Comp-final postnominal RC
   type in V-final languages. But Thomason and Kaufman (1988: 220–1) make
   reference to an example of the 'unattested' Comp-initial prenominal RC
   type, based on Dawkins's (1916) study. The Asia Minor Greek dialects
   spoken in the regions of Sílli, Cappadocia and Phárasa are heavily influenced
   by Turkish, one of the borrowed features being RelN order. In Common
   Greek, which is predominantly SVO, the restricting clause follows the head
   noun (i.e. NRel) but in Sílli dialects, for instance, the converse is frequently
   the case (i.e. RelN) as in Turkish. Compare:

   (i) Sílli
        kịát   íra   perí
        COMP saw-I boy
        'the boy who(m) I saw'

   (ii) Common Greek
        tò peðì pû   to îða
        the boy COMP it saw-I
        'the boy who(m) I saw'

   (iii) Turkish
        gör-düğ-üm   oğlan
        see-NR-1.SG.POSS boy(son)
        'the boy who(m) I saw'

   Note that the invariant complementizer *kịát* in Sílli, like that in Common
   Greek, is maintained at the onset of the RC in spite of the fact that the
   restricting clause precedes the head noun (i.e. RelN). Thus the RC in Sílli
   runs counter to Hawkins's (1994: 327) claim that the Comp-initial prenominal RC is unattested. This also highlights the role of language contact
   in linguistic typology and language universals research (cf. Campbell 1997).

5

Causatives

5.1   Introduction

The causative construction generally represents a linguistic expression which denotes a complex macro-situation consisting of two micro-situations or component events (cf. Nedjalkov and Silnitsky 1973: 1, Comrie 1989: 165–6): (i) the causing event in which the causer does or initiates something in order to bring about a different event (i.e. the caused event), and (ii) the caused event in which the causee carries out an action or undergoes a change of condition or state as a result of the causer's action. The following English sentence thus denotes a causative situation, for instance.

(1)   Elizabeth made the chef eat the leftovers.

In (1), having the desire or wish to have the leftovers consumed, the causer (or *Elizabeth*) did (or said) something, and as a result of that action the causee (or *the chef*) in turn carried out the action of eating the leftovers, thereby satisfying the causer's desire or wish. Note that in (1) the fact that the causer had had the desire or wish is not explicitly indicated at all but rather simply assumed to be antecedent to the causer's action (see 5.9 for discussion).

   Further observations about the causative construction can be made on the basis of the example in (1). First, the causer's action is expressed by the predicate of cause *made*, and the causee's action by the predicate of effect *eat*; these predicates happen to be separate lexical verbs in (1). Second, the actual action performed by the causer, as opposed to the action performed by the causee, is highly 'abtractized' down to the simple expression of causation. In other words, '[a]ll that is expressed by the predicate representing the causing event . . . is the pure notion of cause . . . without more specific lexical content' (Kemmer and Verhagen 1994: 117). Third, the causer NP and the predicate of cause are 'foregrounded' in opposition to the causee NP and the predicate of effect. That is, in (1) the causer NP is the subject NP of the whole causative sentence and the predicate of cause the main verb of that sentence. The causee NP and the predicate of effect, on the other hand, are 'backgrounded' in the sense that they do not occupy as prominent positions in the sentence as do the causer NP and the predicate of cause. For instance, the causee NP in (1) behaves grammatically as the direct object NP; it can potentially appear as the subject NP of the corresponding passive sentence (i.e. *The chef was made to eat the leftovers by Elizabeth*). The predicate of effect is also not a full-fledged verb, lacking the ability to host verbal markings, e.g. tense, number, etc. (e.g. **Elizabeth makes the chef eats the leftovers*).

In this chapter only linguistic expressions that exhibit the aforementioned properties will be regarded as exemplifying or instantiating the causative construction. Thus the sentence in (2), for example, does not constitute an instance of the causative construction.

(2)   The chef ate the leftovers because Elizabeth burnt his meal.

In common with (1) the sentence in (2) does denote two separate events, the causing event (denoted by the subordinate clause, *because Elizabeth burnt his meal*) and the caused event (denoted by the main clause, *The chef ate the leftovers*). Each of these events also happens to be indicated by a separate lexical verb, *ate* or *burnt*. Note, however, that in (2) the predicate of cause has a very specific lexical content with the effect that the causing event is clearly characterized or identified, i.e. burning. Moreover, both the causer NP and the predicate of cause are placed in the background as opposed to the causee NP and the predicate of effect. The causer NP is not the subject NP of the main clause, nor is the predicate of cause the main verb. The causee NP and the predicate of effect instead are the subject NP and the verb of the main clause, respectively. For these reasons the sentence in (2) does not represent or instantiate the causative construction but rather what may be referred to broadly as the causal construction. The causative construction (e.g. (1)), not the causal construction (e.g. (2)), will be the topic of the present chapter.

Kemmer and Verhagen (1994: 115–16) point out correctly that the study of causative constructions 'has inspired what is probably one of the most extensive literatures in modern linguistics' (also Song 1996: 1–2). This is indeed no overstatement although it is not unfair to say that it has perhaps not spawned as many works in linguistic typology as in, for instance, generative grammar. The study of causatives has, as a matter of fact, been carried out within linguistic typology with respect mainly to the hierarchy of grammatical relations, which was introduced in Chapter 4 in the form of Keenan and Comrie's (1977) Accessibility Hierarchy. It has been claimed that the utility of this hierarchy is not confined to the study of relative clauses but actually extends to that of causative constructions. Thus a similar (streamlined) hierarchy of grammatical relations, i.e. Comrie's (1975, 1976) *Case Hierarchy* (or hereafter CH), has been invoked in order to account for the syntax of causative constructions or, to be more precise, the grammatical relation of the causee NP. In fact, this has long been the focus of typological research on causative constructions and has been referred to in numerous – typological or otherwise – works (for a most recent reference to it see Palmer 1994: 218–21, for example). Part of the present chapter will thus be devoted to a critical – albeit very brief – discussion of the CH in relation to causative constructions (for a full critical discussion see Song (1996: chapter 6)).

Apart from the syntax of the causee NP there is another important parameter in terms of which the causative construction has been studied. Different (semantic and/or pragmatic) causation types, e.g. direct vs. indirect causation, have been identified, usually in relation to various formal types of causative construction and also to the case marking of the causee. There is, for instance, a strong correlation between the formal types of causative construction (i.e. lexical, morphological and syntactic), and the semantic types of causation to the extent that the formal distance between the predicate of cause and that of effect is claimed to be motivated iconically by the conceptual distance between the cause and the effect, and between the causer and the causee (Haiman 1985a: 108–11; also Comrie 1989: 171–4). It is also suggested that the case marking of the causee is determined by the type of causation, which is in turn related to other semantic and/or pragmatic factors such as agency, control, affectedness and topicality (e.g. Cole 1983, Comrie 1989: 181–3, Kemmer and Verhagen 1994). Discussion of these and other related issues in the present chapter will, unfortunately, only be somewhat fragmentary and far from conclusive due primarily to lack of large-scale cross-linguistic studies (as evident in word order typology, for instance). Nonetheless the general conclusions to be arrived at in the present chapter seem to be at least representative or typical of the languages of the world. In other words, no serious counterexamples to the general patterns are known to exist in the literature (but cf. Song 1992).

Finally, mention must also be made of one consequence of the prominence of the morphological causative type in the typological – and also general – literature on the causative construction. The causative types other than the morphological type have been poorly treated or neglected, if not ignored, in the literature. For this reason alone a few brief words about one recently proposed typology of causative constructions which has made a deliberate attempt to fill this empirical lacuna (i.e. Song 1996) seem to be in order.

5.2 The morphologically based typology of causative constructions

It does not seem inappropriate to embark on the main discussion of the present chapter by first examining the traditional morphologically based typology of causative constructions as it has served as the basis for many

studies of causatives. The parameter in terms of which this typology is conceived of is formal or morphological fusion between the predicate of cause
and that of effect. As a matter of fact, this is the same parameter of fusion
that is also often used to characterize the morphological profile of individual
languages (cf. 1.6 and 7.4). There are at least three prototypical or ideal types
based on this parameter of fusion: (i) isolating or analytic; (ii) agglutinating;
and (iii) fusional or inflectional. In isolating languages there is an equi-
valence relationship between word and morpheme with the effect that a
morpheme can be taken to be a word or *vice versa*. In agglutinating languages
a word may consist of more than one morpheme and may not be impervious
to the conventional morpheme-by-morpheme analysis. Finally, in fusional
or inflectional languages a single morpheme bears more than one meaning
or represents more than one grammatical category.

Directly from this parameter of fusion follow three different types of
causative: (i) lexical; (ii) morphological; and (iii) syntactic. These three types
of causative then constitute the traditional morphologically based typology
of causatives. The lexical causative type involves suppletion. There is no
formal similarity between the basic verb and the causative counterpart. In
other words, the formal fusion of the predicate of cause and that of effect is
'maximal' with the effect that the causative verb is not formally analysable
into two separate morphemes. This causative type is thus fusional or inflectional in nature. For example, in Russian the basic verb meaning 'to die'
is *umeret*, whereas the causative verb meaning 'to kill' is *ubit*. Languages
which exhibit the lexical causative type also include, e.g. German *sterben* 'to
die' vs. *töten* 'to kill', Japanese *sin-* 'to die' vs. *koros-* 'to kill', Mixtec *kúù* 'to
die' vs. *ka?ni* 'to kill' and English *die* vs. *kill*.

The second causative type is the morphological type, in which the predicate of cause is in the form of a derivational morpheme or an affix, with the
predicate of effect realized by the basic lexical verb, to which that affix is
attached. Single lexical verb though it is, the morphological causative verb
consists of two morphemes, which can easily be identified as such. In this
sense the morphological causative type is agglutinating. In Basque, for example,
the causative morpheme or suffix *-erazi* can apply to both intransitive and
transitive verbs to derive causative verbs (Saltarelli 1988: 220–2).

(3)   Basque
      azken-ean kotxe-a   ibil-eraz-i   d-u-te
      end-LOC car-SG.ABS walk-CS-PFV 3SG.ABS(-PRS)-AUX-3PL.ERG
      'Finally, they have made the car work.'

The causative morpheme can be in the form of not only suffixes but also
prefixes (e.g. Jinghpaw (Maran and Clifton 1976: 444)), infixes (e.g. Nancowry
(Radhakrishnan 1981: 49, 58–60)) and circumfixes (e.g. Alutor (Koptjevskaja-
Tamm and Muravyova 1993: 295)).

(4) Jinghpaw
     Ma Naw gaw Ma Gam hpe sha-tsap   ai
     Ma Naw SBJ Ma Gam OBJ CP-stand.up DECL
     'Ma Naw causes Ma Gam to stand up.'

(5) Nancowry
     paloʔ 'to lose'   vs. pumloʔ 'to cause to lose'
     paʔũy 'bad smell' vs. pumʔũy 'to cause to smell bad'

(6) Alutor
     unyunyu-ta Ø-t-imŋul-avə-tkə-nin   əlla
     child-ERG 3SG.A-C-miss-C-PRS-3SG.P mother.ABS
     'The child makes Mother miss him/her.'

There is no clear indication in the literature as to the distribution of the types of causative affix in the languages of the world. But given the overall predominance of suffixes over prefixes and the infrequency of infixes and circumfixes (see Hawkins and Gilligan 1988 and Bybee *et al*. 1990 for further discussion; also cf. 2.6) one would also expect causative suffixes to be far more frequent than the other types of causative affix. Croft (1995: 105), however, makes reference to Dryer's (unpublished) suggestion that causatives do not seem to display a suffixing preference. Song (1996: 25), on the other hand, makes an informal observation, based on his 613-language database, that far more languages employ causative suffixes than the other types of causative affix.

Finally, the syntactic causative type is an exponent of the isolating or analytic type in the morphologically based typology in that the predicate of cause and that of effect are separate lexical verbs. This type has already been exemplified by the English causative sentence in (1) above. But a far clearer example may come from a somewhat contrived version of (1):

(7) Elizabeth brought it about that the chef ate the leftovers.

Babungo also provides a good example of the syntactic type (Schaub 1985: 211):

(8) Babungo
     vɨ́   yàa yɨ́sə̀   (laa) ŋwə̀ gə̌   ntó'
     they-IPFV PST make-PFV (that) he go-PFV palace
     'They made him go to the palace.'

It is to be borne in mind that the three causative types must only be understood to serve as reference points (cf. Comrie 1989: 169–70) very much as do the cardinal vowels in the vowel quadrilateral for transcribing vowels. There may be languages which fall somewhere between any two of the prototypical types. For instance, Japanese lexical causative verbs may perhaps lie between the ideal lexical type and the ideal morphological type because, although they cannot in a clear-cut, consistent fashion be analysed into the basic verb and the causative morpheme or suffix, these lexical causative verbs do exhibit varying degrees of physical resemblance – from almost identical to totally different – to their corresponding basic verbs, e.g. *tome-* 'to make (someone/something) stop' vs. *tomar-* 'to stop', *nokos-* 'to leave behind' vs. *nokor-* 'to stay behind', *oros-* 'to bring down' vs. *ori-* 'to come down', *age-* 'to raise' vs. *agar-* 'to rise', *koros-* 'to kill' vs. *sin-* 'to die' and *ine-* 'to put in' vs. *hair-* 'to come in' (Shibatani 1976b: 17; also cf. English *seat* vs. *sit*, *fell* vs. *fall* and *kill* vs. *die*). Romance languages such as French, Spanish and Italian, on the other hand, have causative constructions that may best be described as intermediate between the ideal morphological type and the ideal syntactic causative type. The predicate of cause and that of effect in the so-called 'quasi-morphological' causatives (Song 1996: 161) in these languages are separate lexical verbs. However, these two verbs in question do behave like a cohesive unit in a number of respects, albeit not always (for a full discussion see Comrie 1976: 296–303). For one thing, they must appear next to each other so that, for instance, the causee NP is prevented from intervening between them as demonstrated in the following Italian examples (Comrie 1976: 298):

(9)   Italian
       Faccio baciare le   ragazze a   Carlo
       I-make kiss   the girls   to Carlo
       'I make Carlo kiss the girls.'

(10)   Italian
       *Faccio Carlo baciare le   ragazze
       I-make Carlo kiss   the girls

Moreover, object (clitic) pronouns must precede the whole unit regardless of which of the two verbs they may be associated semantically or logically with. For instance, *le ragazze* is the patient of the predicate of effect, whereas *Carlo* is the agent of the predicate of effect (as well as the causee). Nevertheless they must both be placed to the left of the entire sequence of the predicates of cause and effect if and when appearing in pronominal form as demonstrated in (11) and (12).

(11)   Italian
       Glie-le   faccio baciare
       to.him-them I-make kiss
       'I make him kiss them.'

(12)   Italian
　　　*Lo faccio baciar-le
　　　him I-make kiss-them

There may also be some causative types that are not very easy to classify in terms of the traditional morphologically based typology. The notion of causation may be expressed, for instance, by a segmental or suprasegmental feature, not by a morpheme or a word. In Lahu, Hayu and Pengo, for example, the voice quality of a consonant of the basic verb is changed in order to express causation. In Lushai and Lahu a tonal change to the basic verb is all that is required to indicate the causative meaning. In these languages, thus, it is impossible to analyse the causative verb into the basic verb and the causative morpheme or affix. These causative verbs may not belong strictly to the morphological type or to the lexical causative type although they may arguably be intermediate between these two causative types.

Few and far between though they may be, so-called 'anti-causatives' may likewise pose a difficult problem of classification for the traditional morpho-logically based typology in that it is the non-causative or basic verb, not the causative verb, that bears an additional morpheme or affix. In Swahili, for example, the basic verb *vunj-ik-a* 'to become broken' contains the anti-causative suffix *-ik-* as opposed to the causative verb *vunj-a* 'to make (something) break' (but cf. *-chek-a* 'to laugh' vs. *-chek-esh-a* 'to make (someone) laugh', and *chem-k-a* 'to boil' vs. *chem-sh-a* 'to bring to a boil' in the same language (Nedjalkov and Silnitsky 1973: 3)). It does not seem to be entirely appropriate to treat the causative verb *vunj-a* in Swahili as an example of the morphological causative type. Nor does it seem to be correct to classify it as an example of the lexical causative type because of its transparent relationship to the basic verb *vunj-ik-a*. Nonetheless the form *vunj-a* is taken to be a causative verb by the absence of *-ik-*, whereas the form *vunj-ik-a* is recognized as a basic non-causative verb by the presence of *-ik-*.[1] The term 'anti-causative' is, thus, satisfactory only to the extent that it describes the reverse direction of morphological derivation between the basic verb and the causative verb.

5.3　The syntax of the causee NP: the Case Hierarchy

The syntax of the causee NP has, as already pointed out, been the main theme in typological research on causative constructions. In two most influ-ential articles Comrie (1975, 1976) sets out to determine the cross-linguistic patterns in the grammatical behaviour of the causee NP, or the grammatical relation which the causee NP assumes in the – morphological or quasi-morphological – causative construction. In so doing he makes an attempt to extend to causative constructions the same hierarchy of grammatical relations that Keenan and Comrie (1972, 1977, 1979) claim is operative cross-linguistically in relativization. Comrie's (1975, 1976) data consist mainly of morphological causatives, wherein the predicate of cause is fused morphologically with the predicate of effect or the basic verb, thereby creating a new single, albeit derived verb. However, he makes a theoretical assumption that these causatives are made up of two separate clauses, one (expressing the caused event) embedded in the other (expressing the causing event), at some abstract level. This means that, when the main clause and the embedded clause are 'amalgamated' into a single clause, the causee NP must abdicate its original subject relation of the embedded clause and must instead be 'mapped onto' a different grammatical relation because subject relation is reserved for the causer NP – otherwise, the causer NP will be backgrounded (see 5.1). Thus the grammatical relation which the causee NP will assume in morphological causativization can in principle be predicted strictly by reference to the CH in (13).

(13)   *The Case Hierarchy*
       Subject > Direct Object > Indirect Object > Oblique

If the basic verb is intransitive with one core NP, the causee NP will assume direct object relation because that grammatical relation is the next highest available one on the CH, with subject relation taken by the causer NP. If the basic verb is transitive, requiring two core NPs, the causee NP will be mapped onto indirect object relation because that is the next topmost available position on the CH, with the causer NP assuming subject relation and the direct object NP of the basic verb retaining its direct object relation. If the basic verb is ditransitive, with three core NPs, i.e. subject, direct object and indirect object, the grammatico-relational fate of the causee NP is predicted to be the lowest position of the CH, i.e. oblique, which is the 'highest' vacant position on the CH. These predictions are clearly borne out by Turkish, an example of what Comrie (1975, 1976) refers to as 'the paradigm case' – which conforms perfectly to the CH (Comrie 1975: 5–6).

(14)   Turkish
       a.   Hasan öl-dü
            Hasan die-PST
            'Hasan died.'
       b.   Ali Hasan-ı   öl-dür-dü
            Ali Hasan-DO die-CS-PST
            'Ali killed Hasan.'

(15)   Turkish
       a.   müdür   mektub-u imzala-dı
            director letter-DO sign-PST
            'The director signed the letter.'

b. dişçi   mektub-u müdür-e   imzala-t-tı
   dentist letter-DO director-IO sign-CS-PST
   'The dentist made the director sign the letter.'

(16) Turkish
   a. müdür Hasan-a   mektub-u göster-di
      director Hasan-IO letter-DO show-PST
      'The director showed the letter to Hasan.'

   b. dişçi   Hasan-a   mektub-u müdür tarafından
      dentist Hasan-IO letter-DO director by
      göster-t-ti
      show-CS-PST
      'The dentist made the director show the letter to Hasan.'

Further evidence that Turkish is a perfect exponent of the paradigm case comes from non-causative two-place verbs that require their non-subject core NP to be indirect object. This means that in sentences with this type of non-causative verb only the subject and indirect object positions will be occupied by the core NPs, thus leaving the direct object position skipped over, and that in the corresponding causative sentences the causee NP will assume none other than direct object, i.e. the topmost vacant position on the CH. This is illustrated by the following pair of sentences (Comrie 1975: 5):

(17) Turkish
   a. çocuk okul-a   başla-dı
      child school-IO start-PST
      'The child started school.'

   b. dişçi   çocuğ-u okul-a   başla-t-tı
      dentist child-DO school-IO start-CS-PST
      'The dentist made the child start school.'

Thus the validity of the CH is supported by evidence from languages such as Turkish. It is also claimed to be strengthened by independent confirmation of the hierarchy from a different area of syntax, i.e. relativization (Comrie 1976: 264; but cf. Fox 1987, and also 4.4 and 4.8).

As is pointed out by Song (1996: 160), however, the biggest weakness of the CH theory of causative constructions is exactly that there are too few languages which, like Turkish, behave in accordance with predictions made by the CH theory. Many languages do deviate from the paradigm case. They do so in two major ways. First, there are languages in which the causee NP occupies a lower position on the CH than is predicted by the CH theory. Comrie (1975, 1976) refers to this type of deviation as 'extended demotion'. In Finnish, for example, although it is predicted to assume indirect object relation, the causee NP is marked by adessive case – which expresses instrument role – when the basic verb is transitive (Comrie 1975: 22). (But note that, when intransitive verbs are morphologically causativized, the causee NP is marked as direct object as is predicted by the CH theory.)

(18) Finnish
      minä rakennutin talo-n   muurarei-lla
      I   build-CS   house-DO bricklayers-INST
      'I make the bricklayers build the house.'

There are also languages in which the causee NP may 'double up' on the grammatical relation that is already taken up by one of the other core NPs of the basic verb. Comrie (1975, 1976) refers to this second type of deviation as 'doubling'. In Ewenki, for example, direct object relation is borne not only by the causee NP but also by the direct object NP of the basic transitive verb (Comrie (1976: 285) based on Konstantinova (1964: 157–8); but see 5.5).

(19) Ewenki
      ynīn-in   xuty-wī awun-mī baka-pkān-yn
      mother-his son-DO cap-DO find-CS
      'The (lit. his) mother made her son find his cap.'

Apart from these deviations from the paradigm case there are other equally significant issues that must be taken into account when the syntax of the causee NP is being studied (Song 1996: 170–4, 179–81). It has long been noted (e.g. Nedjalkov and Silnitsky 1973) that languages tend to apply causative affixes to intransitive verbs more often than to transitive verbs, or to transitive verbs more often than to ditransitive verbs. To put it differently, transitive verbs are harder to causativize morphologically than intransitive verbs; and ditransitive verbs are harder to causativize morphologically than transitive verbs. For instance, there are languages which completely refrain from adding causative affixes to transitive verbs (e.g. Lamang, Uradhi, Urubu-Kaapor, Moroccan Berber, Kayardild, etc.). Languages such as Abkhaz and Basque, on the other hand, may restrict their causative affixes to both intransitive and transitive verbs, with ditransitive verbs failing to undergo morphological causativization. Note, however, that there is nothing inherent in the CH theory that actually predicts this particular distributional pattern of causative affixes.

The conclusion that must be drawn from the preceding discussion is that the maximum number of core NPs per clause (or MCNP hereafter) may range from two to three regardless of whether a given clause is a simple non-causative or morphological causative one. In other words, morphological causatives may be subject to the same case marking system that ordinary non-causative clauses are. For instance, some languages may not accommodate more than two core NPs per clause; these languages may restrict causative affixes to intransitive verbs in order to avoid morphological causativization of non-intransitive verbs, which will certainly give rise to more than two core NPs. If causative affixes apply to transitive verbs, the total number of core NPs in the morphological causative sentence will increase to three. But some languages may tolerate as many as three core NPs per clause. Indeed there are languages such as Abkhaz and Basque which extend application of causative affixes to transitive verbs. Morphological causativization of ditransitive verbs, however, will result in four core NPs, with which few languages may be able to cope in a single clause, be it causative or not. The general distributional pattern of causative affixes thus arises out of the fact that languages maintain the MCNP in morphological causatives as strictly as in simple non-causative clauses.

This suggests strongly that extended demotion may also be regarded as a possible mechanism that languages may draw upon in order to maintain the MCNP. In extended demotion the causee NP appears in oblique positions which, more often than not, agent phrases also assume in passive clauses. As is evident in Comrie (1975, 1976), extended demotion only takes place when the grammatical relation predicted by the CH for the causee NP is indirect object, not direct object. To put it differently, extended demotion does not seem to occur when the basic verb is intransitive. Morphological causativization of intransitive verbs really causes no problems for the maintaining of the MCNP because it will only give rise to two core NPs, i.e. the causer NP and the causee NP. But, when transitive verbs are morphologically causativized, the total number of core NPs will increase to three. This is not tolerated at all in certain languages, which then encode the causee NP as an adjunct, i.e. a non-core, oblique NP. In the Finnish example in (18), for example, this is exactly what has happened: the causee NP is marked by adessive case as an oblique or adjunct NP. Thus extended demotion is merely one of the ways in which some languages deal with the introduction of one additional core NP – the causer NP – when the basic transitive verb is morphologically causativized.

As for the other type of deviation from the paradigm case, doubling on direct object in causatives parallels doubling on direct object in non-causatives as Comrie (1989: 178) himself confirms that:

[i]t turns out . . . that nearly all languages allowing this possibility [i.e. doubling] in causative constructions are languages that otherwise allow clauses to have two accusative [i.e. direct] objects – it is even conceivable that one should say 'all languages' rather than 'nearly all languages'.

This means that, if doubling is permitted on direct object in simple non-causative clauses, then it is also permitted in morphological causatives (cf. 5.8). As for the indirect object doubling, however, there does not seem to be a similar parallelism although Comrie (1989: 178) notes that it is much more widespread cross-linguistically than is direct object doubling. But this observation should be taken with a degree of caution because, as Comrie (1975: 14, 1976: 277–80) himself notes, the languages that are listed as indirect object doubling languages do seem to disfavour indirect object doubling in causative constructions. As a matter of fact, there are no studies – language-specific or cross-linguistic – that can determine the nature and extent of indirect object doubling in causatives (but cf. Kozinsky and Polinsky 1993, and Polinsky 1994; see 5.5). It remains to be seen, therefore, whether or not indirect object doubling in causatives is as widespread as Comrie (1989: 178) claims it to be.

5.4   Conspiracy in causativization

The tendency for causative affixes to apply more frequently to intransitive verbs than to transitive verbs, and more frequently to transitive verbs than to ditransitive verbs has been interpreted to reflect the way languages manage to comply with the MCNP in morphological causativization as much as in simple non-causative clauses. The restrictions on application of causative affixes may be seen to cheat transitive and/or ditransitive verbs of the opportunity to undergo morphological causativization, as it were.

This does not mean, however, that languages do not have any grammatical means to bypass those strict restrictions imposed on causative affixes. In fact, just as various grammatical devices are pressed into service to create grammatical conditions that are conducive to relativization (see 4.5), there is a number of devices that may be called upon to conspire with morphological causativization. These conspiratorial devices in causativization then enable languages eventually to causativize transitive and/or ditransitive verbs morphologically, while at the same time adhering strictly to the permitted MCNP.

In Blackfoot, for instance, the basic transitive verb is detransitivized by means of the suffix -a:ki before it is causativized by means of the causative suffix, -ippi or -atti. Thus only intransitive verbs – originally or post-detransitivization – are morphologically causativized without a hitch in this Algonquian language. Bandjalang and Halkomelem behave very much like Blackfoot in this respect. In Halkomelem, for example, morphological causativization is permitted only if the non-causative transitive verb is first detransitivized via the antipassive suffix -əm (Gerdts 1984: 194–5). The sentence in (20) is ungrammatical since the causative suffix -st is added directly to the transitive verb root $q'^{w}əl$. In contrast, (21) is grammatical since the transitive verb is antipassivized before undergoing morphological causativization (Gerdts 1984: 194–5).

(20) Halkomelem
*ni   cən q'ʷəl-ət-stəxʷ kʷθə səplíl ʔə ɬə sɬéniʔ
AUX 1SG bake-TR-CS DET bread OBL DET woman
'I had the woman bake the bread.'

(21) Halkomelem
ni   cən q'ʷə́l-əm-stəxʷ θə   sɬéniʔ ʔə kʷθə səplíl
AUX 1SG bake-AP-CS   DET woman OBL DET bread
'I had the woman bake the bread.'

Languages such as Southern Tiwa, on the other hand, must first detransitivize the basic transitive verb by incorporating the direct object into the verb prior to morphological causativization (cf. 3.11.3). This is well illustrated in the example in (22) (Baker 1988: 194–5).

(22) Southern Tiwa
i-'u'u-kur-'am-ban
1SG.SBJ:2SG.OBJ-baby-hold-CS-PST
'I made you hold the baby.'

Note also that both the causer and the causee are represented by the single prefix *i-* on the verb. The verb in Southern Tiwa can register up to two core NPs, the causative verb being no exception to this constraint.[2] This means effectively that, if the direct object NP of the basic verb were not incorporated into the causative verb in (22), there would be no room for that NP in the causative verb. This is precisely why (23) is ungrammatical. In (23) the causative verb has reached its maximum capacity of registering its core NPs, i.e. the causer and causee NP, and yet the direct object NP of the basic verb is expressed fully as a core or non-incorporated NP.

(23) Southern Tiwa
*'u'ude i-kur-'am-ban
baby   1SG.SBJ:2SG.OBJ-hold-CS-PST
'I made you hold the baby.'

Note also that in Southern Tiwa noun incorporation is not called for in causativization of intransitive verbs. This makes sense because morphological causativization of intransitive verbs will give rise to only two core NPs in total, well within the bounds of the MCNP.

Languages such as Afar, Babungo and Songhai may take an even more drastic measure by suppressing or not encoding the causee or some other non-causer NP in morphological causatives. Incidentally, this phenomenon is referred to somewhat misleadingly as 'causative blockage' by Comrie (1975: 9–11, 1976: 264). In Afar and Songhai the causee or some other NP is deleted only in causatives built on transitive verbs as opposed to those built on intransitive verbs (e.g. Afar (Bliese 1981: 129)), or only in causatives built on ditransitive verbs as opposed to those built on intransitive and transitive verbs (e.g. Songhai (Shopen and Konaré 1970: 215)). (Note that this suppression strategy may also give rise to ambiguity in Songhai causatives.)

(24)   Afar
       'oson 'garca gey-siis-ee-'ni
       they thief find-CS-they.PFV-PL
       'They caused the thief to be found' *or*
       'They caused someone to find the thief.'

(25)   Songhai
       garba neere-ndi bari di   musa se
       Garba sell-CS   horse the Musa IO
       'Garba had Musa sell the horse' *or*
       'Garba had the horse sold to Musa.'

Babungo exhibits a slight variation on the suppression strategy in that the direct object NP of the basic verb can be either deleted or expressed as an optional adjunct NP (Schaub 1985: 210).

(26)   Babungo
       ŋwə́ fèe   zɔ̃
       he   fear-PFV snake
       'He was afraid of a snake.'

(27)   Babungo
       mə̀ fèsə̀   ŋwə́ (nə̀ zɔ̃)
       I   fear-CS-PFV him (with snake)
       'I frightened him with a snake.'

The direct object NP in the non-causative sentence in (26), zɔ̃, can appear as part of an adjunct prepositional phrase, nə̀ zɔ̃, or be omitted completely in the corresponding causative sentence in (27).

   The languages that have so far been discussed here all draw upon grammatical devices to which they already have access (for some other original functions) or upon straightforward suppression in order to avoid the possibility of the MCNP being exceeded in morphological causatives. The foregoing discussion raises two important points that further vitiate the CH theory. First, it follows from the CH theory that it is the causee NP that must somehow be mapped onto a 'new' grammatical relation because it is displaced from its original subject relation by the causer NP. But contrary to this prediction the direct object NP of the basic verb, not the causee NP, is omitted in morphological causatives in languages such as Babungo. In other words, if anything happens to one of the NPs of the causative in terms of reassignment of grammatical relations, it is the direct object NP of the basic verb, not the causee NP in Babungo. The same comment can also be made of the direct object NP of the basic verb that must be incorporated into the verb in Southern Tiwa. The causee NP is not at all incorporated into the verb. Thus in these languages the causee NP 'usurps' the grammatical relation of the direct object of the basic verb instead of assuming the next highest grammatical relation on the CH, i.e. indirect object. Second, it is with transitive verbs, not intransitive verbs – or ditransitive verbs, not intransitive and transitive verbs – that omission of the causee NP or the direct object NP of the basic verb takes place. Intransitive verbs never undergo grammatical adjustments that may eventually affect the total number of the core NPs in causatives. Transitive verbs, on the other hand, must first be detransitivized for purposes of morphological causativization in languages such as Blackfoot, Bandjalang and Halkomelem. Theoretically speaking, the causee NP in these languages can and should assume lower grammatical relations on the CH because it is not as if the CH had run out of grammatical relations onto which to map the causee NP. The introduction into causatives of the causer NP via the causative affix is offset neatly by the elimination or downgrading of one of the other core NPs, thereby satisfying the MCNP requirement. The CH theory simply fails to capture, let alone to explain, this intriguing conspiracy in causativization.

5.5 Doubling: coding vs. grammatical relation

If languages are allowed to have up to two or three core NPs per clause, it is reasonable to ask why doubling is permitted in morphological causative clauses in the first place (as well as in simple non-causative clauses). It goes without saying that doubling on direct object only adds to the total number of core NPs. Thus doubling seems to militate against the view advocated here that languages maintain the MCNP not only in non-causative clauses but also in morphological causative clauses. But one first needs to be mindful of what is exactly doubled on in causatives. In the following Ewenki causative sentence direct object relation is claimed to be doubled on as indicated by the fact that both the causee NP and the direct object NP of the basic verb are marked by the same case.

(28) Ewenki
      ynīn-in   xuty-wī awun-mī baka-pkān-yn
      mother-his son-DO   cap-DO   find-CS
      'The (lit. his) mother made her son find his cap.'

The point to be addressed here is this: is it entirely correct to assume that these two NPs also bear the same grammatical relation, i.e. direct object, because they are both marked by accusative case? The position taken in Comrie's (1975, 1976) work is, of course, that they do indeed bear the same grammatical relation, hence doubling on direct object in Ewenki causatives (Comrie 1976: 285).

Recently, however, Polinsky's (1994; also Kozinsky and Polinsky 1993) work has cast doubt on doubling on direct object in causative constructions. The thrust of her argument is that, although they are both marked or coded as direct object NPs, either the causee NP or the direct object NP of the basic verb, not both, may behave syntactically like a genuine direct object NP. In Kinyarwanda, for example, both the causee NP, and the direct object NP of the basic transitive verb are unmarked, appearing as 'bare' nominals without prepositions. Thus they are indistinguishable from each other insofar as coding is concerned (Polinsky 1994: 142).

(29) Kinyarwanda
      umugore y-Ø-uhag-iish-ije   umukoobwa umwaana
      woman   3SG-PST-wash-CS-PFV girl   child
      'The woman made the girl wash the child.'

(30) Kinyarwanda
      umukoobwa y-Ø-uhagi-ye   umwaana
      girl   3SG-PST-wash-PFV child
      'The girl washed the child.'

Polinsky (1994: 140–60) argues, however, that it is the direct object NP of the basic transitive verb, not the causee NP in (29) that can be identified syntactically as a true direct object NP of the causative. As evidence in support she points to the fact that the causee NP, unlike the causer NP and the direct object NP of the basic transitive clause, cannot function as the controller of NP ellipsis across conjoined clauses. This is illustrated in (31) (Polinsky 1994: 150).

(31) Kinyarwanda
      umugore$_i$ y-a-som-eesh-eje   Rusi$_j$ Mariko$_k$
      woman   3SG-PST-kiss-CS-ASP Ruth Mark
      Ø$_{k/*i/*j}$ a-ra-geend-a
      Ø$_{k/*i/*j}$ 3SG-PRS-leave-ASP
      'The woman made Ruth kiss Mark, and (Mark/the woman) left.'

In fact, if the subject NP of the second conjunct clause is intended to be coreferential with the causee NP, it must be repeated in full.

(32)　Kinyarwanda
　　　umugore y-a-som-eesh-eje　　　Rusi Mariko
　　　woman　3SG-PST-kiss-CS-ASP Ruth Mark
　　　Rusi a-ra-geend-a
　　　Ruth 3SG-PRS-leave-ASP
　　　'The woman made Ruth kiss Mark, and Ruth left.'

The direct object NP of the basic verb in the causative 'has more controlling properties than' the causee NP. This is then taken to be in support of the direct object NP of the basic verb being syntactically the direct object NP although it does appear as a bare nominal like the causee NP in the causative (Polinsky 1994: 152).

Moreover, the causee NP, not the direct object NP of the basic verb, must be deleted if and when morphological causativization interacts with other grammatical operations which may engender a 'new' indirect object NP. For instance, the possessor nominal of the possessive phrase (in (33)) can optionally advance to indirect object (in (34)) in Kinyarwanda (Polinsky 1994: 152–8).

(33)　Kinyarwanda
　　　umugore y-a-siimbuk-iish-ije　　　umwaana wa Mariko
　　　woman　3SG-PST-jump-CS-PFV child　　of　Mark
　　　'The woman made Mark's child jump.'

(34)　Kinyarwanda
　　　umugore y-a-siimbuk-iish-iriz-e　　　Mariko umwaana
　　　woman　3SG-PST-jump-CS-APPL-PFV Mark　child
　　　'The woman made Mark's child jump.'

The possessor nominal of the possessive phrase, *Mariko*, is preceded by the preposition, *wa* in (33) but, having advanced to indirect object, it appears without the preposition as a bare nominal in (34) – not to mention its new postverbal position. This advancement is also represented by the applicative suffix *-iriz* on the verb in (34). The causative sentence in (33) is built upon an intransitive verb; thus the causee NP, *umwaana wa Mariko*, in (33) is a direct object NP. When the possessor nominal advances to indirect object in (34), it does not (have to) come into conflict with the causee NP, which is the direct object.

But, when the advancement of the possessor nominal interacts with causativization of transitive verbs, the causee NP must be omitted because Kinyarwanda does not tolerate doubling on indirect object at all. To see how this is so, consider the causative of a transitive verb in (35), in which the direct object NP of the basic verb involves a possessive phrase (Polinsky 1994: 153).

(35)   Kinyarwanda
       umugabo y-Ø-uhag-iish-ije   umukoobwa umwaana
       man   3SG-PST-wash-CS-PFV girl   child
       w'umugore
       of woman
       'The man made the girl wash the woman's child.'

As discussed earlier in relation to NP ellipsis across conjoined clauses, the causee NP is the indirect object NP of the causative, whereas the direct object NP of the basic verb is the direct object NP of the causative in (35). But, when it does advance to indirect object, the possessor nominal in (35) will have to compete with the causee, which is already indirect object. In this case it is the causee NP, not the advanced possessor nominal, that loses out. This is why the causative sentence in (36) is ungrammatical because there are two indirect object NPs in that sentence (Polinsky 1994: 153).

(36)   Kinyarwanda
       *umugabo y-Ø-uhag-iish-iriz-e   umukoobwa umugore
       man   3SG-PST-wash-CS-APPL-PFV girl   woman
       umwaana
       child
       'The man made the girl wash the woman's child.'

Thus the causee NP must be deleted from (36) in order to restore grammaticality of the sentence as in (37). Note that the sentence in (37) does not have the interpretation of 'The man made the girl wash someone's child' because the bare nominals other than the causer in that sentence are meant to be the direct object NP of the basic verb, and the advanced possessor nominal.

(37)   Kinyarwanda
       umugabo y-Ø-uhag-iish-iriz-e   umukoobwa umwaana
       man   3SG-PST-wash-CS-APPL-PFV girl   child
       'The man made (someone) wash the girl's child.'

To conclude, there is no doubling on direct object in Kinyarwanda causatives, the same bare-nominal status of the causee NP and the direct object of the basic verb notwithstanding.

Polinsky (1994: 160–76) arrives at a similar conclusion for Tamil, and Kozinsky and Polinsky (1993) for Korean and Dutch. For instance, Kozinsky and Polinsky (1993) argue that, although in Korean quasi-morphological causatives the causee NP and the direct object NP of the basic verb both appear in accusative case, it is only the causee NP that is syntactically a direct object NP, with the direct object NP of the basic verb being an oblique NP (but cf. Song 1995: 215–19). It should be borne firmly in mind that Polinsky's (1994) and Kozinsky and Polinsky's (1993) findings, based on examination of only four languages, are very far from conclusive. Nonetheless their research draws attention to the important distinction between case marking and grammatical relation: identical case marking or coding may not necessarily be paralleled by 'doubling of grammatical [relations]'.

Moreover, Polinsky's and Kozinsky and Polinsky's works have implications for the other type of doubling. Thus doubling on indirect object may likewise be confined to case marking, not paralleled by doubling on indirect object relation itself. That is to say, although both the causee NP and the indirect object NP of the basic verb are coded identically as indirect object NPs, only one of them may actually be syntactically a genuine indirect object NP. However, no investigation has yet been carried out to extend Polinsky's and Kozinsky and Polinsky's insight to doubling on indirect object in causatives. Note also that their findings at least provide support for the view that morphological causatives are akin to simple non-causative clauses in terms of the MCNP. In Korean the accusative-marked direct object NP of the basic verb is not a core NP but an oblique NP despite the case marking that it bears in common with the causee NP. There are no more than two core NPs in Korean quasi-morphological causatives of transitive verbs, namely the causer NP and the causee NP, well within the bounds of the MCNP.

5.6   Causation types and causative types

The causative construction expresses a macro-situation consisting of two events: (i) the causing event in which the causer does or initiates something in order to bring about another event (that is, the caused event) and (ii) the caused event in which as a result of the causer's action the causee carries out an action or undergoes a change of condition or state. There are two mixed but distinct levels of description in this brief definition of causation: (i) the level of events and (ii) the level of participants. The former level is where the relationship between the causing event and the caused event is captured. The latter level, on the other hand, concerns the relationship between the two major participants of a causative situation, namely the causer and the causee. In fact, most descriptions of semantic causation types revolve around these two different levels of description (e.g. Talmy 1976, Shibatani 1975, 1976b, Haiman 1985a and Kemmer and Verhagen 1994).

There are a number of semantic causation types into which different relations between cause and effect expressed in languages can be categorized. In the present section, however, only two pairs of causation types – (i) the distinction between direct and indirect causation; and (ii) the distinction between manipulative and directive causation – will be examined because these are known to be most highly relevant cross-linguistically to the three causative types, i.e. lexical, morphological and syntactic (Kemmer and Verhagen 1994: 120). The first pair of causation types is based on the level of events and the second on the level of participants.

The distinction between direct and indirect causation hinges on the temporal distance between the causing event and the caused event. If the caused event is temporally connected with the causing event without any other event intervening between them (which will certainly also have a bearing on the caused event), the overall causative situation may be regarded as direct. For example, if X makes Y fall into the river by pushing Y, the causing event of X pushing Y immediately precedes the caused event of Y's falling into the river. There is no intervening or intermediary event that plays a role – however trivial or infinitesimal – in the realization of the caused event.[3] In direct causation the caused event is temporally sequential immediately to the causing event. As a matter of fact, the temporal distance between cause and effect in direct causation may often be so close that it becomes very difficult perceptually, if not conceptually, to divide the whole causative situation clearly into the causing event and the caused event. Thus direct causation represents a causative situation in which the causing event and the caused event abut temporally on each other, the former immediately preceding the latter.

Indirect causation, on the other hand, involves a situation in which the caused event may not immediately follow the causing event in temporal terms. There may thus be an event intervening between the causing and caused events. In order for this to be the case, however, the temporal distance between the two events must be great enough – at least greater than in direct causation – for the whole causative situation to be divided clearly into the causing event and the caused event.[4] For example, X fiddles with Y's car and weeks later Y is injured in a car accident due to the failure of the car. In this situation the causing event is X's fiddling with Y's car and the caused event is Y's getting injured in the accident. But the causing event and the caused event are separated temporally from each other by the intermediary event (i.e. the failure of the car). The intervening event does play an important role in bringing about the caused event. Note that, although this causative situation is indirect, the caused event is connected temporally with the causing event in an inevitable flow or chain of events (Comrie 1989: 172), e.g. Y's accident caused by the failure of the car, and the failure of the car in turn caused by X's fiddling with it. There can potentially be more than one event intervening between the causing event and the caused event in indirect causation. Moreover, in indirect causation the causer may fail to perform an action, thereby effecting the caused event. Think of a situation in which X sees Y in danger of falling off a cliff but X fails to warn Y, and Y falls to his/ her death. In this case 'the ultimate effect [i.e. Y's or the causee's death] is not a direct result of the action of the [X, or the causer], but some other [event, i.e. the killing effect of the fall] which is in turn occasioned or facilitated by the ... *inaction* of the ultimate [causer] [emphasis added]' (DeLancey 1984: 183). The inaction on the part of the causer may thus also permit other events to intervene between the causing event and the caused event as much as does the action on the part of the causer. The causer's inaction is thus taken to be the cause of some other intermediary event which gives rise to the caused event.

The other level of description involves the major participants of the causative situation, i.e. the causer and the causee. Depending on the nature and extent of the causer's relationship with the causee in the realization of the caused event the causative situation may be either manipulative or directive. If the causer acts physically on the causee, then the causative situation is regarded as manipulative. The causer manipulates the causee in bringing about the caused event. The causative situation that was referred to earlier in order to exemplify direct causation actually is also manipulative because the causer physically pushes the causee into the river. In other words, this particular causative situation represents direct and manipulative causation. The causer may also rely on an intermediary physical process or means in effecting the caused event. For example, if X causes Y to fall by pushing a shopping trolley straight into Y, the causer effects the caused event through some physical means as in the case of direct manipulative causation discussed above. But this intermediary physical process does also represent an independent event intervening between the causing event and the caused event – in fact, this intermediary event itself constitutes a causative situation consisting of a causing event (i.e. X exerting physical force directly on the shopping trolley) and a caused event (i.e. the shopping trolley rolling straight into Y) (see Croft 1991: 159–81, and DeLancey 1985 for general discussion of causal chain, or causal order). The causative situation in question may thus be regarded as indirect and manipulative causation.

The causer may also draw upon a non-physical – typically verbal or social – means in causing the causee to carry out the required action or to undergo the required change of condition or state. For example, if X causes Y to lie down by giving Y an instruction or direction to do so – suppose X is a medical doctor and Y is a patient, both involved in a medical examination – the causative situation is directive causation – or inducive causation in Kemmer and Verhagen's (1994: 120) work. This particular situation is also direct in that there is no other event intervening between the causing event and the caused event – Y's lying down is posterior immediately to X's uttering the instruction. Again, directive causation may also be indirect, rather than direct. For example, if X causes Y to type a letter by giving Z an instruction to cause Y to do the typing, then one is dealing with indirect directive causation (e.g. *I had the letter typed by Tim (e.g. by asking Mary to tell him to do so)*). The caused event is separated from the causing event by the intermediary event of Z causing Y to comply with X's original instruction.

Also noteworthy about the distinction between manipulative and directive causation is that in the former causation type the causee may be inanimate or even animate (or human), whereas in the latter the causee may be highly animate and very likely also human. The causer can physically manipulate the inanimate or even animate (or human) causee (against the will of the latter). But the causer may have to appeal to the volition (or cooperation) of the human causee, for example, when giving the latter an instruction to follow. Inanimate entities, however, lack such volition or will to resist or counteract the causer's intended effect (cf. Song 1993).

What is most remarkable about the causation types is that there is a very strong correlation between them and the causative types. Recall from 5.2 that the three different causative types can be interpreted to form a continuum of formal fusion or physical propinquity between the predicate of cause and that of effect. The lexical causative type represents the maximum fusion of the two predicates to the extent that it is impossible to analyse the lexical causative verb into two morphemes. The syntactic causative type represents the minimum fusion of the predicate of cause and that of effect, with the two predicates being separate lexical verbs. The morphological causative type occupies the middle point on the continuum of formal fusion, being susceptible to straightforward morpheme-by-morpheme analysis. These three causative types can thus be placed on the continuum of formal fusion as in (38).

(38) lexical   morphological   syntactic

←————————————————————————————————

a greater degree of fusion

There is a strong tendency for manipulative or direct causation to be mapped onto the causative types to the left of the continuum in preference to those to the right of the continuum. Directive or indirect causation, on the other hand, is far more likely to be expressed by the causative types to the right of the continuum than by those to the left of the continuum. There is, unfortunately, no large-scale work which examines this particular tendency on a firm cross-linguistic basis. In the literature references to languages which actually make the formal distinction between direct and indirect causation, and/or between manipulative and directive causation in the manner described here are but sporadic. Nonetheless discussion of such languages will demonstrate how the noted tendency actually works.

In Mixtec there are at least three different formally identifiable expressions of cause (Hinton 1982: 354–5): the independent lexical verb of cause *sáʔà* and the causative prefixes *sá-* and *s-* – the last two may probably be related historically to the first. The difference between the lexical verb of cause (i.e. the syntactic causative type) and the causative prefixes (i.e. the morphological causative type) reflects the distinction between directive and manipulative causation in this Mixtecan language. Thus in (39) the causer may induce the causee to eat by suggesting that he should eat what has been prepared, for example. In (40), on the other hand, the causer may push food down into the causee's mouth – the latter may refuse to eat food for some reasons or he may be an infant or in a coma.

(39) Mixtec
    sáʔà hà nà kee
    cause NR OPT eat
    'Make him eat.'

(40) Mixtec
    s-kée
    CP-eat
    'Feed him.'

Shibatani (1976b: 33–4) points out that in Japanese the lexical causative verb as in (41) expresses manipulative causation and the morphological causative verb as in (42) directive causation. In (41) the causer exerts physical force directly on the causee in order to effect the caused event, for example, by actually shifting the chair from one location to another, whereas in (42) the causer does not engage in such a physical process in order to effect the caused event. The causer may instead induce the causee to fall down, for example by telling him to do so (as in a play rehearsal).

(41) Japanese
    boku wa isu o ugokasi-ta
    I TOP chair ACC move-PST
    'I moved the chair.'

(42) Japanese
    Taroo wa Ziroo o taore-sase-ta
    Taro TOP Ziro ACC fall.down-CS-PST
    'Taro made Ziro fall down.'

The lexical causative in (41) may also express direct causation in that the caused event immediately follows the causing event in time, whereas the morphological causative in (42) may also encode indirect causation in which the temporal distance between the causing event and the caused event may be great enough for other events to intervene between them. For instance, the causer leaves plastic toys lying around on the floor and the causee trips over them and has a fall. For this situation the morphological, not lexical causative as in (42) will be appropriate, with the contact between the causee and the toys functioning as an intermediary event.

Newari makes a similar formal distinction between manipulative causation and directive causation (DeLancey 1984: 194). In this Tibeto-Burman
language manipulative causation is expressed by means of a partially lexicalized
causative suffix -$k^b al$, whereas directive causation is encoded by a syntactic
causative constructed with the independent lexical verb of cause yat- 'to do'
(and the causative suffix -$k^b e$).[5]

(43)   Newari
       misa-nɔ̃   wo mɔca-yatɔ   cahi-kʰal-ɔ
       woman-ERG the child-DAT walk-CS-PFV
       'A/The woman walked the child.'

(44)   Newari
       misa-nɔ̃   wo mɔca-yatɔ   cahi-kʰe yat-ɔ
       woman-ERG the child-DAT walk-CS do-PFV
       'A/The woman made the child walk.'

DeLancey (1984: 194) points out that the sentence in (43) evokes a picture
of the woman physically dragging the child down the road and the sentence
in (44) may involve the woman ordering the child to walk and the latter
complying with the former. Thus (43) represents manipulative causation and
(44) directive causation.

In Jinghpaw, on the other hand, the causative prefix sha-/ja- is used to
express direct causation and the independent causative verb shangun indirect
causation (Maran and Clifton 1976: 445–6).

(45)   Jinghpaw
       Ma Naw gaw Ma Tu hpe ja-san   ai
       Ma Naw SBJ Ma Tu OBJ CP-die DECL
       'Ma Naw killed Ma Tu.'

(46)   Jinghpaw
       Ma Naw gaw Ma Tu hpe san shangun ai
       Ma Naw SBJ Ma Tu OBJ die cause   DECL
       'Ma Naw caused Ma Tu to die.'

Maran and Clifton (1976: 446) explain that the difference between (45) and
(46) is related to a concept of 'directness of causation'. Thus (45) typically
describes a situation in which Ma Naw himself gave Ma Tu a fatal strike and
(46) a situation in which Ma Naw hired someone to kill Ma Tu (i.e. the
causer's action), or in which Ma Naw failed to come to Ma Tu's aid when
Ma Tu was in danger of, for example, drowning in the river (i.e. the causer's
inaction). In other words, (45) expresses direct causation and (46) indirect
causation.[6]

In Nivkh the lexical and morphological causative types can similarly be distinguished, with the former expressing direct causation and the latter indirect causation. In this language the lexical causative verb involves a non-productive process of initial consonant alternation, whereas the morphological causative verb is built on the basic verb by means of the suffix *-gu* (Comrie 1989: 172–3).

(47) Nivkh
    if lep   seu-d'
    he bread dry
    'He dried the bread.'

(48) Nivkh
    if lep   če-gu-d'
    he bread dry-CS
    'He caused the bread to get dry.'

According to Comrie (1989: 173), (47) will be most appropriate for a causative situation in which the causer deliberately set about drying the bread, for example by putting it in the oven, whereas (48) describes a causative situation in which the causer forgot to cover the bread, which eventually became dry. That is, in (47) the ultimate effect was a direct result of the causer's action (i.e. direct causation), while in (48) the causer's inaction did not prevent the intermediary event (i.e. the drying effect of air) from intervening between the causing event and the caused event (i.e. indirect causation).

Thus there is a strong tendency for direct or manipulative causation to be expressed by the causative types to the left of the continuum of fusion in (38) in preference to those to the right, and for indirect or directive causation to be expressed by the causative types to the right of the continuum in preference to those to the left. This is very often cited in the literature as an excellent example whereby iconic motivation can be shown to be at work in language (but cf. Song 1992, 1996: 102–4 for possible counterexamples from Kammu, Malagasy and Tagalog). Iconic motivation or iconicity represents 'the principle that the structure of language should, as closely as possible, reflect the structure of experience, that is, the structure of what is being expressed by language' (Croft 1995: 129; also Haiman 1985a, Bybee 1985a). Haiman (1985a: 102–47), for instance, proposes that grammatical distance mirrors conceptual distance. In particular, he (1985a: 108–11) suggests that the linguistic or formal distance between the predicate of cause and that of effect is motivated iconically by the conceptual distance between the causing event and the caused event, and between the causer and the causee. In order to measure linguistic distance he (1985a: 105) puts forth the formal scale in (49).

(49)   *Linguistic Distance*
   a.   X # A # B # Y
   b.   X # A # Y
   c.   X + A # Y
   d.   X # Y
   e.   X + Y
   f.   Z [= fusion of X and Y into a single form]
   N.B.: # = word boundary, + = morpheme boundary

If X is the predicate of cause and Y the predicate of effect, (49a–b) may well represent the syntactic causative type, (49e) the morphological causative type and (49f) the lexical causative type. Conceptual distance in turn is defined in (50).

(50)   *Conceptual Distance*
   Two ideas are conceptually close to the extent that they
   a.   share semantic features, properties, or parts
   b.   affect each other
   c.   are factually inseparable and
   d.   are perceived as a unit, whether factually inseparable or not

Manipulative causation, for instance, represents a causative situation which is perceived as a single unit, as it were. In (40) the physical contact between the causer and the causee is very close, so much so that the causer acts directly on the causee, for example, by opening the causee's mouth and pushing the food into the causee's mouth and so on. In (39), which expresses directive causation, there is no such physical contact between the causer and the causee. The causer simply tells the causee to eat the food. In addition, there may possibly be a good temporal distance between the causing event and the caused event. In other words, the two events may not be coterminous in time with each other in (39). The conceptual distance between the causing event and the caused event is greater in (indirect) directive causation (39) than in (direct) manipulative causation (40). This conceptual distance in turn is claimed to be what motivates the corresponding linguistic distance between the predicate of cause and that of effect. In (40) the predicate of cause is attached morphologically to that of effect (i.e. (49e)), whereas in (39) the predicate of cause and that of effect are independent lexical verbs, clearly separated by other linguistic expressions (i.e. (49a)).

In principle, iconic motivation, as is demonstrated by the distribution of the causative types in relation to the semantic causation types, is, in fact, akin to Bybee's (1985a) notion of relevance, which was discussed in 2.6: the more highly relevant to a host grammatical material X is, the more fused to that host X becomes. The formal propinquity of the causative affix to the basic verb, for instance, may reflect the relevance between these two predicates. In manipulative, as opposed to directive, causation the caused event is more closely tied up with the causing event. For instance, the caused event may be brought about by the causing event regardless of the causee's volition or will (to resist the causer's intended effect). The causing event (i.e. the predicate of cause) is, thus, highly relevant to the realization of the caused event (i.e. the predicate of effect). In directive causation, on the other hand, the causee is more likely to be able to decide whether s/he will comply with the causer's non-physical or verbal demand or request. To put it differently, the causing event is less relevant to the realization of the caused event, which is, in fact, mediated or facilitated to a great extent by the causee's own volition or will (or cooperation). This difference in relevance between manipulative and directive causation is then reflected by the formal distinction between the morphological and syntactic causative types, found in Mixtec and Newari, or between the lexical and morphological causative types as in Japanese, for instance. A similar comment can also be made *mutatis mutandis* of the distinction between direct and indirect causation.

5.7   The case marking of the causee NP

As demonstrated in 5.3, the CH theory is built on the assumption that the case marking of the causee is determined strictly by reference to the formal hierarchy of grammatical relations. In addition to the evidence presented against the CH theory in the same section there is also a large amount of cross-linguistic evidence in support of the case marking of the causee being determined by semantic and/or pragmatic factors relating to agency, control, affectedness and even topicality of the main participants of the causative situation.

In Japanese the causee NP – or the subject NP of the basic intransitive verb in the sense of Comrie (1975, 1976) – is marked by either the accusative case *o* or the dative case *ni*. (Note that the two sentences both involve morphological causativization.)

(51) Japanese
Kanako ga   Ziroo o   ik-ase-ta
Kanako NOM Ziroo ACC go-CS-PST
'Kanako made Ziroo go.'

(52) Japanese
Kanako ga   Ziroo ni   ik-ase-ta
Kanako NOM Ziroo DAT go-CS-PST
'Kanako got Ziroo to go.'

There is a clear semantic difference between (51) and (52) in terms of the role of the causee in the overall causative situation. In (51) the causee is understood to exercise a lower degree of control over the caused event, while in (52) it is interpreted to exercise a higher degree of control over the caused event. In other words, the causee in (52) is more agentive than that in (51). The causee in (51) is, in fact, akin conceptually to the patient because the causer does not appeal to the causee's volition or will in effecting the caused event. In (52), on the other hand, the causer is expected to appeal to the causee's volition or will. It may not be unfair to say that the caused event may not come about without the causee's complying with the causer's demand or request. The causee in (51) or (52) is more or less directly affected by the causer's action, respectively. Thus the causative in (51) typically expresses direct, manipulative causation, whereas that in (52) would be more appropriate for the expressing of indirect directive causation. This difference is signalled neatly by the case marking of the causee in (51) and (52).

In Bolivian Quechua the causee NP or the subject NP of the basic transitive verb can be marked either by the accusative case *-ta* or by the instrumental case *-wan* (Cole 1983: 118).

(53)   Bolivian Quechua
    nuqa Fan-ta   rumi-ta   apa-či-ni
    I   Juan-ACC rock-ACC carry-CS-1SG
    'I made Juan carry the rock.'

(54)   Bolivian Quechua
    nuqa Fan-wan   rumi-ta   apa-či-ni
    I   Juan-INST rock-ACC carry-CS-1SG
    'I had Juan carry the rock.'

The sentence in (53) describes a situation in which the causee 'is directly under the [causer's] authority and has no control over whether he will carry the rock' (Cole 1983: 119). This contrasts clearly with (54), which is more appropriate for a situation in which 'the causee retains control over his actions and submits voluntarily to the [causer's] wishes' (Cole 1983: 119). Moreover, in Bolivian Quechua the causee NP can also appear in dative case *-man*. In fact, this dative type of causee marking co-occurs with 'verbs of experience', a language-specific grammatical category, which includes predicates such as *rikʰu-* 'to see', *yuya-* 'to remember', *yaca-* 'to know', *mikʰu-* 'to eat', etc. (Cole 1983: 119). The dative marking of the causee is exemplified in (55).

(55)   Bolivian Quechua
    nuqa runa-man rikʰu-či-ni
    I   man-DAT see-CS-1SG
    'I showed it to the man.'

Involuntary recipient of the experience of the basic verb (i.e. perception) though he is, the causee in (55) is a human and thus *potentially* highly agentive. For instance, the causee may have far more control over perception than is the case in (53), in which the causee has no choice but to carry the rock. (The causee can easily refuse to look at what is shown to him, for instance.) This is essentially what distinguishes the dative causee from either the accusative or the instrumental causee. Thus Cole (1983: 119) suggests that the alternation between instrumental, dative and accusative case reflects the degree of agency or control of the causee as schematized in (56).

(56)   Instrumental > Dative > Accusative

$\longleftarrow \qquad\qquad\qquad \longrightarrow$

more agentive	more patient-like
more control	less control
(less affected)	(more affected)

This hierarchy of agency or control may alternatively be interpreted to reflect the degree of affectedness of the causee. If the causee has more control over his or her action, s/he is likely to be less affected by the causer's action. In contrast, if the causee does not have control over his or her action, s/he is likely to be more affected by the causer's action (cf. Saksena 1980).

Comparable data can be adduced from languages such as Hindi, Hungarian and Kannada in support of (56) (Cole 1983: 120–4, and Kemmer and Verhagen 1994: 131–9, based on Saksena 1980). Consider:

(57)   Hindi
mai-nee raam-koo   masaalaa cakh-vaa-yaa
I-AGT Ram-DAT spice   taste-CS-PST
'I had Ram taste the seasoning.'

(58)   Hindi
mai-nee raam-see   masaalaa cakh-vaa-yaa
I-AGT Ram-INST spice   taste-CS-PST
'I had Ram taste the seasoning.'

(59)   Hungarian
köhögtettem a   gyerek-kel
I-CP-cough the boy-INST
'I had the boy cough.'

(60)   Hungarian
köhögtettem a   gyerek-et
I-CP-cough the boy-ACC
'I made the boy cough.'

(61)   Kannada
avanu   nanage tīyannu kudisidanu
he-NOM me-DAT tea-ACC drink-CS-PST
'He caused me to drink tea.'

(62) Kannada
      avanu   nanninda tīyannu kudisidanu
      he-NOM me-INST tea-ACC drink-CS-PST
      'He caused me to drink tea.'

In these languages, as in the case of Bolivian Quechua, when it is in the
instrumental as opposed to the accusative, the causee NP is interpreted to
retain control over the caused event. In (59) the causee's coughing may have
been 'at the request of the [causer]', whereas in (60) it may have been
induced, for example, 'by blowing smoke in the [causee's] face' (Hetzron
1976: 394, Cole 1983: 124). This difference in control, again, falls out neatly
from the hierarchy in (56). A similar comment can also be made of the
Hindi and Kannada pairs.

Incidentally, the preceding discussion of the variable case marking of the
causee NP may also be seen to provide support for the indexing, as opposed
to discriminatory, view of case marking, discussed in 3.7. The fact that the
case marking of the causee varies between accusative, dative and instrumental
in the same language indicates strongly that the function of case marking –
insofar as the case marking of the causee NP is concerned – is motivated
by the role or integration of the causee in the overall causative event (i.e.
patient ~ experiencer ~ agent). If the causee is affected directly by the causer's
action, it is marked by accusative case just as the patient (or P) is in the
prototypical transitive clause. If it is affected least by the causer's action, the
causee appears in instrumental case, thereby indicating that it is an agentive
participant who has much control over the caused event, perhaps as much
control as, if not more than, the causer may have over the causee. This
indexing view of the case marking of the causee NP is demonstrated most
clearly by the Japanese causatives in (51) and (52). There are only two (core)
NPs in either of the two sentences. Thus there is no reason why the causee
NP should have to be marked in two different ways if the function of the
case marking of the causee is only to distinguish the causee from the causer
in nominative case.

5.8   The conceptual integration of the causee in the causative event

Recently, Kemmer and Verhagen (1994) have reinforced Cole's (1983) work
by (re)interpreting the variable case marking of the causee NP to reflect the
conceptual integration of the causee in the causative event as a whole. The
causee NP in accusative case is more patient-like than the causee NP in dative or instrumental case, 'and therefore central it is to the event as a whole'
(Kemmer and Verhagen 1994: 133). To put it differently, the accusative

causee is to the causer in the causative event what the patient is to the agent in the transitive event. The causer as the agent is seen to act or impinge directly on the causee as the patient in the causative event as a whole. In this very sense the accusative causee is highly integrated in the overall causative event. The causee in dative case is less affected by the causer's action and, in fact, more likely to be affected experientially or mentally than physically, with the focus on the experiencing rather than the undergoing of an effect by the causee (Kemmer and Verhagen 1994: 135; cf. (55)).[7] Thus, while retaining some control over his or her action, the dative causee is still a central – albeit less central than the accusative causee – participant in the overall causative event. The causee in instrumental case, on the other hand, is the least central – or the most peripheral – to the causative event as a whole because it is the most agentive and, therefore, affected least by the causer's action. The instrumental causee has as much control over his or her action, or over the caused event just as the causer has over the causee or over the causing event. The instrumental causee is as agentive as, if not more than the causer. In other words, the focus is 'on nothing more than [the causee's] intermediary role in accomplishing the [caused] event' (Kemmer and Verhagen 1994: 135). Thus the instrumental causee is integrated in the overall causative event much less than either the accusative causee or the dative causee.

This leads Kemmer and Verhagen (1994: 125–31) to take the simple transitive clause as a conceptual (and also structural) pattern on which the causative is built. The causative of intransitive verbs is based conceptually on the transitive clause pattern, e.g. *I ate the cake*, and the causative of transitive verbs on either the ditransitive clause pattern, e.g. *I gave her the apple*, or the transitive clause pattern with an adjunct, e.g. *I hit it with a hammer*. Like the agent of the simple transitive clause the causer in the causative of intransitive verbs represents 'a highly individuated entity capable of volition, and volitionally exerting energy on a second participant'. On the other hand, the causee in the causative of intransitive verbs, like the patient of the simple transitive clause, represents the second participant, who in turn 'absorbs the energy, whereby it undergoes a change of state that would not have taken place without the exertion of energy' (Kemmer and Verhagen 1994: 126). This conceptual similarity between the transitive clause and the causative of intransitive verbs is represented schematically in Figure 5.1.

In the causative of transitive verbs, on the other hand, the causee is akin conceptually to the indirect object – recipients or beneficiaries – in the non-causative ditransitive clause. Thus just like the recipient or beneficiary the dative causee has many experiencer-like properties. Typically, the dative causee is animate and/or human, and thus very likely to be experientially or mentally – rather than physically – affected by the causer's action (Kemmer and Verhagen 1994: 129); cf. (55)). In a typical 'ditransitive' situation (e.g. giving, showing, etc.) the recipient may indeed be as much affected experientially as humans normally are in social interaction (Newman 1996: 51–2).

Figure 5.1: *The direction of impingement in simple transitive and causative constructions*

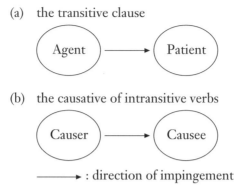

(a)   the transitive clause

Agent ⟶ Patient

(b)   the causative of intransitive verbs

Causer ⟶ Causee

⟶ : direction of impingement

To put it differently, the dative causee can be conceived of as an intermediary who interacts with the causer in realizing the caused event just as the recipient interacts with the giver in carrying out a transfer of an object or thing. Moreover, the giver may also be understood to cause the recipient to come into possession of the patient (or the thing which is given) (for such a view see Tuggy 1988). Hence the conceptual similarity between the prototypical 'ditransitive' situation and the causative of transitive verbs (cf. Newman 1996). As already shown, the causee may also appear in instrumental case. Like a physical instrument (e.g. a hammer) which may be employed by the agent acting on the patient in a typical transitive situation, the causee can also be seen to act as 'a kind of metaphorical instrument, employed by the causer to get the action carried out' (Kemmer and Verhagen 1994: 129). That is, the instrumental causee can be looked upon as the causer's intermediary agent.

This conceptual similarity thus motivates the causee in the causative of transitive verbs to appear in dative or instrumental case in some languages. This is schematized in Figure 5.2. (Note that regardless of whether the causee is in the dative or the instrumental the ultimate endpoint of the causer's action – or what Langacker (1991: 292) refers to as the 'energy sink' – is the patient.)

Kemmer and Verhagen's (1994) proposal that the simple transitive clause pattern serves as a conceptual model for morphological – and probably also for quasi-morphological – causatives fits in very well with the view put forward in 5.3: the 'deviations' from the paradigm case, e.g. extended demotion, doubling, etc., arise out of the different ways in which the same MCNP permitted in simple non-causative clauses is also adhered to in morphological causatives. Insofar as case marking is concerned, the same MCNP serves as the basic conceptual and structural model not only for simple non-causative clauses, but also for morphological causatives.[8]

Figure 5.2: *The direction of impingement in transitive-with-adjunct and causative constructions*

(a) the transitive with a recipient, beneficiary or instrumental adjunct

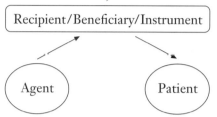

(b) the causative of transitive verbs

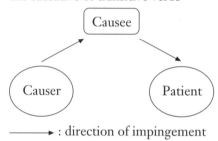

——→ : direction of impingement

In support of the view that the variable case marking of the causee reflects the conceptual – and also structural – integration of the causee in the causative event as a whole Kemmer and Verhagen (1994: 141–2) present statistical data from Dutch. In Dutch causatives direct and less direct (or indirect) causation are differentiated grammatically by means of a choice in the predicates of cause, *laten* 'to let' (e.g. (63)) vs. *doen* 'to do, to make' (e.g. (66)). The predicate of cause *doen* is used to express direct causation and the other predicate of cause *laten* less direct or indirect causation. Moreover, the case marking of the causee fluctuates between zero-marking (Ø) (e.g. (63)), dative (*aan*) (e.g. (64)) and agentive or instrumental (*door*) (e.g. (65)). Thus the distinction between direct and less direct or indirect causation is predicted to correlate with the actual case marking of the causee with the effect that, for example, zero marking of the causee will more frequently be found to co-occur with *doen* than with *laten*.

(63) Dutch
U   kunt ook uw   man   de boodschappen laten doen
you can also your husband the groceries   let   do
'You can also have your husband get the groceries.'

Table 5.1: *Case marking of the causee in Dutch causatives*

	Ø	DAT	AGT/INST
Causatives of intransitive verbs (n = 417):			
with *laten*	100%	–	–
with *doen*	100%	–	–
Causatives of transitive verbs (n = 143):			
with *laten* (n = 118)	47%	6%	47%
with *doen* (n = 25)	100%	–	–

(64) Dutch
    Hij wilde   het aan een collega   laten zien
    he wanted it   to   a   colleague let   see
    'He wanted to show it to a colleague.'

(65) Dutch
    Zij   lieten Woody adopteren door een echtpaar
    they let   Woody adopt   by   a   married-couple
    'They had Woody adopted by a married couple.'

(66) Dutch
    Dit deed de VPRO leden   verliezen
    this did the VPRO members lose
    'This made the VPRO lose members.'

The distribution of the case marking of the causee vis-à-vis the predicates of
cause, reported in Kemmer and Verhagen (1994: 141–5; cf. Verhagen and
Kemmer 1997), is summarized in Table 5.1. (Note that direct object nominal
phrases are zero-marked (i.e. Ø).)
    With the predicate of cause *doen* – as somewhat predicted – it is always
in zero-marking that the causee appears (regardless of whether the basic
verb is intransitive or transitive). Thus only zero marking is used for the
causee in the *doen*-based causative. In the *laten*-based causative of transitive
verbs, on the other hand, the case marking of the causee is polarized between
zero-marking and agentive/instrumental marking, with dative marking attested
in a very limited number of instances. This is claimed to be due to the fact
that the predicate of cause *laten* expresses less direct or indirect, not direct
causation, thereby 'leav[ing] room, as it were, for different case-markings on
the causee that express different degrees of integration [of the causee] in the
event' (Kemmer and Verhagen 1994: 144). It is also worth noting that the
causee in the causative of intransitive verbs in Dutch is always zero-marked

as direct object irrespective of whether the predicate of cause is *laten* or *doen* (cf. Figure 5.1). It seems that in Dutch the causative of intransitive verbs is grammaticized fully into or modelled completely on the transitive clause structure (Kemmer and Verhagen 1994: 138, 142; but cf. Japanese as in (51) and (52)).

Finally, Kemmer and Verhagen's (1994) interpretation also explains the correlation between case marking of the causee as captured in (56) and topicality of the causee. Consider (57) and (58) again.

(57)   Hindi
       mai-nee raam-koo   masaalaa cakh-vaa-yaa
       I-AGT   Ram-DAT spice   taste-CS-PST
       'I had Ram taste the seasoning.'

(58)   Hindi
       mai-nee raam-see   masaalaa cakh-vaa-yaa
       I-AGT   Ram-INST spice   taste-CS-PST
       'I had Ram taste the seasoning.'

In (57), for instance, the causer's aim is to get the causee to taste the seasoning, while in (58) it is to get the tasting done regardless of who actually carries out the tasting task. Thus in (58) it is merely incidental to the whole causative event who tastes the seasoning. To put it differently, the instrumental causee is non-topical, whereas the dative causee is topical. This is also found to be the case with the case marking of the causee in French as clearly demonstrated in Hyman and Zimmer (1976: 199).

(67)   French   *au = à + le*
       j'ai fait   nettoyer les toilettes au   le général
       I   made clean   the toilets   to (DAT) the general
       'I made the general clean the toilets.'

(68)   French
       j'ai fait   nettoyer les toilettes par le   général
       I   made clean   the toilets   by the general
       'I had the toilets cleaned by the general.'

The contrast in topicality is reflected in the English translations of the two sentences in (67) and (68). In (67) what is topically important is that the general was the one that the causer got to do the toilet-cleaning. In (68), on the other hand, what really matters is that the toilet-cleaning was done. In fact, 'the general is incidental to the task' (Hyman and Zimmer 1976: 199). The dative causee in (67) is topical, whereas the instrumental causee in (68) is non-topical.

Thus topicality of the causee also seems to vary in direct proportion to the integration in the overall causative event of the causee (Kemmer and Verhagen 1994: 133). The causee NP in accusative case is central to the causative event as a whole because it is most patient-like and integrated most in the causative event. Therefore, it is topical. The causee NP in instrumental case, on the other hand, is the opposite of the causee NP in accusative case. Being the least patient-like the instrumental causee NP is integrated least in, and peripheral to the causative event as a whole. Therefore, it is non-topical. In fact, the peripherality of the oblique – agentive or instrumental – causee NP is exactly what makes it even dispensable in some cases. The oblique causee NP 'represents a participant that is not prominent in any way in the overall conceptualization of the event' (Kemmer and Verhagen 1994: 136). The dative causee NP may probably fall between the accusative causee NP and the instrumental causee NP in terms of topicality. The hierarchy of the agency or control of the causee in (56) can then also be interpreted as a hierarchy of topicality. This again ties in well with the view put forward in 5.3 that languages may resort to extended demotion of the causee NP to the oblique position on the CH so that the MCNP can be complied with. In extended demotion the causee NP is reduced to non-core or peripheral status. The causee NP is thus put into a position in which it is unable to vie for topical status with the other core NPs including the causer. It is no coincidence, therefore, that the oblique causee NP tends to share the same case marking with the optional – non-topical – agentive phrase of the passive construction. Of course, in languages such as Babungo, Southern Tiwa, etc., it is the direct object NP of the basic verb, not the causee NP, that is demoted to a non-core/peripheral and thus non-topical position.

5.9   Towards a typology of causative constructions

The traditional typology of causative constructions is based crucially on the parameter of formal fusion between the predicate of cause and that of effect as captured in (38). Among the three causative types embodied in this typology the morphological type has over the years received most attention from researchers of various theoretical, including typological orientations. This is probably because the morphological type does indeed pose a number of interesting questions as to how and why the two conceptually separate events – the causing event and the caused event – are expressed by means of a single, albeit derived verb. For instance, the question arises immediately of how the conceptually two-fold event structure can be mapped onto, or related to the grammatically simple structure. Thus Comrie's (1975, 1976) CH theory can better be understood to be an attempt to resolve this fundamental discrepancy between the two levels of structure. The lexical causative type, on the other hand, can without much difficulty be accepted as non-productive, as opposed to the relatively productive morphological causative type. Lexical causative verbs can simply be listed in the lexicon as lexical oddities although it may present the same problem.

This predilection for the morphological causative type notwithstanding discussions of the semantic causation types – which have been correlated directly with the causative types (cf. 5.6) – have shed little light on the nature of causation *per se* although they have unquestionably enriched our understanding of causation. For instance, the temporal distance between the causing event and the caused event – i.e. direct vs. indirect causation – does not provide much insight into what it is that the human mind cognizes as a causative situation. In fact, what seems to be taken for granted in the explicating of the distinction between direct and indirect causation is an understanding of causation itself. The temporal distance between the causing event and the caused event is not equivalent to causation, however. The degree of agency or control exercised by the causee in a causative situation – or the degree of affectedness of the causee for that matter – only pertains to the interaction or (interpersonal) relationship between the causer and the causee, which in itself constitutes only part of a causative situation. The interaction between the causer and the causee is not equivalent to causation, either.

Recently, Song (1996) has demonstrated that the undue emphasis placed on the morphological causative type has contributed to under-determination of the other causative types, especially the syntactic causative type, in the languages of the world. Based on a database of 613 languages he has proposed an alternative typology in which three different types of causative construction are identified: the *COMPACT* type, the *AND* type and the *PURP* type. In particular, his cross-linguistic study has led to the discovery of a far richer variety of the so-called syntactic causative type, under which the *AND* type and the *PURP* type – not to mention various sub-types of them – have been indiscriminately lumped together in the traditional morphologically based typology. Limitations of space, of course, make it impossible to discuss this typology in detail. What follows is, therefore, a very brief introduction. The reader is encouraged to refer to Song (1996) for full discussion.

The *COMPACT* type typically includes the lexical and morphological causative types in that the expression of cause and that of effect are physically contiguous to each other (to varying degrees). This particular type is exemplified, for example, by the lexical causative in English (e.g. *kill*) and by the morphological causatives in Turkish (as in (14)–(17)), or Japanese (as in (42)).

The *AND* type is illustrated by the causative from Vata in (69), for example. In this Kru language the clause of cause and that of effect are coordinated by means of the universal conjunction *le*. Note that the first clause denotes the causing event, and the second clause the caused event, strictly in that order (Koopman 1984: 24–5).

(69) Vata
      ǹ gbā le   yò-ò   lī
      I speak CONJ child-DEF eat
      'I make the child eat.'

In the *AND*-type causative of Kinyarwanda, on the other hand, the clause
of cause and that of effect are juxtaposed to each other without use of an
explicit conjunction, again in that order (Kimenyi 1980: 160–3).

(70) Kinyarwanda
      umukoôbwa y-a-tum-ye   n-á-andik-a   amábárúwa
      girl   she-PST-cause-ASP I-PST-write-ASP letters
      meênshi
      many
      'The girl caused me to write many letters.'

Finally, the *PURP* type of causative construction consists of two clauses,
one denoting event$_x$ carried out for the purpose of realizing event$_y$ denoted
by the other. The purposive element prominent in this type of causative can
be in the form of purposive case markers, verbal markings such as future
tense, irrealis, subjunctive mood, incompletive aspect, etc., or purposive particles. Languages such as Kunjen, Tzotzil and Lahu provide examples of this
type of causative construction, with diverse realizations of the purposive
element.

(71) Kunjen
      arŋg ugŋgaṇiyar   ud il iŋun abm   aṯan-aɣ
      child frighten-SBJ-AGT dog he him person bite-PURP
      ambar
      cause-RLSPST
      'The frightened child caused the dog to bite him.'

(72) Kunjen
      abm   ay egŋ-aɣ   igun   ay lalaŋan
      person I food-PURP go-RLSPRS I uncle-DAT
      'I am going for food for Uncle.'

(73) Tzotzil
      ʔa li Xun-e   l-i-y-ak'-be
      TOP the Xun-CLT CMP-1ABS-3ERG-make-IO
      j-tuch'-Ø   turasnu
      1ERG-cut-SUBJ peach
      'Xun made me cut peaches.'

(74) Tzotzil
      tal   ?elk'aj-uk ta Muk'ta Jok'
      came steal-SUBJ at Muk'ta Jok'
      'They came to steal at Muk'ta Jok'.'

(75) Lahu
      yô cân-pā ší tù   te gâ ve
      he enemy die PURP do want PRT
      'He wants to make the enemy die.'

(76) Lahu
      ɛ́   hɔ̀ ğa tù   mɔ̀ʔ-qɔ qhɔ á-phὲʔ-šī jû̀ʔ   pî ve
      baby cry get PURP mouth LOC hot.peppers pierce give PRT
      yò
      DECL
      'In order to get the baby to cry we stick hot peppers into its mouth.'

In Kunjen the case marker -*aɣ*, which is used to express the purposive role
of the NP *egɣ* in (72), is also employed to mark the clause of effect in the
causative construction in (71) (Sommer 1972: 42, 118). In Tzotzil the ordinary subordinate clause of purpose is marked by the subjunctive mood of the
verb of that clause as in (74). Note that the verb of effect in the causative
construction also appears in subjunctive mood as in (73) (Aissen 1987: 214).
Finally, in Lahu the purposive particle *tù* is used to signal unreal, future,
hypothetical or purposive actions as in (76). The same particle is also used in
the expression of the caused event in the causative construction in (75)
(Matisoff 1976: 438–41).

   One of the findings that have emerged out of Song's (1996) cross-
linguistic survey of causative constructions is the full richness and variety of
causative constructions found in the languages of the world. The proposed
typology also offers an empirical basis on which to build a cognitive model
of causation and also a diachronic model of causative affixes.

   First, with the *COMPACT* type understood to be the type towards which
the other two types tend to gravitate over time, the *AND* type and the *PURP*
type represent the two major types of causative construction in the languages
of the world. The *AND* type expresses two components of causation: a
deliberate attempt to realize a desire or wish (or EVENT); and accomplish-
ment of that desire or wish (or RESULT). In the *AND* type the EVENT
component corresponds to the clause of cause and the RESULT component
to the clause of effect. The *PURP* type, on the other hand, denotes the
EVENT component (i.e. a deliberate attempt to realize a desire or wish) and
also one other component, that is perception of that desire or wish (or
GOAL) – the latter component in the *PURP* type corresponds to the subordinate clause of purpose. These three components can then be assembled
into the temporally based structure or model in (77) (Song 1996: 138–48).

(77)   GOAL → EVENT → RESULT
       where → represents progression of time

The diagram in (77) in turn is claimed to represent the cognitive model of causation, reflected directly in the typology of causative constructions.

Second, proper recognition as a causative construction *par excellence* of the PURP type in particular has implications for diachronic sources of causative affixes. Thus in a large number of languages causative affixes can be plausibly traced back to various purposive case markers, verbal markers of purpose, etc.; in other languages hitherto claimed origins of causative affixes can be fruitfully re-examined (Song 1996: 80–102).

Notes

1. Perhaps the causative verb *vunj-a* may also be analysed as containing a zero causative affix in opposition to the non-causative verb *vunj-ik-a*, that is *vunj-ø-a*.
2. Frantz (1971: 19) notes that with transitive animate verbs (i.e. with both animate actors and undergoers) some agreement suffixes are optional only if the NPs with which they agree are clearly present in the immediate clause.
3. One may argue that even in this case there is an intervening event, that is X's causing his or her limb to push Y. But in the present discussion the limb is regarded as an inalienable part of X. There is thus no intervening event involving entities other than X as the causer.
4. Exactly how great this distance should be is difficult to say, however.
5. Note that DeLancey (1983) reports that in the Newari syntactic causative construction with *yat-* the basic verb is used without the causative suffix (cf. DeLancey 1984: 210).
6. It may be said that (45) also expresses manipulative causation in that the causer was physically involved in carrying out the caused event (i.e. the causee's death).
7. Kemmer and Verhagen (1994: 135) also point out that there is an additional piece of evidence that the notion of experience is of relevance to the causee in dative case. Thus they find that in languages such as Hindi, Dutch, Kannada and Quechua the use of dative case for the causee is restricted to a limited set of verbs or predicates, which all denote experiences on the part of the causee (e.g. 'see', 'read', 'hear', 'notice', etc.).
8. This suggests strongly that, unless doubling is permitted in non-causative transitive clauses, doubling in causative clauses will not be permitted because, as Kemmer and Verhagen (1994) claim, causatives are modelled conceptually and structurally on non-causative clauses.

6

The application of linguistic typology

6.1   Introduction

In the present chapter possibilities of applying linguistic typology to other areas of linguistics – i.e. historical linguistics, first language acquisition (FLA) and second language acquisition (SLA) – will be explored, wherever possible, by referring back to relevant discussions in the preceding chapters. In historical linguistics some linguists have enthusiastically embraced linguistic typology particularly since the publication of Greenberg (1963b); other linguists have sharply criticized and also called into question the application of linguistic typology to linguistic reconstruction. Nonetheless linguistic typology commands excellent prospects of raising fundamental questions about language change, and resolving some of the problems and issues involved in historical linguistics, if and when applied judiciously. In FLA and SLA, on the other hand, linguistic typology in the opinion of the present writer, has not been utilized as much as it should have. This is echoed by the L2 researcher William Rutherford (1984b: 138), who puts it, '[i]t is probably safe to say that the [L2] explanatory framework that is most often mentioned, *though less often actually utilized*, is that of "language universal" [emphasis added].' Indeed, with the notable exception of the work of S. Gass (1979, 1982, 1984a, 1984b), S.M. Gass (1989) and that of a few other FLA and SLA researchers, linguistic typology is not very widely invoked as a viable theoretical framework within which to raise questions about the language acquisition process and also to address some of the theoretical issues emerging from FLA and SLA studies. This, however, should never be understood to imply that linguistic typology has little to offer for these areas of applied linguistics. Nothing is further from the truth as will be shown in the present chapter. For instance, the validity of the Accessibility Hierarchy (AH) has not only been demonstrated in relation to the SLA process in particular but important pedagogical implications for language teaching and learning have also been drawn directly from the relevance of the AH to SLA (see 6.3.2).

6.2   Linguistic typology and historical linguistics

Even before the appearance of Greenberg's (1963b) work on word order correlations the possibility of extending linguistic typology to historical linguistics had been explored or entertained as evident in the earlier works by Greenberg (1957a) and Jakobson (1958). Jakobson (1958), for instance, called into question the validity of the then generally accepted reconstruction of the Proto-Indo-European (PIE) stop system, which contained a series of voiced aspirates, e.g. b^h, but lacked a corresponding series of voiceless aspirates, e.g. p^h. He pointed out that this phonological asymmetry was a typological impossibility (for detailed discussion see Szemerényi 1967, Gamkrelidze and Ivanov 1973, Hopper 1973, and Collinge 1985: 259–69). Put differently, the reconstructed PIE stop system in question did not conform to the implicational universal that the presence of voiced aspirated stops implies the presence of voiceless aspirated stops, e.g. $b^h \supset p^h$ (Greenberg 1995: 145). Jakobson (1958: 528) also made a similar comment on the reconstructed one-vowel system of PIE by pointing to the complete absence of the one-vowel system in the recorded languages of the world (but cf. Allen 1964; also see Comrie 1993: 84–91 for a good assessment of this particular debate). It follows, therefore, that language universals, or what Greenberg (1995: 146) refers to as 'synchronic typologically derived universals' should not be violated in linguistic reconstruction. This actually does not come as a complete surprise because language universals are meant to represent limits on the variation within which languages may differ from one another. Needless to say, languages – reconstructed or not – are expected to fall within the bounds of language universals.

Ideally speaking, languages should belong to one of the occurring types within specific typologies. For example, suppose there are six logically possible types in a given typology, Type A, Type B, Type C, Type D, Type E and Type F, with the last type unattested in the languages of the world. Based on the distribution of the types in question a language universal can then be constructed in order to rule Type F out as impossible in human language and at the same time to recognize all the other types as possible in human language. Language universals are deemed to function as constraints on language types. This in turn has significant implications for linguistic reconstruction just as do implicational universals. Languages can only change from one occurring type into another occurring type. In other words, languages can never change either from or into a non-occurring type – in the present case, Type F. Thus what is possible in human language will not turn into what is impossible in human language; and what is possible in human language will not arise out of what is impossible in human language. This suggests that the constraints that synchronic typology places on language types can also be interpreted as 'constraints on typological change among occurring types within specific typologies' (Greenberg 1995: 147). This dynamic view of synchronic typology is referred to by Greenberg (1978: 77) as 'the dynamicization of typology'.

From what precedes it may be concluded that linguistic typology can potentially have a lot to contribute to linguistic reconstruction and also to our general understanding of linguistic change. Indeed, as has already been illustrated, the potential utility of linguistic typology in historical linguistics is not very difficult to recognize at least at theoretical level. But, unfortunately, linguistic typology was initially extended to linguistic reconstruction without fully understanding the nature of synchronic typology. First, not all languages are likely to be classified neatly into ideal language types within typologies, with there being, for instance, languages intermediate between two ideal types or exhibiting properties of two ideal types. The existence of intermediate or non-ideal-type languages was not taken properly into account or was ignored in earlier attempts at applying linguistic typology to linguistic reconstruction. This inevitably led to the 'Procrustean' approach to linguistic reconstruction (Watkins 1976: 305), whereby proto-languages were taken to have also been of ideal language types. Second, not all language universals are exceptionless; some universals may be absolute universals but many others may only represent universal tendencies among the languages of the world, however strong those tendencies may be (cf. 1.3). Thus absolute universals are formulated to distinguish possible language types from impossible ones, whereas non-absolute universals are designed to differentiate between more probable language types and less probable ones. However, this fundamental difference between absolute and non-absolute universals was not always heeded in the introduction of linguistic typology into linguistic reconstruction. This gave rise to claims being made on the strength of non-absolute universals that proto-languages could not have had typological profiles other than ideal ones. The validity and reliability of these claims can only be open to serious question. No proto-language states can be ruled out as totally impossible on the basis of non-absolute universals. The only difference among potential proto-language states reconstructed on the basis of non-absolute universals is that some proto-language states are more likely than others to have been the case (cf. Hawkins 1983: chapter 6). No more or no less than that. The point is that one cannot predict on the basis of mere tendencies that X is possible or that Y is impossible. It is only when absolute universals are taken into account that one may be in a position to exclude certain proto-language states completely from linguistic reconstruction.

Be that as it may, Haider (1985: 4) argues that it is not a valid procedure in linguistic reconstruction to apply non-absolute universals to reconstruction of a single proto-language because inferences about a single case – or a proto-language – cannot be drawn from non-absolute universals or statistical typological generalizations. For instance, proto-language X is thought to have had property *p* and there is, furthermore, a cross-linguistic tendency for the presence of property p to imply that of property q (i.e. $p \supset q$). In other words, far more languages are likely to be of p & q than of p & $-q$. Then, it is not implausible to claim that proto-language X may also have had property of q. But the possibility that proto-language X may have lacked property q cannot completely be ruled out because proto-language X may possibly have been of p & $-q$, the existence of which has also in the first place motivated the tendency of $p \supset q$ to be formulated as a non-absolute universal. The point is well taken. But this seems to be too extreme a position to take. It is tantamount to saying, for example, that one can never apply to phonological reconstruction of a proto-language the widely observed tendency for voiced stops to weaken to fricatives over time (e.g. $d > ð$; cf. Hock 1991: 80–6) because the reverse direction of change is also at least known to exist (e.g. $ð > d$; cf. Ferguson 1978). But in reality historical linguists will not refrain – unless there is reason to do so – from making use of the tendency of $d > ð$ in reconstructing proto-language phonological systems. It is neither invalid nor unwarranted to apply statistical typological generalizations to a single case. What one wishes to achieve in linguistic reconstruction – regardless of whether or not one employs linguistic typology – is, after all, the most plausible scenario of proto-language states. It seems foolhardy to reject non-absolute universals out of hand when they can contribute precisely to the very task of arriving at the most plausible scenario of proto-language states. The more sensible approach to adopt is, therefore, to recognize non-absolute universals as exactly what they are and also to bear in mind that reconstructions based on non-absolute universals only refer to relative probabilities of proto-language states. As Harris (1984: 183) puts it, 'while some of the more extreme claims made in favour of the utility of a typological approach to historical syntax cannot be upheld, it is nevertheless the case that any theory which ignores the insights gained by such an approach is substantially impoverished by so doing'.

6.2.1   Early attempts at word order reconstruction

It may not be entirely a coincidence that linguistic typology was initially taken up as a possible avenue of linguistic reconstruction of PIE (e.g. Shields 1995, 1997 for recent typological attempts at PIE reconstruction). This may perhaps reflect the amount of research conducted on and the level of scholarly interest in PIE (e.g. Beekes 1995: 4). No other proto-languages may probably have been investigated or worked out more extensively and intensively than has PIE. As has already been mentioned, Jakobson (1958) made one of the initial attempts to demonstrate the utility of linguistic typology in historical linguistics by pointing to the typological anomalies of the reconstructed PIE phonological system. Moreover, it was precisely PIE basic word order that Greenberg's (1963b) word order typology was first extended to. For instance, W.P. Lehmann (1973, 1974, 1978b, 1978c) made a number of claims about the PIE word order on the basis of his abstract re-interpretation of Greenberg's (1963b) word order typology.

As the reader recalls from 2.2.2, W.P. Lehmann (1973, 1978b, 1978c) takes the verb (or V) and the object (or O) to be the primary concomitants of each other within the sentence. In W.P. Lehmann's word order typology there are only two basic word order types, OV and VO. Based on the relative positioning of the primary concomitants within the sentence predictions are made of where in the sentence modifiers of V and of O will appear. In particular, W.P. Lehmann's Fundamental Principle of Placement (FPP) stipulates that modifiers be placed on the opposite side of V or O from its primary concomitant. What this means for linguistic reconstruction is that, once the basic word order type of a proto-language has been determined, other word order properties of that proto-language can also easily be characterized. If the proto-language had OV order, verbal modifiers must all have appeared to the right of V, whereas nominal modifiers must all have occurred to the left of O. If, on the other hand, the proto-language had VO order, verbal modifiers must all have been placed to the left of V and nominal modifiers to the right of O. Conversely, if there is evidence that in a given proto-language modifiers may have been placed to the right of V and to the left of O, it may also be suggested that the proto-language may have had OV order. For instance, W.P. Lehmann (1974: 30–56) reconstructs PIE to have (S)OV order on the basis of other word order properties of early Indo-European languages (e.g. Vedic Sanskrit, Hittite, etc.). In Vedic the order of the restricting clause and the head noun, for instance, was RelN, rather than NRel; it is in OV languages that nominal modifiers are expected to appear to the left of O. Hence OV word order in PIE. Predictions like this can, of course, only be made on the basis of the assumption that all (proto-)languages are typologically consistent. Thus the basis of W.P. Lehmann's application of word order typology to historical reconstruction is typological consistency: word order properties are expected to be consistent with either of the basic word order types, OV and VO. This, however, is also precisely what makes W.P. Lehmann's reconstruction of PIE – reconstruction of any other proto-language for that matter – wholly untenable. There is no reason to believe that PIE was typologically consistent in the way that W.P. Lehmann claims it to have been – any more than are the majority of the languages of the world. In fact, in the light of Greenberg's (1963b) sample – which W.P. Lehmann's work is based on – over half of the languages of the world will probably prove to be typologically inconsistent (Comrie 1989: 211); by a different estimation only about 40 per cent of languages are typologically consistent in terms of six word order properties including basic clausal word order (Mallinson and Blake 1981: 379). Thus, as Comrie (1989: 212) puts it, 'other things being equal, we would actually expect a slightly greater possibility that [PIE] followed the majority, and was typologically inconsistent'. This fact alone indeed casts serious doubt on

W.P. Lehmann's reconstruction of PIE word order patterns. Moreover, there is a fundamental problem with the PIE basic word order itself, from which all other word order properties are presumed to fall out, as it were. For instance, Friedrich (1975) believes that PIE had SVO rather than SOV, whereas Watkins (1976) argues that the debate about PIE basic word order is but a 'pseudo-problem', with the fact that languages tend to exhibit both marked and unmarked word order not taken into consideration in the overall process of reconstruction. Not surprisingly, W.P. Lehmann's reconstruction of the PIE (S)OV word order is not accepted by all historical linguists.

In common with W.P. Lehmann, Vennemann (1974a) adopts the OV–VO typology because he likewise dismisses subject from his word order theory. But, unlike W.P. Lehmann, Vennemann reduces all word order patterns including OV and VO to the ordering of operators and operands (for detailed discussion see 2.2.2). Thus he invokes the Principle of Natural Serialization (PNS), whereby operators and operands tend to be placed in one or the other order, namely either operators before operands, or operands before operators. The consistent ordering of operators and operands is, then, claimed to be natural or preferred in languages. This indeed has strong implications for historical reconstruction of word order patterns. If the serialization of operators and operands is to be the natural state of language, then proto-languages may probably also have been no exceptions to the serialization. But, of course, not all languages of the world are typologically consistent. In the majority of the languages of the world typological inconsistency is much closer to the truth.

The question also arises of why consistent languages ever become inconsistent in the first place: why do (proto-)languages have to depart from their natural or preferred states at all? As the reader recalls from 2.2.2, W.P. Lehmann does not explain why his FPP predicts what it predicts; he is not in a position to explain why languages shift from typological consistency to typological inconsistency except for being able to say that 'when languages change, patterns of the new type are introduced and gradually become established, while the language becomes increasingly consistent' (W.P. Lehmann 1978c: 409). Vennemann (1974b: 347), on the other hand, offers an answer to the question posed above by attempting to explain, for instance, how SOV may change into SVO. He points out that languages tend to topicalize constituents by moving them to sentence-initial position. In SOV languages – if they move topicalized constituents to sentence-initial position – topicalization will give rise to a marked OSV order. However, the unmarked SOV order and the topicalized OSV order may not be differentiated from each other in terms of syntactic categories because both word orders will come out as a linearization of NP-NP-V. As Greenberg's (1963b) Universal 41 states, however, there is a very strong tendency for SOV languages to have a case system, whereby S and O are marked differently (cf. 3.14 for further discussion). Thus there really is no real risk of confusing S and O in

SOV languages owing to case marking. However, case marking is also known to erode away over time. This erosion is claimed to have serious implications for disambiguation of S and O in SOV languages. If and when case marking has finally decayed into zero, the unmarked SOV order and the topicalized OSV order will no longer be distinguished in terms of syntactic categories; both will be represented by the same linear sequence of NP-NP-V, with these two NPs 'unmarked' for case. There thus now arises the functional need to distinguish S from O by some other means. In order to compensate for the loss of case marking, Vennemann claims, SOV languages may then shift V into a position between S and O, thereby adopting 'new' SVO order. Indeed in SVO word order, even if O is topicalized and moved to sentence-initial position, the topicalized OSV order will be different from the unmarked SVO order in terms of syntactic categories; SVO will come out as NP-V-NP, and OSV as NP-NP-V. This new SVO order will increasingly become more and more rigid or fixed over time. If typologically consistent SOV languages undergo such a drastic change to SVO, then this will no doubt give rise to typological inconsistency. This inconsistency in turn is claimed to trigger these languages into gradually restoring typological consistency in line with the now unmarked SVO order. For instance, once a given typologically consistent SOV language has adopted SVO order due to internal development or due to contact with neighbouring SVO languages, other word order properties consistent with SOV, e.g. GN, postpositions, etc., will also change into the corresponding properties consistent with SVO, e.g. NG, prepositions, etc., one after another until the language in question has metamorphosed itself into a typologically consistent SVO language.[1]

There are a number of problems with Vennemann's explanation of word order change, however. First, Vennemann's theory does not explain why languages can afford to undergo such a complete or large-scale typological overhaul when simple devices potentially can be found or developed in order to differentiate between the unmarked SOV order and the topicalized OSV order. Topic marking, for instance, is a far more economical or less drastic way to carry out the same task of disambiguation especially when languages have already been exposed to use of case marking (cf. Hawkins 1983: 240). Languages may also choose to restore case marking, thereby nipping the typological inconsistency in the bud, so to speak. Second, there are languages which had previously had SOV order without case marking but which subsequently developed SVO order, anyway. For instance, Comrie (1989: 214) points out that Proto-Niger-Congo had SOV order and no case marking, whereas many of its descendants have changed basic word order to SVO. Third, Comrie (1989: 214–15) refers to Baltic and Slavonic languages, which are known to have adopted VO order while retaining their case marking for S and O. This highlights the point that erosion of case marking may not be the only factor that can potentially initiate the change from SOV to SVO. Fourth, Vennemann – and also W.P. Lehmann – suggests that inconsistent

languages merely happen to be in transition from one typologically consistent type to the other, not having undergone necessary changes yet. Typological consistency will eventually be restored because there is pressure towards
typological consistency (cf. Mallinson and Blake 1981: 402–7). But, as N.V.
Smith (1981: 49) points out correctly, this may be nothing but an escape-
hatch for the theory. The concept of languages in a process of drift is rendered
completely vacuous unless one can explain, for instance, why languages have
not yet undergone necessary changes to reclaim typological consistency,
how long it will take to restore typological consistency, etc. (cf. Comrie 1989:
212). Note that this point applies as much to Vennemann as to W.P. Lehmann
(see above). Finally, there are a number of well-documented languages which
may continue to 'put up with' typological inconsistency without taking
steps to restore typological consistency. For instance, Persian is reported to
exhibit stable V-final order although it has adopted a number of SVO properties over several centuries (Comrie 1989: 211). N.V. Smith (1981: 50)
also points out that Amharic is known to retain prepositions although it has
changed its basic word order from SVO – or perhaps VSO – to SOV (cf.
6.2.2), whereas Chinese 'is still vacillating between SVO and SOV after 2000
years with little sign of consistency in the whole of that period'. Note that
this in turn leads to an additional problem with Vennemann's theory of word
order change. As Comrie (1989: 213) puts it, '[i]f a language can remain this
long in an inconsistent state, then the pressure towards conformity cannot
be that strong'. To put it differently, typological consistency must at the same
time be considered to be strong and weak (Hawkins 1979: 641). It must be
weak enough to permit incongruous word order properties to be incorporated into typologically consistent languages in the first place and it must
also be strong enough to remedy the resulting situation by bringing all
remaining old word order properties into line with the new ones. This is
a serious logical problem, indeed.

In W.P. Lehmann's and Vennemann's typological approach proto-
languages must be fitted into the 'intellectual straightjacket' of the two ideal
word order types (Watkins 1976: 306). In fact, their attempts to apply word
order typology to word order reconstruction were doomed to failure from
the start. Their theories of word order change derived directly from their
respective word order typologies, which in turn chose not to take into consideration inconsistent language types present in Greenberg's (1963b) expanded sample. As was pointed out in 2.2.2, the elegance and simplicity of
W.P. Lehmann's and Vennemann's word order typologies had been achieved
only at the expense of the empirical validity of Greenberg's universal statements. In other words, their ideal word order types at best merely reflect
two universal tendencies of a not high statistical grade. But these ideal word
order types are interpreted to represent the very typological consistency
towards which inconsistent languages may eventually drift, whereby the
universal tendencies are by fiat elevated to the status of non-statistical state-

ments concerning word order change. Thus it really comes as no surprise that their theories of word order change should run into the same kinds of empirical problem that their synchronic word order typologies are beset with.

6.2.2   Linguistic typology as a control on, and a tool in, reconstruction

It is generally accepted that W.P. Lehmann's and Vennemann's applications of Greenberg's word order typology to linguistic reconstruction have failed dismally for the reasons explained above. This, unfortunately, has also led some linguists (e.g. N.V. Smith (1981)) to draw the hasty, sweeping conclusion that the validity and reliability of the typological approach to reconstruction itself are highly questionable.[2] But it must be borne in mind that W.P. Lehmann and Vennemann made an attempt to apply linguistic typology to word order reconstruction alone. There are many other areas of historical linguistics to which linguistic typology is yet to be extended in a productive manner. W.P. Lehmann's and Vennemann's failure in word order reconstruction is never to be taken to portend the failure of the typological approach to linguistic reconstruction and, more generally, to historical linguistics. As Harris (1984: 186) counsels caution in this regard, 'one should be careful not to equate doubts about the application of a theory to one particular task with doubts about the theory itself'.

Linguistic typology can profitably be utilized in order to determine the possibility or probability of reconstructions (cf. Comrie 1993). For instance, a given reconstruction may represent an unattested language type in a typology, in which case the validity of that reconstruction needs to be questioned or reconsidered. Recall, for instance, that this is precisely what Jakobson (1958) has to say about the reconstructed PIE phonological system. There being two (or more) competing reconstructions, linguistic typology may also enable the historical linguist to identify one reconstruction as more probable and the other as less probable – with all other things being equal. The language type represented by the former reconstruction may be very frequently attested and/or stable whereas the one represented by the latter reconstruction may be extremely rare and/or unstable. Indeed the role of linguistic typology in linguistic reconstruction is clearly pronounced in its early formulations (Greenberg 1957: 77; also Jakobson 1958: 528):

> [The typology of languages] clearly adds to our understanding of linguistic historical change and our predictive power since from a given synchronic system certain developments will be highly likely, others have less probability, and still others may be practically excluded.

> (Greenberg 1957: 77)

[Thus o]ur 'predictive power' in reconstruction gains support from typological studies.

(Jakobson 1958: 528)

Linguistic typology can thus be used as a control on linguistic reconstruction, thereby identifying some reconstructions as typologically improbable or even impossible, for instance. It is precisely in this spirit that Gamkrelidze (1997: 31) looks upon linguistic typology and related language universals as 'verificational criteria' for proposed reconstructions (also see Comrie 1993 and Shields 1997: 372).

One will not only be able to justify one's linguistic reconstruction based on language universals or universal tendencies (i.e. a control on reconstruction) but also to take advantage of them in the actual process of reconstruction (i.e. a tool in reconstruction) (cf. Fox 1995: 252). In other words, reconstruction itself can also be carried out in line with the diachronic interpretation of language universals or universal tendencies. Take absolute universals, for instance. They represent language states which languages are never meant to violate. Otherwise, they will not be exceptionless or inviolable. The advantage of utilizing absolute universals for linguistic reconstruction is glaringly obvious. First, languages can only be seen to move from one permitted language state to another. Second, no change will ever give rise to language states which are not permitted by absolute universals.

Recall that one of the primary objectives that Hawkins (1983) sets out to achieve in his study is to (re-)discover exceptionless word order universals, based initially on Greenberg (1963b), and also on his own sample. From such exceptionless universals Hawkins (1983: chapter 5) is able to draw a number of diachronic inferences about language change. For instance, the implicational universal of $p \supset q$ permits three co-occurrence types and rules out one co-occurrence type. The permitted ones are p & q, $-p$ & $-q$ and $-p$ & q; the illicit one is p & $-q$, which contradicts the very nature of the original universal, $p \supset q$.

This suggests that languages may change between the three permitted co-occurrence patterns but that no language will develop out of or into the illicit co-occurrence pattern. The diachronic interpretation or dynamicization of the exceptionless implicational universal $p \supset q$ predicts, therefore, that no languages will be arrested in the state of p & $-q$. From this it can be inferred that languages with $-p$ & $-q$ will acquire the property of q before the property of p, or both properties at the same time. No languages with $-p$ & $-q$ will acquire the property of p before the property of q; otherwise, the illicit co-occurrence of p & $-q$ will not be avoided. Thus languages may undergo the series of changes in either (1a) or (1b), but never that in (1c).

Table 6.1: *GN/NG and RelN/NRel orders in Gathic Avestan and Younger Avestan*

Gathic Avestan (SOV)	Younger Avestan (SOV)
GN (n = 27)/NG (n = 20)	GN (n = 8)/NG (n = 11)
RelN (n = 11)/NRel (n = 20)	RelN (n = 2)/NRel (n = 13)

n = quantities of competing word orders

(Adapted from Hawkins 1983: 220)

(1) a. $-p$ & $-q$ → $-p$ & q → p & q
     b. $-p$ & $-q$ → p & q
     c. $-p$ & $-q$ → $^*p$ & $-q$ → p & q

Note that languages do not acquire properties overnight. Thus if languages undergo a change from $-p$ to p, what really is meant by this is that both of the two properties may for a long period vie with each other – length of the period should be understood in relative, not absolute terms – and that $-p$ will gradually and eventually give way to p. For the sake of exemplification, take one of Hawkins's (1983: 83) simple exceptionless universals:

(2) NG ⊃ NRel

The dynamic interpretation of this particular implicational universal enables one to make a number of diachronic inferences. For example, languages with GN order and RelN order can only change to NG order if they have first acquired NRel order or taken on both NG and NRel order at the same time. To put it differently, NG order cannot be acquired prior to NRel order because that will be in complete violation of the implicational universal in (2) (i.e. *NG & RelN). Hawkins (1983: 220–1) tests the validity of this particular dynamic interpretation of (2) on the basis of Friedrich's (1975: 44–5) study of the diachronic data from Gathic Avestan (*circa* 900 BC), and from Younger Avestan (the fifth or fourth century BC). The relevant data are presented in Table 6.1.

In Gathic Avestan GN and NRel are more frequent than NG and RelN, respectively, whereas in Younger Avestan NG and NRel are more frequent than GN and RelN, respectively. There are two important things that Table 6.1 unequivocally demonstrates. First, between Gathic Avestan and Younger Avestan the dominant ordering of N and G clearly changed from GN to NG. Second, in Gathic Avestan RelN had already given way to NRel, the latter dominating over the former by 2 to 1. By the time of Younger Avestan – a lapse of several centuries – this dominance did increase threefold to 6:1, thereby 'almost removing [RelN order] from the language' (Hawkins 1983: 221). It was in Younger Avestan that NG exceeded GN in frequency in line with the change from RelN to NRel, which had already been well under way in Gathic Avestan. In other words, the change from GN to NG was preceded by that from RelN to NRel. This is exactly the prediction that is made by the dynamic interpretation of the implicational universal NG ⊃ NRel: between Gathic Avestan and Younger Avestan the acquisition of NG was 'driven' by the acquisition of NRel, not the other way round.

Moreover, if a proto-language is reconstructed on the basis of independent evidence to have the property of $-q$, it can be deduced that it may also have had the property of $-p$. However, it cannot be reconstructed to possess the property of p because this will violate the implicational universal of $p \supset q$. For instance, one of the cross-linguistic observations made in Dryer's monumental work (1991: 455–6, 1992: 86–7) can be formulated in the form of an almost absolute implicational universal, i.e. VO ⊃ NRel (see 4.9 for discussion); as a matter of fact, there is only one instance in his very large database of a genus containing VO languages that have RelN order, namely Chinese. There is thus an extremely high level of probability of VO languages exhibiting NRel order. Campbell (1997: 60–1), for instance, takes advantage of this particular universal – accurately speaking, Hawkins's (1983) earlier version – in reconstructing the basic word order of Proto-Finno-Ugric as SOV. Balto-Finnic is reported to exhibit SVO, whereas the rest of the Finno-Ugric languages have the basic word order of SOV. Thus it is quite possible that Proto-Finno-Ugric may have had either SOV or SVO as its basic word order. Campbell also points out that, although the SOV languages of Finno-Ugric have RelN, Balto-Finnic – with its SVO word order – has both NRel and RelN. In view of the almost absolute implicational universal of VO ⊃ NRel one can arrive at the conclusion, as has Campbell (1997: 61), that the presence of RelN (i.e. $-q$) in Balto-Finnic suggests strongly that Proto-Finno-Ugric must have had (S)OV basic word order (i.e. $-p$) because VO word order does not co-occur with RelN.

The dynamic interpretation of $p \supset q$ is also claimed to make it possible to ascertain which of the two competing properties in a given language may be the earlier historical relic and which may be the more recently innovated property. For instance, the exceptionless implicational universal of $p \supset q$ will predict that in the attested co-occurrence of p & $q/-q$ the property of q is the innovated property, whereas the property of $-q$ is the original property or historical relic. This is because no languages will undergo innovations which result in direct violation of absolute implicational universals. It is less risky or speculative to take this position than to claim that the property of q is the historical relic, with the property of $-q$ innovated only to wreak havoc with the implicational universal itself. This reasoning may also be based to some extent on the tendency for historical relics to be irregular, inconsistent and incongruous. Thus given the absolute universal of $p \supset q$ it is less implausible to take the property of $-q$, rather than the property of q, to be the historical relic precisely because it is inconsistent with the property of p. In support of this inference Hawkins (1983: 222) provides statistical data from Late Common Germanic based on the work by J.R. Smith (1971). Late Common Germanic was 100 per cent SOV and 100 per cent prepositional; it also exhibited 100 per cent NA order. But it did fluctuate between GN (50 per cent) and NG (50 per cent). Hawkins (1983: 265) claims that in Late Common Germanic GN was the earlier historical relic, whereas NG was the innovated order. This is based on the diachronic interpretation of his (1983: 67) own exceptionless implicational universal in (3).[3]

(3)   Prep & –SVO $\supset$ (NA $\supset$ NG)

The implicational universal states that, if a language has prepositions and any clausal word order other than SVO then, if the adjective follows the noun, the genitive likewise follows the noun. Following the reasoning discussed above, GN could not have been the more recently innovated order because that would mean that Late Common Germanic had innovated the co-occurrence of *Prep & –SVO & NA & GN, which is ruled out by (3) as impossible. But if, on the other hand, NG is taken to have been innovated, then Late Common Germanic may only have shifted completely to the permitted co-occurrence of Prep & –SVO & NA & NG. Thus GN must have been the earlier historical relic which had somehow persisted well into Late Common Germanic.

The reader may wonder why in Late Common Germanic GN still remained in competition with NG whereas all the other word order properties of (3) had already been in full accordance with NG. Recall that given the implicational universal $p \supset q$ no languages will acquire the property of p prior to the property of q. This means that, if in Late Common Germanic NG was the innovated order, the other properties, Prep, SOV and NA, must only have been acquired either simultaneously with or after NG but not before NG. Thus NG must have had as much time to develop into a dominant word order as, if not more than, the other word order properties. Then, the question arises as to why NG and GN were distributed equally in terms of frequency, while there was no indication of fluctuation in the case of the other word order properties. Hawkins (1983: 245) makes an attempt to explain this anomaly away by pointing out that the dynamic interpretation of $p \supset q$ makes no predictions concerning the relative timing of structures lost, as opposed to that of structures acquired. He claims that it is possible for languages to retain the property of $-q$ even after the property of p has now been established as the only option available though it is q that has motivated the appearance of *p* in the first place. 'The laws of word order loss are . . . different from those of word order acquisitions', and 'archaic word orders are often retained in a language to perform certain grammatical functions' (Hawkins 1983: 245). Be that as it may, this seems to vitiate the strength of Hawkins's original claim unless it is also possible to explain, for instance, why it is –*q*, not –*p*, that has been retained as a historical relic, and at least to answer the question of when retention of earlier word order properties does or does not occur.

Another positive contribution made by Hawkins's (1983) work to the dynamicization of linguistic typology is that the concept of probability has been brought right back into the purview of the typological approach to reconstruction. W.P. Lehmann and Vennemann do not recognize the graduated distinction between more probable and less probable language states because in their view languages should be of either of the two ideal word order types – if not, they will eventually change into either type, anyway. For them, therefore, the question of probability of word order change does not arise. Hawkins, on the other hand, does not suffer from this rigidity because he also takes inconsistent languages into account. In this respect, Hawkins's work lives up to the spirit of the typological approach to reconstruction as is captured in the quotation of Greenberg (1957) above: '. . . from a given synchronic system certain developments will be highly likely, others have less probability and still others may be practically excluded'.

The synchronic basis for Hawkins's concept of probability in word order change is the Principle of Cross-Category Harmony (PCCH) (cf. 2.2.3 for detailed discussion of it). The thrust of this principle is that the number of languages exemplifying a given co-occurrence type is directly proportional to the number of phrasal categories in that co-occurrence type in which operators are consistently positioned relative to their operands. In other words, if in a given type all operators are consistently serialized in one direction, then that type is represented by more languages than other types which may deviate in one or more respects from fully consistent serialization. From the PCCH, Hawkins (1983: 253–5) also deduces that the greater the number of phrasal categories there are in which operators are not positioned consistently relative to their operands the more likely languages are to change from one word order type to another. In other words, the greater deviation from ideal serialization is, the greater the pressure to restore cross-category harmony is. This prediction, however, needs to be borne out by empirical historical investigation.

Finally, it must be remembered that linguistic typology is never meant to be the sole criterion for linguistic reconstruction. The reason for this is not a very difficult one to fathom. Absolute language universals, just as generalizations in all scientific disciplines, are subject to confirmation or falsification in the light of new data. For instance, not all the languages of the world have been described by linguists; nor have they all been taken into account in typological research – for obvious reasons, one might add. Thus, as our understanding of the languages of the world increases, so does our understanding of language universals. This, unashamedly, is a fact of life in scientific endeavour. Typological research is no exception. Typological consideration can only be employed as one of the arguments for or against a particular reconstruction. For instance, typologically plausible reconstructions must be preferred to typologically implausible reconstructions, all other things being equal. Moreover, if both non-typological, and typological evidence do converge on one reconstruction in preference to others, then one can be said to hold a far stronger case for that reconstruction than otherwise. Even if typological evidence goes against the reconstruction that is preferred by all other types of consideration, the worst one can do is to reconsider that reconstruction more carefully. What all this boils down to is that linguistic typology serves as a very useful control on linguistic reconstruction insofar as it is utilized in conjunction with other reconstruction criteria.

This important point is made very clearly by Hawkins (1983: 261–2, 273–4), who states: '[t]he selection of one (or very occasionally none) of the variants as the proto[-]language property is then based on an inferencing procedure which draws on numerous reconstruction criteria'; and '[w]hat weight is to be given to [typological] evidence must then depend on the other reconstruction criteria'. By way of illustration, consider Greenberg's (1980, 1995) attempt to reconstruct Proto-Ethiopian Semitic (PES) word order patterns. A number of Ethiopian Semitic languages are found to make use of circumpositions, that is a combination of prepositions and postpositions, e.g. Amharic *bä-bet wasṭ* 'in-house interior'. Moreover, contrary to the cross-linguistic tendency for prepositions and postpositions to co-occur with NG and GN, respectively, some Ethiopian Semitic languages do exhibit 'a typologically rare sort of genitive construction' in which the genitive (or G) of GN is marked by a preposition, not a postposition, e.g. Amharic *yä-saw bet* 'of-man house'. Greenberg interprets these unusual properties to have come into existence as a direct result of the gradual change of Ethiopian Semitic languages from the earlier – that is, PES – prepositional type to the postpositional type. The use of circumpositions is taken to reflect the intermediate stage of development between preposition and postposition, whereas the appearance of prepositions on the genitive of GN is claimed to be due to the persistence of prepositions in spite of the fact that GN has now taken over from NG. Thus Greenberg is led to postulate that PES was prepositional, and also had NG and NA order, with the daughter languages showing deviations from these word order patterns to varying degrees, e.g. Tigre with NA and AN, Tigrinya with NG and GN, etc. Furthermore, Greenberg subscribes to the view that PES must also have had VSO order since languages with Pr & NG & NA are very frequently VSO (e.g. Greenberg 1963b, Hawkins 1983: 65–9). Thus PES is reconstructed to possess the word order properties of VSO & Pr & NG & NA.

But PES could well instead be reconstructed to have SOV & Po & GN & AN, an almost mirror image of Greenberg's reconstructed PES word order patterns. As a matter of fact, most of the Ethiopian Semitic languages that are studied by Greenberg do have SOV order, with only Ge'ez (the liturgical language of the Ethiopian Christian Church) exhibiting VSO as the most frequent order, albeit free in large measure. Moreover, even if PES is reconstructed to have SOV & Po & GN & AN, it is still possible to explain the presence of the unusual word order properties in Ethiopian Semitic. For instance, it can be argued that the use of circumpositions is due to the ongoing or incomplete change from postposition to preposition, and that the appearance of prepositions on the genitive of GN may simply reflect the increasing dominance of prepositions over postpositions.

In order to resolve this problem Greenberg thus draws upon non-typological evidence. First, the basic word order of the whole Semitic family is considered. The basic word order of the Semitic family is VSO, with the exception of Akkadian, whose SOV order is generally believed to be due to Sumerian influence. Second, evidence arising from written records in Ge'ez, Amharic and Harari also generally points to the direction of change put forth by Greenberg. Third, evidence from grammaticalization theory and sociolinguistic considerations also provide additional support for the change from preposition to postposition. In Amharic *bä-bet wäṣṭ* 'in-house interior', for instance, the preposition actually is a prefix whereas the postposition is an independent word. This difference in phonological fusion indicates strongly that the preposition is older than the postposition. Moreover, the preposition *bä* tends to be reduced to *ʔǝ* and also to zero, leaving the independent word *wäṣṭ* alone in colloquial speech. This is taken to suggest that the preposition is older than the postposition since the former is more likely to occur in formal than informal style. Thus when different types of evidence 'all point to the same conclusion, we are clearly on strong ground' (Greenberg 1995: 156). Indeed this is precisely the spirit in which linguistic typology must be utilized for purposes of linguistic reconstruction.

6.2.3   Linguistic typology and linguistic prehistory

In an epoch-making book Nichols (1992) develops linguistic typology into a population science that enables one to detect genetic and/or areal connections at considerable time depths and to probe into linguistic prehistory and also possibly into human prehistory. Based on population genetics this kind of linguistic typology is referred to as 'population typology'. Linguistic typology, as has so far been demonstrated in the present book, is concerned with the study of variation of structural features across languages with a view to placing limits on variation within human language. When applied to historical linguistics, for instance, linguistic typology serves as a plausibility control on reconstructions. In common with linguistic typology population typology does also operate with structural typology. However, unlike linguistic typology population typology seeks to discover 'principles governing the [geographical or areal] distribution of structural features among the world's languages' with a view to making inferences about migration and spread of languages, and thus to contributing to our understanding of linguistic pre-history (Nichols 1992: 2). Population typology also diverges from the classic comparative-historical method in that it does not deal with individual languages or individual etyma but rather with populations of languages and geographical distributions of structural features and types (Nichols 1992: 280).

The primary advantage of utilizing population typology lies in its ability to extend 'the purview of historical linguistics back to at least the dawn of the Neolithic and perhaps to the beginning of human expansion over the globe [or 60,000 to 30,000 years BP]' (Nichols 1992: 7). Population typology can take us so far back in time because it reads a temporal interpretation into the geographical distribution of structural features. The comparative method, on the other hand, is generally thought to reach back only to time depths no greater than about 8,000 years. Unlike the comparative method population typology does not establish genetic sub-groupings. This, however, is no disadvantage because at time depths of 60,000–30,000 years 'the issue of interest is migration and spread of languages rather than the reconstruction of proto[-]languages per se'; at any rate it will probably never be possible to draw 'a complete picture of genetic relatedness for all languages and all areas' (Nichols 1992: 3, 231).

Nichols (1992) evaluates a number of structural types and features in terms of four measures of central tendency and divergence – i.e. (i) mean, (ii) range, (iii) standard deviation of feature values or type frequencies and (iv) the percentage of languages in a genetic or areal group departing from the modal type – so as to determine if they have reliable genetic and/or areal stability. For purposes of these measurement tests Nichols works with eight genetic stocks and nine areas or areal groupings.[4] For instance, the mean number of alignment or case marking types per stock is 1.6, compared to 2.3 per area, thereby suggesting strongly that alignment has strong genetic stability. In contrast, the mean number of word order types per stock is 2.1, and the mean number of word order types per area drops down to 1.6. This implies that word order is strongly areal, not genetic. Then, Nichols proceeds to establish structural affinities or non-affinities between areas in terms of the structural types and features. This is an important part of doing population typology because, as has already been alluded to, at time depths to which the comparative method cannot reach back it really is impossible to differentiate between genetic inheritance and areal connections. For instance, the stocks of a continental-sized area are bound to retain not only deep – too deep to be detected by the comparative method – genetic connections to one another but also deep-seated areal connections to one another as a consequence of millennia on the same continent (Nichols 1992: 184). Among these structural features and types, four or possibly five structural features – inclusive/exclusive oppositions in first-person pronouns, plurality neutralization, adpositional phrases, inalienable possession and noun classes – stand out in that their geographical distributions must be characterized as global. For instance, the distribution of the inclusive/exclusive distinction in first-person pronouns is such that 'it increases from area to area on a cline going from west to east, and [also] with a clear distinction between Old World and colonized areas' (Nichols 1992: 185, 196–8, 278). This global west-to-east cline, with a substantial difference between the Old World and the colonized areas, is manifested, for instance, by the respective percentages of languages having the distinction in question in the three macroareas – into which the areas can conventionally be classified: Old World (22 per cent), New World (48 per cent) and Pacific (57 per cent). Note also that the global west-to-east cline proposed here holds only in the sense that the Pacific is understood to be east of the New World (see below for further discussion). The same cline is also observed within each of the three macroareas; within the New World, for instance, the frequency of the inclusive/exclusive distinction rises gradually from North America to Mesoamerica to South America. Similar comments can also be made of the other structural features referred to above.

Nichols (1992: 208) takes the fact that the four or five structural features display the same global west-to-east cline to be highly significant. It cannot be accidental or coincidental. In order to explain this she (1992: 209) relies on the assumption that the more slowly a given structural feature – if and when it does – changes the more widely around the globe it will spread before dying away or changing into something else. In other words, there is a correlation between diachronic stability and geographical distribution. The fact that the inclusive/exclusive distinction in first-person pronouns is observed from the Old World to the New World does attest to the diachronic stability of this particular structural feature. This assumption is the very basis of Nichols's temporal interpretation of geographical distribution. There are two potential interpretations of this global west-to-east cline as Nichols (1992: 210–15) puts forth: one based on dialect geography and the other based on population genetics.

First, one may argue that the lack of the inclusive/exclusive distinction in first-person pronouns was an innovation which emanated from the far west of the Old World, namely (western) Europe and (northern) Africa. This innovation, or the lack of the inclusive/exclusive distinction may then have spread eastward from this centre but it has not yet reached the peripheral continents in the Pacific and the New World, where the distinction is prominently preserved. Most crucial for the interpretation based on dialect geography is the Pacific, in which the frequency of the inclusive/exclusive distinction fluctuates, depending on whether it is New Guinea (26 per cent) or Australia (89 per cent). This very difference in frequency suggests that the innovation reached New Guinea but really not Australia. From this it follows that the spread to the Pacific of the innovation must postdate the post-glacial sea-level rise. The process of glaciation, which began 16,000 years BP and was completed 8,000 years BP, gave rise to the bifurcation of the landmass known as Sahul into New Guinea and Australia. These inferences suggest strongly that the lack of the inclusive/exclusive distinction in first-person pronouns cannot possibly have been a structural feature associated with the first human expansion out of Africa or the original peopling of the globe. It must instead have spread much more recently, possibly after the end of glaciation. For purposes of her investigation Nichols (1992: 274–5) assumes three stages for the peopling of the world. The first stage begins with the origin of the human species probably in Africa and over 100,000 years BP. The second stage, which can be dated to approximately 60,000 to 30,000 years BP, is the period of human expansion out of the Old World tropics into the rest of the globe, i.e. Europe, inner Asia, New Guinea-Australia (or then Sahul) and finally the New World. The third stage is marked by the end of glaciation. In terms of this chronology, then, the spread of the innovation in question pertains to the third stage beginning with the Neolithic, or approximately 12,000 (±4,000) years BP (Nichols 1992: 278). Relatively shallow as it may be, this dating is further back into the past than is ever possible under the traditional comparative method.

This interpretation, however, tells us little about the distribution of the inclusive/exclusive distinction prior to the spread of the innovation referred to above, especially in Australia and the New World. Nichols (1992: 213, 215) also discusses one serious problem with the interpretation based on dialect geography. In this interpretation the centre of diffusion is located in the far west of the Old World. Though this centre of diffusion falls nicely in the vicinity of the North Africa-Southwest Asia centre of Neolithic revolution, there are other independent centres of early grain agriculture, e.g. Southeast Asia, the Pacific and Mesoamerica, with New Guinea identified as the earliest centre of agriculture (Nichols 1992: 213). There are no known typological distributions originating from these centres, however. They are not in the least centres of spread as opposed to the far west of the Old World. Therefore, the question arises of whether or not the Old World was a centre of spread for the innovation in question.

The second interpretation that Nichols (1992: 213–15) offers in preference to the first one is modelled on population genetics, in which it is understood that one of the factors driving evolution is the tendency of genes to reach equilibrium in populations. How this actually happens is dependent crucially on two variables: (i) size of populations; and (ii) initial frequencies. The smaller the population, the sooner frequencies stabilize at 100 per cent or 0 per cent; and 100 per cent for high initial frequencies or 0 per cent for low initial frequencies. Based on this reasoning Nichols postulates the skewing of the inclusive/exclusive distinction in the initial population of languages (in the far west of the Old World), with less than half of the western languages with the distinction, and more than half of the eastern languages with the distinction. Then, just like biological genes the skewing of frequencies has over time played it out on an increasingly larger and larger scale, while stabilizing at 0 per cent or 100 per cent at the extreme periphery. The initial diversity, which may have been confined to the sub-continental far west of the Old World, has thus developed to the extent that the west-to-east cline is now clearly discernible at the global level. It follows that the different frequencies of the inclusive/exclusive distinction in Australia (89 per cent) and New Guinea (26 per cent) are only part of the overall global cline, with the extreme peripheral areas of Europe and (northern) Australia – also an extreme peripheral area – ending up with a zero frequency and a 100 per cent frequency, respectively. The size of these peripheral areas must also have contributed to the stabilization in question because stabilization occurs earlier in sub-continental populations than in larger populations (Nichols 1992: 214). This leads Nichols (1992: 214) to claim that '[t]he entire time span representing the age of our species has produced only the first stage of stabilization, with extreme frequencies reached only in the smaller populations at the periphery'. Thus the initial skewing of frequencies in the far west of the Old World must belong to the end of the first stage, or the beginning of the second stage of the peopling of the world (Nichols 1992: 279). The dating of the inclusive/exclusive distinction in first-person pronouns can well be pushed back into the Paleolithic era.

The primary advantage of the second interpretation over the first one lies in that it does not suffer from 'the Eurocentric defect of assuming all innovations come from the western Old World' (Nichols 1992: 215). The lack of the inclusive/exclusive distinction in first-person pronouns did not originate from the far west corner of the Old World and then spread eastward into where the distinction had already been in existence but rather both the distinction and the lack of it were part and parcel of the initial linguistic diversity 'that earlier hominid language had developed' (Nichols 1992: 275). More importantly, the global west-to-east cline also mirrors the directionality or the vector of the human expansion itself. Thus this global cline should go back to the beginning of the second stage of the peopling of the world or the stage of human expansion (Nichols 1992: 275). This chronology is possible in the second interpretation, not in the first.

However, there are problems with Nichols's population-typological approach to linguistic prehistory. Being related to sampling, interpretation of data, etc. (cf. Blake 1993, Heath 1994 and Siewierska 1994), most of these problems can without much difficulty be sorted out in future investigations. But some may be more serious than these. For instance, it was noted earlier that the global west-to-east cline can be identified as such only if the Pacific is treated as though it were east of the New World. In order to explain

better why this may be so Nichols (1992: 215–29) performs additional informal cluster analysis and determines inter-areal typological affinities and
divergences. Based on this cluster analysis she (1992: 221–5) arrives at the
discovery that the Pacific bears affinities to both the Old and New Worlds,
with New Guinea and Oceania more akin to the New World than to the
Old World, and with Australia more akin to the Old World than to the New
World. In other words, the Pacific displays a great deal of typological differ-
entiation, or structural diversity, compared with the Old and New Worlds.
Nichols (1992: 224) interprets this to suggest that the Pacific was colonized
from the Old World, and that the New World in turn was colonized from
the Pacific, especially from New Guinea. Features of the Eurasian linguistic
population that initially colonized ancient Sahul are better preserved in
Australia than in New Guinea, whereas features of the South-East Asian
linguistic population, which subsequently penetrated not only into Sahul,
but also into Asia and, then, the New World, are better represented in New
Guinea than in Australia (Nichols 1997: 165). New Guinea and the New
World represent the secondary centre of colonization (Nichols 1992: 225).
This, however, does not sit comfortably with what is known about human
biology. As Nichols (1992: 225) admits, the physiological or biological characteristics of the human population of the New World do without doubt
have much in common with those of the human population of Mongolia
and Siberia, not of New Guinea – due to mainly coastal people entering the
New World through Beringia (Nichols 1992: 228, 1997: 165). Nichols (1992:
225) makes an attempt to explain this discrepancy by claiming that 'the
linguistic affinities of the New World reach as far as Melanesia, while the
biological affinities extend only to Northern Asia'. To put it differently,
linguistic features travel farther and faster than do biological ones. This,
however, is one thorny issue that needs to be resolved, particularly in view of
the fact that Nichols frequently draws from typological distributions inferences not only about linguistic prehistory but also about the peopling of the
globe and human migration movements.

Nonetheless one cannot but concur with Nichols (1992: 230) when
she says that '[w]hat is striking about these patterns [i.e. the parallel global
west-to-east clines for the structural features referred to in this section] is
not the particular view of early human expansion they support, but the fact
that modern linguistic evidence can have anything to say about such an early
stage of human prehistory'. Indeed what the population-typological interpretation of the global clines tells us about human prehistory is neither new
nor insightful. What is new and insightful about Nichols's (1992) work is
her utilization of structural typology for purposes of reconstructing linguistic
prehistory and perhaps also learning about human prehistory, and her application of population genetics to geographical distributions of structural features. This is what makes Nichols's population typology uniquely innovative
and truly fascinating.

6.3 Linguistic typology and language acquisition

Language acquisition is a vast field of intellectual inquiry in its own right, with FLA and SLA regarded as two (almost) autonomous areas within linguistics. Needless to say, it is beyond the scope of the present book to provide a comprehensive review – let alone a critical evaluation – of the role in language acquisition research of linguistic typology. A review like that will, in fact, demand more than a chapter, if not a book (see Ingram 1989 for a general introduction to FLA, and Slobin 1985a, 1985b, 1992, 1997 for a cross-linguistic study of FLA; and Ellis 1985, 1994, Larsen-Freeman and Long 1991, Gass and Selinker 1994 and Sharwood Smith 1994 for general discussion of SLA). What will instead be done here is to concentrate on one particular grammatical phenomenon which has been reasonably thoroughly investigated in linguistic typology and which has also attracted – and will continue to attract – attention from FLA/SLA researchers and, then, to expatiate upon what insight, if any, such an investigation has provided into both the first language (or L1) and second language (or L2) acquisition processes. The grammatical phenomenon selected for this particular purpose is accessibility to relativization (i.e. the AH), investigated by Keenan and Comrie (1977) and discussed in detail in 4.4. Moreover, an exploratory discussion of two other areas in FLA and SLA to which linguistic typology can potentially be applied will be provided.

The relationship between language universals and FLA – if not SLA – was clearly identified very early on in the development of modern linguistic typology as was first enunciated by Jakobson in his 1941 monograph, *Kindersprache, Aphasie und Allgemeine Lautgesetze* (published again in 1968 in English under the title of *Child language, aphasia and phonological universals*). He assumed that the implicational universal of $p \supset q$ can be dynamically interpreted with the effect that acquisition of phonological property q will precede acquisition of phonological property p, for instance; otherwise, the implicational universal of $p \supset q$ will be violated, namely p & $-q$. Hawkins (1987) makes an attempt to improve on Jakobson's nascent interpretation by arguing that all that can be predicted by the implicational universal of $p \supset q$ actually is that acquisition of property q will either precede, or occur simultaneously with, acquisition of property p because there are already numerous languages with both p and q as well as languages with q only. For instance, children may acquire p and q at the same time, 'thereby mirroring the adult languages that have both [p, and q]' (Hawkins 1987: 458). Moreover, Hawkins (1987) demonstrates that the dynamic interpretation of $p \supset q$ applies not only to L1 acquisition but also to L2 acquisition. Thus the implicational universal of $p \supset q$ can be understood to place a strong constraint on both the L1 and L2 acquisition processes to the effect that the progressions of (4a), and (4b) are permitted, whereas that of (4c) is not.

(4)   a. $-p \, \& \, -q \to -p \, \& \, q \to p \, \& \, q$
      b. $-p \, \& \, -q \to p \, \& \, q$
      c. $-p \, \& \, -q \to {}^{*}p \, \& \, -q \to p \, \& \, q$

This then leads Hawkins (1987: 457) to formulate what he refers to as *the Principle of Universal Consistency in Acquisition* (PUCA): at each stage in their evolution L1s and L2s remain consistent with implicational universals that are derived from current synchronic evidence. The conceptual basis of this principle is not new at all but, in fact, is shared with Hawkins's own dynamic interpretation of implicational universals for language change (cf. (1) in 6.2.2).

Taking his cue again from Jakobson (1941), Hawkins (1987: 463–6) also adds a quantitative dimension to the dynamic interpretation for the order of L1/L2 acquisition of the implicational universal of $p \supset q$ defined in (4). Given $p \supset q$, the quantity of successful production and comprehension instances in L1 or L2 of property q is predicted to be greater than, or equal to, the quantity for property p. When applied to the AH, for instance, this quantitative formulation of $p \supset q$ enables one to predict that L1 acquirers and L2 learners will correctly produce or comprehend direct object relativization more often than, or at least as often as, indirect object relativization, for example. This is the kind of prediction that has actually been tested in a number of FLA/SLA studies of the AH.

The discussion that will ensue is divided into two sections, one on FLA and the other on SLA. The rationale for this division comes from evidence that suggests that affinities between them notwithstanding, e.g. similar, but not necessarily identical, developmental sequences in L1 and L2 (see Dulay and Burt 1972, 1974, Bailey, Madden and Krashen 1974 and Dulay, Burt and Krashen 1982; cf. Eckman 1984, 1996), there are differences between the L1 and L2 acquisition processes. Perhaps it is not very difficult to see why this may be so. L2 learners already possess (i) a mature semantic, pragmatic and syntactic system; (ii) a great deal of world knowledge; (iii) the option of using some or all of their L1 system as a starting point for building the L2 grammar and (iv) the ability to produce sentences using the few L2 words and the L1 grammar as a skeleton for those L2 words (Sharwood Smith 1994: 46–7; also see Berman (1984), Schachter (1988) and Bley-Vroman (1989) for detailed discussion).[5] Thus in SLA, unlike in FLA, '[w]e cannot speak of conceptual [or cognitive] development or conversational immaturity delaying the onset of acquisition and we cannot speak of one-word or two-word stages in the language of more mature learners' (Sharwood Smith 1994: 46). For instance, young children acquiring L1 may in the first instance pay little or no attention to certain grammatical distinctions made in L1 because of the particular way that they construct the world around them – differently from mature L2 learners. The animacy distinction in Polish and Russian object nouns is a relatively late acquisition, with one accusative inflection used not only for animate but also for inanimate nouns in child speech (Slobin 1985c: 1186–7). This may perhaps be due to the fact that 'many inanimate objects in the child's world are grammatically [or conceptually] classified as animate, such as stuffed animals and dolls' (Slobin 1985c: 1187). This certainly will not be the case with L2 learners of Polish or Russian, however. More importantly, children may undergo different maturational stages during L1 acquisition. But presumably L2 learners – at least adolescents and adults – do not have to go through such maturational stages of language acquisition (e.g. Gass and Ard 1980, Clahsen 1984, Felix 1984 and Ellis 1985: 201–2 for further discussion). Cognitive and perceptual development may affect young children's (or L1 acquirers') linguistic development. So much so that Cook (1985: 11), for instance, goes so far as to characterize SLA as 'acquisition minus maturation'. Thus 'it is conceivable that some properties of first language acquisition might reflect properties of maturational stages that are subsequently lost, i.e. do not form part of the adult human language potential' (Comrie 1989: 230). By pointing to as many as nine differences between (child) L1 and (adult) L2 acquisition ranging from the lack of general success or failure in acquisition to the role of affective factors Bley-Vroman (1989, 1990) also argues that L1 and L2 involve fundamentally different acquisition processes, the former mediated by the (innate) domain-specific acquisition system and the latter by knowledge of L1 and also by a general abstract problem-solving system (also see Schachter 1988).

In the next two sections, accordingly, accessibility to relativization will be examined separately in FLA and SLA. The results of relevant L1 and L2 studies turn out to be rather disappointingly contradictory to the point of implying that L1 acquisition may indeed involve a number of developmental and/or environmental factors that L2 learners may not have to deal with during L2 acquisition. It must also be said at the outset that accessibility to relativization in FLA and SLA has only been tested on the basis of a relatively small number of languages. Thus the conclusions to be reached at the end of each of the sections should be considered tentative at best.

6.3.1   Accessibility to relativization in FLA

Children's acquisition of relative clauses (or RCs) has been examined largely by testing their comprehension; children were asked to 'act out' sentences with RCs by manually manipulating small toy animals, e.g. *The sheep that jumps over the rabbit stands on the lion* (Sheldon 1974, Harada, Uyeno, Hayashibe and Yamada 1976, Solan and Roeper 1978, de Villiers, Tager Flusberg, Hakuta and Cohen 1979, Tavakolian 1981, Hakuta 1981, Goodluck and Tavakolian 1982, Clancy, Lee and Zoh 1986; for discussion of children's acquisition of RCs in writing see Perera 1984: 236–41). Languages that have been looked at in these studies are mainly English, Japanese and Korean. What strikes one as most remarkable about these comprehension tests is that they have produced mostly inconsistent or at best inconclusive evidence insofar as accessibility to relativization is concerned. For instance, Harada *et al.*'s (1976) study of six-year-old Japanese children indicates that sentences with subject relativization were interpreted correctly about 80 per cent of the time, whereas those with object relativization were understood correctly only about 60 per cent of the time. Hakuta (1981: 213, 219), on the other hand, comes to the opposite conclusion in his experiments, in which children aged 5;3–6;2 were used: at least in left-embedded (or left-branching) restricting clauses object relativization was better understood than subject relativization.[6] English data for the relevance of accessibility to relativization prove to be no less different or, as a matter of fact, 'disappointingly inconsistent' (Clancy *et al.* 1986: 250). Both de Villiers *et al.* (1979) and Tavakolian (1981) report that in their respective studies children understood subject relativization far more often than object relativization but Sheldon's (1974) data motivate her to put forth the parallel function hypothesis, whereby it is predicted that children will find it easier to interpret sentences in which the relativized NP has the same grammatical relation in both the main and restricting clauses (e.g. object relativization as in *The dog stands on the horse that the giraffe jumps over*) than sentences in which the relativized NP has different grammatical relations in the main and restricting clauses (e.g. subject relativization as in *The pig bumps into the horse that jumps over the giraffe*).

   Clancy *et al.* (1986) present a very careful evaluation of most of the studies referred to above. They come to the conclusion that Japanese data provide support only for the anti-interruption hypothesis (Slobin 1973: 354), which predicts that 'the greater the separation between related parts of a sentence, the greater the tendency that the sentence will not be adequately processed (in imitation, comprehension, or production)'. This is, then, taken to explain, among other things, Japanese children's consistent failure to interpret centre-embedded restricting clauses as opposed to left-embedded restricting clauses, and also their strong tendency to interpret sentences with centre-embedded restricting clauses by using the canonical sentence schema, i.e. SOV. However, Clancy *et al.* (1986: 249) find no evidence for the relevance of Keenan and Comrie's (1977) Accessibility Hierarchy (or AH) to Japanese children's comprehension of RCs as, in fact, indirectly manifested by Harada *et al.*'s and Hakuta's contradictory data.

   Clancy *et al.* (1986: 255–6) also come to a similar conclusion about data from English. Not just one strategy but multiple strategies are found to be at work in English-speaking children's comprehension of RCs. For instance, there is evidence in support of sentences with RCs being processed in terms of schemas already developed for conjoined sentences (as most clearly demonstrated by Tavakolian's 1981 study): the superior performance on sentences with the relativized NP with subject relation in both the main and restricting clauses (e.g. *The sheep that jumps over the rabbit stands on the lion*), and the poor performance on sentences with the relativized NP with object relation in the main clause and subject relation in the restricting clause (e.g.

The duck stands on the lion that bumps into the pig) – these sentences will thus be interpreted under the conjoined clause strategy as *The sheep jumps over the rabbit and stands on the lion* and *The duck stands on the lion and bumps into the pig*, respectively. This tendency to rely on the conjoined clause strategy is, incidentally, taken by Clancy *et al.* (1986: 254) to provide partial support for Sheldon's (1974) parallel function hypothesis – albeit not in the strictest sense – because the initial NP is taken to be the subject of both the main and embedded verbs. There is also evidence which points to the importance of the canonical sentence schema strategy (Slobin and Bever 1982; see above). Main clauses were better understood than right-embedded (or right-branching) restricting clauses but the final NVN segment of sentences with the relativized NP having subject relation in both the main and restricting clauses – i.e. $N_S[VN]_S VN$ – was misinterpreted as an SVO unit. Nevertheless, as demonstrated, for instance, by de Villiers *et al.* (1979) and Tavakolian (1981), subject relativization certainly was understood far more often than object relativization (but cf. Sheldon 1974). This may perhaps be taken to be in support of the AH. Clancy *et al.* (1986: 255), however, put this down to the canonical word order of SVO in English because subject relativization creates a canonical SVO sequence in the RC as in ***The sheep*** [S] ***that jumps over*** [V] ***the rabbit*** [O] *stands on the lion*, whereas object relativization gives rise to a non-canonical or unfamiliar OSV sequence in the RC as in ***The lion*** [O] ***that the horse*** [S] ***kisses*** [V] *knocks down the duck*. They (1986: 256) conclude, therefore, that what little evidence in support of the AH there may be 'probably reflects the conformity of subject relativization in English to the canonical SVO word order, rather than demonstrating a direct relevance of the [AH] *per se* to sentence processing'.

Clancy *et al.* (1986) also carry out their own experiment in order to test Korean children's (aged 6;3 to 7;3 years) comprehension of RCs. Very much as they have done with the others' studies, they also interpret their own findings to indicate that there is no single processing strategy that can wholly account for Korean children's comprehension of sentences with RCs. Rather, anti-interruption, canonical sentence schema, parallel function and even intonation each have a role to play in Korean children's comprehension of sentences with RCs, albeit some factors are more significant than others. For example, in SOV order Korean children performed far better on sentences with subject head NPs than on sentences with direct object head NPs, whereas in OSV order they performed far better on sentences with direct object head NPs than on sentences with subject head NPs – Korean allows both SOV and OSV although the former is normally taken to be basic. Because in Korean restricting clauses must precede head NPs (i.e. RelN), in SOV sentences with subject head NPs contain left-embedded restricting clauses, and sentences with object head NPs centre-embedded restricting clauses. The situation is reversed in OSV sentences with RCs, however. This provides a clear piece of evidence in support of Korean children's preference of left-embedded restricting clauses to centre-embedded ones. This in turn provides support for the anti-interruption hypothesis, with centre-embedding giving rise to separation of related parts of the main clause (Slobin 1973). With regard to the AH, however, Clancy *et al.* (1986: 244) point to those cases where object relativization – i.e. with left-embedded restricting clauses – is better understood than subject relativization – i.e. with centre-embedded restricting clauses – as 'partially contradict[ing] predictions of the [AH]' (but cf. Comrie 1984: 19, and Hawkins 1987: 471).

In view of the foregoing discussion one may jump to the conclusion that the AH may shed little light on the way children actually interpret sentences with RCs (but see Keenan and S. Hawkins 1987 for evidence from older children and adults in support of the AH). After all, a number of other processing strategies such as anti-interruption, canonical sentence schema, parallel function, etc. have been found to play a more or less important role in children's performance. It will be injudicious to dismiss the AH out of hand, however. There are at least four reasons for being cautious.

First, the AH involves many grammatical relations other than subject and object relation – i.e. indirect object, oblique, genitive and object of comparison. None of the studies referred to above, however, have actually tested children's comprehension of sentences with the relativized NP having grammatical relations other than subject or object in the restricting clause.[7] Thus it remains to be seen whether or not the AH still has any bearing on children's acquisition of relativization on the lower grammatical relations.

Second, RCs are generally regarded as a very difficult construction for children to produce, comprehend and imitate (Tavakolian 1981: 169); Bloom, Lahey, Hood, Lifter and Fiess (1980: 250) also find in their study of children aged 2–3 that '[r]elativization . . . was the last structure to appear [and] was always infrequent'. It must be noted, however, that this may be more true of some languages than of others. Slobin (1982: 165–6), for instance, reports that Turkish children (up to age 4;8) all failed to act out sentences with RCs but that Yugoslav children at the age of two produced RCs with much ease. He argues that this striking difference in time of acquisition of RCs between these two groups of children is due directly to the difference in linguistic complexity between Turkish and Serbo-Croatian RCs. What this suggests strongly is that there may be language-particular variables that may interfere with the relevance of the AH to children's mastery of relativization in their input language.

Third, there is also evidence that in (English) natural discourse intransitive subject and direct object (i.e. absolutive) are treated preferentially in relativization as opposed to transitive subject (i.e. ergative) (Fox 1987). The reason for this is that, unlike intransitive subject (S) and direct object (P), transitive subject (A) tends to carry given or old information, thereby functioning as an excellent anchor to the preceding discourse. This difference in their discourse roles is claimed to give rise ultimately to the predominance in natural discourse of the relativized NP being in *S* or P function, as opposed to A function, in the restricting clause (refer to 4.8 for detailed discussion). This point is all the more pertinent to the present discussion because sufficient evidence has been accumulated to conclude that adults' linguistic input to children has a direct impact on what they acquire and also on how they acquire what they acquire. For example, Mills (1986) explains that German children's early and frequent use of the infinitive – in comparison with the participle – is due to the fact that it is very prominent in adults' input to children. Moreover, some of children's so-called errors may arise directly from adults' input to children. Bowerman (1985: 1310–11), for instance, makes reference to an error made by a German child, reported by Mills (1985) on the basis of Scupin and Scupin (1910): *die Grossmama* zu *den Affe* 'the grandmother *to* the monkey' (i.e. the monkey's grandmother). The error is the use of the preposition *zu* instead of the appropriate preposition *von*. But she points out that adult German uses *zu* and *von* interchangeably in many constructions, e.g. 'the top *zu/von* this bottle', 'the cover *zu/von* the book' and the like. Thus it is very likely that this type of error is due more to the child's overly productive application of a pattern present in the linguistic input that s/he has already received than to anything else (Bowerman 1985: 1311). Similarly, adults' input to children – at least in English, as Fox's (1987) study has amply demonstrated – may consist of far more sentences with the relativized NP in P (or *S*) function in the restricting clause than sentences with the relativized NP in A function in the restricting clause. It will probably not do much good to test children's interpretation of sentences with RCs unless the distinction between intransitive, and transitive subject in relation to direct object is also maintained strictly in experiments.[8]

Finally, the relevance of the AH to L1 acquisition of RCs must also be tested thoroughly on the basis of children's data from a much wider range of languages, although in some languages, admittedly, it will not always be so easy to collect data from young children as from grammatical descriptions and/or adult speakers (e.g. Tavakolian 1981: 169).

Before ending this section it is worth discussing briefly one general application of linguistic typology to FLA studies. One of the heated debates in FLA is whether or not children start their L1 acquisition with a fixed, pre-structured universal set of semantic notions or meaning categories. Slobin (1973, 1985c) argues that they do (also see Clark and Carpenter 1989, and Clark (in press); but cf. Slobin 1997d: 276, 316–18 for his more recent open-minded position on the status of the universal semantic space); in his view L1 grammatical categories or forms are mapped directly onto such a universal 'semantic space', mediated by linguistic input, and operating principles that children draw upon in order to work out the grammar of L1, e.g. the canonical sentence schema strategy, the conjoined clause strategy and the like.

Bowerman and her associates, however, have called into question the validity of the pre-structured universal semantic space, thereby arguing that it is much more flexible than, and not so invariable cross-linguistically as Slobin (1973, 1985c) claims. For instance, Choi and Bowerman (1991) have convincingly demonstrated that English and Korean children lexicalize differently the components of motion events from as early as 17–20 months. From this they have been able to draw the inference that children do not map spatial words directly onto non-linguistic spatial concepts (i.e. the pre-structured universal semantic space) but that they are very sensitive to the (language-particular) semantic structure of L1 virtually from the onset of their L1 acquisition (also Bowerman 1985, 1996a, 1996b). To put it differently, 'there is diversity in children's starting [form-function mapping] options' (Bowerman 1985: 1305).

However, Bowerman (1985: 1304) admits that it is not the case that 'children are conceptually so flexible that all structure is provided by the input'. She suggests that, although they may initiate their L1 acquisition with different form-function mapping options (both within and across languages), children may do so only within certain limits. Thus starting options are 'structured enough [for linguists] to account for the [diverse] ways in which children depart from the semantic system displayed in the input' (Bowerman 1985: 1304). In particular, she proposes that children's starting options be placed on 'accessibility hierarchies', that is with some options more accessible to children than others, albeit all available right from the beginning of the development of grammar (Bowerman 1985: 1304–5; but cf. Slobin 1985c). But how might this kind of relative accessibility be determined in the first place? In order to answer this Bowerman (1985: 1306) appeals to linguistic typology, thereby arguing that 'the relative accessibility for children of alternative schemes [or starting options] for partitioning meaning in a given conceptual domain is correlated with the *frequency with which these schemes are instantiated in the languages of the world* [italics original]'. As the reader can see, this is partly the way, for instance, the AH is constructed on the basis of the observation that more languages relativize on direct object than on indirect object, more languages relativize on indirect object than on oblique and so forth. Said in a general way, the more frequently a given form or structure occurs in the languages of the world, the more accessible that form or structure is taken to be (see 2.2.3 for a similar example from word order; cf. Hawkins's 1983 distributional universals).

The other important aspect of such accessibility hierarchies as the AH is, of course, that they are meant to be implicational by nature. For instance, the possibility of indirect object relativization in a given language implies that of direct object relativization and also of subject relativization and so forth in that language. Bowerman (1985: 1309) also alludes to this particular aspect of accessibility hierarchies by suggesting that in FLA various L1 sub-systems may 'hang together in a larger, semantically coherent pattern' with the effect that having learned about conceptual domain X children can 'develop expectations about what meaning distinctions will be important' in conceptual domain Y (cf. Hawkins's (1987) interpretation for the order of acquisition of implicational universals as defined in (4) above). This does certainly represent one exciting possibility of applying linguistic typology to L1 acquisition (Bowerman 1985: 1306; see 6.3.3); implications for FLA of it, however, remain to be recognized and fully understood because 'much more research is needed before we can make claims about universal "starting points" for the meanings of grammatical morphemes' (Slobin 1997d: 276).[9]

6.3.2   Accessibility to relativization in SLA

In practical terms it is much more difficult to test the validity of the AH – and of other universals for that matter – in SLA, as opposed to FLA, because SLA does not involve only L1 (or the learner's native language (NL)) but also L2 (or the learner's target language (TL)). The magnitude of L2 research in this respect can easily be appreciated because each language involved in a contact situation can theoretically serve either as L1 or as L2. Thus, if one confines oneself to two languages in contact, one is not dealing only with one possible constellation of X as L1 and Y as L2 but with two possible constellations of X as L1 and Y as L2 on the one hand, and of Y as L1 and X as L2 on the other; if three languages, X, Y and Z, are involved, it means that there are six possible constellations, each language functioning as either L1 or L2 in relation to the others; and so on (i.e. to the order of $n \times (n-1)$). The role of L1 in L2 acquisition is an important one in that L1 has a bearing on the way L2 is acquired, what part of L2 is acquired earlier rather than later, etc. because, unlike L1 acquirers, L2 learners are expected to bring their knowledge of the specific L1 grammar among others to the task of L2 acquisition (Ellis 1985: 201, Schachter 1988: 226–8 and Bley-Vroman 1989: 51–3). As will be demonstrated below, L1 has indeed proven to be a significant variable in the L2 acquisition process insofar as the AH is concerned.

As Comrie (1984: 15) observes, the AH 'has spawned a vast amount of relevant literature in the second language acquisition area, showing how the theoretical conclusions reached by Keenan and Comrie [1977] translate fairly directly into valid predictions about the acquisition of relative clauses in a second language, though also noting more specific points where the fit between the two areas is less than perfect'. Indeed it seems that no other typological properties have been investigated in SLA as thoroughly as has the AH. Moreover, the validity of the AH has been tested much more widely in SLA than in FLA. This may perhaps not be a total accident because linguistic typology has been accepted more enthusiastically – but no less critically – as a viable theoretical framework in SLA than in FLA (e.g. Gass 1989, 1996, Gass and Ard 1980, 1984, Eckman 1984, 1991, 1996, Eckman, Moravcsik and Wirth 1989 *inter alia* in SLA, as opposed to Bowerman 1985 and few other passing references to linguistic typology in FLA).

It was Gass (1979) who first tested the relevance of the AH to L2 acquisition. She carried out two experiments in which seventeen adult L2 learners of English – with nine different NL backgrounds, Arabic, Chinese, French, Italian, Japanese, Korean, Persian, Portuguese and Thai – were asked to give acceptability judgements to the TL (i.e. English) sentences with RCs, and also to perform the task of converting two separate sentences into a single sentence with an RC (for subsequent L2 studies of the AH, see Hyltenstam 1984, Pavesi 1986, Doughty 1991, Aarts and Schils 1995 and Croteau 1995). The most important thing that emerged out of these experiments – especially the combining task – was that the L2 learners' ability to form correctly sentences with RCs decreased regressively from the highest position (i.e. SBJ) to the lowest position (i.e. OCOMP) on the AH with the exception of GEN. (Note that in Gass's 1979 work the positions of IO and OBL were collapsed into one position due to their analogous behaviour in English RCs.)[10] Thus Keenan and Comrie's (1977) AH was relatively well validated by Gass's (1979) L2 data.

Further evidence in support of the AH also comes from the fact that in nearly all instances where the L2 learners failed to form RCs by not following the instructions given – i.e. 'avoidance' in the sense of Schachter (1974) – RCs were formed on higher positions on the AH than the intended ones (Gass and Ard 1984: 47; but cf. Akagawa 1990, who found no comparable evidence from Japanese L2 learners).

In Keenan and Comrie's (1977) original cross-linguistic survey it was discovered that resumptive (personal) pronouns were more likely to be used for lower positions than higher positions on the AH. This was also found to be the case with all the L2 learners of English in Gass's (1979) study irrespective of whether or not their NLs made use of resumptive pronouns in RCs (Gass and Ard 1984: 47–8). But at the same time L2 learners speaking NLs with the pronoun-retention strategy were more likely to employ resumptive pronouns than L2 learners speaking NLs without (cf. 4.3.2). Thus there was also evidence in support of the L1 effect of pronoun retention on at least the three highest positions on the AH, i.e. SBJ, DO and IO/OBL. However, insofar as relativization on the two lowest positions on the AH, i.e. GEN and OCOMP, was concerned, no (statistically) significant differences were noted between the two groups of L2 learners. The use of resumptive pronouns for GEN and OCOMP may thus well be consistent with the predictions of the AH although it cannot be ruled out completely that at least the speakers of languages with the pronoun-retention strategy may still have been 'relying on the patterns of their own NLs' (Gass 1979: 337).

This inverse relationship between the AH and the use of resumptive pronouns in L2 acquisition of RCs, well evident in Gass's data, is further supported generally by Hyltenstam's (1984) investigation of the use of resumptive pronouns in RCs by L2 learners of Swedish, with Spanish, Finnish, Greek and Persian as their NLs. In common with English Swedish does not rely on the pronoun-retention strategy and can relativize on every position on the AH, whereas those NLs differ in the positions that can be relativized on, and also in the optional and obligatory use of resumptive pronouns. Hyltenstam's results conform well with the predictions of the AH, albeit not perfectly. With the positions of GEN and OCOMP inverted, however, the conformity increases to a greater extent (cf. Gass 1979). Overall, the use of resumptive pronouns in the L2 learners' output is inversely related to the AH with the effect that the frequency of occurrence of resumptive pronouns in RCs increases as one moves down the AH.

Hyltenstam's (1984) study also revealed that the frequency of occurrence of resumptive pronouns in the L2 learners' production of Swedish RCs was in direct proportion to the degree to which resumptive pronouns are used in RCs in their NLs. Persian uses resumptive pronouns for more positions on the AH than does Greek, whereas both Spanish and Finnish completely lack the pronoun-retention strategy; Persian speakers were thus found to make the most extensive use of resumptive pronouns in their production of Swedish RCs, followed by Greek, Spanish and Finnish speakers in that order.[11] The point is that the inverse relationship between the AH and the use of resumptive pronouns in the L2 learners' output notwithstanding the effect of L1 on L2 learners' acquisition of RCs was also discernible in Hyltenstam's data, very much as in the case of Gass's original study.

The AH is a chain of implicational universals in that relativizability of any given position on the AH – of course, except for the topmost position of SBJ – implies relativizability of all positions higher than that position. This implicational nature of the AH has also prompted some L2 researchers to explore pedagogical implications of the AH for L2 acquisition. Thus Gass (1982) wonders if it is possible to provide L2 learners with relativization instruction only on a low position on the AH on the assumption that they may be able to make generalizations to the higher positions but not to the lower positions on the AH. This indeed is an intriguing hypothesis, especially in view of the standard pedagogical assumption in at least L2 teaching that instruction on easy structures should precede that on more difficult ones. The question to be asked is whether or not L2 learners are able to 'learn' more than they have been taught. If so, it will surely make more sense to teach students difficult structures first so that they can generalize to easy structures on their own than to teach them easy structures first when it is anticipated that they are unable to make similar generalizations to difficult structures.

This particular hypothesis was tested by Gass (1982) by using two groups of ESL (English as Second Language) classes: one experimental group consisting of thirteen ESL students and one control group consisting of five ESL students. The NLs of these ESL students were Arabic, Italian, Persian, Russian and Spanish. First, both the experimental group and the control group were given two tests – i.e. grammaticality judgement and production

Table 6.2: *Improvement on the production task in the two groups*

Control group		Experimental group	
SBJ	40%	SBJ	30%
DO	30%	DO	39%
IO	0%	IO	42%
OBL	40%	OBL	57%
GEN	10%	GEN	12%
OCOMP	0%	OCOMP	50%

(Adapted from Gass 1982: 138)

tests – with a view to determining their pre-instructional knowledge of English relativization. The tests revealed that neither group possessed much pre-instructional knowledge of RCs; moreover, there was no statistically significant difference between the two groups in terms of performance on the pre-instruction tests. Three days after the tests the experimental group was given instruction only on OBL relativization, whereas the control group was taught along the lines of standard ESL textbooks (e.g. Krohn 1977), that is, instruction first on SBJ, DO and IO relativization, followed by that on GEN relativization with less emphasis. About two days after the conclusion of the instruction the students of the two groups were all tested once again on their knowledge of relativization on all the positions on the AH. The results of the post-instruction tests were quite illuminating. First, the difference between the pre-test and post-test scores of the experimental group was statistically significant, whereas that of the control group was not. Second, with respect to the production task (i.e. combining two separate clauses to form a sentence with an RC) the students in the experimental group did generalize from OBL relativization to relativization on the other positions on the AH with the exception of GEN (cf. Gass 1979). In the control group, on the other hand, learning was limited only to what they had been taught by means of formal instruction. The improvement on the ability of the two groups to relativize on all the positions on the AH between the pre-test and the post-test is summarized in percentage terms in Table 6.2.

It should also be pointed out, however, that, although the students in the experimental group – as opposed to those in the control group – generalized to the positions other than the one for which they actually received instruction, they did make generalizations not only to higher (or more accessible) positions but also to lower (or less accessible) positions, e.g. OCOMP (cf. Doughty 1991: 464). This indeed is problematic for the hypothesis that Gass (1982) originally set up for her investigation. Nonetheless there is marked improvement on the pre-test in the post-test in the case of the experimental group, whereby Gass's (1982) hypothesis is well supported. From these results, therefore, Gass (1982: 139) draws an important implication for language pedagogy to the effect that 'a more efficacious model for syllabus design . . . would be one in which a more difficult structure preceded an easier one' because L2 learners may come into the classroom, not as 'passive' learners but with the 'natural' abilities to make generalizations from more difficult to less difficult structures. This implication, however, needs to be evaluated in the light of the fact that by definition it takes more time and effort to learn difficult structures than easy ones.

Eckman, Bell and Nelson (1988) replicate Gass's (1982) study by further introducing a few elaborations into the latter's testing method and procedures. They carried out their research with three experimental groups instead of one, with each being taught to form RCs on only one AH position, namely SBJ, DO or OBL but, unlike in Gass (1982), they administered no instruction on relativization to the control group. The results of the pre-test were taken into account along with NLs and English proficiency level in order to assign ESL students randomly to one of the four groups. The three experimental groups were then given appropriate instruction on relativization between the two tests, with the control group receiving instruction on sentence combining techniques not related to RCs. Two days after the instruction all of the students were given the post-test. The most prominent aspect of the results of the post-test is that the group who performed the best was the OBL group, followed by the DO group, the SBJ group and the control group in that order. Moreover, although the SBJ experimental group generalized somewhat to DO, neither the SBJ group nor the DO group generalized to OBL. Nearly all generalizations were made in the direction of the higher (or more accessible) positions on the AH. These results do indeed seem to confirm the pedagogical hypothesis put forth by Gass (1982). Thus Eckman *et al.* (1988) come to the conclusion that learners actually 'learn' more than they have been taught, thereby challenging the assumption that learners know only what they are taught.

Though the foregoing results are very impressive and reasonably consistent in support of the validity of the AH in L2 acquisition, in contrast to L1 acquisition (cf. 6.3.1), it goes without saying that more research – better planned and constructed – must be carried out in order to draw firm conclusions about the relevance of the AH to L2 acquisition. To that end two comments can be put forward here. First, as in the case of FLA no studies have actually examined L2 acquisition of RCs, with the distinction in mind between transitive subject and intransitive subject in opposition to direct object (cf. Fox 1987). Indeed there is some indication that the distinction may be of vital importance for a better understanding of the role in L2 acquisition of the AH. For example, Aarts and Schils (1995: 53, 57) observe that their Dutch L2 learners of English actually performed better on DO relativization than on SBJ relativization although the difference was statistically non-significant. A quick look at their test questions reveals that SBJ relativization seemed to involve not only intransitive subject but also transitive subject. Eckman *et al.* (1988: 12) also note that there was, contrary to the predictions of the AH, no difference in performance between SBJ and DO relativization. They admit that they have no explanation for this apparent counterexample to the AH. On closer inspection, however, Eckman *et al.*'s pre-test and post-test questions on SBJ relativization involved only transitive subject despite the fact that their relevant instruction on SBJ relativization did not concern only transitive subject but also intransitive subject. It is not entirely clear at the moment how to interpret this discrepancy between the instruction and test questions in terms of its effect on Eckman *et al.*'s students' performance. But what is clear is that in future research on L2 learners' acquisition of RCs it may be beneficial to pay due attention to the distinction between transitive subject and intransitive subject relative to direct object.

Second, there is also some evidence, albeit inconclusive, that linear proximity between the head NP and the relativized position may also bear upon L2 learners' acceptance of RCs with resumptive pronouns.[12] Thus Tarallo and Myhill (1983) find that English 2 learners of right-branching languages such as German and Portuguese incorrectly accepted RCs with resumptive pronouns more often for DO than for SBJ, whereas English L2 learners of left-branching languages such as Chinese and Japanese incorrectly accepted RCs with resumptive pronouns for SBJ more often than for DO. Tarallo and Myhill (1983: 71) impute this difference to the fact that in right-branching languages the physical distance between the head NP and the relativized position (indicated by the resumptive pronoun) is shorter in SBJ than DO relativization, whereas in left-branching languages it is the other way around (cf. Dryer 1992 and 2.4). They suggest that linear proximity between the head NP and the relativized position may play a more important role in L2 learners' acquisition of RCs than the AH. However, their data also indicate clearly that in the case of Chinese and Japanese – both left-branching languages – the rates of acceptance of RCs with resumptive pronouns for IO (42 per cent) and for OBL (50 per cent) (i.e. preposition *with*) are very similar to the rate for SBJ (49 per cent) (cf. Hamilton 1995: 103), thereby suggesting that something else is at work here. Nevertheless the role in the L2 acquisition of RCs of linear proximity between the head NP and the relativized position awaits further investigation (cf. R. Hawkins 1989, Hamilton 1995).

As has been done in the previous section on FLA, it may also be well worth briefly discussing one general contribution of linguistic typology to SLA studies. Linguistic typology has indeed played not a small role in perhaps one of the most debated issues in SLA: the role of L1 in L2 acquisition (for a brief survey see Gass 1996). There are two extreme views in conflict. At one end there are those who believe that the role of L1 in L2 acquisition is so significant that '[t]hose elements [in the TL] that are similar to [the NL] will be simple for [the L2 learner], and those elements [in the TL] that are different [from the NL] will be difficult' (Lado 1957: 2). This view is embodied in *the Contrastive Analysis Hypothesis* (CAH) (for full discussion, see James 1980). At the other end there are those who argue, in reaction to the CAH, that the role of L1 in L2 acquisition is very minimal and that there is, in fact, no real difference between L1 and L2 acquisition, with the latter being guided by the same language acquisition device responsible for the former. This view is captured in *the Creative Construction Hypothesis* (CCH), in which the role of L1 in L2 acquisition is heavily discounted, if not completely thrown out (e.g. Dulay and Burt 1972, 1974).

Eckman (1977) makes an attempt to reconcile these two opposing views by appealing to 'markedness differential'. This notion is based precisely on the very logical nature of implicational universals that, if the presence of p unilaterally implies the presence of q (i.e. $p \supset q$), p is marked relative to q, whereas q is unmarked relative to p (cf. (4) above; and Hawkins 1987). The empirical basis of implicational universals is in turn none other than the relative frequency of structural properties across the languages of the world (Eckman 1996: 198; cf. 6.3.1; and Bowerman 1985). Thus for Eckman markedness is typological markedness. From this the inference can be drawn that those areas of the TL that differ from and are more marked than the NL will be difficult for the L2 learner, whereas those areas of the TL that differ from but are not more marked than the NL will not be difficult. The advantage of this approach, or *the Markedness Differential Hypothesis* (MDH) as Eckman calls it, is its ability to explain most of the main problems with which the CAH is beset (cf. James 1980: chapter 7 for a review of these problems): e.g. why some differences between the NL and the TL do not lead to difficulty in learning L2, and also why some L2 errors resemble those that are made during the acquisition of the TL as an L1.

However, there is still something that the MDH cannot account for. There are areas of difficulty that do not arise from NL-TL differences at all (e.g. Dušková 1969, Sciarone 1970). For instance, recall that Hyltenstam (1984) pointed to Spanish and Finnish L2 learners' use of resumptive pronouns in Swedish RCs despite the lack of the pronoun-retention relativization strategy in both the NLs and the TL. In other words, there is no difference between the NLs and the TL insofar as the absence of the pronoun-retention strategy is concerned. Nevertheless Spanish and Finnish learners did actually produce RCs by using resumptive pronouns. This type of 'error pattern' has led Eckman (1984, 1991, 1996; also see Eckman, Moravcsik and Wirth 1989) to abandon the MDH in favour of *the Structure Conformity Hypothesis* (SCH), whereby it is now claimed that all language universals that are true of L1s (or primary languages in the sense of Lamendella 1977) are also true of L2s (or interlanguages in the sense of Selinker 1972). Given this characterization, the SCH can readily be likened to Hawkins's (1987) PUCA referred to earlier (cf. 6.3; also see Adjémian 1976).

Finally, Ellis (1994: 429) claims, following Rutherford (1984b) and Gregg (1989), that 'until it is possible to determine the precise source of specific universals, the typological approach will not be capable of explaining L2 acquisition'. This is an extraordinary assessment indeed. First, one cannot but wonder if there really are any other approaches that are even close to being capable of explaining L2 acquisition. Ellis seems to be unjustifiably harsh on the typological approach. In point of fact, he (1994: 429) seems to give preference to 'an approach that concentrates on the nature of the abstract knowledge that determines the structure of any particular language'. But what he is mindless of here is that the nature of such abstract knowledge in turn demands explanation of a higher order. Thus linguistic typology is no different from any other intellectual or scientific approaches to empirical problems (e.g. L2 acquisition) in that it finds itself pushing the need for explanation of language universals one stage further back (Comrie 1989: 25). It is never indifferent to the explanatory basis of language universals (Hawkins 1987: 469) as has amply been attested by the preceding chapters.

6.3.3   Two potential FLA/SLA areas of application

Because the preceding discussion of the application of linguistic typology to FLA and SLA has been limited to the AH, mention can perhaps be made of two other potential areas on which linguistic typology can be utilized to shed light: acquisition of case marking and of number marking. Recall from 3.5 that under the discriminatory view the function of case marking is to distinguish 'who' (A) from 'whom' (P) in 'who is doing X to whom'. This particular view of case marking may lead one to predict that case marking of A or P will be acquired prior to, or simultaneously with, case marking of S. The basis of this prediction is that there is no functional need to mark S as distinct from either A or P because the former co-occurs with neither of the latter two, whereas there is the immediate need to distinguish between A and P because they co-occur in the same clause. Of course, case marking of S will differ depending on whether the NL or the TL has nominative-accusative or ergative-absolutive case marking, for instance.

There seem to be no sufficient L1 or L2 data against which to test this particular prediction, however. What little evidence from L1 acquisition there is actually seems to cast doubt on the discriminatory view of case marking itself (cf. various studies in Slobin 1985a, 1985b, 1992, 1997a, 1997b). Clancy (1985), for instance, observes that young Japanese children use case marking after nouns 'in a semantically and pragmatically unmotivated way' (Bowerman 1985: 1267). Particularly detrimental to the discriminatory view is the most common type of error in which both A and P are marked by nominative *ga* in transitive clauses (Clancy 1985: 389). This type of error persisted not only at the early stages of acquisition but also in the speech of much older children aged 4 to 6 (Clancy 1985: 390). As in the case of the

AH there may perhaps also be other 'extra-linguistic exigencies' that bear directly upon the L1 acquisition of case marking. Nonetheless the prediction in question remains to be tested thoroughly on both L1 and L2 acquisition.

Another potential area to which linguistic typology can be fruitfully applied is acquisition of the animacy distinction in conjunction with number marking (cf. Comrie (1989: 219) on the diachronic interaction of animacy and case marking). In 3.3.1 reference was made to the so-called Nominal Hierarchy, which is based largely on animacy (see Figure 3.2). There is a strong cross-linguistic correlation between animacy and the presence vs. absence of the number distinction. Noun phrases higher in animacy have the distinction whereas those lower in animacy do not (Comrie 1989: 189–90). To put it differently, the presence of number marking in noun phrases lower in animacy implies the presence of number marking in noun phrases higher in animacy. Thus predictions can be made as to how acquisition of number marking will proceed. Number marking for entities of higher animacy is predicted to be acquired prior to, or simultaneously with, number marking for entities of lower animacy. This is an interesting prediction that – to the best of the present writer's knowledge – has not yet been tested out thoroughly on either L1 or L2 acquisition although there is a modicum of evidence from a different context that the animacy distinction may be a relatively late L1 acquisition, whereas number marking may not be (for example, see Slobin 1985c: 1186–7, and Schieffelin 1985: 543 *inter alia*).

6.3.4   Closing remarks

The relevance of the AH to L2 acquisition seems to have been much better substantiated than the relevance of the AH to L1 acquisition. The data from L1 acquisition have turned out to be disappointingly inconsistent when compared with those from L2 acquisition. In L2 acquisition, however, there is a respectable amount of agreement between the predictions of the AH and the data. Linguistic typology has certainly proven to be a competitive theoretical framework within which questions or issues pertaining to language acquisition cannot only be raised but also be better understood. Even in FLA the testing of the AH itself has shed much light on the L1 acquisition process by contributing indirectly to discovery of processing strategies that L1 acquirers draw upon during the acquisition of L1.

Before closing the present chapter, however, it may be worth (re-)thinking about the disparity between L1 and L2 acquisition (of RCs in particular). Though it falls outside the purview of the book to explore this in any depth, there are at least three things which promptly present themselves as contributing factors. First, L1 acquirers or young children learn their L1 at the same time when cultural, social, perceptual and cognitive systems are being developed (Gass and Ard 1980: 445). Certainly, this is not the case with L2 learners – at least post-pubescent adults and probably also adolescents.

There may thus be a good variety of 'extra-linguistic exigencies' to which L1 acquirers must attend during the acquisition of L1. As has already been demonstrated in 6.3.1, factors other than the AH, for example, preference for anti-interruption, use of canonical schemas, dispreference of centre-embedding, etc., do have a great impact on the way young children comprehend RCs, for instance. In fact, so much so that Gass and Ard (1980: 445) go so far as to suggest that 'patterns in [SLA] may . . . correspond more closely to language universals than do patterns in [FLA]'. Second, unlike L1 acquirers L2 learners very often undergo formal instruction on relativization in the TL. This is, as a matter of fact, true of at least the L2 learners in all the studies that have been discussed or mentioned in the previous section, with the partial exception of Pavesi (1986). L1 acquirers, on the other hand, never receive exposure to relativization in their NLs through formal instruction. This difference must thus also have a bearing on the way L2 learners performed the way they actually did in the L2 studies in question. Last but not least, the role of L1 in L2 acquisition, as evident particularly in Gass's (1979) and Hyltenstam's (1984) studies, should never be discounted as irrelevant. In view of these and other differences between L1 and L2 acquisition one must be careful enough to tease out those extra-linguistic exigencies that 'might at times override the predictions made [for instance] by the [AH] on its own' (Comrie 1984: 19) so that the role or the validity of language universals in L1 and L2 acquisition can be accurately determined.

Notes

1. W.P. Lehmann (1972) seems to believe that what triggers this typological overhaul is word order change at the clausal level, i.e. OV → VO, or VO → OV. Vennemann (1974: 352–4), on the other hand, allows for the possibility of word order change at the phrasal level triggering word order change at the clausal level (cf. Mallinson and Blake 1981: 402–7). But W.P. Lehmann (1978c) admits of word order properties undergoing typological changes without word order at the clausal level being similarly affected.

2. Ironically, this negative attitude towards the typological approach to reconstruction is expressed forcibly by none other than Vennemann (1984: 605) himself, who makes the claim that '[t]ypologies do not even have a heuristic value in the study of language change' because linguistic typology itself is not a general theory of language, let alone part of it. But linguistic typology never pretends to be a general theory of language, and it has never done so. Instead linguistic typology concerns itself directly with the study of variation across languages, on the basis of which 'the study of language universals [in turn] aims to establish limits on variation within human language' (Comrie 1989: 33–4). It is the study of language universals, not

linguistic typology, that constitutes a general theory of language, with language universals feeding on linguistic typology.

3. Actually, the implicational universal in (3) is not exceptionless. Dryer (1991: 450) points out that there are two counterexamples to (3) in his database, namely Kilivila and Garawa, both being Prep & VOS & NA & GN. Nevertheless the implicational universal in (3) is a very strong universal tendency. In other words, it can safely be said at least that GN is more likely to have temporally preceded NG in Late Common Germanic than the other way round.

4. The eight stocks are: Afroasiatic, Niger-Kordofanian, Indo-European, Uralic-Yukagir, Pama-Nyungan, Austronesian, Uto-Aztecan and Penutian. The areas include: Ethiopia & Kenya, Near East, Caucasus, Europe, Interior Siberia, North Pacific coast of Asia, Oceania, Southeastern US and Mesoamerica.

5. For example, Schachter (1988: 222) proclaims in no uncertain terms that '[t]he facts of second language acquisition are *nowhere* near the same as those of first language acquisition' (emphasis added).

6. In Hakuta's (1981) study Japanese children almost never processed centre-embedded RCs correctly. Thus it was not possible to test accessibility to relativization. Clancy *et al.* (1986: 247–8) put forth a possible explanation for this by pointing out that the embedded verb in Japanese RCs bears morphological marking indistinct from that which appears on the main verb (cf. 4.6).

7. Note that in studies such as Clancy *et al.* (1986) NPs that appear immediately after verbal expressions such as *jump over*, *bump into*, *stand on*, etc. are treated as object NPs. In other words, the verbal expressions are analysed as transitive verbs.

8. Hakuta (1981) actually tests children's comprehension of sentences with the relativized NP having intransitive subject relation in the restricting clause but he does not compare this directly with their performance on sentences with the relativized NP having transitive subject or direct object relation in the restricting clause. The same comment can be made of Goodluck and Tavakolian (1982).

9. Slobin (1997d: 276) is firmly of the view that the basis of accessibility hierarchies should ultimately be sought in terms of cognitive and processing variables (e.g. children's cognitive development), not by mere statistical sampling of languages as suggested by Bowerman (1985). No linguistic typologists will argue against this view but it must also be borne in mind that the relative accessibility of starting options must first be determined prior to turning to cognitive and processing variables for possible explanation. Moreover, mere statistical sampling of languages may turn out to be a more efficient, and productive way of determining the relative accessibility of starting options than by collecting child acquisition data from a wide range of languages.

10. Incidentally, the exceptional behaviour of GEN in Gass's (1979) data was taken to be a TL factor in that in English the genitive relative marker

whose is 'particularly unusual and hence more salient' because it is restricted to GEN. Moreover, Gass (1979: 341) points out that, being positioned immediately after the head NP and before the possessed (e.g. *The man whose son just came home . . .*), the GEN relative pronoun and the possessed may have been treated as a single unit, thereby functioning either as SBJ or as DO – positions higher on the AH – in the restricting clause. Gass (1979: 341) is of the opinion that this may explain why her L2 learners performed better on GEN than on DO and IO.

11. As indicated earlier, Spanish and Finnish do not draw upon the pronoun-retention strategy but in Hyltenstam's data Spanish learners of Swedish made use of resumptive pronouns over five times as often as Finnish learners of Swedish. Hyltenstam (1984: 51–2) explains this 'anomaly' by pointing out that certain colloquial varieties of Spanish are known to use resumptive pronouns in RCs.

12. By the relativized position is meant the position in which the head NP would appear within the restricting clause if the latter were not a restricting clause but rather a full independent clause. For example, in *Lee bought the car that Megan had sold Ø two years ago* or *The man who Ø came to see you was a New Zealander* the relativized position is marked by Ø.

7

European approaches to linguistic typology

7.1   Introduction

The preceding chapters have been concerned mainly with discussion and exemplification of what may broadly be characterized as Greenbergian linguistic typology. This type of linguistic typology is represented either by linguists who follow directly in the footsteps of Joseph H. Greenberg, or by linguists who endorse or adopt his philosophy of linguistic typology in carrying out their own research. As it happens, the majority of the leading figures in Greenbergian linguistic typology – including Greenberg himself – are or were based in the US. For this very reason Greenbergian linguistic typology is often also referred to by non-American outsiders (e.g. Nedjalkov and Litvinov 1995: 255) as American linguistic typology. But this should never be understood to imply that Greenbergian linguistic typology is practised only in the US. Nothing is further from the truth. There are a sizeable number of linguists elsewhere in the world whose work may suitably be categorized as Greenbergian. In Europe, however, the situation actually is more complicated than in the rest of the world in that in addition to linguists who have embraced Greenbergian linguistic typology there are linguists who have developed their own schools of linguistic typology based on the same European tradition of linguistic typology as that in which Greenbergian linguistic typology has its roots (cf. 1.6). It is probably not unfair to say that most of such European schools of linguistic typology – especially those in the former East European Communist bloc – have for most of their existence evolved in more or less complete isolation. They had scarcely made contact with one another or with their American counterparts until very recently (or *vice versa*), for instance. In this respect alone these European schools may be said to be on a par with Greenbergian linguistic typology.

In the present chapter three European schools of linguistic typology will be introduced with a view not only to discussing their similarities to, and differences from, Greenbergian linguistic typology in particular but also to highlighting the vivacity of linguistic typology itself in a more global context. The three European schools of linguistic typology to be discussed are (in no particular order): (i) the Leningrad Typology Group; (ii) the Cologne UNITYP Group; and (iii) the Prague School Typology.[1] The objectives and methodologies of each of these schools will be in turn briefly examined with some of their achievements also discussed, albeit in a selective fashion. Because they are not well known outside their own countries of origin, the statuses in linguistic typology of these European schools do not seem to have been properly recognized, if not misunderstood. For example, one American critic writes disdainfully that 'one has to wonder whether any of these [European approaches to linguistic typology] will lead anywhere but into their own cul-de-sacs' (Steele 1997: 387). This less than constructive view may have been avoided if their research had been made more widely available to the linguistic community, especially in the West, and if the critic had also found an opportunity to read more of their works. The fact that members of these schools tend to publish their works in languages other than English and through local publishers – which is quite understandable – does also interfere with dissemination of their ideas and findings. As a matter of fact, members of the Leningrad Typology Group and the Prague School Typology have only fairly recently begun to publish (only a small fraction of) their research in English, whereas the Cologne UNITYP Group has mainly released its research – very often written in German but also in English – either in the form of in-house publication or through German publishers.[2] These European schools of linguistic typology must thus be afforded some space in a book like the present one in order to alert the reader to their existence, if not to familiarize him or her thoroughly with their research.

It should be emphasized that there may be other approaches to linguistic typology which equally well deserve to be discussed or at least mentioned in a book like the present one, e.g. the Paris RIVALC (*Recherche interlinguistique sur les variations d'actance et leur corrélats*) Group (e.g. Lazard 1994, 1995), the research group led by Östen Dahl in Sweden (e.g. Dahl 1985), the Italian linguist Paolo Ramat (1987) and the Russian linguist G.A. Klimov (e.g. Klimov 1977, 1983).[3] Limitations of space preclude discussion of these and other approaches to linguistic typology, however. Moreover, in the present writer's opinion the Leningrad Typology Group, the Cologne UNITYP Group and the Prague School Typology stand out from the rest – save Greenbergian linguistic typology – in terms of depth or breadth of their typological investigations and, more importantly, in terms of theoretical coherence of their respective approaches to linguistic typology.

7.2   The Leningrad Typology Group

The Leningrad Typology Group (or LTG hereafter) was initially set up in the early 1960s as the Group for the Typological Study of Languages at the Institute of Linguistics at the USSR (now Russian) Academy of Sciences in Leningrad (now St Petersburg), with Aleksandr A. Xolodovič (1906–77) as its inaugural head. From its inception the LTG was conceived of as a team made up of a leader (or a coordinator), theorists and specialists, all working together on projects, not as a mere collection of single-minded scholars pursuing their own individual projects. In the LTG the leader first decides on projects, which are then discussed thoroughly by the leader and the theorists in terms of theoretical issues, literature review, relevant facts to be covered in specialists' reports and the like. This discussion then forms the theoretical foundation of a questionnaire, which in turn serves as the bounds within which the specialists are expected to describe languages of their specialization. The end product of this type of collective research effort normally is an anthology of articles which are uniform and coherent in terms of scope and content. The original conception of this research method – referred to aptly as the 'Collective Method in Typology' – is attributed to none other than Xolodovič himself (Nedjalkov and Litvinov 1995: 215–19).

In the eyes of the reader who is more familiar with individualistic research common in the West this collective method may seem to be far too rigid or even insalubrious for individual creativity. But it is actually said to be 'flexible rather than dogmatic' in that the questionnaire and its under-lying theoretical assumptions 'guide, but do not constrain, the investigations into individual languages' (Knott 1988: 1). In fact, prior to the writing up of the questionnaire members of the LTG do undergo seminars, discussions and brainstorming sessions to thrash out their theoretical or ideological conflicts with the effect that projects can eventually be 'regarded as their own programme[s] rather than one[s] imposed upon them from outside' (Nedjalkov and Litvinov 1995: 218). Theoretical or ideological conflicts, different views and opinions, however, do not find their way into the LTG's published volumes because they are merely part of 'a natural path to know-ledge, not to be displayed in the final result' (Nedjalkov and Litvinov 1995: 257). Leaving aside the issue as to whether or not definition and illustration are preferable to argumentation (e.g. Nichols 1979a) it does seem that the LTG is doing a serious disservice to those outside the LTG by not explain-ing how its final result has actually been arrived at. It is as important to be fully conscious of the path to knowledge as it is to possess knowledge because the former necessarily bears upon the latter.

For almost four decades the LTG has produced a good number of collect-ive volumes, the most important ones of which may include: *Tipologija kauzativnyx konstrukcij: Morfologičeskij kauzativ* 'The Typology of Causative

Constructions: Morphological Causatives' (Xolodovič 1969); *Tipologija passivnyx konstrukcij: Diatezy i zalogy* 'The Typology of Passive Constructions: Diatheses and Voices' (Xolodovič 1974); *Tipologija rezul'tativnyx konstrukcij: rezul'tativ, stativ, passiv, perfect* 'The Typology of Resultative Constructions: Resultative, Stative, Passive, Perfect' (Nedjalkov 1983; revised and expanded English edition published in 1988 under the title of *Typology of Resultative Constructions*); *Kategorii glagola i struktura predloženija: Konstrukcii s predikatnymi aktantami* 'Verbal Categories and Sentence Structure: Constructions with Predicate Actants' (Xrakovskij 1983); and *Tipologija iterativnyx konstrukcy* 'The Typology of Iterative Constructions' (Xrakovskij 1989).

In common with many other modern typological approaches the LTG is decidedly a practitioner of partial, as opposed to holistic, typology (for discussion of partial vs. holistic typology, see 1.6) as is clearly evident in the titles of the publications listed above. Its collective projects all involve individual grammatical systems ranging from causative to iterative. Linguists in the LTG do not seek to discover possible connections or links between different grammatical systems, for instance. That is not their intention or objective at all. What they are instead interested in doing is to define a given grammatical system X by providing a complete illustration of X. Features or properties by which X is identified in languages under investigation must thus all be included in the definition of X to the effect that they can ultimately be utilized in order to construct a calculus of all logically possible types of X. Not all logically possible types of X may actually be attested in the languages of the world, however. Moreover, members of the LTG are not predisposed to discover potential connections between different properties within one and the same grammatical system, either. This means that the LTG does actually practise much more partial typology than does Greenbergian linguistic typology. In the latter, for instance, reference has been made to many correlations between different parameters in one and the same domain of basic word order, e.g. V-initial word order, and the presence of prepositions. To bring such correlations to light is, in fact, one of the main objectives of Greenbergian linguistic typology. It is true, however, that more frequently than not researchers of the LTG also find themselves making generalizations which are reminiscent of Greenbergian implicational universals. For example, in their investigation of causatives they have made an observation that, if a language has an affix to causativize transitive verbs, it also has an affix to causativize intransitive verbs (i.e. $p \supset q$; cf. 5.3). But implicational statements like this one are few and far between in the LTG tradition of linguistic typology. Even when they do appear in the LTG work, they are not given prominence but mentioned only *en passant*. In the words of two spokespersons for the LTG (Nedjalkov and Litvinov 1995: 254):

the main effort of the LTG has been concentrated on typology; concern with universals was not lost, but it was of secondary importance. A search for universals was not part of the intention in any of the principal LTG monographs; the ultimate goal has always been to devise an adequate model of obtaining a coherent and uniform description of heterogeneous linguistic material.

To go beyond the level of systematic typological description is not the brief of the LTG, as it were. This is one fundamental difference between the LTG and the Greenbergian tradition of linguistic typology. In the latter, cross-linguistic generalizations, or language universals are formulated with a view to establishing constraints or limits on variation in human language. These constraints or limits in effect characterize possible, as opposed to impossible, human language. In the LTG tradition of linguistic typology, on the other hand, typological description is utilized to describe concrete or actual human languages, not possible human language (Dezsö 1982: 254).

Moreover, researchers in the LTG are normally not concerned with distribution of types in a given typology. To determine distribution of types is part and parcel of Greenbergian typological investigation. For example, there may be a sheer preponderance of some types over others as in the case of the distribution of the basic word order types in favour of S-initial languages as opposed to V-initial or O-initial languages. This skewed distribution will then immediately lead to formulation of a cross-linguistic generalization, or a universal statement, which will in turn call for principled explanation (e.g. Tomlin 1986, Dryer 1992 and Hawkins 1994). In the LTG tradition of linguistic typology, however, distribution of types is hardly sought after or determined (cf. Khrakovsky and Ogloblin 1993: 122).

The reason for giving prominence to typology in lieu of universals, or generalizations is that '[w]hen a search for universals comes to be taken for the central task, typology is demoted to a subordinate position' (Nedjalkov and Litvinov 1995: 258). So much so, in fact, that '[v]ariation is *lost* if explained via universals [emphasis added]' (Nedjalkov and Litvinov 1995: 259). Therefore, 'theory in the LTG is subordinated to typology' (Nedjalkov and Litvinov 1995: 259). This position is not easy to accept, however. In Greenbergian linguistic typology language universals are grounded firmly in typological description; without typology universals research can never be initiated or maintained, the latter feeding on the former. It is not as if typology would be put aside and forgotten once language universals have been worked out. Far from it! From typology language universals research is merely the next logical step forward in Greenbergian linguistic typology. Variation is *not* lost if explained via universals *pace* Nedjalkov and Litvinov (1995: 259); variation is *embodied* in universals. Typological description does not need to be subordinated to language universals research even if 'a search for universals comes to be taken for the central task'.

The LTG's emphasis on typology to the near exclusion of universals may probably be the reason why the LTG displays almost complete lack of concern for explanation – highly valued in the Greenbergian tradition of linguistic typology.[4] Said simply, there will be little or no explaining to do with no generalizations or universals formulated in the first place. The LTG's focus on typology may be due ultimately to the nature and role of theory in the LTG research. What theory does in the LTG investigation is not to make generalizations or 'assertions' about data but rather to generate a coherent set of questions as to how data are to be collected and processed into a systematic typological description. As Nedjalkov and Litvinov (1995: 259) put it, 'theory is behind the questionnaire, thus lending meaning to it', and as a consequence it 'is viewed [only] as an intermediate step in obtaining a typological description . . . [and] *is meant to be used as a tool* [emphasis added]'. For most linguists outside the LTG this may actually not even count as theory but rather as a set of pre-theoretical assumptions or concepts to be employed for purposes of theory-building (but cf. Nedjalkov and Litvinov 1995: 259–60, who are at pains to argue for their LTG theory being theory). In a nutshell the role of theory in the LTG research lies only in the establishing of a typology that represents empirical reality or data. From this it also follows that the best theory may be the one that offers 'an adequate unified typological scheme for handling diverse language data', not the one that attempts to achieve 'the coherence of its constituent claims' (Nedjalkov and Litvinov 1995: 227) as in the case of Greenbergian linguistic typology, for instance.

There may also be a systemic or inherent property of the LTG's Collective Method in Typology that militates against explanatory theory as promoted in Greenbergian linguistic typology. It seems that the LTG research team is dissolved once typological description has been produced for a given project. Thus there is no mechanism in place for a 'post-mortem' procedure within the LTG. No opportunities seem to be available for members of the team to sit down and try to make sense of what they have collectively produced.

Perhaps it is no accident that names of grammatical constructions (e.g. causatives) rather than corresponding cognitive or conceptual domains (e.g. causation) appear prominently in the titles of the LTG monographs. The main preoccupation of the LTG is not theory, explanation or universals but typology, as has been pointed out. In Greenbergian linguistic typology cognitive or conceptual properties very often constitute an avenue for explanation. In view of the LTG's lack of concern for explanation it does indeed come as no surprise that cognitive or conceptual domains are not part of the titles of publications by the LTG.

This may also suggest that the LTG relies upon structural features or properties (i.e. form) rather than upon meaning (i.e. function) in order to identify and to typologize grammatical constructions. For instance, in their investigation of passive constructions researchers of the LTG focus on the system of formal correspondences between semantic roles and grammatical relations, or on what is generically referred to in the LTG as 'diathesis' (Xolodovič 1974). For example, some languages may only have passive constructions with Subject = Patient correspondence (e.g. *The child was kissed by the chef*), others with Subject = Patient and also with Subject = Recipient (e.g. *The child was given a flower by the chef*), but with Subject ≠ Beneficiary (e.g. */?The child was made a cake by the chef*) and so on. The calculus of formal correspondences like these will then constitute the basis for the LTG typology of passives. Note that there is no principled semantic or 'notional' definition of passive in use here, such semantic roles as patient, recipient or beneficiary notwithstanding. The LTG's official position is that typology must be approached from form not from meaning because otherwise one 'may lose the subject of typological analysis proper and degrade it into an appendix to quasi-universal semantics' (Nedjalkov and Litvinov 1995: 225; cf. Keenan and Comrie's 1977 investigation of relative clause formation based primarily on meaning; also see 1.5.1 and 4.1). In practice, however, it really does not seem to be very important 'whether the approach should be exclusively from form to meaning or from meaning to form' (Nedjalkov and Litvinov 1995: 243). For instance, Nedjalkov and Sil'nickij (1969) draw mainly on a notionally based definition of the causative situation in their investigation of causatives.[5] Thus it is not inaccurate to say that the LTG vacillates between the two opposing approaches (cf. Knott 1988: 2–3; also Khrakovsky and Ogloblin 1993: 119–20).

Finally, in contrast to the Greenbergian tradition of linguistic typology language sampling methodology never seems to be an issue of importance in the LTG. There are few fleeting indirect references to the need for language sampling as Nedjalkov and Litvinov (1995: 244–5), for example, admit readily that: '[o]ne can hardly regard this sample of languages [in Xolodovič (1974)] as sufficient'. It is, in fact, impossible to avoid the distinct impression that language sampling is a non-issue within the LTG. Looking at the list of languages surveyed for each of the LTG's collective volumes, for instance, one cannot escape the conclusion that it probably reflects – more than anything else – the research interests of the LTG members, especially specialists, who happened to have been invited or selected for a given project. There is no evidence of either discussion or consideration of language sampling methodology, be it in genetic or areal terms. It must, however, be mentioned in fairness to the LTG that, although only a small number of languages – e.g. twenty-two languages in Nedjalkov (1988) – are examined in each LTG collective monograph, each and every language, based primarily on collaborative work between specialists and language consultants, is treated in far greater depth than in the Greenbergian tradition of linguistic typology, in which written grammatical descriptions, albeit in huge numbers, are drawn heavily upon (cf. Haspelmath 1991: 494).

7.3   The Cologne UNITYP Group

The Cologne UNITYP Group (or CUG hereafter) was founded by Hansjakob Seiler in the early 1970s within the Institute of Linguistics at the University of Cologne in the former Federal Republic of Germany. Like the LTG the CUG is made up of typologists collaborating in projects. But it does seem to have a less rigid hierarchy than does the LTG. There is no distinction between theorists and specialists as in the case of the LTG, for instance. As a matter of fact, Seiler and Brettschneider (1985: xi) identify all participants of the CUG including the founder himself only as members.

The CUG is as much a practitioner of partial typology as is the LTG. As has been demonstrated in 7.2, the primary objective of the LTG is the typologizing of specific individual grammatical constructions such as causatives, passives and resultatives, among others. The CUG is also interested in investigating individual linguistic phenomena although it does not seem to be wholly insensitive to discovery of connections or links between them (e.g. Heine, Lehmann and Reh 1985: 36). But unlike the LTG the CUG deals with cognitive-conceptual domains such as 'possession', 'apprehension', 'determination', 'numeration', 'participation', etc. (see below) rather than grammatical constructions. Thus the CUG is orientated very much towards human cognition, with individual cognitive-conceptual domains being the starting point of its investigation. This is not completely unexpected because the CUG maintains a 'teleonomic' view of language: language is looked upon as a problem-solving system, the goal of which is not only to achieve cognition but also to represent cognition (Seiler 1995: 300).

In this respect the CUG is said to have 'strong conceptual ties' with Greenbergian linguistic typology because cognition plays a prominent role in both approaches (cf. Moravcsik 1997: 112). Insofar as the unity of human languages is concerned, cognition has indeed frequently been looked to in Greenbergian linguistic typology as an avenue of explaining the nature of human language. This similarity may perhaps be more apparent than real, however. In Greenbergian linguistic typology one of the main objectives is to discover and characterize the unity of human languages by means of also discovering and characterizing the diversity of human languages. To put it differently, not only unity but also diversity is something to be defined in a most rigorous manner. In the CUG framework, on the other hand, neither diversity nor unity is to be defined or explained. In fact, both diversity and unity are what the CUG will not deal with because they are taken to be given or presupposed. 'It is a fact that, although languages differ significantly and considerably indeed, [. . .] they have something in common: [h]ow else could they be labelled "language"?' (Seiler 1990: 156). Thus there is no point in explaining either unity or diversity. While the Greenbergian tradition of linguistic typology and the CUG may both appeal to cognition (or more generally to function), the context in which cognition plays a role could not be more different in these two approaches.

But if neither diversity, nor unity is what the CUG is interested in explaining, what is its primary object of inquiry? It is the pathways from unity to diversity, or from diversity to unity that need to be investigated or discovered in the CUG framework. The main objective of the CUG is 'to explain the way in which language-specific facts are connected with a unitarian concept of language – *"die Sprache"*, *"le langage"*' (Seiler 1995: 299). Note that by the pathways from unity to diversity, or *vice versa* is meant language as a dynamic, not static, object. Thus language is conceived of not as a formal or abstract object made up of features, elements, constructions and what not, as in Greenbergian linguistic typology, but as a *process* of moving from unity to diversity, or *vice versa*. For instance, this process is claimed to describe how the speaker/hearer construes and then represents cognitive-conceptual domains in individual languages (i.e. the onomasiological view), or how the speaker/hearer deals with structural properties of individual languages in order to retrieve or understand the cognitive concepts that they represent (i.e. semasiological view) (Seiler 1995: 302–3). Therefore, the focus of the CUG is placed firmly on language as an activity (or *enérgeia*), not on language as a product (or *érgon*). This particular philosophical underpinning of the CUG is, incidentally, attributed directly to W. von Humboldt (Seiler 1995: 299; cf. Robins 1997: 163–4 for a brief discussion of W. von Humboldt's philosophy of language).

To say the least, the CUG's conception of language is very abstract, in fact so abstract that it may not be very easy to come to grips with the CUG framework without actually discussing at least part of its research in some detail. One of the most prominent topics that the CUG has investigated is the cognitive-conceptual domain of 'possession'. 'Possession' is defined deductively 'as a relation of appurtenance between two substances' (Seiler 1995: 277). In other words, 'possession' is a relationship between the possessor (i.e. 'prototypically [+animate], and more specifically [+human], and still more specifically [+EGO] or close to the speaker'), and the possessum (i.e. 'either [+animate] or [−animate]') (Seiler 1995: 277). That relationship is also characterized as 'biocultural'. From this definition of 'possession' it can further be inferred that the relationship between the possessor and the possessum can be either inherent or established. Being given or taken for granted, inherent relationship of 'possession' does not need to be described or predicated (hence inherent), whereas established relationship of 'possession' cannot simply be indicated or pointed out but needs to be described (hence established). On the basis of this notional definition of 'possession', mediated by the logically conceived functional/operational principles of indicativity (=inherent) and predicativity (=established) relevant data either from a single language or from a variety of languages are analysed inductively with a view to identifying various 'techniques' or 'sub-dimensions' (e.g. 'classified possession'), by which the cognitive-conceptual domain of 'possession' is represented linguistically, both in terms of form and meaning.[6] These techniques or sub-dimensions are then placed on a continuum in a certain order, thereby constituting the overall dimension of 'possession'.[7] The techniques or sub-dimensions in turn correspond to formal devices or constructions which actually carry out the expressing of 'possession' (e.g. the construction of possessor-possessive classifier-possessum for the technique of 'classified possession'). Note that the continuum of the dimension is 'bi-directional' with one of the two principles increasing, while the other decreasing over the whole continuum (Seiler 1990: 160, 1995: 283–4). For example, technique X will be higher than technique Y in terms of indicativity, or conversely technique Y will be higher than technique X in terms of predicativity – i.e. the two principles working in an inverse relationship. Each technique of the dimension of 'possession' thus represents the speaker/hearer's unique blend of the two functional/operational principles of indicativity and predicativity. Languages can also be seen to range over the whole continuum of the dimension of 'possession' as 'each language represents a particular choice of techniques out of the total range of possible techniques corresponding to such an overall function as that of' 'possession' (Seiler 1990: 160).

The main research objective of the CUG is, then, to identify and reconstruct 'the mental operation' that mediates between the cognitive-conceptual domain and the techniques or sub-dimensions (i.e. blends of the two functional/operational principles). This mental operation does exactly represent the process from unity (i.e. one and the same cognitive-conceptual domain) to diversity (i.e. a variety of techniques), or *vice versa*. The same link between unity and diversity can be discerned also at the level of techniques or sub-dimensions. Each technique or sub-dimension (i.e. unity) is related either to different structural options in one and the same language or to various language-specific structures across languages (i.e. diversity).

In addition to 'possession' the CUG has so far investigated other dimensions or cognitive-conceptual domains: 'apprehension' (i.e. the cognitive-conceptual domain of the object or the thing (Seiler and Lehmann 1982, Seiler and Stachowiak 1982, and Seiler 1986)), 'participation' (i.e. the cognitive-conceptual domain of participation and that which is participated in (Seiler 1989b)), and 'numeration' (i.e. the cognitive-conceptual domain of counting (Seiler 1989a)). The same two functional/operational principles of indicativity and predicativity are claimed to bear directly upon the constitution of each and every one of these dimensions although they may be differently manifested in different dimensions. Indicativity and predicativity are reflected, for instance, in the dimension of 'apprehension' as individualization and generalization, respectively.

There are a few comments to be made about the CUG in comparison with Greenbergian linguistic typology. First, the most striking difference between these two approaches may be the concept of universals itself. In the

CUG framework the functional/operational principles of indicativity and predicativity are taken to be universals. The kind of (implicational) language universal that is prominent in the Greenbergian tradition of linguistic typology – e.g. if a language V-initial, then it is also prepositional – is not regarded as such but merely as a typological generalization (Heine, Lehmann and Reh 1985: 34). To put it in another way, in the CUG framework 'universality' does not exist in substance (e.g. features, elements, constructions, etc.) but in processes or mental operations or, ultimately, in the blending of the two universal principles (Seiler (1995: 301); Seiler and Luis-Iturrioz (1994: 44)). This is so because all cognitive-conceptual domains or dimensions are constituted by the blending of indicativity and predicativity. Note, however, that these functional/operational principles are not inductively derived from empirical generalizations. Rather they are 'rationally [or logically] deduced from intuitive insight into the tasks to be fulfilled by language' (Seiler 1995: 312). In other words, the universal principles fall out directly from the 'teleonomic' function of language itself. This is indeed in stark contrast to the way language universals are discovered in the Greenbergian tradition of linguistic typology. Language universals in the latter approach do only emerge from empirical generalizations.

In the CUG framework dimensions are taken to be continua in nature. The techniques or sub-dimensions of a given dimension are ordered in a certain way on a continuum of that dimension. Perhaps this continuum can be regarded as the type of hierarchy, frequently invoked in Greenbergian linguistic typology (e.g. Keenan and Comrie's (1977) Accessibility Hierarchy). If so, one may wonder if the CUG dimension can also be interpreted in such a way that the presence (or absence) of a given technique is predicted on the basis of the presence (or absence) of another. Indeed Seiler (1995: 313–14) alludes to this very possibility. For instance, in the case of the dimension of 'possession', he observes that 'inner-layer' techniques (i.e. those in the middle range of the continuum) seem to occur in isolation from one another and from 'outer-layer' techniques (i.e. those in the peripheries of the continuum). As an example in support, he points to 'Melanesian' languages, which exhibit possessive classifiers but no possessive verbs (cf. Mosel 1983, who discusses Nguna, in which the emergence of a possessive verb is found to coincide with the disappearance of possessive classifiers). This observation can easily be converted into an implicational statement or possibly a language universal (i.e. $p \supset q$), prominent in Greenbergian linguistic typology: if a language has possessive classifiers, it lacks verbs of possession or (1).

(1)   [+N classifier N] $\supset$ [–N V N]

Implicational statements such as (1) are claimed to be derived directly from the theoretical framework of the CUG 'instead of being arrived at by inductive generalization, i.e. from a sample of languages' (Seiler 1995: 313). This suggests strongly that the whole conception of language within the CUG framework is so notionally or logically based that implicational statements such as (1) simply fall out directly from the theoretical framework itself, not from relevant language data. This, however, seems to be an extraordinary claim considering that implicational statements can be deduced from a given dimension *only* because the techniques of that dimension are placed on a continuum on the basis of empirical data in the first place. In view of this it is patently difficult to accept that implicational statements such as (1) are deducible from the framework.

In common with the LTG the CUG does not seem to be particularly interested in discovering distribution of types. In fact, the type in the CUG framework may be very different from that invoked in Greenbergian linguistic typology. In the CUG framework the type represents something that characterizes a language as a whole (Heine, Lehmann and Reh 1985: 35). This holistic view of type certainly is not what is normally meant by 'type' in the Greenbergian tradition of linguistic typology, e.g. the six word order types in word order typology, or nominative-accusative, ergative-absolutive, etc. in case marking typology. The type in the Greenbergian tradition is more closely related to partial typology than to holistic typology.

It must be pointed out, however, that the CUG's holistic view of type is not compatible with its propensity to produce partial typologies. This apparent anomaly does not seem to have received due attention in the CUG literature although Heine, Lehmann and Reh (1985: 36) do make a passing reference to potential correlations between techniques of different domains. For example, languages with the technique of noun classification within the dimension of 'apprehension' may lack the technique of possessive classifiers within the dimension of 'possession'. They thus seem to be suggesting here that there is room for (more) holistic typology to be developed within the CUG framework. However, inter-dimensional correlations like the one proposed by Heine, Lehmann and Reh (1985) have not been given much prominence in the CUG literature. Nor has cross-linguistic evidence in support been produced.

Moreover, it is not entirely clear whether or not type itself is a vital concept in the CUG framework, in which the primary object of inquiry is the process from unity to diversity, or *vice versa*. But, if one really tries to find something in the CUG framework which is akin to the type invoked commonly in the Greenbergian tradition, the concept of technique, or sub-dimension is the most obvious candidate because '[l]anguages may differ with regard to the techniques they employ' (Heine, Lehmann and Reh 1985: 36). This suggests that distribution of techniques may perhaps be studied in a similar way that distribution of types is in Greenbergian linguistic typology. For instance, languages may be classified into different types of technique, or even different combinations of techniques. The distribution of techniques may in turn form the basis for typological comparison, with techniques or combinations of them constituting types for a given dimension.

Finally, insofar as the issue of language sampling is concerned, the CUG is not very different from the LTG. No discussion seems to have taken place in the context of the CUG framework as to, for instance, what kinds of bias (i.e. genetic, areal and typological) must be avoided in setting up language samples for what reasons, let alone how language sampling must be carried out in order to avoid those biases. One can be forgiven for surmising the CUG's position only from its infrequent comments remotely related to language sampling. For example, Seiler (1995: 312, 1986: 170–1) points out that 'the [CUG framework] is open in the sense that new data from languages hitherto not considered can be integrated in a natural way'. This, however, is nothing more than a position statement that the CUG is willing to accept and accommodate new data, which is minimally required of any kind of scientific discipline, anyway, be it linguistics or genetics. Allusions like this notwithstanding it is safe to conclude that language sampling methodology is not a very important issue in the CUG framework.

7.4   The Prague School Typology

This particular school of linguistic typology is embedded directly in the tradition of the renowned Prague School of structural and functional linguistics, founded by Vilém Mathesius and other linguists in the mid-1920s in Prague, Czechoslovakia (now the Czech Republic). This is no place in which to provide a historical account of the Prague School itself. For information on the Prague School the reader is referred to Vachek (1964, 1966), Sgall (1984a), Luelsdorff (1994a) and Robins (1997: *passim*) *inter alia*. The focus of the present section will be on the research activities of typologists within the Prague School or of the Prague School Typology (or PST hereafter) (Sgall 1995). The PST is associated chiefly with two Czech linguists, Vladimír Skalička and Petr Sgall but often also with one of the founding fathers of modern linguistic typology, Roman Jakobson (e.g. his work (1929) in particular), who was an active member of the Prague School in the early stage of his career (i.e. from his arrival in Czechoslovakia in 1918 till his departure for Scandinavia in 1939).

In contrast to many other modern approaches to linguistic typology (e.g. Greenbergian linguistic typology, the LTG and the CUG) the PST is decidedly an ardent proponent of holistic typology (but cf. 7.5). In fact, it may rightly be said to be a genuine believer in the Gabelentzian ideal (cf. 1.6): it is possible to characterize the entire language on the basis of a handful of grammatical properties, if not a single property. (Indeed Vilém Mathesius, the senior founder/member of the Prague School, was known to have been inspired by Gabelentz's ideas (Luelsdorff: 1994b: 1)). The Gabelentzian ideal is just that, an ideal. There are a number of serious theoretical problems or flaws associated with the basic concept of holistic typology as discussed in 1.6. Typologists of the PST are well aware of this. For instance, Sgall (1995: 71) admits that it is not possible to predict all properties of a language on the basis of a single property or even a small number of properties. Nonetheless he (1995: 71) proposes that different typologies should be evaluated in terms of the degree of 'holism' or in terms of their 'holistic character'. The best possible typology will be the one which predicts the largest number of properties on the basis of a single property, or even a handful of 'dominant' properties (Sgall 1995: 71). In the spirit of the Gabelentzian ideal the PST is thus insistent upon discovering such a holistic property or a cluster of properties. Whether or not such a perfectly holistic typology exists may perhaps be a moot question. After all, an ideal is nothing more or less than a goal towards which one can only arduously work.

With the degree of holism introduced into the discussion of holistic typology, however, one may point out that more or less the same kind of criterion may also be utilized in Greenbergian linguistic typology. For instance, in Dryer (1992) one and the same structural parameter (i.e. ordering of branching and non-branching categories) is claimed to account for a large number of word order correlations ranging from the ordering of verb and object to that of verb and manner adverb. The main advantage of Dryer's theory over previous ones is precisely that it is able to account for *far more* word order properties of language in a uniform manner than hitherto possible. But it is still only a partial typology in the sense that the wide range of correlations of which Dryer's theory attempts to take account pertains to one and the same domain of basic word order (cf. Shibatani and Bynon (1995b: 12)). A similar comment can also be made of DeLancey's (1981) theory of viewpoint and attention flow with respect to different types of case marking, for instance (cf. 3.9).

As already discussed in 1.6, holistic typology was conceived of in the nineteenth century as an intellectual pursuit in the context of the classical (i.e. morphological) typology. The classical typology was 'seized upon as in some sense central to the attempt to characterize the language as a whole' (Greenberg 1974: 36). Thus it does not come as a total surprise that the PST has come to regard the classical typology as an excellent candidate for the best possible holistic typology 'at a time when hardly anyone else continued [or even bothered with] the classical tradition of 19th century typology' (Haspelmath 1996: 514). The classical typology has the right pedigree of holistic typology, so to speak.

It is Skalička who is regarded as the first Praguian linguist to have made an attempt to develop the classical typology – albeit with slight modification – into a holistic typology. First, he recognizes as many as five different types: (i) agglutinative; (ii) inflectional; (iii) isolating (or analytic); (iv) polysynthetic; and (v) introflexive. The first three of these types are indeed descended directly from the nineteenth-century classical typology (cf. Horne 1966,

Greenberg 1974, and 1.6). The polysynthetic type in Skalička's typology should not be confused with the type which bears the same name (Comrie 1989: 45–6) and which is also known as 'incorporating' in the (typological) literature (W. von Humboldt 1825, 1836). In fact, Skalička's polysynthetic type can be subsumed under what is referred to conventionally as the isolating type, which is divided into the isolating type and the polysynthetic type in Skalička's typology. What is referred to as the polysynthetic type in Comrie (1989: 45–6) (e.g. Eskimo) in turn is included in the agglutinative type in Skalička's typology. One of the major differences between the isolating type and the polysynthetic type in Skalička's typology is that the former (as in English, French, Hawaiian, etc.) exhibits grammatical elements, whereas the latter (as in Vietnamese, Thai, Ewe, Yoruba, written Chinese, etc.) has no grammatical elements other than some lexical words used also as function words (but see below). The introflexive type, unique to Skalička's typology, is claimed to be a very marginal type, manifested only when grammatical values (or 'semes') are marked by vowel changes within the root or stem (i.e. metaphony) or by use of infixes (i.e. infixation). This type is reported to be highly evident particularly in Semitic languages (Sgall 1995: 57).

Skalička (1966) proposes that each of the five types is constituted by 'preferred connections' or correlations between properties from different grammatical domains or levels, i.e. phonology, syntax, etc. as well as morphology. Note that properties involved in preferred connections are not confined to one grammatical domain but they belong to different grammatical domains. This is what makes his typology holistic. Central to the typology is the concept of 'mutual favourability'. Properties are thought to be 'favourable' to others in a symmetric manner. Thus if property X is favourable to property Y, then it is also claimed to be the case that property Y is favourable to property X. This simply means that there is a propensity or tendency for X and Y to co-occur with each other. To say the least, the concept of favourability is rather nebulous, however; no precise definition of it seems to be available in the PST literature. This kind of co-occurrence may most probably be motivated by a number of factors – linguistic or otherwise. There is, however, lack of concern for explanation in the PST (see below). It is not totally surprising, therefore, that the concept of favourability is neither defined nor explained in an explicit manner. Moreover, akin to Greenbergian implicational universals (i.e. $p \supset q$) as it may be, Skalička's mutual favourability is bilateral (i.e. $p \supset q$ & $q \supset p$). Recall that the predictive power of Greenbergian implicational universals, on the other hand, is enhanced precisely due to their unilateral nature (i.e. $p \supset q$ & $^*q \supset p$). For instance, in Skalička's bilateral system the co-occurrence type of $-p$ & q will be ruled out – by $q \supset p$ – as impossible, which is not the case in the Greenbergian unilateral system (cf. Hawkins 1983: 35; and also 2.2.2).

While accepting Skalička's revised classical typology, Sgall (1958, 1967, 1995: 63) argues that favourability is not always mutual or symmetric but can rather be unilateral. Thus if property X is favourable to property Y, it is not always the case that property Y is also favourable to property X. For example, he (1995: 63) points out that the abundance of function words – characteristic of the isolating type – is favourable to fixed word order but the converse is not necessarily true. Fixed word order is not always favourable to the abundance of function words in polysynthetic – in Skalička's sense – languages such as Chinese or Vietnamese. From this observation Sgall (1967, 1986, 1995: 64) draws an inference that it may be (theoretically) possible to identify for each of the types a single basic property that is favourable asymmetrically to all other properties. This must be regarded as a significant improvement on Skalička (1966), indeed. The bilateral nature of Skalička's favourability is now replaced by the unilateral nature of Sgall's favourability, the latter being very much closer to the concept of Greenbergian implicational universals.

Sgall (1995: 64, 71; also Sgall 1958, 1967, 1986) is of the view that the best area in which to discover such a basic property is the ways of expression of grammatical values as opposed to lexical units. This is so because, although 'lexical units are conveyed by strings of phonemes in all languages[, . . .] *grammatical* units have different *shapes*, the repertoire of which is *not unlimited* [italics original]' (Sgall 1995: 64–5). Moreover, '[i]t is in the area of this relationship [between expression and grammar] that the degree of arbitrariness of language structure is higher than anywhere else (although not absolute) and gives more room for the clustering of various properties than is the case within any such sub-domains as phonology, syntax, or semantics' (Sgall 1995: 71; but cf. Haiman 1985a). The distinction between grammar and lexicon is already captured in Skalička's typology and, not surprisingly, this is what Sgall also adopts in his own search for holistic typology. Formal properties of grammatical values are taken to be favourable asymmetrically to many other properties not only of morphology but also of other grammatical domains, including phonology and syntax. In the isolating type, for example, grammatical values are expressed by function words. This in turn predicts an abundance of adpositions and auxiliary verbs, use of fixed word order, existence of articles, conversion of word classes, a large number of vowel phonemes and even a high frequency of loan words. The classical typology is now claimed to be the best possible typology because, in Sgall's view (1995: 71–5), it surpasses other partial typologies (e.g. Greenbergian word order typology) in terms of the degree of holism.

Before accepting this claim, however, one needs to take a close look at Sgall's holistic typology. First, it is not entirely clear whether or not expression of grammatical values is the basic property that can be held to be favourable asymmetrically to *all other* properties. In the isolating type fixed word order 'is required by the absence of endings [in turn motivated by the presence of function words]'. In the case of articles in the isolating type Sgall (1995: 65) has this to say: 'articles will also be needed since the [fixed] word order cannot directly express the difference between topic ("given", most often definite) and focus ("new", possibly indefinite)'. Moreover, the existence of a large number of vowel phonemes in the isolating type is due to the presence of many monosyllabic words in that type. Connected ultimately with one another though they may be, it cannot be said that all these properties are predicted directly from the very existence of function words. At best, one property may be related to another, which may in turn be related to yet another as if they were in a network of relationships (i.e. $X \approx Y$, $Y \approx Z$, $Z \approx A$, and so forth, where $\approx$ means 'related to'; cf. Aikhenvald and Dixon (1998)).

Moreover, the five types that constitute the holistic typology must be accurately defined in statistical terms. In other words, quantitative analysis of data is absolutely crucial for distinguishing the types from one another. Impressionistic or subjective evaluations to the effect that language X has more function words than language Y, or that language Z has more inflectional endings than language A will not suffice at all because without a rigorous metric linguists will never be able to agree on whether or not a given language is of one type as opposed to another. Sgall (1995: 60–3, 77) is fully aware of this when he says 'statistical inquiries are necessary'. (They are more indispensable than necessary, it seems.) Based on his earlier work (1960), in fact, Sgall (1995: 60–3) proposes a kind of metric based on the index of the cumulation of functions, for instance (i.e. the ratio of the number of actual morphemes to the number of grammatical values). Apart from the practical question of identifying actual morphemes and grammatical values in individual languages it is not clear, however, where to draw distinctions between the five types. For example, where should the index of the cumulation of functions be set for the inflectional type in distinction to the other four types? This undoubtedly is as difficult a question to resolve as the very question that Sgall's metric is originally set up to address in the first place (cf. Greenberg 1960 for perhaps the clearest demonstration of this problem). Thus it comes as no surprise that Sgall does not indicate exactly where the distinctions between the five types, for instance, in terms of the index of the cumulation of functions should be drawn. It is highly doubtful, in fact, whether arbitrariness can completely be eliminated from such a quantitative analysis as Sgall has in mind.

One of the problems with which the classical typology is beset is the existence of mixed types or hybrids as pointed out in 1.6. This has indeed proven to be one of the primary causes for the decline of the classical typology. To address this problem Sgall (1995: 75) suggests that one of the five types be 'prototypical' for a given language, with other types being marginal. For instance, languages such as English may prototypically be of the isolating type while marginally being of the agglutinative type. The question does immediately arise, however, as to how languages should actually be classified in this manner. In how many areas of grammar should the isolating type be prototypical for a whole language to be regarded as being of the isolating type as opposed to the polysynthetic type? In what areas of grammar should a language exhibit properties of the isolating type in order to qualify as a prototypical example of the isolating type as opposed to a marginal example of the isolating type?; asked differently, are some areas of grammar more important than others for purposes of classification? (This may probably be the case given the network of relationships alluded to above.) Moreover, areas that are relevant to some languages may be irrelevant to other languages. There are many questions like these that remain to be answered in a far more transparent and rigorous manner. In the absence of answers to these questions most of the claims made by the PST can only be regarded as speculative or even unfalsifiable.

To make matters worse, the preferred connections claimed by the PST are 'not backed up by systematic data from a large language sample, so many of them will probably not survive closer examination without significant changes' (Haspelmath 1996: 514). It strikes one as totally incomprehensible to find no systematic data or evidence in support of the holistic typology, which is, after all, supposed to embody cross-linguistic preferred connections, or correlations between properties of different grammatical systems in each of the five types. This also naturally leads to the issue of language sampling methodology in the PST. However there are no visible references to language sampling, let alone discussions of it.

The PST can further be compared with the other schools of linguistic typology. In the eyes of the PST discovery of preferred connections represents the return to the use of the term 'type' or 'typology', that is typology for the sake of typology, not for 'the search for universals' (Sgall 1995: 53). Thus typology in the context of the PST is more akin to that understood by the CUG or the LTG rather than to that employed by practitioners of Greenbergian linguistic typology. Implicational relationships between properties 'can only be stated [in the form of preferred connections], and *no more* [emphasis added]' (Sgall 1995: 71). In other words, the PST looks upon implicational statements merely as typological generalizations, not as language universals in the Greenbergian sense. In fact, language universals fall outside the purview of the PST research. Thus there is also lack of concern for explanation very much as in the LTG. It must also be mentioned that the way preferred connections are interpreted in the PST is probabilistic or statistical. Thus Sgall (1995: 50) points out that one of the defining characteristics of type in the PST is that preferred connections must be understood with the effect that 'if a language has the property A, then it *probably* also has the property B [emphasis added].' This could not be closer to the way most implicational universals are formulated in the earlier Greenbergian tradition of linguistic typology (e.g. Greenberg 1963b in particular).

7.5   Epilogue

The three European schools of linguistic typology have been shown to be similar to, and different from, one another and also the Greenbergian tradition of linguistic typology in a number of respects. There is, however, one respect in which one school of linguistic typology is in stark contrast to the other three: the PST does stand out from the rest in that it persistently pursues holistic typology. Though what is akin to holistic approach – if not to holistic typology – may sometimes be adopted also by the other schools of linguistic typology, it is the PST which has always taken a hard line on holistic typology as its primary research objective. But the 'numerical inferiority' of the PST may potentially lead one to form a hasty conclusion that holistic typology may not be a particularly viable research option among the majority of linguistic typologists. Indeed it may not be unfair to say that holistic typology has been thought to be a thing of the past, more frequently than often in association with the somewhat stigmatized nineteenth-century classical typology (e.g. Comrie 1989: 40). This, however, may very well prove to be premature, if not misconceived, thinking. The final section of the present book will thus be devoted to making a small attempt to dispel that kind of negative perception.

The major 'parameter' in terms of which different approaches to linguistic typology can be evaluated may eventually turn out to be none other than the distinction between holistic typology and partial typology, or what Sgall (1995: 71) refers to aptly as the degree of holism. This is, of course, not to say that the classical typology – whether in pristine or revised form – will be the basis of holistic typology as in the case of the PST. But what can at least be said at this point in time is that more and more attempts will in the future be made to discover 'preferred connections' or correlations between diverse linguistic phenomena in an effort to achieve holistic typology, or at least something close to it. This prediction is based on the *raison d'être* of linguistic typology itself. Thus one is right to ask what is the point of continuing to establish partial typologies when they can hardly be utilized for an understanding of the nature of *language as a whole*. One may produce as many partial typologies as one likes but one must sooner or later stop to ponder where all those partial typologies lead. Revealing as they may be about bits and pieces of language, partial typologies are not very useful, if not completely hopeless, for gaining an overall understanding of language. One of the early comments reflecting dissatisfaction with partial typology actually comes from one of the leading practitioners of Greenbergian linguistic typology (also see Shibatani and Bynon 1995b: 14). Thus Hawkins (1986: 3) points out that:

[. . . partial typology . . .] is probably missing important universal generalisations. It involves examination of a small number of variant linguistic
properties within large numbers of languages. The properties may be
selected word orders, selected morpheme orders within words [. . .], relative clauses [. . .], subjecthood properties [. . .], and so on. In each case,
small pieces of language are plucked out from the overall grammar that
contains them, and the range of attested variation is described, and universal generalisations, or truths, are proposed that are compatible with all and
only the observed patterns. Obviously, the more such pieces of language
we study, the more universal generalisations we gain. *But it is not clear that
we are making much progress towards understanding how the variants that
an individual language selects in one area of grammar are determined by, or
determine, the variants that it selects in another* [emphasis added].

Though Hawkins's point is directed primarily towards partial typologies
based on a very small number of languages (e.g. contrastive linguistics, comparative typology or so-called linguistic characterology), it can also apply
equally well to such partial (universal) typologies as those discussed in the
present book. The same criticism is echoed by typologists working outside
the Greenbergian tradition of linguistic typology. Seiler (1990: 165), for
instance, calls for 'total accountability', by which he means that:

> any typological statement must be assigned its hierarchical level, its domain,
> and *its significance within the total structure of the language or languages it applies
> to*. Why pick word order for a typology? Why relative clauses? Why tenses?
> Why case marking? Why subject – object? *The reasons for such selective
> treatments must be made transparent* [emphasis added].

The point is very well taken. Admittedly, there is a certain degree of arbitrariness in the selection of research areas or topics within Greenbergian
linguistic typology.

There is every indication, however, that linguistic typologists working in
the Greenbergian tradition have already begun to move from partial typology towards holistic typology or at least to take a more holistic approach to
linguistic typology. It may not be inaccurate to say that holistic typology has
never completely been lost sight of by practitioners of Greenbergian linguistic typology. Hawkins's (1994) EIC theory, for instance, is not only
designed to take adequate account of multiple word order correlations (i.e.
one area of syntax) but it is also claimed to be able to explain cross-linguistic
patterns pertaining to the AH in relative clause formation (i.e. another area
of syntax; cf. 4.10). Siewierska and Bakker (1996) also make an attempt to discover correlations between subject and object agreement markers (i.e. morphology) on the one hand, and basic word orders (i.e. syntax) on the other (cf.
2.6). Both Nichols (1992) and Siewierska (1996) investigate possible preferred

connections between basic word order (i.e. syntax) and case marking (i.e. morphology) – Nichols (1986, 1992) does explicitly attribute her scholarly inspiration to the Russian linguist Klimov's (1977, 1983) holistic typology (cf. 1.6), however. The reader will also recall that this particular line of research actually dates back to Greenberg's (1963b) seminal paper in linguistic typology (cf. his Universal 41; and 3.14). Moreover, Nichols (1986, 1992) and Siewierska and Bakker (1996) may be regarded as attempts at providing cross-linguistic evidence in support of correlations between basic word order (i.e. syntax) and head vs. dependent marking (i.e. morphology) (cf. 3.13).[8] Needless to say, none of these individual studies ever qualify as the kind of holistic typology that was envisaged by Georg von der Gabelentz (1901). Nonetheless it may not be presumptuous to say at least that they have all made their own initial small contributions to the laying of the groundwork for realization of the Gabelentzian ideal.

It may perhaps be pointed out in closing the present book that 'recent resurgent moves' (Shibatani and Bynon 1995b: 14) towards holistic typology are but a natural or logical consequence of what makes linguistic typology what it is. One of the defining properties of science is the propensity to discover a single principle or a handful of principles with which to explain an increasingly wider and wider range of (disparate) phenomena (i.e. so-called *Ockham's Razor*). Being part of the scientific discipline of linguistics, linguistic typology is not indifferent to this basic theoretical desideratum. Thus, though such an overarching principle – e.g. in the form of holistic typology – will probably never come within the reach of linguistic typologists, to try and get a little closer and closer to the 'possibility' of discovering it at every turn is what makes linguistic typology not only challenging but also exciting. This perhaps is what Georg von der Gabelentz (1901: 481) may also have had in mind when he exclaimed a century ago:

> [a]ber welcher Gewinn wäre es auch, wenn wir einer Sprache auf den Kopf zusagen dürften: Du hast das und das Einzelmerkmal, folglich hast du die und die weiteren Eigenschaften und den und den Gesammtcharakter! – wenn wir, wie es kühne Botaniker wohl versucht haben, aus dem Lindenblatte den Lindenbaum construiren könnten.
> ([b]ut what an achievement would it be were we to be able to confront a language and say to it: 'you have such and such a specific property and hence also such and such further propeties and such and such an overall character' – were we able, as daring botanists have indeed tried, to construct the entire lime tree from its leaf. [translation by Shibatani and Bynon 1995b: 10])

Notes

1. Leningrad has now reverted to its pre-Revolution name, St Petersburg, in the wake of the collapse of the Soviet Union. But in the present book the name Leningrad will be retained because two of the most prominent scholars from this tradition of linguistic typology (Nedjalkov and Litvinov 1995) continue to use Leningrad in preference to St Petersburg.

2. As to Western linguists' reluctance to acknowledge, let alone familiarize themselves with, non-Western work, Majewicz (1993: 421) has this to say:

    > [m]any linguists in the West struggling with some problem, upon being informed that their problem had somehow been solved or at least that a solution had been proposed, either turned up the whites of their eyes in disbelief or, apparently frightened, asked for bibliographical references. Learning that the publication in question was in Russian, they usually heaved a sigh of evident relief . . . They'd rather go on with their study, however complex and time-consuming, than make any effort to get acquainted with scholarly output about the same problem written in a language unknown to them.

3. Recently members of the European research project called 'Typology of Languages of Europe' (or EUROTYP) commissioned by the European Science Foundation (ESF) have begun to publish their findings in selected areas of grammar (e.g. Siewierska 1998). But this research project team does not represent a school of linguistic typology in any sense as it consists of linguists of diverse theoretical orientations working on different projects. Moreover, its general typological orientation notwithstanding its investigation is confined mainly to the languages of Europe. For these and other reasons, discussion of the EUROTYP project is not included in the present chapter.

    Reference must also be made to the activities of the Research Centre for Linguistic Typology based at the Australian National University in Canberra but to be shifted to La Trobe University in Melbourne in year 2000 (see note 8; its webpage is located at http://www.anu.edu.au/linguistics/typ_centre/). This research centre was founded in late 1996 and is headed by R. M. W. Dixon. It may potentially develop into the first school of linguistic typology in the southern hemisphere but it is too early to tell whether or not it will promote itself into such a fully fledged school, on a par with the schools of linguistic typology to be discussed or mentioned in the present chapter.

    Brief mention can also be made of the Chomskyan principles-and-parameters approach, which has recently begun to pay attention to typological variation in its theory-driven research (cf. Horrocks 1987: 152–3). But its reference to typology notwithstanding the Chomskyan approach does not have any direct historical link with the European tradition of linguistic typology, in which all the typological schools described in the present book have their roots. Moreover, this approach is fundamentally very different in a number of respects from the typological approaches under discussion (cf. Comrie 1989: chapter 1).

4. A few researchers of the LTG have recently begun to address seriously the issue of explanation. For example, Kozinsky (1988: 497) writes that 'the typological study of the resultative has revealed a number of quite unexpected typological regularities, which cry out for explanation'. He goes on to make an attempt to explain some of those regularities very much in the same way as in the American tradition of linguistic typology.

5. It must also be mentioned that Nedjalkov and Sil'nickij (1969) regard constructions with permissive meaning as causative construcions 'despite the fact that permission does not in general fall within the definition of the causative situation'; this is partly because 'causation and permission are so commonly expressed by the same affix (or auxiliary verb)' (Knott 1988: 2). Thus even in a notionally based typological investigation like Nedjalkov and Sil'nickij (1969) there is still evidence of adherence to form.

6. The difference between 'functional' and 'operational' in the functional or operational principles is only the difference between the static and processual aspect of the principles. Similarly, the difference between techniques and sub-dimensions has to do with how they are perceived with respect to the dimension. The term 'technique' emphasizes the processual aspect relative to the dimension, whereas the term 'sub-dimension' highlights the hierarchical aspect relative to the dimension. Also note that in Seiler (1995) the functional/operational principle of iconicity, which is based on similarity, is proposed in addition to indicativity and predicativity. In the present discussion it will be ignored in line with other major CUG publications.

7. There are four types of evidence for ordering techniques or sub-dimensions on a continuum of a single dimension (Seiler 1995: 292–4): (i) similarity or affinity of adjacent positions, e.g. one technique substituting for another; (ii) the amount of information (e.g. contrasts) that structures convey with respect to a given cognitive-conceptual domain; (iii) situational or contextual markedness; and (iv) degree of grammaticalization.

8. One of the most wide ranging typological investigations (also cf. Klimov 1977, 1983) has very recently emerged from the Centre for Linguistic Typology at the Australian National University. Though not associated with any particular school of linguistic typology, Aikhenvald and Dixon (1998) develop a network model of dependencies between eight grammatical systems – polarity, tense, aspect, evidentiality, person, reference classification, number and case – based on a convenience sample of more than five hundred languages. In this model some dependencies may be unidirectional, whereas others may be bidirectional. For instance, they suggest that there is a unidirectional dependency between polarity and case, with the latter depending on the former but never the other way around. There seems to be a bidirectional dependency between number and case, on the other hand. Aikhenvald and Dixon (1998: 73–5) suggest that the network of dependencies between the eight grammatical systems is related to dependencies in grammatical organization. For instance, polarity does not depend on the

other systems, whereas the latter depend on the former. This is claimed to be due to the fact that polarity 'is unequivocally associated with the unit clause, in every language' (Aikhenvald and Dixon 1998: 73) whereas the other systems, e.g. aspect and number, are related to the constituent units of the clause, e.g. the predicate and the predicate argument, respectively (cf. Foley and Van Vain 1984). Although their findings are tentative and suggestive, Aikhenvald and Dixon's work is very reminiscent of a holistic approach to linguistic typology, if not of holistic typology, evident in the PST. Also note that their concept of dependency, both bidirectional and unidirectional, is very similar to favourability, both mutual and asymmetric, invoked in the PST.

Bibliography

Abbreviations used below:

AJL Australian Journal of Linguistics
AL Applied Linguistics
BLS Berkeley Linguistic Society
CLS Chicago Linguistic Society
IJAL International Journal of American Linguistics
JL Journal of Linguistics
LI Linguistic Inquiry
LL Language Learning
SiL Studies in Language

AARTS, F. and E. SCHILS (1995) 'Relative clauses, the Accessibility Hierarchy and the Contrastive Analysis Hypothesis', *International Review of Applied Linguistics* 33: 47–63.

ADJÉMIAN, C. (1976) 'On the nature of interlanguage systems', *LL* 26: 297–320.

AIKHENVALD, A.Y. and R.M.W. DIXON (1998) 'Dependencies between grammatical systems', *Language* 74: 56–80.

AISSEN, J.L. (1987) *Tzotzil clause structure*. D. Reidel: Dordrecht.

AKAGAWA, Y. (1990) 'Avoidance of relative clauses by Japanese high school students', *JACET Kiyo* 21.

ALLÉN, S. (ed.) (1980) *Text processing, text analysis and generation, text typology and attribution: proceedings of Nobel Symposium 51*. Almqvist & Wiksell International: Stockholm.

ALLEN, W.S. (1964) 'On one-vowel systems', *Lingua* 13: 111–24.

ANDERSEN, R.W. (ed.) (1984) *Second languages: a cross-linguistic perspective*. Newbury House: Rowley, MA.

ANDERSON, S.R. (1976) 'On the notion of subject in ergative languages', in C.N. Li (ed.) (1976).

ANDREWS, A. (1975) Studies in the syntax of relative and comparative clauses. Unpublished PhD dissertation, MIT.

ANTINUCCI, F., A. DURANTI and L. GEBERT (1979) 'Relative clause structure, relative clause perception, and the change from SOV to SVO', *Cognition* 7: 145–76.

BAILEY, N., C. MADDEN and S. KRASHEN (1974) 'Is there a "natural sequence" in adult second language learning?', *LL* 24: 235–43.

BAKER, M.C. (1988) *Incorporation: a theory of grammatical function changing*. University of Chicago Press: Chicago.

BARTSCH, R. and T. VENNEMANN (1972) *Semantic structures: a study in the relation between semantics and syntax*. Athenaum: Frankfurt (Main).

BAVIN, E.L. (1998) 'Factors of typology in language acquisition: some examples from Warlpiri', in A. Siewierska and J.J. Song (eds) (1998).

BEEKES, R.S.P. (1995) *Comparative Indo-European linguistics: an introduction*. John Benjamins: Amsterdam.

BELL, A. (1978) 'Language samples', in J.H. Greenberg *et al.* (eds) (1978a).

BERG, T. (1996) 'Review of J.A. Hawkins, *A performance theory of order and constituency*', *Linguistics* 34: 1247–53.

BERMAN, R. (1978) *Modern Hebrew structure*. University Publishing Projects: Tel Aviv.

BERMAN, R.A. (1984) 'Cross-linguistic first language perspectives on second language acquisition research', in R.W. Andersen (ed.) (1984).

BERINSTEIN, A. (1990) 'On distinguishing surface datives in K'ekchi', in P.M. Postal and B.D. Joseph (eds), *Studies in Relational Grammar 3*. University of Chicago Press: Chicago.

BIRD, C. (1968) 'Relative clauses in Bambara', *Journal of West African Languages* 5: 35–47.

BISHOP, Y.M.M., S.E. FIENBERG and P.W. HOLLAND (1975) *Discrete multivariate analysis: theory and practice*. MIT Press: Cambridge, MA.

BLAKE, B.J. (1976) 'On ergativity and the notion of subject: some Australian cases', *Lingua* 39: 281–300.

BLAKE, B.J. (1977) *Case marking in Australian languages*. Australian Institute of Aboriginal Studies: Canberra.

BLAKE, B.J. (1987) *Australian Aboriginal grammar*. Croom Helm: London.

BLAKE, B.J. (1990) *Relational grammar*. Routledge: London.

BLAKE, B.J. (1993) 'Review of J. Nichols, *Linguistic diversity in space and time*', *Languages of the World* 6: 50–3.

BLAKE, B.J. (1994) *Case*. Cambridge University Press: Cambridge.

BLEY-VROMAN, R. (1989) 'What is the logical problem of foreign language learning?', in S.M. Gass and J. Schachter (eds) (1989).

BLEY-VROMAN, R. (1990) 'The logical problem of foreign language learning', *Linguistic Analysis* 20: 3–49.

BLIESE, L.F. (1981) *A generative grammar of Afar*. SIL and University of Texas at Arlington.

BLOOM, L., M. LAHEY, L. HOOD, K. LIFTER and K. FIESS (1980) 'Complex sentences: acquisition of syntactic connectives and the semantic relations they encode', *Journal of Child Language* 7: 235–61.

BOSSONG, G. (1984) 'Review of H. Seiler, *Possession as an operational dimension of language*', *Lingua* 64: 229–33.

BOWERMAN, M. (1985) 'What shapes children's grammars?', in D.I. Slobin (ed.) (1985b).

BOWERMAN, M. (1996a) 'The origins of children's spatial semantic categories: cognitive versus linguistic determinants', in J.J. Gumperz and S.C. Levinson (eds), *Rethinking linguistic relativity*. Cambridge University Press: Cambridge.

BOWERMAN, M. (1996b) 'Learning how to structure space for language: a crosslinguistic perspective', in P. Bloom, M.A. Peterson, L. Nadel and M.F. Garrett (eds), *Language and space*. MIT Press: Cambridge, MA.

BRESNAN, J. and L. MOSHI (1990) 'Object asymmetries in comparative Bantu syntax', *LI* 21: 147–85.

BRICKER, V.R. (1978) 'Antipassive constructions in Yucatec Maya', in N.C. England (ed.), *Papers in Mayan linguistics*. University of Missouri: Columbia.

BYBEE, J.L. (1985a) *Morphology: a study of the relation between meaning and form*. John Benjamins: Amsterdam.

BYBEE, J.L. (1985b) 'Diagrammatic iconicity in stem-inflection relations', in J. Haiman (ed.) (1985b).

BYBEE, J.L. (1988) 'The diachronic dimension in explanation', in J. A. Hawkins (ed.) (1988a).

BYBEE, J.L., W. PAGLIUCA and R.D. PERKINS (1990) 'On the asymmetries in the affixation of grammatical material', in W. Croft, K. Denning and S. Kemmer (eds), *Studies in typology and diachrony*. John Benjamins: Amsterdam.

BYBEE, J.L., R. PERKINS and W. PAGLIUCA (1994) *The evolution of grammar: tense, aspect, and modality in the languages of the world*. University of Chicago Press: Chicago.

CAMPBELL, L. (1997) 'Typological and areal issues in reconstruction', in J. Fisiak (ed.) (1997).

CAMPBELL, L., V. BUBENIK and L. SAXON (1988) 'Word order universals: refinements and clarifications', *Canadian Journal of Linguistics* 33: 209–30.

CAMPBELL, L., T. KAUFMAN and T.C. SMITH-STARK (1986) 'Meso-America as a linguistic area', *Language* 62: 530–70.

CATFORD, I. (1976) 'Ergativity in Caucasian languages', *North Eastern Linguistic Society Papers* 6: 37–48.

CHAFE, W.L. (ed.) (1980) *The pear stories: cognitive, cultural, and linguistic aspects of narrative production*. Ablex: Norwood, NJ.

CHOI, S. and M. BOWERMAN (1991) 'Learning to express motion events in English and Korean: the influence of language-specific lexicalization patterns', *Cognition* 41: 83–121.

CHOMSKY, N. (1970) 'Remarks on nominalization', in R.A. Jacobs and P.S. Rosenbaum (eds), *Readings in English transformational grammar*. Ginn and Co.: Waltham, MA.

CLAHSEN, H. (1984) 'The acquisition of German word-order: a test case for cognitive approaches to L2 development', in R. Andersen (ed.) (1984).

CLANCY, P.M. (1985) 'The acquisition of Japanese', in D.I. Slobin (ed.) (1985a).

CLANCY, P.M., H. LEE and M.-H. ZOH (1986) 'Processing strategies in the acquisition of relative clauses: universal principles and language-specific realizations', *Cognition* 24: 225–62.

CLARK, E.V. (in press) 'Emergent categories in first language acquisition', in M. Bowerman and S. Levinson (eds), *Language acquisition and conceptual development*. Cambridge University Press: Cambridge.

CLARK, E.V. and K.L. CARPENTER (1989) 'The notion of source in language acquisition', *Language* 65: 1–30.

CLARK, H.H. and E.V. CLARK (1977) *Psychology and language: an introduction to psycholinguistics*. Harcourt Brace Jovanovich: New York.

COLE, P. (1983) 'The grammatical role of the causee in universal grammar', *IJAL* 49: 115–33.

COLE, P. and S.N. SRIDHAR (1977) 'Clause union and relational grammar: evidence from Hebrew and Kannada', *LI* 8: 700–13.

COLLINGE, N.E. (1985) *The laws of Indo-European*. John Benjamins: Amsterdam.

COLLINGE, N.E. (1994) 'Historical linguistics: history', in R.E. Asher (ed.), *The Encyclopedia of Language and Linguistics*. Pergamon Press: Oxford.

COMRIE, B. (1973) 'The ergative: variations on a theme', *Lingua* 32: 239–53.

COMRIE, B. (1975) 'Causatives and universal grammar', *Transactions of the Philological Society* (1974): 1–32.

COMRIE, B. (1976) 'The syntax of causative constructions: cross-language similarities and divergences', in M. Shibatani (ed.) (1976a).

COMRIE, B. (1977) 'Subjects and direct objects in Uralic languages: a functional explanation of case-marking systems', *Études Finno-Ougriennes* 12: 5–17.

COMRIE, B. (1978) 'Ergativity', in W.P. Lehmann (ed.) (1978a).

COMRIE, B. (1980) 'Morphology and word order reconstruction: problems and prospects', in J. Fisiak (ed.), *Historical morphology*. Mouton: The Hague.

COMRIE, B. (1984) 'Why linguists need language acquirers', in W.E. Rutherford (ed.) (1984a).

COMRIE, B. (1985) 'Causative verb formation and other verb-deriving morphology', in T. Shopen (ed.), *Language typology and syntactic description III: grammatical categories and the lexicon*. Cambridge University Press: Cambridge.

COMRIE, B. (1988) 'Linguistic typology', *Annual Review of Anthropology* 17: 145–59.

COMRIE, B. (1989) *Language universals and linguistic typology*. Second edition. Blackwell: Oxford.

COMRIE, B. (1993) 'Typology and reconstruction', in C. Jones (ed.), *Historical linguistics: problems and perspectives*. Longman: London.

COMRIE, B. and K. HORIE (1995) 'Complement clauses versus relative clauses: some Khmer evidence', in W. Abraham, T. Givón and S.A. Thompson (eds), *Discourse grammar and typology*. John Benjamins: Amsterdam.

COMRIE, B. and M. POLINSKY (eds) (1993) *Causatives and transitivity*. John Benjamins: Amsterdam.

COOK, V.J. (1985) 'Chomsky's Universal Grammar and second language learning', *AL* 6: 2–18.

COOREMAN, A. (1994) 'A functional typology of antipassives', in B. Fox and P.J. Hopper (eds), *Voice: form and function*. John Benjamins: Amsterdam.

CRAIG, C.G. (1976) 'Properties of basic and derived subjects in Jacaltec', in C.N. Li (ed.) (1976).

CRAIG, C.G. (1987) 'The Rama language: a text with grammatical notes', *Journal of Chibchan Studies* 5.

CROFT, W. (1990) *Typology and universals*. Cambridge University Press: Cambridge.

CROFT, W. (1991) *Syntactic categories and grammatical relations: the cognitive organization of information*. University of Chicago Press: Chicago.

CROFT, W. (1995) 'Modern syntactic typology', in M. Shibatani and T. Bynon (eds) (1995a).

CROTEAU, K.C. (1995) 'Second language acquisition of relative clause structures by learners of Italian', in F.R. Eckman *et al.* (eds) (1995).

CROWLEY, T. (1978) *The Middle Clarence dialects of Bandjalang*. Australian Institute of Aboriginal Studies: Canberra.

CUTLER, A., J.A. HAWKINS and G. GILLIGAN (1985) 'The suffixing preference: a processing explanation', *Linguistics* 23: 723–58.

DAHL, Ö. (1985) *Tense and aspect systems*. Blackwell: Oxford.

DAVIES, A., C. CRIPER and A.P.R. HOWATT (eds) (1984) *Interlanguage*. Edinburgh University Press: Edinburgh.

DAWKINS, R.M. (1916) *Modern Greek in Asia Minor: a study of the dialects of Sílli, Cappadocia and Phárasa with grammars, texts, translations, and glossary*. Cambridge University Press: Cambridge.

DAYLEY, J.P. (1978) 'Voice in Tzutujil', *Journal of Mayan Linguistics* 1: 20–52.

DAYLEY, J.P. (1985) *Tzutujil grammar*. University of California Press: Berkeley.

DeLANCEY, S. (1981) 'An interpretation of split ergativity and related patterns', *Language* 57: 626–57.

DeLANCEY, S. (1983) 'Agentivity and causation: data from Newari', *BLS* 9: 54–63.

DeLANCEY, S. (1984) 'Notes on agentivity and causation', *SiL* 8: 181–213.

DeLANCEY, S. (1985) 'Lhasa Tibetan evidentials and the semantics of causation', *BLS* 11: 65–72.

DERBYSHIRE, D.C. and G.K. PULLUM (1981) 'Object-initial languages', *IJAL* 47: 192–214.

DERBYSHIRE, D.C. and G.K. PULLUM (eds) (1986) *Handbook of Amazonian languages*. Mouton de Gruyter: Berlin.

DE VILLIERS, J.G., H.B. TAGER FLUSBERG, K. HAKUTA and M. COHEN (1979) 'Children's comprehension of relative clauses', *Journal of Psycholinguistic Research* 8: 499–518.

DEZSÖ, L. (1982) *Studies in syntactic typology and contrastive grammar*. Mouton: The Hague.

DIXON, R.M.W. (1972) *The Dyirbal language of North Queensland*. Cambridge University Press: Cambridge.

DIXON, R.M.W. (ed.) (1976) *Grammatical categories in Australian languages*. Humanities Press: Atlantic Highlands, NJ.

DIXON, R.M.W. (1979) 'Ergativity', *Language* 55: 59–138.

DIXON, R.M.W. (1980) *The languages of Australia*. Cambridge University Press: Cambridge.

DIXON, R.M.W. (1994) *Ergativity*. Cambridge University Press: Cambridge.

DOUGHTY, C. (1991) 'Second language instruction does make a difference: evidence from an empirical study of SL relativization', *Studies in Second Language Acquisition* 13: 431–69.

DOWNING, B.T. (1973) 'Corelative relative clauses in universal grammar', *Minnesota Working Papers in Linguistics and Philosophy of Language* 2: 1–17.

DOWNING, B.T. (1978) 'Some universals of relative clause structure', in J.H. Greenberg *et al.* (ed.) (1978b).

DOWNING, P. (1985) Classifier constructions and referentiality marking in Japanese. Paper presented at the Conference on Japanese Language and Linguistics, University of California, Los Angeles.

DRESSLER, W. (1969) 'Eine textsyntaktische Regel er idg. Wortstellung', *Zeitschrift für Vergleichende Sprachforschung* 83: 1–25.

DRESSLER, W. (1981) 'Notes on textual typology', *Wiener Linguistische Gazette* 25: 1–11.

DRIVER, H.E. and R.P. CHANEY (1970) 'Cross-cultural sampling and Galton's problem', in R. Naroll and R. Cohen (eds), *A handbook of method in cultural anthropology*. Natural History Press: Garden City, NY.

DRYER, M.S. (1980) 'The positional tendencies of sentential noun phrases in universal grammar', *Canadian Journal of Linguistics* 25: 123–95.

DRYER, M.S. (1986) 'Primary objects, secondary objects, and antidative', *Language* 62: 808–45.

DRYER, M.S. (1988) 'Object-verb order and adjective-noun order: dispelling a myth', *Lingua* 74: 185–217.

DRYER, M.S. (1989) 'Large linguistic areas and language sampling', *SiL* 13: 257–92.

DRYER, M.S. (1991) 'SVO languages and the OV:VO typology', *JL* 27: 443–82.

DRYER, M.S. (1992) 'The Greenbergian word order correlations', *Language* 68: 81–138.

DRYER, M.S. (1995) 'Frequency and pragmatically unmarked word order', in P. Downing and M. Noonan (eds), *Word order in discourse*. John Benjamins: Amsterdam.

DRYER, M.S. (1997) 'On the six-way word order typology', *SiL* 21: 69–103.

DRYER, M.S. (1998) 'Aspects of word order in the languages of Europe', in A. Siewierska (ed.) (1998).

Du BOIS, J.W. (1985) 'Competing motivations', in J. Haiman (ed.) (1985b).

Du BOIS, J.W. (1987) 'The discourse basis of ergativity', *Language* 63: 805–55.

DULAY, H. and M. BURT (1972) 'Goofing, an indicator of children's second language strategies', *LL* 22: 234–52.

DULAY, H. and M. BURT (1974) 'Natural sequences in child second language acquisition', *LL* 24: 37–53.

DULAY, H., M. BURT and S. KRASHEN (1982) *Language Two*. Oxford University Press: New York.

DURIE, M. (1988) 'Preferred argument structure in an active language: arguments against the category "intransitive subject"', *Lingua* 74: 1–25.

DUŠKOVÁ, L. (1969) 'On sources of errors in foreign language learning', *International Review of Applied Linguistics* 7: 11–36.

EBELING, C.L. (1966) 'Review of Chikobava and Cercvadze, *The grammar of literary Avar*', *Studia Caucasica* 2: 58–100.

ECKMAN, F.R. (1977) 'Markedness and the contrastive analysis hypothesis', *LL* 27: 315–30.

ECKMAN, F.R. (1984) 'Universals, typologies and interlanguage', in W.E. Rutherford (ed.) (1984a).

ECKMAN, F.R. (1988) 'Typological and parametric views of universals in second language acquisition', in S. Flynn and W. O'Neil (eds) (1988).

ECKMAN, F.R. (1991) 'The structural conformity hypothesis and the acquisition of consonant clusters in the interlanguage of ESL learners', *Studies in Second Language Acquisition* 13: 23–41.

ECKMAN, F.R. (1996) 'A functional-typological approach to second language acquisition theory', in W.C. Ritchie and T.K. Bhatia (eds) (1996).

ECKMAN, F.R., L. BELL and D. NELSON (1988) 'On the generalization of relative clause instruction in the acquisition of English as a second language', *AL* 9: 1– 20.

ECKMAN, F.R., D. HIGHLAND, P.W. LEE, J. MILEHAM and R.R. WEBER (eds) (1995) *Second language acquisition theory and pedagogy*. Lawrence Erlbaum: Mahwah, NJ.

ECKMAN, F.R., E.A. MORAVCSIK and J.R. WIRTH (1989) 'Implicational universals and interrogative structures in the interlanguage of ESL learners', *LL* 39: 173–205.

ELLIS, R. (1985) *Understanding second language acquisition*. Oxford University Press: Oxford.

ELLIS, R. (1994) *The study of second language acquisition*. Oxford University Press: Oxford.

ENGLAND, N.C. (1983) 'Ergativity in Mamean (Mayan) languages', *IJAL* 49: 1–19.

ENGLAND, N.C. (1986) Mamean voice: syntactic and narrative considerations. Ms, University of Iowa.

FELIX, S.W. (1984) 'Maturational aspects of universal grammar', in A. Davies *et al.* (eds) (1984).

FERGUSON, C.A. (1978) 'Phonological processes', in J.H. Greenberg, C.A. Ferguson and E.A. Moravcsik (eds), *Universals of human language, vol. II: phonology*. Stanford University Press: Stanford.

FINCK, F.N. (1899) *Der deutsche Sprachbau als Ausdruck deutscher Weltanschauung*. Elwert: Marburg.

FISIAK, J. (ed.) (1984) *Historical syntax*. Mouton: Berlin.

FISIAK, J. (ed.) (1997) *Linguistic reconstruction and typology*. Mouton de Gruyter: Berlin.

FLYNN, S. and W. O'NEIL (eds) (1988) *Linguistic theory in second language acquisition*. Kluwer: Dordrecht.

FODOR, J.A., T.G. BEVER and M.F. GARRETT (1974) *The psychology of language: an introduction to psycholinguistics and generative grammar*. McGraw Hill: New York.

FOLEY, W.A. and R.D. VAN VALIN (1984) *Functional syntax and universal grammar*. Cambridge University Press: Cambridge.

FOLEY, W.A. and R.D. VAN VALIN (1985) 'Information packaging in the clause', in T. Shopen (ed.), *Language typology and syntactic description, I: clause structure*. Cambridge University Press: Cambridge.

FOX, A. (1995) *Linguistic reconstruction: an introduction to theory and method*. Oxford University Press: Oxford.

FOX, B.A. (1987) 'The Noun Phrase Accessibility Hierarchy reinterpreted: subject primacy or the absolutive hypothesis?', *Language* 63: 856–70.

FRANTZ, D. (1971) *Toward a generative grammar of Blackfoot*. SIL/University of Oklahoma: Norman.

FRAZIER, L. (1979) 'Parsing and constraints on word order', *University of Massachusetts Occasional Papers in Linguistics* 5: 177–98.

FRAZIER, L. (1985) 'Syntactic complexity,' in D. Dowty, L. Karttunen and A. Zwicky (eds), *Natural language parsing: psychological, computational, and theoretical perspectives*. Cambridge University Press: Cambridge.

FRIEDRICH, P. (1975) *Proto-Indo-European syntax: the order of meaningful elements*. Montana College of Mineral Science and Technology: Butte.

GABELENTZ, G. von der (1901) *Die Sprachwissenschaft: Ihre Aufgaben, Methoden und bisherigen Ergebnisse*. Chr. H. Tauchnitz: Leipzig.

GAMKRELIDZE, T.V. (1997) 'Language typology and linguistic reconstruction', in J. Fisiak (ed.) (1997).

GAMKRELIDZE, T.V. and V.V. IVANOV (1973) 'Sprachtypologie und die Rekonstruktion der gemeinindogermanischen Verschlüsse', *Phonetica* 27: 150–6.

GARCÍA-BERRIO, A. (1980) 'Textual typology and universals of discourse', in S. Allén (ed.) (1980).

GASS, S. (1979) 'Language transfer and universal grammatical relations', *LL* 29: 327–44.

GASS, S. (1982) 'From theory to practice', in M. Hines and W. Rutherford (eds), *On TESOL '81*. TESOL: Washington, DC.

GASS, S. (1984a) 'A review of interlanguage syntax: language transfer and language universals', *LL* 34: 115–32.

GASS, S. (1984b) 'The empirical basis for the universal hypothesis in interlanguage studies', in A. Davies *et al.* (eds) (1984).

GASS, S. (1996) 'Second language acquisition and linguistic theory: the role of language transfer', in W.C. Ritchie and T.K. Bhatia (eds) (1996).

GASS, S. and J. ARD (1980) 'L2 data: their relevance for language universals', *TESOL Quarterly* 14: 443–52.

GASS, S. and J. ARD (1984) 'Second language acquisition and the ontology of language universals', in W.E. Rutherford (ed.) (1984a).

GASS, S.M. (1988) 'Second language acquisition and linguistic theory: the role of language transfer', in S. Flynn and W. O'Neil (eds) (1988).

GASS, S.M. (1989) 'Language universals and second-language acquisition', *LL* 39: 497–534.

GASS, S.M. and J. SCHACHTER (eds) (1989) *Linguistic perspectives on second language acquisition*. Cambridge University Press: Cambridge.

GASS, S.M. and L. SELINKER (1994) *Second language acquisition: an introductory course*. Lawrence Erlbaum: Hillsdale, NJ.

GAZDAR, G., G.K. PULLUM and I.A. SAG (1982) 'Auxiliaries and related phenomena in a restrictive theory of grammar', *Language* 58: 591–638.

GERDTS, D.B. (1984) 'A relational analysis of Halkomelem causals', in E.D. Cook and D.B. Gerdts (eds), *Syntax and semantics 16: the syntax of native American languages*. Academic Press: New York.

GIVÓN, T. (1971a) 'Historical syntax and synchronic morphology: an archaeologist's field trip', *CLS* 7: 394–415.

GIVÓN, T. (1971b) 'Some historical changes in the noun-class system of Bantu, their possible causes and wider implications', in C.W. Kim and H. Stahlke (eds), *Papers in African linguistics*. Linguistic Research: Edmonton.

GIVÓN, T. (1973) Pronoun attraction and subject postposing in Bantu. Ms, Department of Linguistics, University of California, Los Angeles.

GIVÓN, T. (1975) 'Serial verbs and syntactic change: Niger-Congo', in C.N. Li (ed.) (1975).

GIVÓN, T. (1976a) 'Topic, pronoun and grammatical agreement', in C.N. Li (ed.) (1976).

GIVÓN, T. (1976b) 'On the SOV reconstruction of southern Nilotic: internal evidence from Toposa', *Studies in African Linguistics* 6: 73–81.

GIVÓN, T. (1979) *On understanding grammar*. Academic Press: New York.

GIVÓN, T. (1984) *Syntax: a functional–typological introduction, vol. I*. John Benjamins: Amsterdam.

GOODLUCK, H. and S. TAVAKOLIAN (1982) 'Competence and processing in children's grammar of relative clauses', *Cognition* 11: 1–27.

GREENBERG, J.H. (1954) 'A quantitative approach to the morphological typology of language', in R.F. Spencer (ed.), *Method and perspective in anthropology*. University of Minnesota Press: Minneapolis. (Reprinted as Greenberg 1960.)

GREENBERG, J.H. (1957a) 'The nature and uses of linguistic typologies', *IJAL* 23: 68–77.

GREENBERG, J.H. (1957b) 'Order of affixing: a study in general linguistics', in J.H. Greenberg, *Essays in Linguistics*. University of Chicago Press: Chicago.

GREENBERG, J.H. (1960) 'A quantitative approach to the morphological typology of language', *IJAL* 26: 178–94.

GREENBERG, J.H. (ed.) (1963a) *Universals of language*. MIT Press: Cambridge, MA.

GREENBERG, J.H. (1963b) 'Some universals of grammar with particular reference to the order of meaningful elements', in J.H. Greenberg (ed.) (1963a).

GREENBERG, J.H. (1974) *Language typology: a historical and analytic overview*. Mouton: The Hague.

GREENBERG, J.H. (1978) 'Diachrony, synchrony and language universals', in J.H. Greenberg *et al.* (eds) (1978a).

GREENBERG, J.H. (1980) 'Circumfixes and typological change', in E. Traugott, R. Labrum and S. Shepherd (eds), *Papers from the 4th International Conference on Historical Linguistics*. John Benjamins: Amsterdam.

GREENBERG, J.H. (1991) 'Typology/universals and second language acquisition', in T. Huebner and C.A. Ferguson (eds), *Crosscurrents in second language acquisition and linguistic theories*. John Benjamins: Amsterdam.

GREENBERG, J.H. (1995) 'The diachronic typological approach to language', in M. Shibatani and T. Bynon (eds) (1995a).

GREENBERG, J.H., C.A. FERGUSON and E.A. MORAVCSIK (eds) (1978a) *Universals of human language, vol. I: method and theory*. Stanford University Press: Stanford.

GREENBERG, J.H., C.A. FERGUSON and E.A. MORAVCSIK (eds) (1978b) *Universals of human language, vol. IV: syntax*. Stanford University Press: Stanford.

GREGG, K.R. (1989) 'Second language acquisition theory: the case for a generative perspective', in S.M. Gass and J. Schachter (eds) (1989).

HAIDER, H. (1985) 'The fallacy of typology: remarks on the PIE stop-system', *Lingua* 65: 1–27.

HAIMAN, J. (1980) *Hua, a Papuan language of the Eastern Highlands of New Guinea*. John Benjamins: Amsterdam.

HAIMAN, J. (1985a) *Natural syntax: iconicity and erosion*. Cambridge University Press: Cambridge.

HAIMAN, J. (ed.) (1985b) *Iconicity in syntax*. John Benjamins: Amsterdam.

HAKUTA, K. (1981) 'Grammatical description versus configurational arrangement in language acquisition: the case of relative clauses in Japanese', *Cognition* 9: 197–236.

HALE, K. (1976) 'The adjoined relative clause in Australia', in R.M.W. Dixon (ed.) (1976).

HALL, C.J. (1988) 'Integrating diachronic and processing principles in explaining the suffixing preference', in J.A. Hawkins (ed.) (1988a).

HALL, C.J. (1992) *Morphology and mind*. Routledge: London.

HAMILTON, R.L. (1995) 'The Noun Phrase Accessibility Hierarchy in SLA: determining the basis for its developmental effects', in F.R. Eckman *et al.* (eds) (1995).

HARADA, S.I., T. UYENO, H. HAYASHIBE and H. YAMADA (1976) 'On the development of perceptual strategies in children: a case study on the Japanese child's comprehension of the relative clause constructions', *Annual Bulletin of the Research Institute Logopedics Phoniatrics* (University of Tokyo) 10: 199–224.

HARRIS, A.C. (1985) *Diachronic syntax: the Kartvelian case*. Academic Press: Orlando.

HARRIS, A.C. (1997) 'Review of R.M.W. Dixon, *Ergativity*', *Language* 73: 359–74.

HARRIS, M. (1984) 'On the strengths and weaknesses of a typological approach to historical syntax', in J. Fisiak (ed.) (1984).

HASPELMATH, M. (1991) 'Review of V.S. Xrakovskij (ed.), *Tipologija iterativnyx konstrukcij*', *SiL* 15: 494–9.

HASPELMATH, M. (1992) 'Review of V.P. Nedjalkov (ed.), *Typology of resultative constructions*', *SiL* 16: 240–8.

HASPELMATH, M. (1996) 'Review of M. Shibatani and T. Bynon (eds), *Approaches to language typology*', *JL* 32: 513–17.

HAWKINS, J.A. (1979) 'Implicational universals as predictors of word order change', *Language* 55: 618–48.

HAWKINS, J.A. (1980) 'On implicational and distributional universals of word order', *JL* 16: 193–235.

HAWKINS, J.A. (1983) *Word order universals*. Academic Press: New York.

HAWKINS, J.A. (1986) *A comparative typology of English and German: unifying the contrasts*. Croom Helm: London.

HAWKINS, J.A. (1987) 'Implicational universals as predictors of language acquisition', *Linguistics* 25: 453–73.

HAWKINS, J.A. (ed.) (1988a) *Explaining language universals*. Blackwell: Oxford.

HAWKINS, J.A. (1988b) 'Explaining language universals', in J.A. Hawkins (ed.) (1988a).

HAWKINS, J.A. (1988c) 'On generative and typological approaches to universal grammar', *Lingua* 74: 85–100.

HAWKINS, J.A. (1990) 'A parsing theory of word order universals', *LI* 21: 223–61.

HAWKINS, J.A. (1994) *A performance theory of order and constituency*. Cambridge University Press: Cambridge.

HAWKINS, J.A. (1998) 'Some issues in a performance theory of word order', in A. Siewierska (ed.) (1998).

HAWKINS, J.A. and A. CUTLER (1988) 'Psycholinguistic factors in morphological asymmetry', in J.A. Hawkins (ed.) (1988a).

HAWKINS, J.A. and G. GILLIGAN (1988) 'Prefixing and suffixing universals in relation to basic word order', *Lingua* 74: 219–59.

HAWKINS, R. (1989) 'Do second language learners acquire restrictive relative clauses on the basis of relational or configurational information?: the acquisition of French subject, direct object and genitive restrictive relative clauses by second language learners', *Second Language Research* 5: 158–88.

HEATH, J. (1994) 'Review of J. Nichols, *Linguistic diversity in space and time*', *Anthropological Linguistics* 36: 92–6.

HEINE, B. and U. CLAUDI (1986) *On the rise of grammatical categories: some examples from Maa*. Dietrich Reimer: Berlin.

HEINE, B., U. CLAUDI and F. HÜNNEMEYER (1991) *Grammaticalization: a conceptual framework*. University of Chicago Press: Chicago.

HEINE, B., C. LEHMANN and M. REH (1985) 'Twelve questions on language typology and possible answers', in H. Seiler and G. Brettschneider (eds) (1985).

HEINE, B. and M. REH (1984) *Grammaticalization and reanalysis in African languages*. Helmut Buske: Hamburg.

HETZRON, R. (1976) 'On the Hungarian causative verb and its syntax', in M. Shibatani (ed.) (1976a).

HEWITT, B.G. (1979) *Abkhaz*. North-Holland: Amsterdam.

HINTON, L. (1982) 'How to cause in Mixtec', *BLS* 8: 354–63.

HOCK, H.H. (1991) *Principles of historical linguistics*. Second edition. Mouton de Gruyter: Berlin.

HOCK, H.H. (1992) 'Reconstruction and syntactic typology: a plea for a different approach', in G.W. Davis and G.K. Iverson (eds), *Explanation in historical linguistics*. John Benjamins: Amsterdam.

HOHEPA, P. (1969) 'The accusative to ergative drift in Polynesian languages', *Journal of the Polynesian Society* 78: 295–329.

HOPPER, P.J. (1973) 'Glottalized and murmured occlusives in Indo-European', *Glossa* 7: 141–66.

HOPPER, P.J. and S.A. THOMPSON (1980) 'Transitivity in grammar and discourse', *Language* 56: 251–99.

HOPPER, P.J. and E.C. TRAUGOTT (1993) *Grammaticalization*. Cambridge University Press: Cambridge.

HORNE, K.M. (1966) *Language typology: 19th and 20th century views*. Georgetown University Press: Washington, DC.

HORROCKS, G. (1987) *Generative grammar*. Longman: London.

HUMBOLDT, W. von (1825) 'Über das Entstehen der grammatischen Formen, und ihren Einfluss auf die Ideeentwicklung', *Abhandlungen der hist. phil. Klasse* (Königliche Akademie der Wissenschaften: Berlin), 401–30.

HUMBOLDT, W. von (1836) *Über die Verschiedenheit des menschlichen Sprachbaues: vol. I* of *Über die Kawispache auf der Insel Java*. Königliche Akademie der Wissenschaften: Berlin.

HUNTER, P.J. and G.D. PRIDEAUX (1983) 'Empirical constraints on the verb-particle construction in English', *Journal of the Atlantic Provinces Linguistic Association* 5: 3–15.

HYLTENSTAM, K. (1984) 'The use of typological markedness conditions as predictors in second language acquisition: the case of pronominal copies in relative clauses', in R.W. Andersen (ed.) (1984).

HYMAN, L.M. and K.E. ZIMMER (1976) 'Embedded topic in French', in C.N. Li (ed.) (1976).

INGRAM, D. (1989) *First language acquisition: method, description and explanation*. Cambridge University Press: Cambridge.

INOUE, A. (1991) A comparative study of parsing in English and Japanese. Unpublished PhD dissertation, University of Connecticut, Storrs.

JAKOBSON, R. (1929) 'Remarques sur l'évolution phonologique du russe', *Travaux du Cercle linguistique de Prague 2*.

JAKOBSON, R. (1941) *Kindersprache, Aphasie, und allgemeine Lautgesetze*. Uppsala Universitets Aarskrift: Uppsala.

JAKOBSON, R. (1958) 'Typological studies and their contribution to historical comparative linguistics', in *Proceedings of the Eighth International Congress of Linguists*. Oslo University Press: Oslo.

JAKOBSON, R. (1968) *Child language, aphasia and phonological universals*. Mouton: The Hague.

JAMES, C. (1980) *Contrastive analysis*. Longman: Harlow.

JOHNSON, D.E. (1974) 'On the role of grammatical relations in linguistic theory', *CLS* 10: 269–83.

JOSEPHS, L.S. (1975) *Palauan reference grammar*. University Press of Hawaii: Honolulu.

JUSTESON, J.S. and L.D. STEPHENS (1990) 'Explanation for word order universals: a log-linear analysis', in *Proceedings of the XIV International Congress of Linguists*. Mouton de Gruyter: Berlin.

KEENAN, E.L. (1972) 'Relative clause formation in Malagasy', in P.M. Peranteau *et al.* (eds) (1972).

KEENAN, E.L. (1976) 'Towards a universal definition of "subject"', in C.N. Li (ed.) (1976).

KEENAN, E.L. (1978) 'Language variation and the logical structure of universal grammar', in H. Seiler (ed.) (1978).

KEENAN, E.L. (1979) 'On surface form and logical form', *Studies in Linguistic Sciences* 8.2: 1–41.

KEENAN, E.L. (1984) 'Semantic correlates of the ergative/absolutive distinction', *Linguistics* 22: 197–223.

KEENAN, E.L. (1985) 'Relative clauses', in T. Shopen (ed.), *Language typology and syntactic description II: complex constructions.* Cambridge University Press: Cambridge.

KEENAN, E.L. (1987) *Universal grammar: 15 essays.* Croom Helm: London.

KEENAN, E.L. and B. COMRIE (1972) Noun phrase accessibility and universal grammar. Paper presented at the Annual Meeting of the Linguistic Society of America, Atlanta.

KEENAN, E.L. and B. COMRIE (1977) 'Noun phrase accessibility and universal grammar', *LI* 8: 63–99.

KEENAN, E.L. and B. COMRIE (1979) 'Data on the Noun Phrase Accessibility Hierarchy', *Language* 55: 333–51.

KEENAN, E.L. and S. HAWKINS (1987) 'The psychological validity of the Accessibility Hierarchy', in E.L. Keenan (1987).

KEMMER, S. and A. VERHAGEN (1994) 'The grammar of causatives and the conceptual structure of events', *Cognitive Linguistics* 5: 115–56.

KENNY, J.A. (1974) *A numerical taxonomy of ethnic units using Murdock's 1967 World Sample.* University Microfilms: Ann Arbor.

KHRAKOVSKY, V.S. (1973) 'Passive constructions', in F. Kiefer (ed.) (1973).

KHRAKOVSKY, V. and A. OGLOBLIN (1993) 'The Kholodovich School of Linguistic Typology: 1961–1991', *The Petersburg Journal of Cultural Studies* 1.2: 125–43, 1.3:113–26.

KIBRIK, A.E. (1990) 'As línguas semanticamente ergativas na perspectiva da tipologia sintática geral', *Cadernos de estudos lingüísticos* 18: 15–36.

KIEFER, F. (ed.) (1973) *Trends in Soviet theoretical linguistics.* D. Reidel: Dordrecht.

KIMENYI, A. (1980) *A relational grammar of Kinyarwanda.* University of California Press: Berkeley.

KLIMOV, G.A. (1974) 'On the character of languages of active typology', *Linguistics* 131: 11–25.

KLIMOV, G.A. (1977) *Tipologija jazykov aktivnogo stroja.* Nauka: Moscow.

KLIMOV, G.A. (1983) *Principy kontensivnoj tipologii.* Nauka: Moscow.

KNOTT, J.M. (1988) *The Leningrad Group for the Typological Study of Languages: introduction and translations.* School of Oriental and African Studies, University of London: London.

KONSTANTINOVA, O.A. (1964) *Evenkijskij jazyk: fonetika, morfologija.* Nauka: Moscow-Leningrad.

KOOPMAN, H. (1984) *The syntax of verbs: from verb movement rules in the Kru languages to universal grammar.* Foris: Dordrecht.

KOPTJEVSKAJA-TAMM, M. and I.A. MURAVYOVA (1993) 'Alutor causatives, noun incorporation, and the Mirror Principle', in B. Comrie and M. Polinsky (eds) (1993).

KOZINSKY, I.S. (1988) 'Resultative: results and discussion', in V.P. Nedjalkov (ed.) (1988).

KOZINSKY, I.S., V.P. NEDJALKOV and M.S. POLINSKAJA (1988) 'Antipassive in Chukchee: oblique object, object incorporation, zero object', in M. Shibatani (ed.), *Passive and voice.* John Benjamins: Amsterdam.

KOZINSKY, I. and M. POLINSKY (1993) 'Causee and patient in the causative of transitive: coding conflict or doubling of grammatical relations?', in B. Comrie and M. Polinsky (eds) (1993).

KROHN, R. (1977) *English sentence structure*. University of Michigan Press: Ann Arbor.

KUNO, S. (1972) 'Natural explanations for some syntactic universals', in *Report NSF-28 to the National Science Foundation*. Harvard University Computation Laboratory: Cambridge, MA.

KUNO, S. (1973) *The structure of the Japanese language*. MIT Press: Cambridge, MA.

KUNO, S. (1974) 'The position of relative clauses and conjunctions', *LI* 5: 117–36.

KUNO, S. and E. KABURAKI (1977) 'Empathy and syntax', *LI* 8: 627–72.

LADO, R. (1957) *Linguistics across cultures: applied linguistics for language teachers*. University of Michigan Press: Ann Arbor.

LAMENDELLA, J. (1977) 'General principles of neurofunctional organization and their manifestations in primary and non-primary language acquisition', *LL* 27: 155–96.

LANGACKER, R.W. (1987) *Foundations of cognitive grammar, vol. I: theoretical prerequisites*. Stanford University Press: Stanford.

LANGACKER, R.W. (1991) *Foundations of cognitive grammar, vol. 2: descriptive application*. Stanford University Press: Stanford.

LARSEN, T.W. (1981) 'Functional correlates of ergativity in Aguacatec', *BLS* 7: 136–53.

LARSEN, T.W. and W.M. NORMAN (1979) 'Correlates of ergativity in Mayan grammar', in F. Plank (ed.) (1979).

LARSEN-FREEMAN, D. and M.H. LONG (1991) *An introduction to second language acquisition research*. Longman: London.

LASS, R. (1980) *On explaining language change*. Cambridge University Press: Cambridge.

LASS, R. (1997) *Historical linguistics and language change*. Cambridge University Press: Cambridge.

LAZARD, G. (1994) *L'Actance*. Presses Universitaires de France.

LAZARD, G. (1995) 'Typological research on actancy: the Paris RIVALC Group', in M. Shibatani and T. Bynon (eds) (1995a).

LEE, K. (1975) *Kusaiean reference grammar*. University Press of Hawaii: Honolulu.

LEHMANN, C. (1982) *Thoughts on grammaticalization: a programmatic sketch*. Institut für Sprachwissenschaft, Universität zu Köln: Köln.

LEHMANN, C. (1984) *Der Relativsatz: Typologie seiner Strukturen, Theorie seiner Funktionen, Kompendium seiner Grammatik*. Gunter Narr: Tübingen.

LEHMANN, C. (1986) 'On the typology of relative clauses', *Linguistics* 24: 663–80.

LEHMANN, W.P. (1973) 'A structural principle of language and its implications', *Language* 49: 47–66.

LEHMANN, W.P. (1974) *Proto-Indo-European syntax*. University of Texas Press: Austin.

LEHMANN, W.P. (ed.) (1978a) *Syntactic typology: studies in the phenomenology of language*. University of Texas Press: Austin.

LEHMANN, W.P. (1978b) 'The great underlying ground-plans', in W.P. Lehmann (ed.) (1978a).

LEHMANN, W.P. (1978c) 'Conclusion: toward an understanding of the profound unity underlying languages', in W.P. Lehmann (ed.) (1978a).

LEWY, E. (1942) 'Der Bau der europäischen Sprachen', in *Proceedings of the Royal Irish Academy*, volume 48, section C, nr. 2 (Dublin).

LI, C.N. (ed.) (1975) *Word order and word order change*. University of Texas Press: Austin.

LI, C.N. (ed.) (1976) *Subject and topic*. Academic Press: New York.

LI, C.N. and S.A. THOMPSON. (1989) *Mandarin Chinese: a functional reference grammar*. University of California Press: Berkeley.

LIGHT, R.J. and B.H. MARGOLIN (1971) 'An analysis of variance for categorical data', *Journal of the American Statistical Association* 66: 534–44.

LIGHTFOOT, D.W. (1982) *The language lottery: toward a biology of grammars*. MIT Press: Cambridge, MA.

LINDENFELD, J. (1973) *Yaqui syntax*. University of California Press: Berkeley.

LONGACRE, B.E. (1980) 'Discourse typology in relation to language typology', in S. Allén (ed.) (1980).

LUELSDORFF, P.A. (ed.) (1994a) *The Prague School of structural and functional linguistics: a short introduction*. John Benjamins: Amsterdam.

LUELSDORFF, P.A. (1994b) 'Introduction', in P.A. Luelsdorff (ed.) (1994a).

McKAY, G.R. (1976) 'Rembarnga', in R.M.W. Dixon (ed.) (1976).

MAJEWICZ, A.F. (1993) 'Review of V.P. Nedjalkov (ed.), *Typology of resultative constructions*', *Linguistics* 31: 421–4.

MALLINSON, G. and B.J. BLAKE (1981) *Language typology: cross-linguistic studies in syntax*. North-Holland: Amsterdam.

MANNING, A.D. and F. PARKER (1989) 'The SOV > . . . > OSV frequency hierarchy', *Language Sciences* 11: 43–65.

MARAN, L.R and J.M. CLIFTON (1976) 'The causative mechanism in Jinghpaw', in M. Shibatani (ed.) (1976a).

MARTINET, A. (1962) *A functional view of language*. Clarendon Press: Oxford.

MASICA, C.P. (1976) *Defining a linguistic area*. University of Chicago Press: Chicago.

MATISOFF, J.A. (1973) *The grammar of Lahu*. University of California Press: Berkeley.

MATISOFF, J.A. (1976) 'Lahu causative constructions: case hierarchies and the morphology/syntax cycle in a Tibeto-Burman perspective', in M. Shibatani, (ed.) (1976a).

MATSUMOTO, Y. (1989) 'Japanese-style noun modification . . . in English', *BLS* 15: 226–37.

MATSUMOTO, Y. (1997) *Noun-modifying constructions in Japanese: a frame-semantic approach*. John Benjamins: Amsterdam.

MAXWELL, D.N. (1979) 'Strategies of relativization and NP accessibility', *Language* 55: 352–71.

MILLER, G.A. and N. CHOMSKY (1963) 'Finitary models of language users', in R.D. Luce, R.R. Bush and E. Galanter (eds), *Handbook of Mathematical Psychology, vol. 2*. Wiley: New York.

MILLS, A.E. (1985) 'The acquisition of German', in D.I. Slobin (ed.) (1985a).

MILLS, A.E. (1986) *The acquisition of gender: a study of English and German*. Springer Verlag: Berlin.

MITHUN, M. (1984) 'The evolution of noun incorporation', *Language* 60: 847–94.

MITHUN, M. (1987) 'Is basic word order universal?' in R. Tomlin (ed.), *Coherence and grounding in discourse*. John Benjamins: Amsterdam.

MITHUN, M. (1991) 'Active/agentive case marking and its motivations', *Language* 67: 510–46.

MITHUN, M. (1992) 'Is basic word order universal?', in D.L. Payne (ed.) (1992).

MOORE, T.E. (1972) 'Speeded recognition of ungrammaticality', *Journal of Verbal Learning and Verbal Behavior* 11: 550–60.

MORAVCSIK, E.A. (1978) 'On the case marking of objects', in J.H. Greenberg *et al.* (ed.) (1978b).

Moravcsik, E.A. (1997) 'Review of M. Shibatani and T. Bynon (eds), *Approaches to language typology*', *Linguistic Typology* 1: 103–22.

Mosel, U. (1983) 'Adnominal and predicative possessive constructions in Melanesian languages. *Arbeiten des Kölner Universalien-Projekts* 50.

Murdock, G.P. (1967) *Ethnographic Atlas*. University of Pittsburgh Press: Pittsburgh.

Nedjalkov, V.P. (ed.) (1983) *Tipologija rezul'tativnyx konstrukcij: rezul'tativ, stativ, passiv, perfect*. Nauka: Leningrad.

Nedjalkov, V.P. (ed.) (1988) *Typology of resultative constructions*. John Benjamins: Amsterdam.

Nedjalkov, V.P. and V.P. Litvinov (1995) 'The St Petersburg/Leningrad Typology Group', in M. Shibatani and T. Bynon (eds) (1995a).

Nedjalkov, V.P. and G.G. Sil'nickij (1969) 'Tipologija kauzativnyx konstrukcij', in A.A. Xolodovič (ed.) (1969).

Nedjalkov, V.P. and G.G. Silnitsky (1973) 'The typology of morphological and lexical causatives', in F. Kiefer (ed.) (1973).

Newman, J. (1996) *Give: a cognitive linguistic study*. Mouton de Gruyter: Berlin.

Newmeyer F.J. (1980 [1986]) *Linguistic theory in America*. Academic Press: New York.

Nichols, J. (1979a) 'The meeting of East and West: confrontation and convergence in contemporary linguistics', *BLS* 5: 261–76.

Nichols, J. (1979b) 'Syntax and pragmatics in Manchu-Tungus languages', in P.R. Clyne, W.F. Hanks and C.L. Hofbauer (eds), *The elements: a parasession on linguistic units and levels*. Chicago Linguistic Society: Chicago.

Nichols, J. (1984) 'Functional theories of grammar', *Annual Review of Anthropology* 13: 97–117.

Nichols, J. (1986) 'Head-marking and dependent-marking grammar', *Language* 62: 56–119.

Nichols, J. (1992) *Linguistic diversity in space and time*. University of Chicago Press: Chicago.

Nichols, J. (1993) 'Diachronically stable structural features', in H. Andersen (ed.), *Historical linguistics, 1993*. John Benjamins: Amsterdam.

Nichols, J. (1997) 'Sprung from two common sources: Sahul as a linguistic area', in P. McConvell and N. Evans (eds), *Archaeology and linguistics: Aboriginal Australia in global perspective*. Oxford University Press: Melbourne.

Oates, L.F. (1964) *A tentative description of the Gunwinggu language*. Oceania Linguistic Monograph no. 10. University of Sydney: Sydney.

Palmer, F.R. (1994) *Grammatical roles and relations*. Cambridge University Press: Cambridge.

Pavesi, M. (1986) 'Markedness, discoursal modes, and relative clause formation in a formal and an informal context', *Studies in Second Language Acquisition* 8: 38–55.

Payne, D.L. (1985a) Aspects of the grammar of Yagua: a typological perspective. Unpublished PhD dissertation, University of California, Los Angeles.

Payne, D.L. (1985b) 'Review of J.A. Hawkins, *Word order universals*', *Language* 61: 462–6.

Payne, D.L. (1990) *The pragmatics of word order: typological dimensions of verb initial languages*. Mouton de Gruyter: Berlin.

Payne, D.L. (ed.) (1992) *Pragmatics of word order flexibility*. John Benjamins: Amsterdam

Peranteau, P.M., J.N. Levi and G.C. Phares (eds) (1972) *The Chicago which hunt*. Chicago Linguistic Society: Chicago.

PERERA, K. (1984) *Children's writing and reading: analysing classroom language*. Blackwell: Oxford.

PERKINS, R.D. (1980) The evolution of culture and grammar. Unpublished PhD dissertation, SUNY, Buffalo.

PERKINS, R.D. (1988) 'The covariation of culture and grammar', in M. Hammond, E.A. Moravcsik and J.R. Wirth (eds), *Studies in syntactic typology*. John Benjamins: Amsterdam.

PERKINS, R.D. (1989) 'Statistical techniques for determining language sample size', *SiL* 13: 293–315.

PERKINS, R.D. (1992) *Deixis, grammar and culture*. John Benjamins: Amsterdam.

PERLMUTTER, D.M. and P.M. POSTAL (1983) 'Toward a universal characterization of passivization', in D.M. Perlmutter (ed.), *Studies in Relational Grammar 1*. University of Chicago Press: Chicago.

PLANK, F. (ed.) (1979) *Ergativity: towards a theory of grammatical relations*. Academic Press: London.

PLANK, F. (1991) 'Hypology, typology: the Gabelentz Puzzle', *Folia Linguistica* 25: 421–58.

PLATERO, P. (1974) 'The Navajo relative clause', *IJAL* 40: 202–46.

POLINSKAJA, M.S. (1989) 'Object initiality: OSV', *Linguistics* 27: 257–303.

POLINSKY, M. (1994) 'Double objects in causatives: towards a study of coding conflict', *SiL* 19: 129–221.

PRIMUS, B. (1987) *Grammatische Hierarchien: eine Beschreibung und Erklärung von Regularitäten des Deutschen ohne grammatische Relationen*. Wilhelm Fink: Munich.

PRIMUS, B. (1991) 'Hierarchiegesetze der Universalgrammatik ohne grammatische Relationen', in S. Olsen and G. Fanselow (eds) (1991), *Det, Comp und Infl: Zur Syntax Funktionaler Kategorien und grammatischer Kategorien*. Max Niemeyer: Tübingen.

PRINCE, E. (1981) 'Toward a taxonomy of given-new information', in P. Cole (ed.), *Radical pragmatics*. Academic Press: New York.

PRIOR, M.H. (1985) Syntactic universals and semantic constraints. Unpublished thesis, University of London.

PULLUM, G.K. (1981) 'Languages with object before subject: a comment and a catalogue', *Linguistics* 19: 147–55.

PULLUM, G.K. and D. WILSON (1977) 'Autonomous syntax and the analysis of auxiliaries', *Language* 53: 741–88.

QUAKENBUSH, J.S. (1992) 'Word order and discourse type: an Austronesian example', in D.L. Payne (ed.) (1992).

RADHAKRISHNAN, R. (1981) *The Nancowry word: phonology, affixal morphology and roots of a Nicobarese language*. Linguistic Research Inc.: Carbondale.

RAMAT, P. (1986) 'Is a holistic typology possible?', *Folia Linguistica* 20: 3–14.

RAMAT, P. (1987) *Linguistic typology*. Mouton de Gruyter: Berlin.

RAMAT, P. (1995) 'Typological comparison: towards a historical perspective', in M. Shibatani and T. Bynon (eds) (1995a).

RIJKHOFF, J., D. BAKKER, K. HENGEVELD and P. KAHREL (1993) 'A method of language sampling', *SiL* 17: 169–203.

RITCHIE, W.C. and T.K. BHATIA (eds) (1996) *Handbook of second language acquisition*. Academic Press: San Diego

ROBINS, R.H. (1997) *A short history of linguistics*. Fourth edition. Addison Wesley Longman: London.

ROTH, W.E. (1897) *Ethnological studies among the north-west-central Queensland Aborigines.* Government Printer: Brisbane.

RUHLEN, M. (1975) *A guide to the languages of the world.* Language Universals Project: Stanford.

RUHLEN, M. (1987) *A guide to the world's languages, 1: classification.* Stanford University Press: Stanford.

RUTHERFORD, W.E. (ed.) (1984a) *Language universals and second language acquisition.* John Benjamins: Amsterdam.

RUTHERFORD, W.E. (1984b) 'Description and explanation in interlanguage syntax: state of the art', *LL* 34: 127–55.

SAKSENA, A. (1980) 'The affected agent', *Language* 56: 812–26.

SAKSENA, A. (1982) 'Contact in causation', *Language* 58: 820–31.

SALTARELLI, M. (1988) *Basque.* Croom Helm: London.

SAPIR, E. (1921) *Language: an introduction to the study of speech.* Harcourt, Brace and World: New York.

SCANCARELLI, J.S. (1985) 'Referential strategies in Chamorro narratives: preferred clause structure and ergativity', *SiL* 9: 335–62.

SCHACHTER, J. (1974) 'An error in error analysis', *LL* 24: 205–14.

SCHACHTER, J. (1988) 'Second language acquisition and its relationship to universal grammar', *AL* 9: 219–35.

SCHACHTER, P. (1983) 'Explaining auxiliary order', in F. Heny and B. Richards (eds), *Linguistic categories: auxiliaries and related puzzles, II: the scope, order, and distribution of English auxiliary verbs.* D. Reidel: Dordrecht.

SCHAUB, W. (1985) *Babungo.* Croom Helm: London.

SCHIEFFELIN, B.B. (1985) 'The acquisition of Kaluli', in D.I. Slobin (ed.) (1985a).

SCIARONE, A.G. (1970) 'Contrastive analysis: possibilities and limitations', *International Review of Applied Linguistics* 8: 115–31.

SCUPIN, E. and G. SCUPIN (1907/1910) *Bubis erste Kindheit, vols 1 & 2.* Dürr: Leipzig.

SEILER, H. (ed.) (1978) *Language universals.* Gunter Narr: Tübingen.

SEILER, H. (1986) *Apprehension: language, object, and order.* Gunter Narr: Tübingen.

SEILER, H. (1989a) 'A dimensional view on numeral systems', *Arbeiten des Kölner Universalien-Projekts* 79.

SEILER, H. (1989b) 'The dimension of participation', *Función* 7.

SEILER, H. (1990) 'Language typology in the UNITYP model', in *Proceedings of the Fourteenth International Congress of Linguists.* Akademie-Verlag: Berlin.

SEILER, H. (1995) 'Cognitive-conceptual structure and linguistic encoding: language universals and typology in the UNITYP framework', in M. Shibatani and T. Bynon (eds) (1995a).

SEILER, H. and G. BRETTSCHNEIDER (eds) (1985) *Language invariants and mental operations.* Gunter Narr: Tübingen.

SEILER, H. and C. LEHMANN (eds) (1982) *Apprehension: das sprachliche Erfassen von Gegenständen, Teil I: Bereich und Ordnung der Phänomene.* Gunter Narr: Tübingen.

SEILER, H. and J. LUIS-ITURRIOZ (1994) 'Interview with Hansjakob Seiler on UNITYP', *Languages of the World* 8: 43–7.

SEILER, H. and F.-J. STACHOWIAK (eds) (1982) *Apprehension: das sprachliche Erfassen von Gegenständen, Teil II: die Techniken und ihr Zusammenhang in Einzelsprachen.* Gunter Narr: Tübingen.

SELINKER, L. (1972) 'Interlanguage', *International Review of Applied Linguistics* 10: 209–31.

SGALL, P. (1958) *Vývoj flexe v indoevropských jazycích.* Academia: Prague.

SGALL, P. (1960) 'Soustava pádových koncovek v češtině', *Acta Universitatis Carolinae-Philologica* 1–2, *Slavica Pragensia* 2: 65–84.

SGALL, P. (1967) 'Typology and the development of the Indo-European languages', *Actes du dixième congrès international des linguistes* (Académie de la République Socialiste de Roumanie) 3: 505–11.

SGALL, P. (ed.) (1984a) *Contributions to functional syntax, semantics, and language comprehension.* John Benjamins: Amsterdam.

SGALL, P. (1984b) 'On the notion of "Type of Language"', in P. Sgall (ed.) (1984a)

SGALL, P. (1986) 'Classical typology and modern linguistics', *Folia Linguistica* 20: 15–28.

SGALL, P. (1995) 'Prague School Typology', in M. Shibatani and T. Bynon (eds) (1995a).

SHARWOOD SMITH, M. (1994) *Second language learning: theoretical foundations.* Addison Wesley Longman: London.

SHELDON, A. (1974) 'The role of parallel function in the acquisition of relative clauses in English', *Journal of Verbal Learning and Verbal Behavior* 13: 272–81.

SHIBATANI, M. (1975) *A linguistic study of causative constructions.* Indiana University Linguistics Club: Bloomington.

SHIBATANI, M. (ed.) (1976a) *Syntax and semantics 6: the grammar of causative constructions.* Academic Press: New York.

SHIBATANI, M. (1976b) 'The grammar of causative constructions: a conspectus', in M. Shibatani (ed.) (1976a).

SHIBATANI, M. and T. BYNON (eds) (1995a) *Approaches to language typology.* Clarendon Press: Oxford.

SHIBATANI, M. and T. BYNON (1995b) 'Approaches to language typology: a conspectus', in M. Shibatani and T. Bynon (eds) (1995a).

SHIELDS, K. (1995) 'On the origin of the Indo-European feminine gender category', *Indogermanische Forschungen* 100: 101–8.

SHIELDS, K. (1997) 'Linguistic typology and reconstruction: the animacy hierarchy and its implications for the Indo-European inflectional number category', *Word* 48: 367–74.

SHOPEN, T. and M. KONARÉ (1970) 'Sonrai causatives and passives: transformational versus lexical derivations for propositional heads', *Studies in African Linguistics* 1: 211–54.

SIEWIERSKA, A. (1988) *Word order rules.* Croom Helm: London.

SIEWIERSKA, A. (1993) 'Syntactic weight vs information structure and word order variation in Polish', *JL* 29: 233–65.

SIEWIERSKA, A. (1994) 'Review of J. Nichols, *Linguistic diversity in space and time*', *Linguistics* 32: 148–53.

SIEWIERSKA, A. (1996) 'Word order type and alignment type', *Sprachtypologie und Universalienforschung* 49: 149–76.

SIEWIERSKA, A. (ed.) (1998) *Constituent order in the languages of Europe.* Mouton de Gruyter: Berlin.

SIEWIERSKA, A. and D. BAKKER (1996) 'The distribution of subject and object agreement and word order type', *SiL* 20: 115–61.

SIEWIERSKA, A. and J.J. SONG (eds) (1998) *Case, typology and grammar: in honor of Barry J. Blake.* John Benjamins: Amsterdam.

SILVERSTEIN, M. (1976) 'Hierarchy of features and ergativity', in R.M.W. Dixon (ed.) (1976).

SILVERSTEIN, M. (1980) Of nominatives and datives: universal grammar from the bottom up. Ms, University of Chicago: Chicago. (Reprinted as Silverstein 1993).

SILVERSTEIN, M. (1981) 'Case marking and the nature of language', *AJL* 1: 227–44.

SILVERSTEIN, M. (1993) 'Of nominatives and datives: universal grammar from the bottom up', in R.D. Van Valin (ed.) (1993a).

SKALIČKA, V. (1935) *Zur ungarischen Grammatik*. Prague.

SKALIČKA, V. (1966) 'Ein "typologisches Konstrukt"', in *Travaux linguistiques de Prague* 2: 157–64.

SKALIČKA, V. and P. SGALL (1994) 'Praguian typology of languages', in P.A. Luelsdorff (ed.) (1994a).

SLOBIN, D.I. (1973) 'Cognitive prerequisites for the development of grammar', in C.A. Ferguson and D.I. Slobin (eds), *Studies of child language development*. Holt, Rinehart and Winston: New York.

SLOBIN, D.I. (1982) 'Universal and particular in the acquisition of language', in E. Wanner and L. Gleitman (eds), *Language acquisition: the state of the art*. Cambridge University Press: Cambridge.

SLOBIN, D.I. (ed.) (1985a) *The crosslinguistic study of language acquisition, volume 1: the data*. Lawrence Erlbaum: Hillsdale, NJ.

SLOBIN, D.I. (ed.) (1985b) *The crosslinguistic study of language acquisition, volume 2: theoretical issues*. Lawrence Erlbaum: Hillsdale, NJ.

SLOBIN, D.I. (1985c) 'Crosslinguistic evidence for the language-making capacity', in D.I. Slobin (ed.) (1985b).

SLOBIN, D.I. (ed.) (1992) *The crosslinguistic study of language acquisition, volume 3*. Lawrence Erlbaum: Mahwah, NJ.

SLOBIN, D.I. (ed.) (1997a) *The crosslinguistic study of language acquisition, volume 4*. Lawrence Erlbaum: Mahwah, NJ.

SLOBIN, D.I. (ed.) (1997b) *The crosslinguistic study of language acquisition, volume 5: expanding the contexts*. Lawrence Erlbaum: Mahwah, NJ.

SLOBIN, D.I. (1997c) 'The universal, the typological, and the particular in acquisition', in D.I. Slobin (ed.) (1997b).

SLOBIN, D.I. (1997d) 'The origins of grammatical notions: beyond the individual mind', in D.I. Slobin (ed.) (1997b).

SLOBIN, D.I. and T.G. BEVER (1982) 'Children use canonical sentence schemas: a crosslinguistic study of word order and inflections', *Cognition* 12: 229–65.

SMITH, J.R. (1971) Word order in the Older Germanic dialects. Unpublished PhD dissertation, University of Illinois.

SMITH, N.V. (1981) 'Consistency, markedness and language change: on the notion "consistent language"', *JL* 17: 39–54.

SMITH, W. (1987) Preferred argument structure in spoken Hebrew discourse. Ms, University of California, Los Angeles.

SOLAN, L. and T. ROEPER (1978) 'Children's use of syntactic structure in interpreting relative clauses', *University of Massachusetts Occasional Papers in Linguistics* 4: 107–26.

SOMMER, B.A. (1972) *Kunjen syntax: a generative view*. Australian Institute of Aboriginal Studies: Canberra.

SONG, J.J. (1991a) 'On Tomlin, and Manning and Parker on basic word order', *Language Sciences* 13: 89–97.

SONG, J.J. (1991b) 'Korean relative clause constructions: conspiracy and pragmatics', *AJL* 11: 195–220.

SONG, J.J. (1992) 'A note on iconicity in causatives,' *Folia Linguistica* XXVI: 333–8.

SONG, J.J. (1993) 'Control and cooperation: adverbial scope in Korean morphological causatives', *Acta Linguistica Hafniensia* 26: 161–74.

SONG, J.J. (1994) 'The verb-object bonding principle and the pronominal system: with special reference to Nuclear Micronesian languages', *Oceanic Linguistics* 33: 517–65.

SONG, J.J. (1995) 'Review of B. Comrie and M. Polinsky (eds), *Causatives and trans-itivity*', *Lingua* 97: 211–32.

SONG, J.J. (1996) *Causatives and causation: a universal-typological perspective*. Addison Wesley Longman: London.

STASSEN, L. (1985) *Comparison and universal grammar*. Basil Blackwell: Oxford.

STEELE, S. (1978) 'Word order variation: a typological study', in J.H. Greenberg *et al.* (eds) (1978b).

STEELE, S. (1997) 'Review of M. Shibatani and T. Bynon (eds), *Approaches to language typology*', *Language* 73: 385–7.

STEWART, A. (1984) A glance at preferred argument structure in Conchucos Quechua. Ms, University of California, Los Angeles.

SUGITA, H. (1973) 'Semitransitive verbs and object incorporation in Micronesian languages', *Oceanic Linguistics* 12: 393–406.

SZEMERÉNYI, O. (1967) 'The new look of Indo-European: reconstruction and typology', *Phonetica* 17: 65–99.

TAGASHIRA, Y. (1972) 'Relative clauses in Korean', in P.M. Peranteau *et al.* (eds) (1972).

TALLERMAN, M. (1990) 'Relativization strategies: NP accessibility in Welsh', *JL* 26: 291–314.

TALMY, L. (1976) 'Semantic causative types', in M. Shibatani (ed.) (1976a).

TARALLO, F. and J. MYHILL (1983) 'Interference and natural language processing in second language acquisition', *LL* 33: 55–76.

TAVAKOLIAN, S.L. (1981) 'The conjoined-clause analysis of relative clauses', in S.L. Tavakolian (ed.), *Language acquisition and linguistic theory*. MIT Press: Cambridge, MA.

THOMASON, S.G. and T. KAUFMAN (1988) *Language contact, creolization, and genetic linguistics*. University of California Press: Berkeley.

THOMPSON, S.A. (1998) 'A discourse explanation for the cross-linguistic differences in the grammar of incorporation and negation', in A. Siewierska and J.J. Song (eds) (1998).

TOMLIN, R. (1983) 'On the interaction of syntactic subject, thematic information, and agent in English', *Journal of Pragmatics* 7: 411–32.

TOMLIN, R. (1986) *Basic word order: functional principles*. Croom Helm: London.

TOMLIN, R. and W.A. KELLOGG (1986) Theme and attention orientation in pro-cedural discourse. Department of Linguistics and the Cognitive Science Program, University of Oregon and IBM T.J. Watson Research Center.

TUGGY, D.H. (1988) 'Náhuatl causative/applicatives in cognitive grammar', in B. Rudzka-Ostyn (ed.), *Topics in cognitive linguistics*. John Benjamins: Amsterdam.

ULTAN, R. (1969) 'Some general characteristics of interrogative systems', *Working Papers on Language Universals* 1: 41–63.

VACHEK, J. (ed.) (1964) *A Prague School reader in linguistics*. Indiana University Press: Bloomington.

VACHEK, J. (1966) *The linguistic school of Prague: an introduction to its theory and practice*. Indiana University Press: Bloomington.

VAN VALIN, R.D. (ed.) (1993a) *Advances in Role and Reference Grammar*. John Benjamins: Amsterdam.

VAN VALIN, R.D. (1993b) 'A synopsis of Role and Reference Grammar', in R.D. Van Valin (ed.) (1993a).

VENNEMANN, T. (1973) 'Explanation in syntax,' in J.P. Kimball (ed.), *Syntax and semantics 2*. Seminar Press: New York.

VENNEMANN, T. (1974a) 'Analogy in generative grammar: the origin of word order', in *Proceedings of the Eleventh International Congress of Linguists*. Il Mulino: Bologna.

VENNEMANN, T. (1974b) 'Topics, subjects, and word order: from SXV to SVX via TVX', in J.M. Anderson and C. Jones (eds), *Historical linguistics I: syntax, morphology, and internal and comparative reconstruction*. North-Holland: Amsterdam.

VENNEMANN, T. (1975) 'An explanation of drift,' in C.N. Li (ed.) (1975).

VENNEMANN, T. (1984) 'Typology, universals and change of language', in J. Fisiak (ed.) (1984).

VERHAGEN, A. and S. KEMMER (1997) 'Interaction and causation: causative constructions in modern standard Dutch', *Journal of Pragmatics* 27: 61–82.

VITALE, A.J. (1981) *Swahili syntax*. Foris: Dordrecht.

VOEGELIN, C.F. and F.M. VOEGELIN (1966) 'Index to languages of the world', *Anthropological Linguistics* 8, no. 6 & 7.

VOEGELIN, C.F. and F.M. VOEGELIN (1977) *Classification and index of the world's languages*. Elsevier: New York.

WACHOWICZ, K. (1976) 'On the typology of causatives,' *Working Papers on Language Universals* 20: 59–106.

WALSH, M.J. (1976) The Murinypata language of north-west Australia. Unpublished PhD thesis, Australian National University.

WATKINS, C. (1976) 'Towards Proto-Indo-European syntax: problems and pseudo-problems', in S.B. Steever, C.A. Walker and S.S. Mufwene (eds), *Papers from the parasession on diachronic syntax*. Chicago Linguistic Society: Chicago.

WEBER, D.J. (1989) *A grammar of Huallaga (Huánuco) Quechua*. University of California Press: Berkeley.

WHALEY, L.J. (1997) *Introduction to typology: the unity and diversity of language*. Sage Publications: Thousand Oaks.

WIERZBICKA, A. (1980) *The case for surface case*. Karoma: Ann Arbor.

WIERZBICKA, A. (1981) 'Case marking and human nature', *AJL* 1: 43–80.

WOLFART, H.C. (1973) 'Plains Cree: a grammatical study', *Transactions of the American Philosophical Society* 63, part 5. American Philosophical Society: Philadelphia.

WOODBURY, A. (1977) 'Greenlandic Eskimo, ergativity, and relational grammar', in P. Cole and J. Sadock (eds), *Syntax and semantics 8: grammatical relations*. Academic Press: New York.

XOLODOVIČ, A.A. (ed.) (1969) *Tipologija kauzativnyx konstrukcij: morfologičeskij kauzativ*. Nauka: Leningrad.

XOLODOVIČ, A.A. (ed.) (1974) *Tipologija passivnyx konstrukcij: diatezy i zalogy*. Nauka: Leningrad.

XRAKOVSKIJ, V.S. (ed.) (1983) *Kategorii glagola i struktura predloženija: konstrukcii s predikatnymi aktantami*. Nauka: Leningrad.

XRAKOVSKIJ, V.S. (ed.) (1989) *Tipologija iterativnyx konstrukcij*. Nauka: Leningrad.

ZUBIN, D. (1979) 'Discourse function of morphology: the focus system in German', in T. Givón (ed.), *Syntax and semantics 12: discourse and syntax*. Academic Press: New York.

Author Index

Aarts, F., 327, 330
Adjémian, C., 332
Aikhenvald, A.Y., 354, 360, 361
Aissen, J.L., 144, 295
Akagawa, Y., 327
Allen, W.S., 298
Anderson, S.R., 164
Andrews, A., 217
Antinucci, F., 115, 250
Ard, J., 320, 326, 327, 334, 335

Bailey, N., 319
Baker, M.C., 191, 269
Bakker, D., 32, 34, 35, 36, 37, 38, 48,
    128, 129, 130, 131, 155, 201, 202,
    204, 357, 358
Bartsch, R., 58
Beekes, R.S.P., 300
Bell, A., 17, 18, 20, 21, 22, 23, 27, 33,
    34, 36, 38, 69
Bell, L., 330, 331
Berg, T., 110
Berinstein, A., 182
Berman, R., 161
Berman, R.A., 319
Bever, T.G., 76, 322
Bird, C., 215
Bishop, Y.M.M., 32
Blake, B.J., 8, 12, 40, 49, 50, 53, 58, 59,
    62, 72, 75, 78, 79, 95, 98, 131, 139,
    140, 143, 145, 148, 150, 153, 155,
    158, 159, 161, 162, 164, 166, 167,
    170, 171, 186, 187, 190, 192, 193,
    194, 203, 207, 208, 209, 213, 234,
    242, 243, 244, 246, 247, 248, 249,
    251, 252, 253, 301, 304, 316, 335

Bley-Vroman, R., 319, 320, 326
Bliese, L.F., 270
Bloom, L., 323
Bowerman, M., 324, 325, 326, 332,
    333, 336
Bresnan, J., 191
Brettschneider, G., 345
Bricker, V.R., 189, 236
Brugman, K., 47
Bubenik, V., 133, 137
Burt, M., 319, 332
Bybee, J.L., 30, 38, 39, 55, 98, 119,
    123, 124, 125, 126, 127, 132, 260,
    281, 282
Bynon, T., 43, 44, 48, 351, 356, 358

Campbell, L., 19, 133, 137, 253, 256,
    260, 308
Carpenter, K.L., 324
Catford, I., 186
Chafe, W.L., 178
Chaney, R.P., 26
Choi, S., 325
Chomsky, N., 88, 102
Clahsen, H., 320
Clancy, P.M., 320, 321, 322, 323, 333,
    336
Clark, E.V., 77, 324
Clark, H.H., 77
Claudi, U., 123, 124
Clifton, J.M., 260, 280
Cohen, M., 320, 321, 322
Cole, P., 259, 284, 285, 286
Collinge, N.E., 47, 298
Comrie, B., 9, 12, 13, 19, 20, 44, 46,
    47, 48, 49, 50, 51, 54, 59, 61, 62, 63,

Language Index

Subject Index